NEGOTIATING THE PAST

Negotiating the Past

The Historical Understanding of Medieval Literature

LEE PATTERSON

The University of Wisconsin Press

Published 1987

The University of Wisconsin Press
114 North Murray Street
Madison, Wisconsin 53715

The University of Wisconsin Press, Ltd.
1 Gower Street
London WC1E 6HA, England

First printing

Printed in the United States of America

For LC CIP information see the colophon

ISBN 0-299-11040-0 cloth; 0-299-11044-3 paper

To the Memory of
JIM RENWICK

Contents

Preface

The utterly sincere need to understand the past as well as possible without any admixture of one's own is the only thing that can make a work history. . . . Contemporary man is a traitor to the spirit of his own culture if he creates myths in the knowledge that they are, or rather pretend to be, myths. Our culture's form of intellectual cognition is that of critical scholarship.

—JOHAN HUIZINGA

I am accused of causing young people to acquiesce in subjectivity. Maybe, for a moment. But how would it be possible to eliminate all the phantoms of objectivity that act as an audience, etc., except by stressing the category of the separate individual? Under the pretext of objectivity the aim has been to sacrifice individualities entirely. That is the crux of the matter.

—SØREN KIERKEGAARD

HUIZINGA'S NAIVE faith in objectivity set against Kierkegaard's disingenuous privileging of the individual—here are citations that figure two apparently exhausted modes of thought, two archaic discourses to be consigned to the ash heap of premodernist thinking. And yet for all their evident blindness, they also speak an inescapable truth. For they figure an opposition—or set of oppositions—that continues to haunt the historicist project. While wanting to do justice to the otherness of a distant past, the historian is unavoidably conditioned by his own historical situation; while concerned to incorporate and understand as much of the material relevant to his chosen problem as he can, he is also aware that that material is never raw data but rather produced by elaborate processes of interpretation—many of which are so much second nature as to be unrecognizable as interpretations at all; and while attentive to the particularity and detail in which the significance of the past resides, he also knows that for detail to be significant at all it must be located within a larger, totalizing context. These are oppositions that can never, in my view, come to resolution; on the contrary, they must be continually negotiated and renegotiated. Like Freud's civilization, historicism both issues from and entails discontent: the insufficiency of the present directs us to the past, but what we recover fails to satisfy. And so history continues to be written.

That the contradictions implicit in historicism cannot be theoretically resolved does not, however, absolve us from the need to theorize. On the contrary, the negotiations that issue in historical understanding can best be conducted in a context informed with the self-awareness that theoretical thinking promotes. But what sort of theoretical thinking? Fredric Jameson argues that "no working model of the functioning of language, the nature of communication or of the speech act, and the dynamics of formal and stylistic change is conceivable which does not imply a whole philosophy of history"—a claim of virtually paralyzing scope.[1] Conversely, Clifford Geertz more modestly suggests that while all interpretive activities should articulate the assumptions that guide their procedures, they must also recognize that the theoretical formulations they engender "hover so low over the interpretations they govern that they don't make much sense or hold much interest apart from them. This is so, not because they are not general . . . but because, stated independently of their application, they seem either commonplace or vacant."[2] By temperament and capacity I am drawn to Geertz's formulation, and yet it is Jameson who rightly insists on the priority of the political in governing our interpretive activities. Indeed, it is probably the case that only by pushing our theoretical thinking beyond the point of comfort can we make clear to ourselves the nature of the imperatives that govern our activity.

In the course of writing these essays I have become progressively more convinced that the various forms of resolution at which historicist negotiations arrive are governed neither by empirical necessity, nor (least of all) by theoretical correctness, but by values and commitments that are in the last analysis political. As a medievalist not trained in but inevitably influenced by the objectivist methodologism typical of the institutionalized Medieval Studies that largely dominates the field, this was a conclusion that I resisted. Yet writing an essay on the history of Chaucer criticism—an essay that has become Chapter 1 of the present book—

---

1. Fredric Jameson, *The Political Unconscious* (Ithaca: Cornell University Press, 1981), p. 59.
2. Clifford Geertz, *The Interpretation of Cultures* (New York: Basic Books, 1973), p. 25.

persuaded me that the definition and development of the field were and still largely are governed by an agenda first put into place during the politically motivated recovery of the national literatures in the nineteenth century. Broadly speaking, there is a Middle Ages of the right and of the left, and they entail allegiances that govern most if not all of the critical work at the present time. Moreover, within nineteenth-century historicism there also developed two ways of figuring the relation of the written text to the nonverbal events, structures, material conditions, and so on, that constitute its historical context. Again speaking broadly, one was a positivism that assumed a causal pressure of context on text, the other a *Geistesgeschichte* that understood all cultural objects as the symptomatic expression of a single, historically specific essence. Dominant across the field, these paradigms entailed a criticism that enforced the priority of context over text, a tyranny that was finally thrown off in the early 1950s with the development of an aggressively ahistoricist New Criticism.

But formalism is now in turn discredited, and for all the remarkable resilience of the earlier historicist paradigms they remain, for reasons that I review at the beginning of Chapter 2, no longer persuasive agencies for scholarly work. The rest of this chapter is devoted to exploring a third way of defining the context/text relationship, a model of cultural activity that is not dialectical (cause/effect, essence/symptom—nor even base/superstructure) but symbolic, in which cultural products are seen as full participants in a historical world that is equivalently densely symbolized. There are two means of approach to this third way. One is through the Frankfurt School, with its insistence that, to quote Adorno, "mediation is in the object itself, not something between the object and that to which it is brought," an insistence that in effect seeks to do away with dualism altogether, as Raymond Williams makes admirably clear.[3] The other is the New Historicism that now flourishes in Renaissance studies, which draws its inspiration from such non-Marxist sources as Michel Foucault and anthropologists like Marshall Sahlins. It is this third way, in both its forms, that seems to me to offer the brightest prospects for historicism. Yet I also want to argue that the Foucauldian allegiances of much New Historicist work allow for an effacement of the subject that threatens its effort to rescue texts from the tyranny of context. Indeed, the current stigmatizing of humanism as simply the false consciousness of a complacent bourgeoisie seems to me bad for both scholarship and politics, and it is part of the purpose of Chapter 2 to argue

---

3. Theodor Adorno, "Thesen zur Kunstsoziologie," *Kölner Zeitschrift für Soziologie und Sozialpsychologie* 19 (March 1967); cited by Raymond Williams, *Marxism and Literature* (Oxford: Oxford University Press, 1977), p. 98.

that the idea of the subject is an interpretive category that contemporary scholarship can ill afford to do without.

After these initial two essays, the book turns to specific cases. Chapter 3 deals with the methodological struggle between subject and object in the history of textual criticism by focusing on the recent, controversial edition of *Piers Plowman* produced by George Kane and E. Talbot Donaldson. My purpose is not only to describe the place of this remarkable edition in the history of textual criticism, but also to show that the methods by which the original poem is extracted from the scribal detritus in which it is embedded are governed by the formalist assumptions that modern criticism has inherited from Romanticism. I do not mean, however, to impeach these assumptions by uncovering their historical nature (for what is not historical?), but on the contrary to argue that the detailed and scrupulous arguments deployed by Kane and Donaldson vindicate their edition against the objections of both old- and new-style critics—objections that are tellingly similar.

Chapter 4 directs the book's metacritical interest toward a particular act of interpretation by reading a medieval text that itself both represents, and prescribes, an act of reading. The text is a late-fifteenth-century treatise for women religious in which the clerical author first uses Chaucer's *Troilus and Criseyde* to illustrate certain spiritual teachings and then recommends it to his cloistered audience. The apparent oddity of this recommendation might lead us to believe that the poem was understood in accordance with a narrowly defined spiritualism, and that this understanding represents an "original" reading, or at least as close to one as we are now likely to get. But in fact such an interpretation seems to me unsatisfactory, for when the text is allowed to define, and to be defined by, its historical context, it reveals a far more subtle and nuanced hermeneutic. In short, our reading of this text must be as capacious as it itself shows medieval reading to have been. Moreover, this chapter argues that the problematic character of reading to which so many prominent writers of the later Middle Ages bear witness is vividly at work in more humble contexts as well, that the drama of interpretation that they fictively stage found a historical enactment in the lives of less famous men and women.

At least since Nietzsche it has been assumed that historicism is a modern phenomenon, that in some sense it defines modernity itself. The final two essays argue otherwise, for I mean my subtitle—"The Historical Understanding of Medieval Literature"—to be both objective and subjective: topics that preoccupy modern historicism are themselves present, in different but recognizable forms, in the Middle Ages, a period that has too often been designated as prehistorical. Chapter 5 shows the way in which two twelfth-century narratives—the anonymous *Roman d'Eneas,* and *Erec et Enide* by Chrétien de Troyes—confront in their different ways the model of linear historicity established, in an already problematic form, by the *Aeneid.* The final chapter discusses the Alliterative *Morte Arthure,* a late-fourteenth-century poem that retells the Arthurian story first narrated by Geoffrey of Monmouth in the 1130s, so as to expose the dilemmas that necessarily afflict the historical imagination in a culture dominated by a transcendentalizing spirituality. The conclusion toward which these readings urge us is not, then, a specific historicist theory or methodology but rather a renewed awareness that historicism is always discontented. Historicist speculation continually and inevitably refigures the same topics: the difference between past and present must be both absolute and yet, if history is to be written at all, negotiable; the present is the custodian of the past, and yet its obsessive interest and unwitting reenactments allow the slave to become the master; the poetic text is created by history and yet continually proclaims a transhistorical value—a paradox that also governs the relation of subjectivity to the material world from which it derives; and so on. All of us concerned with the recovery of the past continue to confront these problems in a wide variety of forms, a ceaseless contestation that only the end of history itself could possibly terminate.

Two of the following chapters were originally written at the request of colleagues: a preliminary version of Chapter 1 was delivered in the Chaucer section of the MLA meeting in December 1983 at the invitation of Charles Owen; and Chapter 3 was first prepared as a contribution to the Caltech/Weingart Conference in the Humanities in March 1982 organized by Jerome McGann, and it was published, in a rather different form than it appears here, in the proceedings of that conference edited by Professor McGann, *Textual Criticism and Literary Interpretation* (Chicago: University of Chicago Press, 1985). Two other chapters have been previously published: Chapter 4, in a slightly different form, in *Speculum* 53 (1979), and Chapter 6, also now somewhat revised, in the *Journal of Medieval and Renaissance Studies* 13 (1983). I am grateful to the publishers for permission to reprint them, and especially to my colleagues for their invitations to think about these matters in public and for their editorial labors on my behalf. I am also grateful to the National Endowment for the Humanities, and to the colleagues who supported me in my application, for crucial fellowship support.
    Of the many other friends who have also read these essays and offered welcome if not always heeded encouragement and advice, I want to thank particularly Winthrop Wetherbee and Peter Travis, who provided

prompt, detailed and very helpful readers' reports, and Stanley Fish, Del Kolve, Frank Lentricchia, Anne Middleton, Ira Sadoff, and Gabrielle Spiegel, each of whom offered specific and thoughtful suggestions. Mark Rasmussen provided expert assistance and helpful advice that went way beyond the editorial tasks that were his responsibility, and Barbara Hanrahan of the University of Wisconsin Press shepherded a fretful author with just the right amounts of patience and urgency. Finally, Annabel Patterson alone knows how much she has contributed to this book—with the exception, that is, of its author, who here records, for future reference, his deep and abiding gratitude.

This book is dedicated to the memory of Jim Renwick, Deputy Leader of the New Democratic Party of Ontario and Member of the Legislative Assembly for Riverdale (Toronto) from 1964 until his death in November 1984. A thoughtful, even meditative man in a profession that rarely rewards such virtues, he knew that the principles that give politics meaning paradoxically enjoin us to respect the stubborn reality that so often frustrates their enactment. That he is no longer alive to read this book is a source of grief, but it is consoling to think that perhaps his spirit in some measure informs its pages.

I. HISTORICISM AND ITS DISCONTENTS

1. Historical Criticism and the Development of Chaucer Studies

AT THIS moment in the history of literary studies, the word *historicism*—indeed, the very word *history*—has become highly charged both in the specific field of Medieval Studies and in literary criticism generally. And yet the charge is in each instance of a different valence: for the medievalist the phrase "historical criticism" is a code word for a densely annotated and narrowly argued reading of an often aggressively moralistic cast; while for critics concerned with other periods, criticism that advertises itself as historical raises expectations of politically engaged readings of a progressive if not explicitly Marxist kind. Why this should be so—why the historicism of the medievalist should so sharply differ from that of critics working in later periods—is the subject of this chapter. The answer, I believe, is itself historical, and is inscribed with particular clarity in the history of Chaucer criticism. Hence the focus of my attention here is upon the two great critical formations, Exegetics and New Criticism, that have served Chaucer studies for the past twenty-five years as the most effective vehicles for critical work and that continue to exert a conditioning influence upon the field. Despite their hostility, these two attitudes—one aggressively historical, the other by and large indifferent to questions of historical understanding—are bound by their shared participation in the historical development of English studies. Their struggle is essentially sibling in nature, and all the more violent for that. Here, as often, the history of scholarship presents the features of a family ro-

mance, and its postures and polemics articulate no simple pattern of thesis and antithesis but a complex interweaving of piety with rebellion,
covert borrowings entwined with ostentatious declarations of independence.[1] This dynamic is especially evident in Chaucer studies, where
New Criticism and Exegetics (and their successors) have not been on
speaking terms for some twenty-five years, although each critical camp
remains oddly and even obsessively aware of the other's presence. Indeed, as I hope to show, it is this breakdown in communication, rather
than the controversy itself, that is of crucial importance for the current
state of Chaucer studies in North America.

When in the 1950s and early 1960s the work of D. W. Robertson first
established Exegetics as a major force in the study of medieval literature,
most medievalists hastened to position themselves vis-à-vis this new critical formation.[2] Some issued anathemas (Donaldson, Utley), some offered less global but still severe strictures (Bloomfield, Howard), some
rather gingerly signed up as co-workers in the Exegetical vineyard
(Kaske).[3] Without exception, however, these responses remained true to
the empirical temper of American criticism by engaging Exegetics at the
level of practice, attacking it for historical misrepresentation and interpretive inadequacy or, conversely, seeing in it new possibilities for
critical work. Indeed, as Talbot Donaldson candidly acknowledged, such
an approach was forced on the opposition by its inability to frame a
theoretical objection.[4] The result of this pragmatism was that, despite

---

1. In *Parler du moyen âge* (Paris: Editions de Minuit, 1980), Paul Zumthor not only
speaks of "le médiévisme de papa" (p. 31) but suggests as well that the antiquarianism that
has traditionally motivated so much medieval scholarship is itself expressive of profound
psychic impulses: "l'érudition devient le refuge des Oedipes ratés" (p. 29) who are denied
a more direct return to the maternal origin.

2. A bibliography of Professor Robertson's writings through 1977 is available in his
Essays in Medieval Culture (Princeton: Princeton University Press, 1980), pp. 283–84.

3. E. Talbot Donaldson, "Patristic Exegesis in the Criticism of Medieval Literature:
The Opposition," in Dorothy Bethurum, ed., *Critical Approaches to Medieval Literature*
(New York: Columbia University Press, 1960), pp. 1–26, reprinted in *Speaking of Chaucer*
(New York: Norton, 1970), pp. 134–53, along with the analogous "Medieval Poetry and
Medieval Sin," pp. 164–74; Francis Lee Utley, "Robertsonianism Redivivus," *Romance Phil-
ology* 19 (1965), 250–60, reprinted as "Chaucer and Patristic Exegesis" in A. C. Cawley,
ed., *Chaucer's Mind and Art* (Edinburgh: Oliver and Boyd, 1969), pp. 69–85; Morton W.
Bloomfield, "Symbolism in Medieval Literature," *Modern Philology* 56 (1958), 73–81, re-
printed in *Essays and Explorations: Studies in Ideas, Language, and Literature* (Cambridge:
Harvard University Press, 1970), pp. 82–95; Donald R. Howard, "Medieval Poems and
Medieval Society," *Medievalia et Humanistica* n.s. 3 (1972), 99–115; Robert E. Kaske, "The
Defense," in *Critical Approaches to Medieval Literature*, pp. 27–60, and "Chaucer and Medie-
val Allegory," *ELH* 30 (1963), 175–92.

4. Donaldson opens his attack on Exegetics with a disarming admission that in fact
serves as a familiar empiricist enabling move: "I am not aware of any valid theoretical

and even because of the devastating force of the practical objections, a confrontation with Exegetics at the level of theory was foreclosed. Moreover, the silent but powerful New Critical reliance upon the educated sensibility as the final arbiter of interpretive common sense—a silence all the more impenetrable because of the necessary implicitness of sensibility itself—ensured that those opposed to Exegetics would continue to decline to articulate a program of medieval literary studies to challenge Exegetics' easily replicated paradigm.

The result has been that Exegetics remains, apparently against all odds, the great unfinished business of Medieval Studies. The point is not simply that the Exegetical method continues to be practiced but that it continues to arouse passions. Unable to absorb Exegetics and move on, Chaucer studies instead circles back almost compulsively to an apparently irrepressible scandal, a recursiveness that itself bespeaks a scandalous limitation to its own critical creativity. Despite having attained a healthy maturity, Exegetics remains as combative and polemical as ever, while its opponents decline the passé title of New Critics but continue to denigrate a critical approach that is presumably beneath their notice.[5]

---

objection to the use of patristic exegesis in the criticism of medieval literature," says Donaldson, thereby protecting his own practice from theoretical examination and launching an appeal to shared standards of value that remain powerfully unarticulated. A theoretical attack on Exegetics was in fact offered by Ronald S. Crane in "On Hypotheses in 'Historical Criticism': Apropos of Certain Contemporary Medievalists," *The Idea of the Humanities* (Chicago: University of Chicago Press, 1967), 2.236–60. Crane's claim is that Robertsonian exegesis violates canons of interpretive correctness, a claim that contemporary criticism, with its stronger sense of the conventional nature of all interpretive activity, would be less likely to make.

5. Recent examples of the persistently polemical nature of Exegetics include the critical writings of Judson B. Allen, *A Distinction of Stories* (Columbus: Ohio State University Press, 1981) (with Theresa Anne Moritz) and *The Ethical Poetic of the Later Middle Ages* (Toronto: University of Toronto Press, 1982), and John V. Fleming, *Reason and the Lover* (Princeton: Princeton University Press, 1984). While it is true that in *A Distinction of Stories* Allen and Moritz "state bluntly and categorically" that they are not "Robertsonian" (p. 34 n. 20), both this book and Allen's *Ethical Poetic* are premised on the assumptions of Robertson's brand of historicism and are directed against the Robertsonian targets of "modern critical expectations" (*Distinction*, p. x) and the "solipsism" and "mere aestheticism" that is said to characterize contemporary modes of critical understanding (*Ethical Poetic*, pp. xi and 38). Fleming, Robertson's student and successor at Princeton, opens his new book on the *Roman de la rose* with an anathema against what he calls "The Ithacan Heresy" promoted by such irreligious Cornellians as Winthrop Wetherbee and Thomas D. Hill. On the other side, critical anxiety about the historicist claims of Exegetics are ubiquitous; two examples, chosen not because they are egregious but because they are at once typical and oblique, are recent comments by Donald R. Howard in *The Idea of the Canterbury Tales* (Berkeley: University of California Press, 1976) and Jill Mann in "Troilus' Swoon," *Chaucer Review* 14 (1980), 319–35. Throughout his book Howard skirmishes with Exegetics but evades direct engagement in favor of nervous dismissal: "It is all very dreary" (p. 51). Analogously, Mann concludes her fine discussion with an apparently superfluous dismissal of "self-

Hence criticism has failed to define a strategy of interpretation that would preserve both the indisputable scholarly findings of Exegetics and the humanist values that, as I hope to show, Exegetics seeks to annul. Faced with the Exegetical meaning of the Miller's bagpipes, for example, or the Wife of Bath's deafness, or the Pardoner's eunuchry, critics opposed to Exegetics are largely silent, turning away from these iconographical details in favor of other, less apparently unilateral textual elements.[6] This evasion is especially marked in relation to the medieval tradition of exegetical reading itself, a tradition that Professor Robertson has almost single-handedly brought to the attention of literary scholars but which criticism has sought to quarantine.

The task of a fully informed Chaucerian criticism is not, however, to fend off Exegetical findings but rather to place them within a more inclusive understanding. Exegetical reading is, as everyone would agree, an authentically medieval mode of understanding; and it is one that is inscribed within Chaucerian poetry. Chaucer's poems both invite and, I believe, finally resist exegetical processing; and his characteristic poetic strategies are designed not only to evade but to explore the hegemonic power of institutionalized modes of medieval interpretation. Exegesis, in short, is itself one of Chaucer's subjects, and so vulnerable to his characteristic irony; and a fully responsive criticism must accommodate both

---

conscious historicism" (p. 332) in favor of a more direct emotional response, a conclusion that makes sense only in terms of an unarticulated but powerfully felt antagonism to the explicitly historicist claims of Exegetics. Again, throughout his recent *Chaucer and the Imagery of Narrative* (Stanford: Stanford University Press, 1984), V. A. Kolve takes great pains to distinguish his interpretive use of visual materials from that of the Exegetes, with the perhaps predictable result that he has been chided by reviewers for not being exegetical enough: see James I. Wimsatt in *South Atlantic Quarterly* 85 (1986), 98–101.

6. There are of course exceptions to this general avoidance. A positive valence for the Miller's bagpipes has been demonstrated both by Robert Boenig, "The Miller's Bagpipe: A Note on the *Canterbury Tales* A 565–566," *English Language Notes* 21 (1983), 1–6, and by V. A. Kolve, *Chaucer and the Imagery of Narrative*, p. 75. As for the Wife of Bath's deafness and the Pardoner's eunuchry, in both cases the exegetical meaning of these details ought to be set in opposition to their narrative function. For example, the Wife's deafness is read by Exegetics as an iconographical detail that defines her as one of those who have ears and hear not (Psalm 113); hence her deafness comments on her "rampant 'femininity' or carnality" (Robertson, *A Preface to Chaucer* [Princeton: Princeton University Press, 1963], p. 321). But the narrative of the Prologue tells us that in the course of her violent struggles with Jankyn over his book of wicked wives "he smot me so that I was deef" (III.668), a narrative detail that defines the deafness as an effect not of female inadequacy but of male violence. It is also an evidently enabling handicap: unable to hear the overbearing discourse of male superiority in all its authority, the Wife reproduces instead a parody that inscribes and legitimizes female difference. In showing how male authority undoes itself, then, the literal narrative of the Wife's deafness both offers an explanation in terms other than the exegetical ones prescribed by the dominant clerical culture and demystifies that very dominance by disclosing the violence upon which it is based.

this interest and the skepticism with which it is regarded. The failure of criticism to accomplish this task is perhaps most vividly shown by the continued production of readings motivated by a wholly unmediated Exegetics. Books and articles continue to appear that not only explicate the details of Chaucer's poetry in the terms established by Exegetics, but place these explications in the service of total interpretations determined by Exegetical norms.[7] In sum, in current criticism, as John Fleming has said, Chaucer "is now widely though not universally regarded as a *conservative* Catholic Christian of his time"—the epithet (which I have emphasized) meaning to imply that Chaucer's religious beliefs are not simply part of his cultural situation, like his status as a royal servant or his residence in London, but the central concern of his writing.[8]

However much this assumption may foreclose fresh initiatives in Chaucer criticism, it will doubtless remain in force as long as Exegetics is allowed to stand as the only fully articulated model of specifically *historical* criticism current in Chaucer studies. This is to say, again, not that there are not many different kinds of work (most of them implicitly ahistorical) being practiced in Chaucer studies today, but rather that not only is there no widely known and generally acknowledged paradigm of historical criticism to be set against that defined by Exegetics, but that the issue of historical understanding per se has received virtually no general discussion within the context of Medieval Studies.[9] This is not,

7. To cite only recent books, see John P. Hermann and John J. Burke, eds., *Signs and Symbols in Chaucer's Poetry* (University: University of Alabama Press, 1981); David Lyle Jeffrey, ed., *Chaucer and Scriptural Tradition* (Ottawa: University of Ottawa Press, 1984); Chauncey Wood, *The Elements of Chaucer's Troilus* (Durham: Duke University Press, 1984); and Paul A. Olson, *The Canterbury Tales and the Good Society* (Princeton: Princeton University Press, 1986). Even a book as critically au courant as R. A. Shoaf's powerful *Dante, Chaucer, and the Currency of the Word* (Norman: Pilgrim Books, 1983) is directed (and, in my view, hamstrung) by the norms of Exegetical interpretation.

8. John V. Fleming, "Chaucer and Erasmus on the Pilgrimage to Canterbury: An Iconographical Speculation," in Thomas J. Heffernan, ed., *The Popular Literature of Medieval England,* Tennessee Studies in Literature, 28 (Knoxville: University of Tennessee Press, 1985), p. 152.

9. The obvious exception is the work of Hans Robert Jauss; see his *Aesthetic Experience and Literary Hermeneutics,* trans. Michael Shaw (Minneapolis: University of Minnesota Press, 1982), *Toward an Aesthetic of Reception,* trans. Timothy Bahti (Minneapolis: University of Minnesota Press, 1982), and the influential essay "The Alterity and Modernity of Medieval Literature," trans. Timothy Bahti, *New Literary History* 10 (1979), 181–229, from *Alterität und Modernität der mittelalterlichen Literatur* (Munich: Fink, 1977). Broadly speaking, Jauss attempts to reconcile the tradition of humanist hermeneutics deriving from Dilthey with the *wissenschaftliche* positivism of traditional literary history; hence he insists on "intersubjective communication" as the defining quality of literary understanding ("Art History and Pragmatic History," *Toward an Aesthetic of Reception,* p. 52), yet designates as the object of a truly historical literary study (i.e., one that respects the work's "alterity") not the work itself but the work's "horizon of expectation," by which he means the expecta-

to be sure, a failure unique to medievalists. The inhospitality of Anglo-American literary culture as a whole to a philosophically informed historicism has largely condemned historical criticism to the benighted positivism of the nineteenth century, a darkness that is only now gradually yielding before the arrival of phenomenological hermeneutics, Marxism, and other European imports. Hence it is within the context of the development of historical criticism per se that Exegetics has played a progressive role, not merely by its uncompromising insistence on the historicity of medieval poetry but by its careful articulation of the way in which such a program might be accomplished. And if the program is, as I hope to show, undermined by systematic weaknesses, it nonetheless remains the only game in town. Indeed, the opponents of the Exegetical project are for the most part united only by their opposition to Exegetics.

My purpose here, despite this polemical introduction, is less to argue a position—the next chapter will take up that task—than to offer an analysis of precisely this opposition. If Exegetics remains unfinished business, an unassimilated challenge to the mainstream of Chaucer studies, perhaps a step toward resolution can be made by understanding why this should be so. There are, I think, a number of interrelated reasons, but all of them have their nexus in the question of what it means to be a medievalist. This is itself a historical and—above all—political question, and I therefore offer this chapter, like the book as a whole, as an exercise in what Professor Robertson would call historical criticism. And while I do not agree with his thinking that historicism either can or should be a

---

tions of the work's original readers. This "horizon" is to be discovered by three means: "first, through familiar norms or the immanent poetics of the genre; second, through the implicit relationships to familiar works of the literary-historical surroundings; and third, through the opposition between fiction and reality, between the poetic and the practical function of language, which is always available to the reflective reader during the reading as a possibility of comparison." "Literary History as a Challenge to Literary Theory," *Toward an Aesthetic of Reception,* p. 24. What this amounts to is traditional literary history (items one and two mean comparing the work to others of its kind and to other literary works) supplemented with a comparison of the work to "reality," a reality whose constitution Jauss does not specify. Moreover, Jauss declines to confront the historicity of the observer. In "The Alterity and Modernity of Medieval Literature," the modern reader is described as being able to recognize both the culturally confirmatory aspects of the medieval text (its alterity) and its disruptive elements (its modernity) because both these aspects correspond to an analogous opposition within the modern situation—an analogy that remains unexamined. As Robert Holub says, in *Reception Theory* (London: Methuen, 1984), "In contradistinction to Gadamer's insistence on historicality, we are asked [by Jauss] to ignore or bracket our own historical situatedness. Despite his struggle to escape a positivist-historicist paradigm, then, Jauss, in adopting objectivity as a methodological principle, appears to fall back into the very errors he criticizes" (p. 60). In sum, Jauss's work seems to me to represent a sophisticated reconceptualization of the problems of historicism that promises a theoretical solution that neither it nor any scheme can deliver.

disinterested project, the story that I wish to tell has, I hope, its own kind of truth.

I

The story begins with the medieval revival of the later eighteenth and nineteenth centuries and its relation to the scholarly effort to recover the vernacular literature of the Middle Ages. While no brief narrative can accommodate all the details, it is nonetheless possible to draw some basic distinctions and outline some affiliations. Popular medievalism in England divided into two major schools or attitudes, the most powerful representing the Middle Ages as universalist, institutional, and deeply conservative. Bishops Hurd and Percy, Sir Walter Scott, Coleridge and Wordsworth, Southey, Carlyle, Kenelm Henry Digby, Disraeli and the Young Englanders—these enthusiasts of things medieval celebrated the Middle Ages as a time when a harmonious society was held together by bonds of common faith and an unquestioned social order.[10] As the leading Young Englander, Sir John Manners, put it in his poem *England's Trust* (1841),

> Each knew his place—king, peasant, peer or priest—
> The greatest owned connexion with least;
> From rank to rank the generous feeling ran,
> And linked society as man to man.[11]

Manners articulated the program of the Young Englanders in, as he said, "a word": "let society take a more feudal appearance than it presents now."[12] These medievalists wanted a return to the past not merely in terms of vague ideals or romanticized trappings but institutionally, in the form of a strengthened national church and an authoritarian, hierarchically ordered society.[13]

---

10. On nineteenth-century medievalism in England, see the general study by Alice Chandler, *A Dream of Order: The Medieval Ideal in Nineteenth-Century English Literature* (Lincoln: University of Nebraska Press, 1970). The best account of the conservative strain of medievalism is by Mark Girouard, *The Return to Camelot: Chivalry and the English Gentleman* (New Haven: Yale University Press, 1981). Girouard stresses the crucial importance of Kenelm Henry Digby's *The Broad Stone of Honour* (1823) in forming the nineteenth-century ideology of chivalry by which the class and economic violence of the nineteenth century was successfully mystified.

11. Cited by Girouard, *Return to Camelot*, p. 83, and by Chandler, *Dream of Order*, p. 161.

12. From a letter of 1842, cited by Chandler, *Dream of Order*, p. 164.

13. The Oxford Movement—which Matthew Arnold characterized as one of the "last enchantments of the Middle Ages"—ought to be enrolled among the promoters of a conservative medievalism, and Manners' explicitly reactionary program can be tellingly

In opposition to this conservative model the nineteenth century also saw the development of a conception of the Middle Ages as pluralist, primitivist, and above all else, individualist. This was the view made popular by Ruskin and Morris and, to a lesser extent, by the Pre-Raphaelites. Ruskin's enormously popular "The Nature of Gothic" argued that the medieval cathedral represented not a corporate Christian consciousness but the "out-speaking of the strong spirit" of the men of the north, and that its value resided less in its embodiment of religious values than in the rough imperfection that testified to the unconstrained labor of its individual makers.[14] Similarly, William Morris saw the great virtue of the Middle Ages in a heroic individuality that resisted "the degradation of . . . sordid utilitarianism." In line with a traditional liberal praise of Anglo-Saxon freedom and the native social forms through which it was expressed, Morris celebrated a voluntary "Fellowship of Men" that characterized medieval life at its best, and that found its finest (and last) expression in the gathering of the commons for the failed revolution of 1381.[15] For Ruskin and Morris, and for others like them, the

matched with an equivalently obscurantist comment uttered by the future Cardinal Newman: "I do not shrink from uttering my firm conviction that it would be a gain to the country were it vastly more superstitious, more bigoted, more gloomy, more fierce in its religion than at present it shows itself to be." Cited by Basil Willey, *Nineteenth-Century Studies* (New York: Columbia University Press, 1949), p. 75; for the citation from Arnold, see p. 73.

14. John Ruskin, "The Nature of Gothic," *Works*, ed. E. T. Cook and Alexander Wedderburn (London: George Allen, 1904), 10.188. Given the complexity of his personality and career, it would be wrong to ascribe to Ruskin any single attitude toward the Middle Ages. Despite his commitment to the Working Men's College in Red Lion Square in the 1860s, the vehicle for educational and social reform that Ruskin proposed in the 1870s was the Guild of St. George, an organization governed by the laws of quattrocento Florence—an image of medieval society radically at odds with that represented in "The Nature of Gothic" in 1852. Indeed, "The Nature of Gothic" is discontinuous with itself, juxtaposing a primitivist Gothicism with a careful iconographical exegesis of St. Mark's Cathedral in Venice. For Ruskin's exegetical interests, see George P. Landow, *The Aesthetic and Critical Theories of John Ruskin* (Princeton: Princeton University Press, 1971), pp. 319–457. The curriculum of Ruskin's St. George's schools was to consist in books by seven authors: Moses, David, Hesiod, Virgil, Dante, Chaucer, and St. John the Divine. Significantly, however, all of Chaucer's works (including the spurious) were to be read *except* the *Canterbury Tales*; see *Fors Clavigera* 61 in *Works* 28.500. For Ruskin the Companions of St. George are "a band of achieving knights—not churls needing deliverance." See Margaret E. Spence, "The Guild of St. George: Ruskin's Attempt to Translate His Ideas into Practice," *Bulletin of the John Rylands Library* 40 (1957), 156.

15. Morris' *A Dream of John Ball* is an attack on "the degradation of the sordid utilitarianism that cares not and knows not of beauty and history" in the name of "the Fellowship of Men" that motivated the Peasant's Revolt and that, Morris asserts, "shall endure." See *Collected Works*, ed. May Morris (London: Longmans, 1910–15), 16.215, 284. In *William Morris: Romantic to Revolutionary* (New York: Monthly Review Press, 1961), E. P. Thompson describes *The Dream of John Ball* as perhaps Morris' "greatest meditation upon the

Middle Ages were valuable not because of their powerful institutions of control and order but despite them. Spared both the classical importations that falsified Renaissance England and the dehumanizing industrialism that was currently disfiguring the nation, the medieval spirit was able to fulfill itself in forms hospitable to its original native vigor. More profoundly, in returning to the primitive origins of the nation these writers sought to recuperate an undergirding identity of spirit that could serve as an ideal of social coherence and unity to set against a contemporary society stratified by class divisions and riven by economic warfare. Rejecting the eighteenth-century idea of culture as the discriminating mark of social superiority, Romantic medievalists instead defined culture as an elemental and universal value that is the birthright of every member of the nation, and one from which too many had been alienated by a postmedieval history that should now be set aside.[16]

---

meaning of life, both in its individual and its historical context" (p. 836). For the appeal to the tradition of Saxon liberty, see Christopher Hill, "The Norman Yoke," in John Saville, ed., *Democracy and the Labour Movement* (London: Lawrence and Wisehart, 1954), pp. 11–66, reprinted in *Puritanism and Revolution* (London: Secker and Warburg, 1958), pp. 50–122. Morris' conception of the Germanic origins of English society is matched by the picture of Saxon life presented by the Anglo-Saxonist J. M. Kemble and the "Whig" historians J. R. Green and E. A. Freeman; see J. W. Burrow, *A Liberal Descent: Victorian Historians and the English Past* (Cambridge: Cambridge University Press, 1981), pp. 155–92. The politically ambiguous medievalism of Morris' Pre-Raphaelite colleagues is examined by John Dixon Hunt, *The Pre-Raphaelite Imagination* (Lincoln: University of Nebraska Press, 1968). As for Tennyson's *Idylls of the King,* Swinburne's suggestion that it be retitled the *Morte D'Albert* neatly crystallizes the poem's political valence (as if its dedication to the Queen were not sufficient indication).

16. For an account of this strain in nineteenth-century medievalism, see Lionel Gossman, "Literature and Education," *New Literary History* 13 (1982), 341–71, and, more generally, Raymond Williams, *Culture and Society, 1780–1950* (Harmondsworth: Penguin Books, 1961), pp. 137–61, 187–91. While beyond the scope of this discussion, it should be stressed that the link between a primitivist reading of medieval culture and liberal commitment to the unification of society is of crucial importance to the development of Medieval Studies on the Continent. The intense politicization of the Middle Ages in France, for example, and its cooption by a conservative state apparatus, had the result of driving liberal medievalists like Michelet into mediaphobia. As a countermeasure, scholars who wished to remain loyal both to the Middle Ages and to their liberal principles insisted that what validated modern interest in the medieval past was not an admiration for its political or religious values but the immediacy with which both a common human nature and a shared national culture were represented in medieval art. A good example here is Gaston Paris, son of the Paulin Paris who was holder of the first chair of medieval French at the Collège de France (1863), and himself holder of the first chair in the same subject at the Ecole Pratique des Hautes Etudes (1872). Throughout his writings Paris insists that medieval literature can be all things to all readers because it offers a full representation of the French nation in its original form; see, e.g., his comments at two of the early meetings of the Société des Anciens Textes Français in the *Bulletin de la Société des Anciens Textes Français* 3 (1877), 53–58, and 5 (1879), 46–52, and the manifesto of *Romania,* founded in the dark days of 1871 and seen as an agency by which France could reunite itself to withstand the

Although this conception of the Middle Ages was a minority view in nineteenth-century England, it was particularly congenial to the pioneers of early English studies. There are several reasons for this. One was the relative lack of state and institutional support for medieval scholarship in England, which meant that it was less easily appropriated by a conservative political apparatus. Nineteenth-century medieval scholarship in England tended to be an entrepreneurial activity, and the self-reliant individuals who engaged in it were naturally admiring of rugged individuality.[17] Another, more profound, reason was the congruence between the methods of German scientific historicism and liberal values. German scholars were themselves largely committed to a liberal political program that opposed both the absolutism of the right and the egalitarianism and revolutionary rationalism of the left. Their central political value was the protection of individual liberties, which they saw threatened by both church and monarchy and protected only by a powerful secular state.[18]

---

challenge of a monolithic Germany: *Romania* 1 (1872), 1–22. For the politicization of the Middle Ages in nineteenth-century France, see Janine Dakyns, *The Middle Ages in French Literature, 1851–1900* (Oxford: Oxford University Press, 1973), and now Hans Ulrich Gumbrecht, " 'Un souffle d'Allemagne ayant passé': Friedrich Diez, Gaston Paris, and the Genesis of National Philologies," *Romance Philology* 40 (1986), 1–37. This process went so far that Fustel de Coulanges could actually claim that the disasters of 1870–71 were the result of the divisions brought about by partisan misrepresentations of the Middle Ages. Hence, "La connaissance du moyen âge, mais la connaissance exacte et scientifique, sincère et sans parti-pris, est pour notre société un intérêt de premier ordre" (cited Dakyns, p. 196). It was by recuperating a Middle Ages unified by a national spirit or character rather than by institutions that were by their very nature divisive that a unified France could be recovered.

17. Complaints about the government's neglect of historical records and monuments are a persistent feature of nineteenth-century scholarly writing; brief overviews are offered by Thomas P. Peardon, *The Transition in English Historical Writing, 1760–1830* (New York: Columbia University Press, 1933), and by Dom David Knowles, *Great Historical Enterprises* (London: Nelson, 1964), whose parallel accounts of the Monumenta Germaniae Historica and the Rolls Series provide a dismaying insight into English neglect and disorganization. For the state control of medievalism in France, see, e.g., William R. Keylor, *Academy and Community: The Foundation of the French Historical Profession* (Cambridge: Harvard University Press, 1975), and Paul Léon, *La vie des monuments français: destruction, restauration* (Paris: Picard, 1951). In England, the feebleness of the aristocratic Royal Society of Antiquaries should be set against the vigor of the voluntary publishing and scholarly societies (which should themselves be distinguished from antiquarian book clubs like the Roxburghe): see Joan Evans, *A History of the Society of Antiquaries* (Oxford: Oxford University Press, 1956) and Harrison Ross Steeves, *Learned Societies and English Literary Scholarship* (New York: Columbia University Press, 1913). On the independent scholar of nineteenth-century England, general surveys are offered by John Gross, *The Rise and Fall of the Man of Letters* (London: Macmillan, 1969), and Richard D. Altick, *The Scholar Adventurers* (New York: Macmillan, 1960).

18. On the politics of the leaders of the historicist movement, see Georg G. Iggers, *The German Conception of History* (Middletown: Wesleyan University Press, 1968) and Peter

At a methodological level, they insisted that history is the sphere of the unique, of an irreducible individuality that must be grasped in all its specificity. And they privileged individuality not only as the object of study but also as the subject who studies, the scientific investigator who is able to arrive by painstaking labor at the original truth of things, whether it be the life of Frederick the Great or the *Nibelungenlied* in its authentic form. In sum, there was a profound affinity between German historical scholarship and liberal progressivism and individualism.[19]

This affinity can be seen in an explicit form in England in politically liberal scholars like J. M. Kemble and F. J. Furnivall. Both of these men became embroiled in controversies that pitted the new methods of German philology against an elitist antiquarianism, Kemble in the so-called Anglo-Saxon controversy of the 1830s, Furnivall in his sulfurous debate with Swinburne about the editing of Shakespeare some forty years later—two technical controversies that were in fact galvanized by political antipathy.[20] Furnivall was profoundly committed to the quintessentially liberal and Arnoldian idea that the study of the literature of the English past could serve to recover the organic unity that the class-divided society of the nineteenth century had lost, and at the opening session of the Working Men's College in Red Lion Square—where he taught for many subsequent years—he distributed copies of Ruskin's "The Nature of Gothic" that he had had printed at his own expense.[21] These instances of explicit political commitment, however, are less important than the fact that the vast majority of nineteenth-century medieval scholars of all political hues shared certain crucial interpretive assumptions. For one thing, despite their commitment to the idea of historical conditioning, these scholars in fact made little effort to corre-

Hanns Reill, *The German Enlightenment and the Rise of Historicism* (Berkeley: University of California Press, 1975).

19. The necessary brevity of this account has constrained me to simplify complex issues that are given full treatment by Hayden White, *Metahistory: The Historical Imagination in Nineteenth-Century Europe* (Baltimore: Johns Hopkins University Press, 1973).

20. Kemble's attack on the Anglo-Saxon establishment is detailed by Hans Aarsleff, *The Study of Language in England, 1780–1860* (Princeton: Princeton University Press, 1967); see also Raymond A. Wiley, "Anglo-Saxon Kemble: The Life and Works of John Mitchell Kemble, 1807–1857, Philologist, Historian, Archaeologist," in S. C. Hawkes, D. Brown, and J. Campbell, eds., *Anglo-Saxon Studies in Archaeology and History*, I, British Archaeological Reports, British Series, 72 (Oxford: British Archaeological Society, 1979), pp. 165–273. The best account of the Swinburne-Furnivall dispute is provided by William S. Peterson, ed., *Browning's Trumpeter: The Correspondance of Robert Browning and Frederick J. Furnivall, 1872–1889* (Washington, D.C.: Decatur House Press, 1979); see also William Benzie, *Dr. F. J. Furnivall, Victorian Scholar Adventurer* (Norman: Pilgrim Books, 1983).

21. Benzie, *Dr. F. J. Furnivall*, p. 48; Peterson, *Browning's Trumpeter*, p. xxiv. For the liberal values that motivated the rise of English studies, see Chris Baldick, *The Social Mission of English Criticism, 1848–1932* (Oxford: Clarendon Press, 1983).

late medieval literature to the institutions, whether social, political or religious, of its period. On the contrary, medieval literature was in large part understood as the expression of a human nature valuably different from our own precisely because it was unconstrained by narrow and dehumanizing institutions. Old English literature was most often understood in the context of a pervasive Germanic primitivism that opposed native Anglo-Saxon values to "the blighting touch of Christianity."[22] So too with Chaucer, whose poetry was read in the very similar terms of an uncritical realism. Chaucer offered, it was thought, a representation of fourteenth-century life unmediated by preconceptions and undistorted by personal commitments; like his latter-day scholarly counterparts, he was above all else an independent individual who saw the truth of things and recorded it accurately. This is the Chaucer of Whig historiography, a disinterested but sympathetic observer, alert to the failings of his time but deeply understanding of the individual lives of his fellow citizens.[23] Far from being engaged in any local polemic, his poetry spoke to concerns that were part of the permanent fabric of human life.

But Chaucer's ability to trace what Blake had called "the Physiognomies or Lineaments of Universal Human Life"[24] required him, paradoxically, to rise above the very historical circumstances that scholars were, from another perspective, attempting to describe in all their specificity. In other words, there was within historicism a largely hidden debate between a conditioning historical context and a transhistorical humanism—a debate that continues in large part to govern current criticism. In the nineteenth century this debate was virtually always silently resolved in favor of an idealist humanism, but in the work of the second generation of Chaucer scholars—for example, Root, Kittredge, Manly, Lowes, Hammond, Tatlock, Patch, Dempster, and Malone—the paradox at the heart of the historicist project began to become visible.[25] These

---

22. Eric Stanley, *The Search for Anglo-Saxon Paganism* (Cambridge: Brewer and Boydell, 1975), p. 8; for the eighteenth-century roots of this primitivism, see Reill's account (*German Enlightenment and the Rise of Historicism*) of the career of the founder of German literary medieval studies, Johann Jacob Bodmer (1698–1783), who was inspired by Thomas Blackwell's *Enquiry into the Life and Writings of Homer* (1735) to search for a German Homeric Age and who then succeeded in discovering/creating one.

23. Whig historiography was first christened by Herbert Butterfield, *The Whig Interpretation of History* (London: G. Bell, 1931); its monuments are perceptively analyzed by Burrow, *Liberal Descent*.

24. "Prospectus of the Engraving of Chaucer's Canterbury Pilgrims," *Poetry and Prose of William Blake,* ed. Geoffrey Keynes (London: Nonesuch Press, 1943), p. 637.

25. Of course there were nineteenth-century exceptions. Early in the century John Wilson, professor of moral philosophy at Glasgow, insisted that Chaucer's poetry was allegorical and motivated by a commitment to "the wonderful political institution of Chivalry," and in his *Encyclopaedia Britannica* article of 1876, William Minto, professor of logic

scholars dominated the field from the death of Furnivall in 1910 until the midpoint of the century. Their work falls into two sharply defined categories, which correspond not to differences among them—almost every scholar is represented in both categories—but to the internal division within historicism itself. On the one hand is an enormous and enormously valuable mass of sheer information, almost always presented in impressively learned articles and now enshrined in the notes to Robinson's edition.[26] This work was accomplished through a laborious attention to detail, polyglot inclusiveness, and mastery of accurate techniques of recovery and restoration—through, that is, those procedures and values that successfully transformed the study of medieval literature from uncritical amateurism into a scientific profession.

But the terms of this success prescribed inevitable and ultimately irremediable limitations upon the whole historicist project as originally conceived—limitations that are for the most part still in force. Believing that natural science was successful because its methodology partook of the certainty and universality of the natural laws it sought to uncover, historicism in its positivist phrase assumed for itself a similar methodological purity. Since the results of its investigations were thus thought to be untouched by human hands, historicism ascribed to them an unqualified objectivity and an explanatory power that no merely thematic interpretation could possibly attain. In thus privileging extratextual data, historical criticism came to depend upon an unreflective factualism that foreclosed interpretive possibilities. Analogous, and equally prejudicial

---

and English at Aberdeen University, argued that "the 'Canterbury Tales' are really in their underlying design an exposition of chivalrous sentiment, thrown into relief by contrast with its opposite." The citations from Wilson (who wrote under the pseudonym "Christopher North") and Minto are taken from Derek Brewer, ed., *Chaucer: The Critical Heritage* (London: Routledge and Kegan Paul, 1978), 2.59, 187. For surveys of Chaucer criticism, see Brewer's introduction to this collection and his essays "Images of Chaucer, 1386–1900," in Brewer, ed., *Chaucer and Chaucerians* (University: University of Alabama Press, 1966), pp. 240–70, and "The Criticism of Chaucer in the Twentieth Century," in *Chaucer's Mind and Art*, pp. 3–28.

26. Examples are John S. P. Tatlock, "The Epilog of Chaucer's *Troilus*," *Modern Philology* 18 (1920–21), 625–59, and "Boccaccio and the Plan of Chaucer's *Canterbury Tales*," *Anglia* 37 (1913), 69–117 (Tatlock published over thirty-five separate items on Chaucer, including seven books); George Lyman Kittredge, "The Authorship of the English Romaunt of the Rose," *Harvard Studies and Notes in Philology and Literature* 1 (1892), 1–65, and "Chaucer's Lollius," *Harvard Studies in Classical Philology* 28 (1917), 47–133 (twenty-two items, three books); John Livingston Lowes, "Chaucer and the *Miroir de Mariage*," *Modern Philology* 8 (1910–11), 165–86, 305–34, and "The Loveres Maladye of Hereos," *Modern Philology* 11 (1913–14), 491–546 (thirty items, one book). Judging from the extent to which the findings and arguments of these great scholars have been inadvertently repeated in later discussions, we are perhaps right in thinking that their role in laying the foundations of Chaucer scholarship has been in recent years neglected.

to the intersubjectivity upon which the humanist recovery of the past depended, was historicism's uncritical indulgence of its inevitable predilection for genetic explanation. After all, much of nineteenth-century historicism had been motivated by a desire to use the past, and specifically the medieval past, to prescribe a future, whether it was the restoration of the ancien régime in France, the reunification of Germany, or the dismantling of industrial techniques of labor management in England. Genetic explanation was virtually the raison d'être of historicism: knowing whence we came, so ran the argument, we would know what we should become. The mission of historicism was quite simply to historicize, to show that the present entities that had previously been understood in terms of universal principles or natural laws were instead the effect of prior causes. And this historicizing applied as much to literary texts as it did to political institutions.

The effect of these cognate aspects of historicism was to decompose the past in the very process of trying to recover it. By so definitively allowing the lines of explanatory force to run vertically, as it were, from the text back into the past that was to account for it, this brand of historicism devalued the possibility of lateral explanation in terms of function within the text itself. The first question it invariably asked of a puzzling element in the text was genetic, while the prevailing factualism disposed the answer to be a newly discovered item whose significance was taken to be self-evident. This procedure was most explicitly at work in the ubiquitous source study that characterized this phase of scholarship, but it was also visible in Manly's attempt to understand the pilgrims in terms of Chaucerian contemporaries, for instance, or in the persistent (and continuing) attempts to tie the poems to specific occasions.[27] In all of these cases Chaucer's poems were seen as effects to be explained by reference to their extratextual causes, explanations that were all the more powerful just because the causes *were* extratextual and therefore thought to be peculiarly objective in comparison to internal or subjective interpretations.

But if historicism was in danger of mummifying the very past it

27. John M. Manly, *Some New Light on Chaucer* (New York: Holt, 1926). Recent examples of occasional criticism are D. W. Robertson, Jr., "The Historical Setting of Chaucer's *Book of the Duchess,*" in John Mahoney and John Esten Keller, eds., *Mediaeval Studies in Honor of Urban Tigner Holmes, Jr.* (Chapel Hill: University of North Carolina Press, 1965), pp. 169–95, reprinted in *Essays in Medieval Culture,* pp. 235–56; Larry D. Benson, "The Occasion of *The Parliament of Fowls,*" in Benson and Siegfried Wenzel, eds., *The Wisdom of Poetry: Essays in Early English Literature in Honor of Morton W. Bloomfield* (Kalamazoo: Medieval Institute Publications, 1982), pp. 123–44; and Larry D. Benson, "The 'Love-Tydynges' in Chaucer's *House of Fame,*" in Julian N. Wasserman and Robert J. Blanch, eds., *Chaucer in the Eighties* (Syracuse: Syracuse University Press, 1986), pp. 3–22.

sought to revive, it remained nonetheless a profoundly humanistic venture. The entire historicist project, we should not forget, was underwritten by the assumption of a transhistorical humanness that at once motivated and legitimized historical study. In the first volume of his *Grundriss der romanischen Philologie,* Gustav Gröber, the high priest of mechanistic positivism, echoed the idealistic Wilhelm von Humboldt in defining the object of philology as "the human spirit in language," and it was that *Geist,* ever varying in its manifestations but identical in its essence, that stood as the goal of historical study.[28] And while the idea of periodization, and the specialization of knowledge that it entailed, radically called into question the continuity between past and present that was at the center of humanist historicism, it never in fact managed to displace it.[29] Hence the other kind of work that the positivist literary historian produced in this period was the explicitly appreciative survey of Chaucer's poetry written by virtually every major scholar. The list begins with Root's *The Poetry of Chaucer* in 1906, includes Kittredge's famous 1915 lectures and Lowes's only slightly less celebrated ones of 1934, and concludes at mid-century with the career-capping books by Patch (1949), Tatlock (posthumously, in 1950), Lawrence (1950), and Malone (1951). Two things stand out about these books. All of them present essentially the same Whig Chaucer as nineteenth-century criticism, and indeed except for greater accuracy could all have been written then. And with only the barest of exceptions none of them makes any real use of the massive historical detail that scholarship had succeeded in accumulating about Chaucer's poetry. In fact, there is in these books by eminent and powerful scholars a marked tendency to devalue scholarship itself.

This paradox is especially striking in perhaps the best of these books, John Livingstone Lowes's *Geoffrey Chaucer and the Development of His Genius* (1934). Lowes begins by assuring his audience that they will be

---

28. Gustav Gröber, *Grundriss der romanischen Philologie,* 2d ed. (Strassburg: Trübner, 1904–6), 1.194: "Die Erscheinung des menschlichen Geistes in der nur mittelbar verständlichen Sprache und seine Leistunge in der künstlerisch behandelten Rede der Vergangenheit also bilden den eigentlichen Gegenstand der Philologie." For Humboldt, see his "Uber die Aufgabe des Geschichtsschreibers," translated as "On the Historian's Task," *History and Theory* 6 (1967), 57–71, esp. 70. The idealism of his project is well discussed by Hayden White, *Metahistory,* pp. 178–87.

29. The crisis of historicism is usually understood as the relativizing of value, but the insistence upon the self-sufficiency of each historical period—"that," in Ranke's famous words, "each period is immediate vis-à-vis God, and that its value depends not at all on what followed from it, but rather on its own existence, on its own self"—also sacrificed the historian's responsibility to connect the past with the present. For the citation from Ranke, and a lucid discussion of this issue, see Jauss, *Toward an Aesthetic of Reception,* pp. 7–8.

spared "the awe-inspiring *chevaux de frise* of technical Chaucerian scholarship" and uses an agricultural metaphor to let us know what he thinks
of it: "technical erudition . . . may safely be left by the lover of poetry
until its results have fertilized the common soil."[30] But having dismissed
the very scholarship to which he had himself made such remarkable con-
tributions, Lowes then offers in his first lecture a masterful summary of
what he calls "the determining concepts of Chaucer's world," by which
he means the kind of medieval astronomical, medical, and geographical
knowledge that C. S. Lewis was later to anatomize in *The Discarded Image*.[31] Furthermore, in the second lecture he offers a biography of the poet
and in the third an account of his reading, with an emphasis on Machaut,
Froissart, and Deschamps. Having now prepared his audience with a
substantial amount of scholarly information, Lowes then reverses his
field again and provides three scintillatingly appreciative lectures on the
poetry that make virtually no reference to the preceding material at all.
In short, historical scholarship and literary understanding have here little
to do with each other. For Lowes, as for his colleagues, there were in
effect two Chaucers: one is the fourteenth-century writer whose every
word requires elaborate annotation, while the other is the purveyor of
God's plenty who, as Root predictably said in 1906, "was in the world,
but not of it," and who speaks with an immediacy that obviates the need
for interpretation.[32] Either an antiquarian curiosity or an occasion for
appreciative paraphrase, Chaucer's poetry fell prey to the ironic law of
positivist historicism that decrees that the more that is known about a
text the less it can be said to mean.

2

It is in the context of the perceived failure of this perhaps uniquely
American brand of historicism that the rise of both New Criticism and
Exegetics should be understood. As a general movement New Criticism
was of course explicit in its opposition to historicism, both as a methodology and as a literary ideology entrenched within the university. Profoundly libertarian in its orientation, New Criticism sought to free poetry from the historicity in which scholarship had mired it so that it
might become once again an agency for cultural reconstruction. For all

30. John Livingstone Lowes, *Chaucer and the Development of His Genius* (Boston:
Houghton Mifflin, 1934), p. 6.
31. C. S. Lewis, *The Discarded Image* (Cambridge: Cambridge University Press,
1964).
32. Robert K. Root, *The Poetry of Chaucer,* 2d ed. (Boston: Houghton Mifflin, 1922),
p. 32.

its celebration of the work of art as a value in and for itself, New Criticism never abandoned the Romantic and Arnoldian claim that literature offers the alienated reader a saving knowledge. Hence it was also opposed to a merely descriptive or appreciative criticism that devalued the capacity of literature to bear significant meaning. Moreover, New Criticism had very specific notions about the kind of meaning that poems could yield. Despite its insistence upon the objectivity of its interpretive procedures, New Critical practice was in fact underwritten by a familiar set of liberal and humanist values. It privileged pragmatic empiricism over a priori theorizing, an ethics of attitude over a code of rules, secular pluralism over doctrinal conformity, and above all else the independence and self-reliance of the individual, who is understood not as conditioned by social practices and institutions but as an autonomous being who creates his historical world through his own self-directed efforts. In effect, New Criticism read all poetry as enacting a continual dramatization of this liberal humanist ideology. For the New Critical "poetics of tension," poetry was a battleground where the abstract certainties of the angelic imagination were subjected to the healthful testing of experience. The formal struggle within the poem between logic and texture (Ransom), or reason and emotion (Winters), or extension and intension (Tate), or the universal and the concrete (Wimsatt) was thematized into what R. S. Crane rightly identified as a set of "reduction terms": order and disorder, reality and appearance, nature and art, emotion and reason, and so on.[33] These are the topoi that the poem was then seen as figuring in a perpetual and irresolvable dialogue, the final meaning being the value of complexity itself. And even beneath this finality was the far bolder claim that meaning itself is a function of a deliberate act of choice. For New Criticism the poetic act is quintessentially the imposition of significance upon that which is otherwise without meaning, a gesture of creation that asserts the autonomy of the individual, just as the act of reading is best undertaken without social or institutional constraints.

While the early 1950s saw the appearance of a number of New Critical readings, it was Talbot Donaldson's edition and commentary of 1958, significantly entitled *Chaucer's Poetry: An Anthology for the Modern Reader,*

---

33. Ronald S. Crane, *The Languages of Criticism and the Structures of Poetry* (Toronto: University of Toronto Press, 1953), pp. 123–24; see Jonathan Culler, *The Pursuit of Signs* (Ithaca: Cornell University Press, 1981), p. 5. On New Criticism, see Murray Krieger, *The New Apologists for Poetry* (Minneapolis: University of Minnesota Press, 1956) and Gerald Graff, *Poetic Statement and Critical Dogma* (Evanston: Northwestern University Press, 1970), among many others. A Marxist reading of New Criticism is offered by John Fekete, *The Critical Twilight: Explorations in the Ideology of Anglo-American Literary Theory from Eliot to McLuhan* (London: Routledge and Kegan Paul, 1977); see also Frank A. Ninkovich, "The New Criticism and Cold War America," *Southern Quarterly* 20 (1981), 1–24.

that marked the full arrival of the New Critical Chaucer.[34] Suppressing all signs of the editorial and philological learning upon which it was based, and eschewing scholarly annotations and bibliographies, Donaldson's text proclaimed Chaucer's liberation from the erudite antiquarianism to which historicism had consigned him. And in his persuasively discreet commentary, Donaldson began to show the subtlety and depth of meaning that Chaucer's poetry could be made to yield when subjected to the interpretive procedures of New Criticism. Not surprisingly, the tenor of this meaning was consistent with the liberal humanism that underwrote the New Critical enterprise itself. Donaldson's Chaucer was a poet who persistently engaged his readers in a debate between the straightforward imperatives of cultural and religious authority, on the one hand, and, on the other, the irreducible complexity of lived experience.

But Donaldson went beyond thematics to argue that this is a debate implicit in Chaucerian form itself. Subscribing to the New Critical conception of poetry as dramatic rather than rhetorical, he both sharpened Kittredge's notion of the *Canterbury Tales* as a collection of monologues and applied the dramatic principle to texts, such as the General Prologue and *Troilus and Criseyde,* which had previously been ascribed to an authorial voice.[35] The effect of this strategy was twofold. First, in opening a gap between author and persona Donaldson allowed entrance to the New Critically sanctified principle of irony. No longer could Chaucerian statement, no matter how orthodox or conventional, be read as unqualified assertion, for it was now subject to the continual negotiations required by context. But secondly, he showed how these negotiations could be brought to a close. For the dramatizing of Chaucerian poetry meant that the referent of every statement was not an extrinsic system of value, whether or not historical, but the fictionalized personality who

---

34. E. Talbot Donaldson, *Chaucer's Poetry: An Anthology for the Modern Reader* (New York: Ronald Press, 1958). Important early New Critical readings were those by Charles Owen, "The Crucial Passages in Five of the Canterbury Tales: A Study in Irony and Symbol," *Journal of English and Germanic Philology* 52 (1953), 294–311, and "Chaucer's *Canterbury Tales:* Aesthetic Design in Stories of the First Day," *English Studies* 35 (1954), 49–56; Charles Muscatine, "Form, Texture, and Meaning in Chaucer's *Knight's Tale,*" *PMLA* 65 (1950), 911–29; Arthur W. Hoffman, "Chaucer's Prologue to Pilgrimage: The Two Voices," *ELH* 21 (1954), 1–16; and the important essays on Chaucerian irony published by Earle Birney in two groups, one in 1939–41 and the other in 1959–60; Birney's essays have now been collected in *Essays on Chaucerian Irony,* ed. Beryl Rowland (Toronto: University of Toronto Press, 1985).

35. E. Talbot Donaldson, "Chaucer the Pilgrim," *PMLA* 69 (1954), 928–36, "The Ending of Chaucer's *Troilus,*" in *Early English and Norse Studies Presented to Hugh Smith* (London: Methuen, 1963), pp. 26–45, both reprinted in *Speaking of Chaucer,* pp. 1–12, 84–101.

spoke it. At the center of Chaucer's poetry was character, and every state-ment should be read in the first instance as a characterizing device. What motivated Chaucerian poetry, then, was an aesthetic impulse toward mi-metic fidelity regardless of the requirements of the absolutist morality of the Christian Middle Ages.

In effect, the New Critical revanche served to rewrite the traditional conception of the Whig Chaucer in terms that would resist the unwitting depredations of positivist historicism while allowing for the articulation of a more complex and powerful poetic meaning than descriptive criti-cism could elicit. Indeed, the New Critical preservation of the traditional image of the Chaucerian author, far from being just a pious gesture to-ward Chaucer scholars of yore, is itself a necessary part of the liberal humanism that New Criticism was anxious to protect. For just as Chau-cer's poetry is an affirmation of the individual self, so must it be itself the effect of a commensurate individuality, of an author who is suitably dis-tanced from his creation but remains the unmoved mover to whom re-sponsibility can ultimately be referred. Even the distance itself is signifi-cant: masked by a series of ironic figurations, the poet is everywhere present but nowhere visible, a displacement that is the authorial equiva-lent of a poetry whose ultimate meaning is always implied but never stated (and hence requires the interpretive ministrations of the reader in order to be made explicit). Similarly, the aesthetic assumptions of New Criticism contained a powerful specific against historicism. As we have seen, the genetic imperative of historicism sought continually to refer the elements of a text back to some prior reality, while its prevailing methodological factualism allowed these referrals to stand as sufficient explanation. But by insisting that the Chaucerian texts found their im-mediate origin in the fictive self of a pilgrim or narrative persona, New Criticism perforce invested their details with human value. No longer was it possible, for instance, to explain the mysterious Lollius as simply the mistranslation of a Horatian line that served to answer Chaucer's need for a Latin *auctor*. On the contrary, since the speaking voice was itself now a character, it too was endowed with a story, and Lollius, whatever his origins, necessarily played a part in it. Once identified, Lollius could no longer drop from critical sight but became a function in the narrative of the poem's telling, part of the speaker's ethical universe. So too, then, for historical scholarship in general. It could be seen as a kind of seman-tics, providing a glossary for Chaucer's topical lexicon but unable to read his poetic syntax, the organizing pattern by which meaning is made. And this was the task that could now be performed by a suitably in-formed criticism.

In its medievalist phase, then, and despite the polemical chasteness of

Donaldson's textbook, New Criticism sought less to extract the poem from its historical context than to find strategies by which to reaffirm the humanist values that had motivated the historicist recovery in the first place. Rejecting the positivist factualism and academic mechanization that had brought about the mutual alienation of scholarship and criticism, this new generation of scholars reinstated the values of liberal humanism at the center of their procedures, using them as the interpretive principles by which they could make sense of the historical materials gathered by their predecessors. Donaldson's situating of character at the origin of Chaucerian discourse was one of the most powerful ways in which the materials of historical scholarship could be interpreted according to the values of liberal humanism. Similarly powerful, and theoretically more explicit, was the historical stylistics promoted by Charles Muscatine in *Chaucer and the French Tradition* (1957), a book that represents the most substantial and influential achievement of this phase of Chaucerian scholarship.[36]

The critical tradition against which Muscatine reacted was, as we have seen, one that privileged realistic immediacy while devaluing a highly figured and rhetoricized poetic, and it read the course of Chaucer's poetic career, and the history of virtually all later medieval poetry, as a progress from an empty courtly artificiality toward a vigorous and democratic realism—a progress, of course, that matched the analogous development of society as a whole. But as the New Critics realized, while such a reading of literary history might make good sense politically, it contained an unwitting and devastating attack upon literature itself. For it assumed that the best kind of art is that which is most like life—and therefore least like art. Committed as they were to defining and defending the literariness of literature as an essential quality that both protected literature from being misjudged by inappropriate standards and established it as an independent *Fach* worthy of professional study, New Critics found any scheme that devalued the artfulness of literary art unacceptable. Hence the announced goal of Muscatine's project was to show that realistic writing, far from representing an unmediated access to the world, was itself a product of verbal art and therefore as conventional as the high style of courtly poetry—which meant by the same token that courtly poetry was worthy of being taken seriously. And as the subtitle of his book suggested ("A Study in Style and Meaning"), he argued that both the high and low styles of medieval literature were best understood as agencies of significance, deliberately chosen means by which values could be articulated.

---

36. Charles Muscatine, *Chaucer and the French Tradition* (Berkeley: University of California Press, 1957); further references will appear in the text.

This does not mean, of course, that Muscatine and his New Critical colleagues wished to attack the Whig account of literary history, with its optimistic story of the emancipation of the poetic imagination from the tyranny of imposed forms. On the contrary, Muscatine's account of medieval literature is underwritten by and supportive of precisely this liberal historiography, although his version is both less explicit and more sophisticated than its nineteenth-century precursors. Attacking in the first instance the fossilizing pressure of positivism, Muscatine insists that both the courtly and bourgeois styles themselves and the values they articulate are unconditioned by any specific historical formation. Each style is "an almost independent literary tool, tied less to a specific social class or specific genres than to a characteristic set of attitudes" (p. 59). "A conventional style," whether it be courtly or bourgeois, highly figured or conversational, is "independent of historical association" (p. 2), precisely because it articulates values that are transhistorical. These values are then themselves defined as expressive of different "levels of human apprehension of experience" (p. 3), apprehensions that are either idealistic or phenomenalistic, committed either to spiritual transcendence or to a practical and materialistic engagement with the world. And while Muscatine locates this opposition at the heart of medieval culture in general and sees it as articulated in the disjunctions and juxtapositions of Gothic form, the very generality with which he describes these values makes it clear that they are in some sense common to all cultural life and that, indeed, their confrontation represents the energy at the heart of cultural history.

It is, in short, by positing a Hegelian conflict of idealist thesis and realist antithesis that Muscatine's humanistic literary history reinstates a realm of value above the world of otherwise inert scholarly facts. As well, the movement from thesis to antithesis tells a story, and one that issues in the triumph of those values that are themselves central to liberal humanism. One of these values is the commitment to the growing emancipation of the individual, expressed here as the developing capacity of medieval writing to represent the self in all its depth and independence. So that while Muscatine agrees that the great weakness of courtly style is its "liability to lose that ultimate, delicate contact with human concerns that gives it meaning," he recuperates a master like Guillaume de Lorris by ascribing to his narrative "a kind of characterization" that is "created less through vagrant excursions into realism than through a richness and complication of the symbolic texture itself" (p. 40). No matter at what distance Guillaume's personification allegory stands from the historical world nor how homogenous its values, it remains validated by "a particular interest in psychology" (p. 40). Given the fact, then, that courtly style is justified by its capacity to represent character, it is inevitably the case that insofar as the bourgeois style articulates that psychology with greater density and detail it will surpass its courtly predecessor. Hence Jean de Meun's representation of La Vieille "shows the poet . . . catching into the web of the discourse elements dictated less by traditional satire than by a sense of the round, complex existence of the speaker herself" (p. 85), while on the contrary Faus-Semblant's disjunctive alternations between hypocrisy and honesty reveal an "abandonment of the literary approach," a failure that is stigmatized as "incomplete dramatization" (p. 92). In sum, Jean's invention of the dramatic monologue is presented by Muscatine as a grounding of traditional discourses in a self that encompasses and ironizes them but that is itself autonomously validated. On this account, the project of Jean's writing, and beyond him of the Chaucer who completes his initiative, is not to judge but to represent a self that stands as an ultimate and irreducible category of understanding, exempt from further analysis.[37]

In thus privileging, like Donaldson, the critical category of character, Muscatine witnesses to a similar loyalty to what a more recent criticism has called the ideology of the subject. This is, in the largest sense, a conception of the self as a self-identical entity defined through its difference from an externalized reality designated as society, or history, or the world; in a literary context, it is a positing of the author as the efficient cause of the text who is also the origin, and the proprietor, of its significance. As the central tenet of liberal humanism, this conception of the largely autonomous individual self is the foundation of Muscatine's literary historiography, where it functions as both object and subject of the poetic process. For when Muscatine defines the goal of the medieval literary project as the representation of individual psychology, he necessar-

---

37. Muscatine's precursor and partial model in thus situating characterization at the heart of stylistic history is Erich Auerbach: see the references to Auerbach in the index to *Chaucer and the French Tradition*, Muscatine's review of *Mimesis* in *Romance Philology* 9 (1956), 448–57, and his acknowledgment of indebtedness in *Poetry and the Age of Chaucer* (Notre Dame: University of Notre Dame Press, 1972), pp. 1–14. It is important to realize that Auerbach's project in *Mimesis* is to understand the formation not of realism per se but rather of a sublime realism that imbues the *sermo humilis* of biblical style with the values of classical humanism. Such a synthesis makes possible what Auerbach calls "realistic works of serious style and character" ([Princeton: Princeton University Press, 1953], p. 556), by which he means above all else Dante's *Commedia*. For Auerbach it is Dante's representation of Farinata and Cavalcante in *Inferno* 10 that stands as the highest achievement of European literature, an achievement that "overwhelms everything else, a comprehension of human realities which spreads as widely and variously as it goes profoundly to the very roots of our emotions, an illumination of man's impulses and passions which leads us to share in them without restraint and indeed to admire their variety and their greatness" (pp. 201–2). For a full and trenchant discussion of Auerbach's work and of the key concept of synthesis, see Paul A. Bové, *Intellectuals in Power: A Genealogy of Critical Humanism* (New York: Columbia University Press, 1986).

ily posits at its source a poet who is motivated by a disinterested quest for mimetic accuracy and is therefore largely uncircumscribed either by programmatic commitments or by more profound social determinants. Chaucer's psychologized representation of the self presumes a corresponding autonomy on his own part: it is because he is free of polemical purpose or conditioning social ideology that he is able to give a sympathetic but carefully distanced representation of his world. Since objectivity is possible only to a dehistoricized and socially unconditioned subject, Chaucerian mimesis stands as the poetic equivalent of the liberal assertion of the freedom of the individual from a determining historical context.[38]

This claim of disinterested sympathy is articulated by Muscatine in terms of the New Critical values of complexity and maturity. Subscribing to the New Critical principle "that the perennial significance of great poems depends on the multiplicity of meanings they interrelate" (p. 9), Muscatine sees Chaucer as the supreme instance of the poet who reconciles opposing values within a supervening order:

> He sees the courtly and bourgeois modes, idealism and practicality, in ironic juxtaposition. He holds them in balance, sympathetically and critically, exploring each for its own essence and for the light it casts on the other. . . . He makes, more than any of his European contemporaries, a capacious, comprehensible order out of his legacy of style and meaning from the French tradition. (P. 120)

But where does Chaucer himself stand as he performs this act of stylistic counterpointing? Far from evading this question, Muscatine gives a forthright and powerful answer: securely within his own time. In defining that time, however, Muscatine turns not to the social conditions of the fourteenth century but to an idealist definition of the Gothic promoted by the Hegelian *Geistesgeschichte* of Wilhelm Worringer and, above all, Max Dvořàk, one that sees Gothicism as an aesthetic characterized by a juxtaposition of disparate forms and a distrust of the singular or monolithic attitude.[39] The effect of this representation of the Chaucerian

---

38. Candor requires that I acknowledge here the influence of Muscatine's example upon my own work—especially in "Chaucerian Confession: Penitential Literature and the Pardoner," *Medievalia et Humanistica* n.s. 7 (1976), 153–73, and " 'For the Wyves love of Bathe': Feminine Rhetoric and Poetic Resolution in the *Roman de la Rose* and the *Canterbury Tales,*" *Speculum* 58 (1983), 656–95—and my own commitment to this kind of humanism. As I argue in the next chapter, what is now required is less the shift to a new paradigm than a rearticulation of the grounds of support for humanist values.

39. Wilhelm Worringer, *Formprobleme der Gotik* (1912), trans. Herbert Read as *Form in Gothic* (London: Putnam, 1927); Max Dvořàk, "Idealismus und Naturalismus in der gotische Skulptur und Malerei," *Historische Zeitschrift* 119 (1919), 1–62, 185–246 (cited by

context is to dehistoricize history, both by defining it at a level of idealistic abstraction and, more tellingly, by reading it as the external reflection of a determining Chaucerian selfhood. Muscatine tells us, in other
words, not how Chaucer is a fourteenth-century poet, but rather how
the fourteenth century is Chaucerian. By thus invoking an idealist definition of Gothicism, Muscatine is able to define a period style that is
simultaneously conditioning and liberating, capable of standing outside
itself and yet preeminently of its time. He defines, in sum, a mode of
historical being that is by definition transhistorical, a paradox that corresponds with brilliant felicity both to a poet who is in but not of his
time and to the needs of a critical tradition that is mired in its own hy-
perhistoricized consciousness and yet aspires to a vision of permanent
truths.

3

It will be clear to all readers of Professor Robertson's work that Exegetics represents a root-and-branch, no-holds-barred, take-no-prisoners
attack upon the liberal humanist ideology that has dominated Anglo-
American literary studies since their inception in the nineteenth century.
It is precisely, I believe, the absoluteness and ferocity of that attack that
make Exegetics valuable, although at the cost of ensuring that it will
never itself become the dominant critical mode. Moreover, I will argue
that the ambiguous *fortuna* of Exegetics derives at least in part from unwitting compromises to both its historicism and its antihumanism, gestures of accommodation that allow the opposition to evade its challenge
by attacking it for violations of humanist values to which it has never
really subscribed in the first place. In large part, I think, these compromises derive from a general resistance to self-understanding that characterizes Exegetical criticism, and especially to an understanding of its own
place in the history of Medieval Studies. This is the most complicated
part of our story, for in seeking to counter the prevailing native values
Exegetics went outside the Anglo-American tradition of medievalism to
more congenial European formations. Specifically, Exegetics' most profound intellectual affiliations are with the European tradition of cultural
history or, more properly, *Geistesgeschichte,* and at a more local level,
with one of the few scholarly projects that harks back to the conservative
medievalism of the nineteenth century, iconography. It is with a sketch

---

Muscatine, *Chaucer and the French Tradition,* p. 258 n. 33). An analogous if less *geistesge-*
schichteliche definition of "Gothic Chaucer," is offered by Derek Brewer in his *Geoffrey*
Chaucer, Writers and Their Background (London: Bell, 1974), pp. 1–32, and by Robert M.
Jordan, *Chaucer and the Shape of Creation* (Cambridge: Harvard University Press, 1967). See
also Brewer's *English Gothic Literature* (New York: Schocken Books, 1983).

of these projects that we can begin to enter on an account of Exegetics
itself.

Despite occasional statements to the contrary, Exegetics was not
originally undertaken to reinstate the historicism of the previous generation that New Criticism sought to displace. On the contrary, Exegetics
shares with New Criticism a distaste for a descriptive historicism that
explains the details of a text in terms of either naive realism or un-
interpretive source study. Perhaps even more than New Criticism, Exegetics is motivated by a passion for meaningfulness, for discovering
within the text a powerfully consistent set of values. But beyond this,
Exegetics wants to see meaningfulness as pervading the historical world
itself, and as motivating those very facts that a positivist historicism re-
gards as wholly objective and therefore exempt from interpretation. It is
because of its fervor for making sense out of materials that less imaginative scholars see as merely natural objects that Exegetics turns away
from the narrow historicism of the Anglo-American tradition and toward the far more capacious and interpretively ambitious historicism of
Geistesgeschichte—but with a difference.

While *Geistesgeschichte* is a multifarious enterprise, we can usefully
enumerate its major premises so as to mark the points at which Exegetics
diverges. In its original form, *Geistesgeschichte* strikingly embodies the
commitment to unity or wholeness that characterizes historicism in its
original, Romantic form. In reaction against the Enlightenment appeal
to timeless laws and analytic reason, historicism insisted that all human
phenomena had to be judged in terms appropriate to the supervening
totality of which they were but parts. In political formulations this totality was the nation, specifically the German state that was struggling toward reunification in the early nineteenth century and whose unity was
justified by appeals to the binding force of customary habits of long du-
ration and, above all, to the underlying identity visible in a pure form in
the Middle Ages. In terms of historical studies as a whole, this wholeness
or *Ganzheit* was possessed by the various cultural periods, however defined. Each historical entity, and especially cultural artifacts, could be
understood only in terms of all the other phenomena that together made
up the period. What *Geistesgeschichte* finally aimed to understand was the
spiritual radix of the historical period, the *diapason* (to use Karl Lamprecht's term) of which each individuality was but a partial and symbolic
expression.[40]

In its traditional formulation, cultural history insisted that this su-

---

40. For a discussion of Lamprecht and his *Kulturgeschichte,* see Karl J. Weintraub, *Visions of Culture: Voltaire, Guizot, Burckhardt, Lamprecht, Ortega y Gasset* (Chicago: University
of Chicago Press, 1966).

preme object of historical knowledge must necessarily remain indeterminate; it was, in Huizinga's words, that "which is always before one's
eyes and is never to be grasped."[41] This is because the crucial values of a
culture are always immanent and dispersed, bespoken but never explicitly stated. The *Weltanschauung* which the individual cultural products of
a period serve to express is necessarily inarticulate, a hidden but all the
more potent spiritual condition that is perforce unknown to the members
of the historical period. No more than a fish can understand the water in
which it swims can a medieval man understand his medievalness. Culture is not learned behavior, inculcated by pedagogy and training, but
an unspoken pattern that conditions the very possibility of life. Karl
Mannheim cites a key statement by Dilthey—"*Weltanschauungen* are not
produced by thinking"—and then comments:

> It needed the anti-rationalist movement within the cultural studies themselves, a
> movement which Dilthey first made a force in Germany, to make people realize
> that theoretical philosophy [i.e., explicit statements of value and meaning] is
> neither the creator nor the principal vehicle of the *Weltanschauung* of an epoch;
> in reality, it is merely only one of the channels through which a global factor—
> to be conceived as transcending the various cultural fields, its emanations—
> manifests itself. . . . As long as *Weltanschauung* is considered as something theo-
> retical, entire vast provinces of cultural life will be inaccessible to historical
> synthesis.[42]

An artist's announced intention and even his explicit *ars poetica* are important not as circumscribing statements of meaning but as signs that
must be themselves interpreted. "We must go beyond this 'immanent'
interpretation and treat the theoretical confession as documentary evidence of something extra-psychic, . . . just as a doctor will take the self-
diagnosis of one of his patients as a symptom rather than as a correct
identification of the latter's illness."[43]

Given this definition of its task, *Geistesgeschichte* necessarily found the
positivist scheme of cause and effect an inadequate methodology. Since
its goal was to explain not the origin or evolution of cultural phenomena
but their symbolic value, its method was consequently not explanatory
but interpretive. Interrogating a wide range of materials in order to uncover their profound interconnectedness, the cultural historian applied

---

41. Johan Huizinga, "The Task of Cultural History," *Men and Ideas,* trans. James S.
Holmes and Hans van Marle (New York: Meridian Books, 1959), p. 76.

42. Karl Mannheim, "On the Interpretation of *Weltanschauung*" (1923), *Essays on the
Sociology of Knowledge,* ed. and trans. Paul Kecskemeti (London: Routledge and Kegan
Paul, 1952), p. 38.

43. Ibid., p. 58.

what Gombrich called "the exegetic method."[44] And as Dilthey and others insisted, this method could not pretend to the objectivity that presumably characterizes the methodology of the natural sciences. Since the object of knowledge was a product of the human spirit, it required of the knower a corresponding spirituality. The very fact that we can know distant cultural objects at all is a function of the shared humanity that undergirds all of history, and to attempt to deny that humanity in the service of an unattainable objectivity is both to try to exempt ourselves from a historicity that conditions all experience and to discredit the very agency of understanding. Hence for Dilthey historical knowledge is the meeting of subjectivities, marked by contemplation (*Anschauung*) and intuition (*Ahnung*). Moreover, this process is necessarily and appropriately circular—the famous hermeneutic circle.[45] Cultural understanding obeys what Edgar Wind has neatly designated "the dialectic of the historical document: that the information which one tries to gain with the help of the document ought to be presupposed for its adequate understanding."[46] Humanistic knowledge proceeds by a dialectical movement from parts to whole and back again, not by a linear accumulation of detail piled upon detail. In his account of the attitude which supports the enterprise of philology (in the largest sense), Leo Spitzer well described the values upon which *Geistesgeschichte* is based, and rightly stressed their essentially religious character:

The philologician must believe in the existence of some light from on high, of some *post nubila Phoebus*. If he did not know that at the end of his journey there would be awaiting him a life-giving draught from some *dive bouteille,* he would not have commenced it: "Tu ne me chercherais pas si tu ne m'avais pas déjà trouvé," says Pascal's God. . . . It is not by chance that the "philological circle" was discovered by a theologian, who was wont to harmonize the discordant, to retrace the beauty of God in this world. This attitude is reflected in the word coined by Schleiermacher: *Weltanschauung:* "die Welt anschauen:" "to see, to cognize the universe *in its sensuous detail.*"[47]

---

44. Ernst Gombrich, *In Search of Cultural History* (Oxford: Clarendon Press, 1969), p. 32. Gombrich represents *Geistesgeschichte,* in Popperian fashion, as a proto-Nazi Hegelianism, an oversimplification that Leo Spitzer took pains to refute in his famous debate with Arthur O. Lovejoy: see *Journal of the History of Ideas* 2 (1941), 257–78; 5 (1944), 191–203, 204–19.

45. On Dilthey and his successors, see David Couzens Hoy, *The Critical Circle* (Berkeley: University of California Press, 1978).

46. Edgar Wind, "Some Points of Contact between History and Natural Science," in Raymond Klibansky and H. J. Paton, eds., *Philosophy and History: Essays Presented to Ernst Cassirer* (Oxford: Clarendon Press, 1936), p. 257.

47. Leo Spitzer, *Linguistics and Literary History* (Princeton: Princeton University Press, 1948), p. 24.

At heart, as Spitzer suggested, then, the humanistic piety that *Geistesge-schichte* displays toward the past is a barely displaced version of religious devotion.

Religious devotion, although in a fully explicit form, is also behind the other, narrower enterprise that Exegetics draws upon, iconography. The conservative medievalism of the nineteenth century gave rise to a wave of architectural Gothicism, with the result that the great bastions of institutional power—government, the church, universities, the courts, and of course prisons—were housed in buildings that bespoke a profound attachment to the feudal past.[48] So, too, in England and especially in France, the restoration of ancient monuments became part of a larger program of political restoration.[49] It was under these auspices that much scholarly work was accomplished in deciphering Gothic symbolism. In England the ecclesiologists of the Cambridge Camden Society not only passed on church restoration and construction, but actually published an edition of Durandus' *Rationale divinorum officiorum*.[50] But it was in France that the most important work was done through the efforts of Napoléon Didron (himself inspired by Châteaubriand's *Génie du christianisme*) and other devout medievalists like the Abbé Cahier, work that culminated in the enormously influential books of Emile Mâle. And it is Mâle and his conception of iconography that stand in the most direct line of descent behind Exegetics. "In medieval art every form clothes a thought," says Mâle, and these thoughts derive from the works of "the theologian, the encyclopaedist, the interpreter of the Bible."[51] The medieval universe is profoundly symbolic—"In the Middle Ages the idea of a thing [is] always more real than the actual thing itself" (p. 158)—and wholly unified: "All the arts united in giving the people the same religious lesson. . . . Liturgy, drama and art teach the same lesson, make manifest the same thought. They reveal the perfect unity of the Middle Ages" (p. 170).

---

48. The most recent account of the Gothic revival is Charles Dellheim, *The Face of the Past* (Cambridge: Cambridge University Press, 1982).

49. See Léon, *Vie des monuments français*. For a German counterpart, see the account of the completion of Cologne Cathedral given by W. D. Robson-Scott, *The Literary Background of the Gothic Revival in Germany* (Oxford: Clarendon Press, 1965), pp. 287–301.

50. James F. White, *The Cambridge Movement: The Ecclesiologists and the Gothic Revival* (Cambridge: Cambridge University Press, 1962), pp. 68–79.

51. Emile Mâle, *The Gothic Image: Religious Art in France in the Thirteenth Century,* trans. Dora Nussey (New York: E. P. Dutton, 1913), p. viii. Mâle's career and impact are discussed by Harry Bober in the Editor's Foreword to *Religious Art in France: The Twelfth Century,* trans. Marthiel Mathes (Princeton: Princeton University Press, 1970); see also André Grabar, "Notice sur la vie et les travaux de M. Emile Mâle," *Académie des Inscriptions et Belles-Lettres, Comptes Rendus,* Séance du 16 Novembre 1962, 328–44.

One useful although admittedly incomplete way of understanding Exegetics is thus as the return of the culturally repressed. The conservative and institutional view of the Middle Ages that Anglo-American liberalism and pragmatic empiricism had not allowed into literary studies has now been introduced through the Trojan horse of French iconography and German *Geistesgeschichte*. For Exegetics articulates the perfect unity of Mâle's Middle Ages through the agency of a totalizing *Weltanschauung*. All elements of medieval culture, according to this view, bespeak the workings of a single radix or diapason. For Professor Robertson this radix is the medieval "tendency to think in terms of symmetrical patterns, characteristically arranged with reference to an abstract hierarchy."[52] Much of the explanatory power of Exegetics derives from both the simplicity of this central conception and the comprehensiveness of its application. Most familiar to readers of Exegetical criticism is the *ethical* hierarchy established by the Augustinian law of charity, a powerful normative tool that unerringly locates all forms of human behavior upon a scale of spiritual value. But equally important are other hierarchies. Medieval *ontology,* for instance, privileges an abstract realm of absolute value over a historical or experiential world that can claim a merely contingent reality. Correspondingly, medieval *aesthetics* promotes meaning over mimesis, the nucleus of *sententia* over a deceptively beautiful cortex. And perhaps most important of all, the Middle Ages manifests throughout a clear *cultural* hierarchy, with the church at the top. As Robertson says, disingenuously, "the dominance of the church in the Middle Ages considerably simplifies the task of the historical critic."[53]

What simplifies it even more is that clerical culture is itself hierarchical, with the ubiquitous Augustine as not merely the leading but virtually the only *auctoritas*. Although Exegetical critics habitually cite an intimidatingly wide range of clerical writings, all are variations on the same Augustinian themes, a fact that far from impeaching the Exegetical

---

52. D. W. Robertson, Jr., *A Preface to Chaucer* (Princeton: Princeton University Press, 1962), p. 6; further citations will be included in the text.

53. D. W. Robertson, Jr., *Essays in Medieval Culture* (Princeton: Princeton University Press, 1980), p. 4; further citations will be included in the text. A more recent expression of the same view of medieval culture is expressed by Judson Boyce Allen, *The Ethical Poetic of the Middle Ages* (Toronto: University of Toronto Press, 1982): "late medieval Europe was a system—a universe with no parts left over, corresponding as a whole, but only as a whole and not part by part, with all other systems. In this late medieval system, texts were made whose textuality we still possess, and which we are pleased to call poems. Between our system and the late medieval one, this textuality persists—an ordered series of words in a particular language. Beyond this, of course, there is nothing—no certain correspondence. Our enterprise must begin by admitting this nothing, lest we impose our categories on the past" (p. 4). The way in which a totalizing view of period consciousness forecloses transhistorical understanding is well illustrated here.

method is entirely consistent with it. As Robertson explicitly argues, writers as divergent in space and time as Boethius, Rhabanus Maurus, Hugh of St. Victor, and Peter Lombard are engaged in providing "transcripts" or "elaborations" of Augustinian doctrines.[54] The inevitable next step in this exposition is then to assert the hegemonic authority of this clerical culture over medieval culture as a whole, an understanding that preempts the modernist opposition between religious or philosophical writing on the one hand, and poetry or literature on the other, in favor of a supervening hierarchy in which *all* medieval writing is "directed towards the establishment and the maintenance of those traditional hierarchies which were dear to the medieval mind" (*Preface,* p. 265). Unlike the babel of modern systems of description, medieval discourse was single and univocal, "able to discuss the goal of personal effort, of social effort, and of religious effort in a single terminology, and to come to an agreement about the general meaning of that terminology." It is ultimately this shared belief in the objectivity of a single set of values that makes possible the coherence, and the success, of medieval culture, and that accounts for the relentlessly normative and didactic nature of all medieval writing.

This catalogue of totalizings is then extended to include, for instance, the relationship between pictorial and literary art, or the capacity of medieval culture to absorb apparently indigestible items such as pagan writings or obscenity, or—most important—the analogous totalizing accomplished by the Exegetical hermeneutic at the level of individual texts. Indeed, the whole point of Robertson's Augustinian exegesis, as of Augustine's, is to harmonize the individual text with a supervening ideology. The central principle of Augustine's hermeneutic is that the text "should be subjected to diligent scrutiny until an interpretation contributing to the reign of charity is produced," and Exegetical readings consist in precisely such a scrutiny.[55] Moreover, the text produced by such an exegesis perfectly replicates the form of medieval culture as a whole, for it subordinates a wide range of disparate and potentially conflicting elements to the authority of an abstract *sententia*. And nothing, of course, could be more totalizing than the fact that that *sententia* is always and everywhere the same; what Robertson says about the final, heaven-directed stanzas of the *Troilus* could equally well be applied to all other

---

54. The dominating influence of Augustine has been recently extended to the *Roman de la rose* by John Fleming, who in *Reason and the Lover* argues that the paradigmatic texts for the poem are Augustine's *Soliloquies*.

55. Saint Augustine, *On Christian Doctrine,* trans. D. W. Robertson, Jr. (Indianapolis: Bobbs-Merrill, 1958), p. 93. On the preemptive nature of this hermeneutic, see below, Chapter 4.

poems and poets throughout the medieval centuries: "This, in effect, is what Chaucer has to tell us about love, not only here but in *The Canterbury Tales* and in the major allegories as well. It is his 'o sentence' " (*Preface,* p. 501). According to Robertson, the key principle of medieval aesthetics is the Augustinian definition of beauty as *convenientia,* which means the harmony that obtains when individual elements are organized according to symmetry and hierarchy in order to form a whole (*Preface,* p. 120). *Convenientia* is beautiful not so much in and of itself but because it replicates the divine order. The most massive medieval expression of *convenientia* is in one sense the Gothic cathedral, which articulates a divine plan through its scrupulous organization. And yet in a deeper sense the most extensive embodiment of *convenientia* is the Middle Ages itself. Imbued with what Robertson calls the "great civilizing concept" of Charity, and rigorously organized according to the "convenient" principles of hierarchy and symmetry, medieval culture itself bespeaks a divine supervision.

But Exegetics goes well beyond simply recuperating for literary studies a conservative, universalist, and institutional view of the Middle Ages. For the central force of its challenge is its antihumanism, that is, its questioning not merely the place of the individual in history but his very existence. For humanism, the individual is the privileged category that must be defended against all challenges. The task of the humanist historian is to define the canon of great writers that constitutes our literary past and to represent them as simultaneously articulating the values of their time and yet rising above them. The humanist's critical purchase upon past historical periods is grounded in an unchanging human nature, a transcendental subjectivity to which his own subjectivity responds and by means of which he understands. But Exegetics wholly rejects this scheme. There is no "unchanging human nature," but rather a humanness that is constituted anew by each cultural period. In contrast to modern assumptions, in the Middle Ages character was conceived not in terms of subjectivity, as a consciousness set over against that which it experiences, but rather in terms of ideology, as a structure of value. Since "psychological theories" are "features of the universe of discourse, and not of the realm of things, [they] do not exist before they are formulated" (*Essays,* p. 3); since the discursive formation of medieval culture did not articulate the idea of a value-free inner self, such an idea was literally unthinkable. Culture not merely conditions individual consciousness but absorbs it entirely; just as each detail of a medieval cathedral witnesses to an underlying *ordo,* so each inhabitant of the medieval centuries articulates a single ideology. This is an effacement of the self that invests medieval discursive practices with absolute authority. Medieval culture is not only fully possessed of its own ideology but endowed with an unqualified self-understanding: able to know nothing other than itself, it is precisely itself that it fully knows. Hence the task of the historian is not to interpret but merely to describe; the past is not a hidden or discarded version of the self but wholly other, an object of knowledge and not a subject. If it is true, as Claude Lévi-Strauss has claimed, that "the ultimate goal of the human sciences [is] not to constitute, but to dissolve man," then Exegetics is an avant-garde movement.[56]

There are many criticisms that can be made of this project, but most of those made to date have served primarily to distract attention from the full power of the Exegetical challenge. One of these criticisms, of course, is to object to the ruthless totalizing that Exegetics accomplishes—an objection that has often, and rightly, been made. Another is to dismiss Exegetics as being merely what Ruskin called a "Gothic opinion," a medievalism constructed to provide arguments in a modern debate. It is unfortunately true that in its least interesting, most vulnerable form Exegetics can be read as simply the nostalgic projection into the past of the values that the modern world has wrongly abandoned. Nor is Exegetics much helped by its habit of characterizing the form of modernism it dislikes (which, typically, it totalizes into modernism per se) in abusive and reductive terms as sentimental, expressionistic, hedonistic, aesthetic and, above all, solipsistic. As the heat of its polemic insists, Exegetics is itself deeply engaged in a contemporary debate, representing an anti-Romantic modernism that is a contemporary analogue to that which it admires in the past.

But perhaps there is a third line of approach that can both respect Exegetical ambitions and yet get us closer to understanding both its practical successes and its exclusion from the mainstream of literary studies. Let us focus for a moment on its own intellectual heritage, both the native historicism that it rejects and the European procedures from which it fashions an alternative. In his not dissimilar attack upon what he calls a humanistic anthropology, Michel Foucault issued a famous dictum: "It is comforting . . . and a source of profound relief to think that man is only a recent invention, a figure not yet two centuries old, a new wrinkle in our knowledge, and that he will disappear again as soon as that knowledge has discovered a new form."[57] In working toward its own new form of knowledge, Exegetics has sharply revised the procedures of the *Geistesgeschichte* from which it derived its initial inspiration. A key principle

56. Claude Lévi-Strauss, *The Savage Mind* (Chicago: University of Chicago Press, 1966), p. 247.

57. Michel Foucault, *The Order of Things* (New York: Vintage Books, 1973), p. xxiii; the next chapter takes up the question of Foucauldian historicism in more detail.

of *Geistesgeschichte,* it should be remembered, is that understanding is necessarily in depth, a quest for a meaningfulness that is by definition unavailable to the individual members of a culture. *Weltanschauungen* are forms of understanding that condition individual consciousness but are necessarily unknown to it, revealed (to cite Charles Peirce) not in the beliefs men parade but in the ones they betray.[58] Now as Foucault has pointed out, this notion of the unknown—the *Unbewusste,* the implicit, the inactual, the sedimented, the unthought—is itself a function of the modern creation of the subject; it is "the shadow cast by man as he emerged in the field of knowledge, . . . the blind stain by which it is possible to know him."[59] Entirely appropriately, therefore, Exegetics rejects the humanist hermeneutic of depth.

But what is to take its place? To judge from Exegetical procedures, the answer is, ironically enough, the very positivist historicism against which Exegetics reacted in the first place. Exegetical interpretations typically display the same reductive geneticism and factualism as dominated this earlier, self-defeating historicism. Not only is a Chaucerian image to be explained in large part by reference to its source, with little or no regard to its function in the poem, but that source is itself exempt from interpretation. Hence by allowing the lines of explanatory force to run only from context to text rather than laterally as well, within the text itself, Exegetics avoids the narrative or literal understanding of an image—much to the dismay of more circumspect critics.[60] More tellingly, in dispensing with the humanist heremeneutics of depth Exegetics is unable to apply its interpretive attention to the explanatory context itself, which remains wholly exempt from interpretation. For Exegetics, for example, what clerical writers said about love is not only an authoritative guide to what Chaucer must have meant but is itself transparent, neither requiring nor yielding to an interpretation that might reveal it as itself determined by unacknowledged imperatives; similarly, not only are hierarchy and symmetry the guiding principles of medieval culture, but they are everywhere stated to be so, statements that are expressions of that which is thought to be simply true rather than elements of a larger cultural articulation. Put bluntly, the *Weltanschauung* of medieval culture is neatly if illegibly printed in the marching columns of Migne's *Patrologia.*[61]

58. Charles Peirce, "Issues of Pragmaticism," *The Monist* 15 (1950), 485; cited by Edgar Wind, "Some Points of Contact between History and Natural Science," p. 258.

59. Foucault, *Order of Things,* p. 326.

60. For a discussion of an instance—the Wife of Bath's deafness—see above, n. 6.

61. The positivizing of *Geistesgeschichte* in literary studies finds a parallel development in art history. In an early discussion of iconology in *Studies in Iconology* (New York: Oxford

This revision of *Geistesgeschichte* in the direction of a positivist historicism is also visible in the Exegetical assumption of what can only be called a naive objectivism. Despite a considerable show of methodological sophistication, Exegetics characteristically defines itself in terms of a simplistic opposition between objective historicism and subjective criticism. For Exegetics, the problem of historical understanding is not epistemological but moral: on the one side are scholars who diligently seek to understand the past in its own terms, however much those terms might run counter to modern sensibilities, while on the other are aesthetes who, wallowing in what Professor Robertson has graphically described as "that rancid solipsistic pit into which the major tendencies of post-romantic thought have thrust us" (*Essays,* p. 82), prefer their own meanings to those of the documents they purport to study. In Robertson's most extended methodological discussion, the ideal scholar is defined as the Stylistic Historian who dispassionately describes the characteristics of other cultures while remaining himself uncircumscribed by any, a suprahistorical consciousness somehow exempt from the historicity that conditions all other forms of life.[62] This resolute refusal to confront the contingency of *all* historical understanding, or even to understand historicism itself as an intellectual formation profoundly shaped by its origins in the Romantic movement, enables the Exegetical recuperation of the positivist methods of its paternal past.

University Press, 1939), Erwin Panofsky defined it as a *geistesgeschichtliche* quest for "those underlying principles which reveal the basic attitude of a nation, a period, a class, a religious or philosophical persuasion" (p. 7) that incorporates a "narrower" iconography concerned only with "specific *themes* or *concepts* manifested in *images, stories* and *allegories*" (p. 6; and see the added comments in *Meaning in the Visual Arts* [Garden City: Doubleday, 1955], pp. 31–32). But Panofsky's *Early Netherlandish Painting* (Cambridge: Harvard University Press, 1953) sets aside this quest for *Weltanschauung* (a goal at the heart of the entire cooperative project initiated by Aby Warburg, himself a pupil of Karl Lamprecht) and restricts iconology simply to iconography—to, that is, the articulation of the intended meaning. This point is well made by Otto Pächt in his review of *Early Netherlandish Painting* in *Burlington Magazine* 98 (1956), 110–16, 267–77. The "premeditated programmes" that motivate Dutch Painting are, according to Pächt, no longer "looked upon as historic data that required interpretation (alongside the stylistic evidence. . . . At least no direct suggestion is made that this interpretation has to be transcended in the search for the intrinsic, inner meaning." This narrowing of analytic focus represents "a clear manifestation of the newly won autonomy of iconographic research" and its triumph over the stylistic approach characteristic of *Geistesgeschichte,* which "rested on the belief that the stylistic data were more reliable guides to the inner meaning, to the true character of a work of art than the most perfect knowledge of its author's intentions could provide" (p. 276). For explicit attacks on *Geistesgeschichte* from the perspective of Anglo-American empiricism, see Ernst Gombrich, *In Search of Cultural History,* Ronald S. Crane, *Critical and Historical Principles of Literary History* (Chicago: University of Chicago Press, 1971), and Jeffrey L. Sammons, *Literary Sociology and Practical Criticism* (Bloomington: Indiana University Press, 1977).

62. "The Allegorist and the Aesthetician," in *Essays,* pp. 85–101.

And it is just this recuperation that makes possible the professional success of Exegetics. For it is by its accommodation of *Geistesgeschichte* to the antitheoretical empiricism of Anglo-American literary scholarship that Exegetics becomes a productive paradigm for literary work. Just as New Criticism offers its adherents an interpretation kit that includes both interpretive techniques and the prescribed result—i.e., a reading contributing to the reign of humanism—so does Exegetics on its side. Endowed with industry and a library card, any competent scholar can produce the prescribed Exegetical reading for any medieval poem. In part, of course, it is just this prescriptiveness and predictability that have kept Exegetics from becoming a truly dominant mode: the paradigm is too easily followed and the range of acceptability too narrowly defined to attract creative minds for long. Yet this kind of stricture really only repeats a familiar liberal lament ("It is all very dreary") while ignoring the continuing (and perhaps increasing) abundance of exegetical readings.[63] And the professional success of Exegetics is important not because it somehow proves the Exegetical representation of the Middle Ages to be correct but because it powerfully illustrates the process of professionalization itself.

As we might expect from its roots in the conservative, institutional medievalism of the nineteenth century, Exegetics has deep affiliations with the modern institution of Medieval Studies. Whether a physical institute, center, or program, or simply a normative idea of the way work on medieval materials ought to be undertaken, it is by means of Medieval Studies that the fundamentally liberal modern university has accommodated a conservative, institutionalist, and universalist conception of culture. That this is the ideology that underwrites the "interdisciplinary" programs of Medieval Studies common throughout North America has been made abundantly clear by the rash of self-explanations proffered by institutionalized medievalism. To cite just one statement among many: in speaking in 1979 at the fiftieth anniversary of the Pontifical Institute of Mediaeval Studies in Toronto, Gerhart Ladner noted the profound affiliation between "the universalist approach to medieval studies" and "the universalism of the Middle Ages" itself, and he eloquently described the "supra-individual and supra-political sense of community" of the Middle Ages that was, he felt, proving so attractive to contemporary students and that was itself embodied in the very institute whose anniversary was being celebrated.[64] Given its commitment to this idea of the

---

63. See above, nn. 5 and 6.

64. Gerhart Ladner, "The Future of Medieval Studies," in *Memory and Promise: From the Special Convocation upon the Fiftieth Anniversary of the Pontifical Institute of Mediaeval Studies, 20 October 1979* (Toronto: Pontifical Institute of Mediaeval Studies), pp. 20, 16.

Middle Ages, its privileging of Latin over the vernacular, its absolutist sense of historical periodization, and its conception of professional training, Exegetics is in theory if not in fact the method of choice for the literary side of Medieval Studies.[65] This means not that the Exegetical method is universally taught in programs of Medieval Studies, which is obviously not the case, but that Exegetics is powerfully in league with the very idea of Medieval Studies—with, that is, a professional superego brandishing paleographical handbooks, dictionaries of arcane tongues, German *wissenschaftliche* tomes, and all the rest of the paraphernalia that simultaneously torments and legitimizes the medievalist. In sum, Exegetics serves to appropriate medieval literature for what has become the dominant institution for the study of the Middle Ages.

Yet for all its trumpeting of popularity and relevance, Medieval Studies appears to many to be more ghetto than enclave, more prison than prelapsarian garden. To nonmedievalists, it must be admitted, the isolation of medievalism from the mainstream of Anglo-American literary studies is a self-evident fact, and even the most pious pilgrim must have twinges of doubt as he winds his way to Kalamazoo. The point is less the resistance of individual medievalists to the winds of change—indeed, one can cite a range of feminist, Marxist, and deconstructionist initiatives now emerging in the field—than the marginalizing of medieval literature as a force within literary studies as a whole. Its irrelevance is especially striking because it was, after all, in the name of the Middle Ages that the stranglehold of classical studies over nineteenth-century education was first broken, allowing vernacular literature to become an academic subject. As the work of Auerbach, Spitzer, and Curtius testifies, medieval literature was once at the center of the old humanist program. Now that that program is breaking up, will medieval literature disappear into an enclave of bureaucratized positivism, protected only by an increasingly dessicated erudition?

While to lay the embarrassment of a marginalized Middle Ages at the door of Exegetics would be unfair, one must also recognize that the insistence of institutionalized Medieval Studies upon the otherness of the Middle Ages has perforce contributed to its alienation from the mainstream of literary studies. Moreover, by treating medieval literature as a fixed object of study that stands over against the scholar rather than as an element within an ongoing and unfinished history in which he too is

---

65. For Robertson's proposals for "a new professionalism in graduate training," see *Essays,* pp. 83–84. A useful survey, with a full if perhaps unwitting articulation of the ideology at issue, is provided by Francis G. Gentry and Christopher Kleinhenz, eds., *Medieval Studies in North America: Past, Present, and Future* (Kalamazoo: Medieval Institute Publications, 1982).

involved, both Exegetics and Medieval Studies as a whole have not only encouraged a naive positivism but have, more seriously, evaded the essentially political nature of the values that govern the modern definition of the Middle Ages. While the debate between Exegetics and New Criticism has followed a nineteenth-century agenda, its concerns continue to be deeply relevant to contemporary American life. The great contribution of Exegetics to the study of medieval literature was that it promised to lay bare the political nature of this debate. With its virulent antimodernism, its polemical attack on the humanistic pieties of New Criticism, and its insistence upon the historicity of value, Exegetics articulated a conservative position with a force that not even a blandly pluralistic liberalism could evade.[66] And yet in the last analysis Exegetics has itself blunted its own attack. Refusing to take the problematics of historical understanding seriously, Exegetics has reinstituted a naive objectivism that both exempts it from the need to acknowledge its own place in the history of medieval studies and leads it to adopt the methods and values of an uncritical positivism. The result is that the debate over values that is at the heart of the confrontation with New Criticism has been sadly remystified, in part by being displaced into arguments about whether it is liberal pluralism or a committed dogmatism that most fundamentally characterizes the profession, in part by being figured as an argument between up-to-date critical sophistication and old-fashioned erudition. Given these positions, New Criticism (and its successors) are always going to win, and Exegetics must necessarily retreat into the bastion of Medieval Studies. Hence the current stalemate, which divides medievalists both among themselves and from the profession as a whole. The alternative, I think, is not some sort of false truce in this critical cold war, nor the badgering polemics that characteristically disfigure academic disputes, but a debate that fully articulates the fundamental values at issue and that aspires not to victory but to clarity. For it is only by understanding exactly where we are (and how we got there) that we will be able to decide where we might go.

---

66. A discussion that makes clear the relation of the Exegetical Middle Ages to conservative political values is Judson Boyce Allen's characteristically forthright essay, "The Education of the Public Man: A Medieval View," in *Medieval Studies in North America*, pp. 179–99.

2. Historical Criticism and the Claims of Humanism

I

THE PREVIOUS chapter has argued that the critical impasse between New Criticism and Exegetics that continues, in a variety of refigured forms, to dominate Chaucer criticism finds its source in the ideological struggles of the nineteenth century. This is a fact that might lead us to conclude that the dead hand of the past must simply be thrown off, that a new start must be definitively made. But in revealing the conditioning power of the historical moment, this account has sought to demonstrate just how inescapably political criticism always is. To be sure, this is not a recognition that either literary criticism in general or Medieval Studies in particular finds easy to make. On the contrary, criticism has habitually understood itself as an activity engendered simply by its object of study, a form of knowledge brought into being by the need to know about an entity called literature. But as recent theory has rightly insisted, literature as a specific object of study is in fact constituted by the institution of criticism itself, despite the secondary and dependent posture it assumes.[1] There is no inherent, ahistorical essence that marks one written document as literary and another as nonliterary; literariness, as a special quality possessed by a certain category of writing, is a self-justifying idea

---

1. For detailed versions of this argument, see Raymond Williams, *Marxism and Literature* (Oxford: Oxford University Press, 1977), pp. 45–54; Tony Bennett, *Formalism and Marxism* (London: Methuen, 1979), pp. 14–17, and passim; Terry Eagleton, *Literary Theory: An Introduction* (Minneapolis: University of Minnesota Press, 1983), pp. 1–53; and for important historical details, Chris Baldick, *The Social Mission of English Criticism, 1848–1932* (Oxford: Clarendon Press, 1983).

generated by a criticism that seeks to mystify its own grounding within social institutions that carry an undeniably political valence. The refusal of criticism to acknowledge this fact, and its counterclaim that it is called into being by an object that exists wholly apart from itself, is simply an effect of its reluctance to reflect upon the political nature of its authority.[2] And nowhere is this reluctance more powerfully in force than in a Medieval Studies heavily endowed with the ostensibly value-free procedures and materials of objectivist scholarship.

The emptiness of this claim to objectivity should by now be abundantly clear. In endowing the observer with an ability to step outside his historical situation that it must necessarily deny to the object he scrutinizes, objectivist methodology is self-condemned to an irresolvable self-contradiction. Moreover, it must ignore the correlative fact that the objects with which the human sciences deal can never be wholly other from the interpreting self over against which they stand; on the contrary, they are themselves constituted by means of the very subjectivity that characterizes the interpreter.[3] Rather than a dangerous intruder that must not be allowed to contaminate the procedures of historical research, subjec-

---

2. It is important to be clear about exactly what is at issue here. To accuse literary criticism of political bad faith because of its attempt to naturalize and dehistoricize its activity is one thing; to take a further step and stigmatize the concept literature as per se an instrument of political oppression is an illegitimate other. Of course it can be, as when it is used to construct a canon that excludes the dispossessed and the suspect. But this need not be the case, and the development of the concept of literature in the Middle Ages should properly be seen as a progressive activity: see, in general, Raymond Williams, *Writing in Society* (London: Verso Editions, [1984]), pp. 203–4, and Bennett, *Formalism and Marxism,* pp. 82–92; and for the way in which the recovery of classical texts enabled twelfth-century writers to free writing from a clerical transcendentalism, see Chapter 5, below. In *Marxism and Literature,* Williams cogently describes the unhappy reversal that has taken place in the use of the concept: "It is in no way surprising that the specialized concept of 'literature,' developed in precise forms of correspondence with a particular social class, a particular organization of learning, and the appropriate particular technology of print, should now be so often invoked in retrospective, nostalgic, or reactionary moods, as a form of opposition to what is correctly seen as a new phase of civilization. The situation is historically comparable to that invocation of the divine and the sacred, and of divine and sacred learning, against the new humanist concept of literature, in the difficult and contested transition from feudal to bourgeois society" (p. 54).

3. Dilthey's distinction between the objects of the natural and the human sciences is crucial here: "The human sciences are distinguished from the natural sciences in that the latter take as their object features which appear to consciousness as coming from outside, as phenomena, and as given in particulars; for the former, in contrast, the object appears as coming from within, as a reality, and as a vivid original whole. It follows therefore that for the natural sciences an ordering of nature is achieved only through a succession of conclusions by means of linking of hypotheses. For the human sciences, on the contrary, it follows that the connectedness of psychic life is given as an original and general foundation. Nature we explain, the life of the soul we understand." Cited by Roy J. Howard, *Three Faces of Hermeneutics* (Berkeley: University of California Press, 1982), pp. 14–15.

tivity is in fact the condition of *all* understanding: if texts are to be understood at all they must be capable of being taken up into consciousness and rendered part of the subject. And as Heidegger long ago said, in a classic statement worthy of repetition,

If, when one is engaged in a particular kind of interpretation, in the sense of exact textual interpretation, one likes to appeal to what "stands there," then one finds that what "stands there" is in the first instance nothing other than the obvious undiscussed assumption of the person who does the interpreting.[4]

We have seen how the power of undiscussed political assumptions is writ large in the history of Chaucer studies; clearly it is past time for them to become an acknowledged part of the interpretive activity itself.

The extent to which political values operate even at the microlevel of historicist methodology—which is, after all, the level at which most literary scholars lead their professional lives—can be made clear by returning to the vexed question of anachronism. Since the governing assumption of *all* historical criticism is that a text can be understood only in terms of some larger context, it is often assumed that the task of the literary historian is to reconstruct that context in all its detail in order to arrive at a valid (i.e., historically authentic) interpretation. Historical context is thought to function as a court of interpretive appeal, while interpretations that slight it are considered—at least within Medieval Studies—to be by definition illegitimate.[5] The theoretical assumptions

---

4. Martin Heidegger, *Being and Time,* trans. John Macquarrie and Edward Robinson (New York: Harper, 1962), pp. 191–92.

5. That such strictures are still very much in force in contemporary Medieval Studies can be illustrated by reference to the theoretical pronouncements of one of the most productive of recent historical critics, Alastair Minnis. In his *Medieval Theory of Authorship: Scholastic Literary Attitudes in the Later Middle Ages* (London: Scolar Press, 1984), Minnis complains that modern critics have ignored medieval literary opinions in preference to "concepts from modern literary theory . . . which have no historical validity as far as medieval literature is concerned" (p. 1); and in a review of Judson Allen's *The Ethical Poetic of the Later Middle Ages* (Toronto: University of Toronto Press, 1982) in *Speculum* 59 (1984), he attacks " 'New Critical' approaches to medieval literature" for an "often pleasant but ultimately limiting anachronism" (p. 366). But "facts should not be ignored," we are chided. Again, in *Chaucer and Pagan Antiquity* (Cambridge: D. S. Brewer, 1982), Minnis offers his work as proceeding from "a wish for some degree of certainty in literary interpretation, in a period in which new interpretations, approaches and critical theories seem to appear almost daily. . . . I am hoping to demonstrate that historical criticism can check the drift towards solipsism and channel imaginative energy into areas of possible interpretation which may be validated by reference to the ideas, thought-structures and literary traditions available to the author" (p. v). Anyone who doubts the tenaciousness of positivist modes of thought in contemporary Medieval Studies need only be directed to the program of the Chaucer section at the MLA Convention of 1986: two of the three sections (the equivalent of six papers) were devoted to the question whether Alison of Bath murdered

that underwrite these opinions have been most fully articulated by E. D. Hirsch in *Validity in Interpretation,* a book that has been subjected to a series of withering attacks in recent years and yet whose arguments remain the theoretical lingua franca of historical scholarship. While acknowledging that "the text itself . . . must always be the final authority," Hirsch asserts that "the interpreter should make an effort to go beyond his text whenever possible" in order to collect "extrinsic data" with which to "verify" his interpretation. It is only by correcting his subjective understanding of the text by reference to an objective historical context that the interpreter can avoid "a vicious circularity."[6] But in fact the knowledge we gain from sources other than the text, however essential to our understanding, is no more objective, and therefore of no greater authority, than that provided by the text itself. The appeal to "history" so commonly made in current critical discourses of all varieties is necessarily always to a reconstruction fabricated according to processes of interpretation that are identical to those applied to the "not-history" of the literary text. Whether we rely upon previous texts, social and political formations, or a period consciousness, we are turning not to "extrinsic data," in the sense of something instantly apprehensible and self-evidently meaningful, but rather to a mass of material, almost all of it textual, that requires interpretation before it can enter into the process of historical understanding. Indeed, however much we may be committed to the idea of original meaning, we must finally acknowledge that, in every way that counts, "original meaning" is indistinguishable from "meaning to us." And the reason it is indistinguishable is that the instrument to which we have recourse in order to draw that distinction—"history"—stands itself within the very interpretive process it is being called upon to judge.

There is, in short, no such thing as an objectively determined, self-evident, original context that can reveal the original meaning of the text. And a criticism that conceives of its task as being the construction of such a context in order to validate interpretation inevitably if implicitly adopts a political stance vis-à-vis the nature of social reality. For the assumption that history can provide an objective norm of judgment set over against a subjectively known text carries with it a correlative as-

---

her fourth husband. Perhaps the Shakespeare sections can now be persuaded to investigate the number of Lady Macbeth's children.

6. E. D. Hirsch, *Validity in Interpretation* (New Haven: Yale University Press, 1967), p. 241. For a general attack upon Hirsch's position, see Stanley Fish, *Is There a Text in This Class?* (Cambridge: Harvard University Press, 1980); and for a more recent discussion of his conception of meaning, see William Ray, *Literary Meaning: From Phenomenology to Deconstruction* (Oxford: Basil Blackwell, 1984), pp. 90–103.

sumption about relative degrees of complexity. Since it serves as a privileged norm of objectivity, history must also be assigned a clarity and
straightforwardness—even, as we have seen in the case of Exegetics, a
uniformity—that can then function to elicit a corresponding clarity from
an otherwise enigmatic text. Knowing what history means, we know
what the text means. Established as an interpretive grid, this inevitably
oversimplified history thus serves to stigmatize discordant textual elements as interpretive errors, modern subjectivities to be put down to a
failure of historical knowledge, what one medievalist has recently characterized as "often pleasant but ultimately limiting anachronism[s]."[7] As
in the realm of politics, the effect of this kind of historiographical totalization is to annul opposition. Not only is the possibility that a text might
stand against the cultural hegemony of its historical moment rendered
improbable, but the historical moment itself (and especially if it is the
Middle Ages) is endowed with a monolithic uniformity that effaces the
contradictions and disruptions that made, and can continue to make, social change possible. In sum, then, the methodological assumption that
historical context can produce interpretive correctness inevitably serves
to stigmatize the discordant, the variant, and the deviant as incorrect—
as, in effect, nonexistent. Social incongruities, like textual discontinuities, are treated as mistakes that arise from error, infractions that could
not (or should not) have happened.

Rather than conceive of history as a completed product capable of
being examined by a detached observer, the alternative is instead to recognize that the unfinished nature of the historical process, however disabling to the quest for methodological correctness, endows the critic's
activity with historical consequence: the past we reconstruct will shape
the future we must live. Nowhere has this recognition been more acutely
sustained than in Marxist historicism. In a world and a profession that
persistently seeks to suppress the political, Marxist criticism has traditionally been—and remains—the most tenacious voice to insist upon its
inescapability. It is also a voice that has rarely been heard in Chaucer
criticism, or in Medieval Studies generally, where historicism has assumed a habitually conservative posture.[8] In opposition to the harmoni-

---

7. The phrase is Alastair Minnis'; see above, n. 5.

8. An early, now almost forgotten work of progressive social criticism is the book by
Margaret Schlauch, *English Medieval Literature and Its Social Foundations* (New York: Cooper
Square, 1971 [1956]); Schlauch, who taught for most of her career at New York University,
emigrated to Poland in the early 1950s. More recent Marxist criticism is provided by Stephen Knight in his "Chaucer and the Sociology of Literature," *Studies in the Age of Chaucer*
2 (1980), 15–51, in "Politics and Chaucer's Poetry," in *The Radical Reader* (Sydney: Wild
and Wooley Press, 1982), and, especially, in *Geoffrey Chaucer* (Oxford: Basil Blackwell,

ous cultural unities promoted by an idealist *Geistesgeschichte*—what Benjamin pungently called "the phantasmagoria of 'cultural history,' in which the bourgeoisie savors its false consciousness to the last"[9]—Marxism defines history as a continual class struggle impelled forward by the instabilities of its own contradictions. And instead of the methodologism and empiricism that foreclose theoretical reflection on the historiographical practice of history, Marxism diligently, even relentlessly, theorizes the problematic of historical-textual relations. Whatever limitations may impede its own theoretical program, and they are major ones, Marxist thought lays bare essential questions that all historicist thinking must confront. Moreover, and most important, Marxism refuses to allow the fascinated gaze of the aesthete or the self-absorptions of the scholar to evade the gross and painful social inequalities that make such pleasures possible. "There is no document of civilization which is not at the same time a document of barbarism," to cite Benjamin again; "The mansion of culture is built on dogshit" is Brecht's bitter version of the same truth.[10] For all these reasons, then, Marxism commands our attention.

But there are difficulties that must be confronted at the outset. Most centrally at issue is the concept of "totality," the importance of which was vigorously proclaimed in Georg Lukács' *History and Class Consciousness* (1923), the founding document of Western Marxism:

It is not the primacy of economic motives in historical explanation that constitutes the decisive difference between Marxism and bourgeois thought, but the point of view of totality. The category of totality, the all-pervasive supremacy of the whole over the parts, is the essence of the method which Marx took over from Hegel and brilliantly transformed into the foundations of a wholly new science. . . . Proletarian science is revolutionary not just by virtue of its revolutionary ideas which it opposes to bourgeois society, but above all because of its method. *The primacy of the category of totality is the bearer of the principle of revolution in science.*[11]

1986); and by Sheila Delany in a series of essays, especially those collected in *Writing Woman: Women Writers and Women in Literature Medieval to Modern* (New York: Schocken Books, 1983). A less programmatically Marxist but nonetheless politically progressive criticism is provided by David Aers, *Chaucer, Langland and the Creative Imagination* (London: Routledge and Kegan Paul, 1980). A good index of the lack of sympathy with which explicitly political criticism is received by medievalists is provided by the reviews of Aers's book: see Elton Higgs in *Studies in the Age of Chaucer* 3 (1981), 121–24, and Barbara Nolan in *Speculum* 58 (1983), 139–41. Nolan begins: "This is a book which, despite an occasionally remarkable aperçu, is severely limited by an anachronistic thesis."

9. Walter Benjamin, "Paris, Capital of the Nineteenth Century," *Reflections,* ed. Peter Demetz, trans. Edmund Jephcott (New York: Schocken Brooks, 1986), p. 158.

10. Cited by Martin Jay, *Adorno* (Cambridge: Harvard University Press, 1984), pp. 36 and 19.

11. Cited by Martin Jay, *Marxism and Totality: The Adventures of a Concept from Lukács*

The revolutionary force of totality derives from its opposition to capitalist reification. Relentlessly commodifying value, capitalism shatters the wholeness of life into atomistic particulars, not only fragmenting the individual's lived experience but, more grievously, occluding his understanding. The knowledge of totality thus provides the necessary counterawareness of the individual's place in history, a history understood both synchronically, as the current social whole, and diachronically, as the unfolding development of the historical process. In effect, the total is the Real, a knowledge of which is the sine qua non for revolutionary praxis; as Lukács says, "Only in this context, which sees the isolated facts of social life as aspects of the historical process and integrates them in a *totality,* can knowledge of the facts hope to become knowledge of *reality.*"[12] Moreover, the very concern for a totalized understanding witnesses to the desire for an authentic totality, an impulse that however utopianist is nonetheless a necessary precondition for revolutionary action.

Given its Hegelian heritage, however, it is not surprising that the Marxist concept of totality suffers from shortcomings similar to those that afflict the idealist *Geistesgeschichte* to which it is opposed. For one thing, Marxist totalization inevitably subordinates local and contingent actions to the historical character of the whole; and for another, it endows the critic's knowledge of the totality with the capacity to predetermine the historical context that brings the cultural object into being and that consequently governs its interpretation. Indeed, for all its rejection of positivism's fetishizing of the facts, the priority of the idea of totality has traditionally directed Marxist hermeneutics toward interpretive procedures that are similarly preemptive. The text serves not as the source of the historian's knowledge but merely as an occasion for its deployment. The interpreter possesses a knowledge of the Real (apparently derived from wholly extratextual sources) with which he will unmask the evasions and repressions that empower the text; he can say that which the text must always silence because he already knows that which the text

<hr>

to *Habermas* (Berkeley: University of California Press, 1984), p. 103; italics in the original. My subsequent discussion of Marxist totalization is indebted to Jay's masterful account.

12. Georg Lukács, *History and Class Consciousness,* trans. Rodney Livingstone (Cambridge: MIT Press, 1971), p. 8, cited by Jay, *Marxism and Totality,* p. 104; and see as well the citation from Lukács' *Lenin: A Study of His Thought,* trans. Nicholas Jacobs (Cambridge: MIT Press, 1971), p. 18: "For every genuine Marxist there is always a reality more real and therefore more important than *isolated* facts and tendencies—namely, *the reality of the total process,* the totality of social development" (cited p. 122). The revolutionary value of the Lukácsian concept of totality has been well described by Edward Said, "Traveling Theory," *The World, the Text, and the Critic* (Cambridge: Harvard University Press, 1983), pp. 226–47.

refuses to (but, from another angle, must inevitably) say.[13] Paradoxically but predictably, then, the historicism of the left comes round to meet that of the right: history (the Marxist Real, the positivist context) tyrannizes the text and constrains its meanings within predetermined limits.

These are serious debilities, and cannot be set aside as simply ungenerous misinterpretations; indeed, they typically constitute the central topics of Marxist theorizing itself, which consists largely of efforts to avoid the reductiveness of its own premises by finding the outer limit to which Marxism can be elaborated and revised without ceasing to be Marxism altogether. By tracing out this process in two major restatements of Marxist critical thought—Fredric Jameson's *The Political Unconscious* and Raymond Williams' *Marxism and Literature*—I hope to illuminate both the powers and limitations of theory per se when applied to the problem of historical understanding. Specifically, I wish to argue that historical criticism must abandon the hope of any theoretical foundation and come to rest instead upon its own historically contingent moment, and upon convictions that find their final support within experience. While this may indeed seem a distressingly unstable basis for historical knowledge, I would ask the reader to reflect upon the possibilities of any other. Moreover, it is a foundation that is bracketed or set aside only at our peril. In the last part of this chapter I wish to discuss the innovative development within Renaissance studies known as the New Historicism, in part because it offers powerful lessons from which Medieval Studies could benefit, but in part because it suggests the vulnerabilities that trouble even the most theoretically aware critical formations when they allow a fear of dogmatism to subvert their deepest political instincts.

2

The project of *The Political Unconscious* is to define what Jameson calls a "totalizing, properly Marxist ideal of understanding,"[14] and its remarkable force derives not just from the power and flexibility of Jameson's mind but from his desire to locate his interpretive activity within the text itself:

---

13. Two widely influential books that promote this kind of program are Pierre Macherey, *A Theory of Literary Production,* trans. Geoffrey Wall (London: Routledge and Kegan Paul, 1978 [1966]), and Terry Eagleton, *Criticism and Ideology* (London: New Left Books, 1976). For a brief summary, see Eagleton's "Machery and Marxist Literary Theory," *Against the Grain* (London: New Left Books, 1986), pp. 9–21.

14. Fredric Jameson, *The Political Unconscious* (Ithaca: Cornell University Press, 1981), p. 10; all further citations will be included within the text.

Rightly or wrongly, a totalizing criticism has been felt to be transcendent in the bad sense, or in other words to make appeal, for its interpretive content, to spheres and levels outside the text proper. . . . [But] it can be argued that this type of interpretation, while containing a transcendent moment, foresees that moment as merely *provisionally* extrinsic, and requires for its completion a movement to the point at which that apparently external content (political attitudes, ideological materials, juridical categories, the raw materials of history, the economic processes) is then at length drawn back within the process of reading. (P. 57; italics in the original)

Jameson is here setting himself in opposition to the kind of upside-down Platonism typical of certain forms of Marxist literary theory, in which the epiphenomenal literary text becomes merely an imitation of an imitation of the Real: first the historical real, then its signification as ideology, and then the literary text, marked by its historical matrix but unable itself to understand that history. According to Terry Eagleton, whose *Criticism and Ideology* espouses this position, literature has "history as its object" but only "in the last instance, [and] in ways apparent not to the text but to criticism."[15] Jameson, on the contrary, wants to make literature itself, in Walter Benjamin's phrase, "the organon of history." If it is true that history produces literature—and, after all, what else could?—it is also true that literature is capable of understanding the conditions of its own production. Yet this principle, in the course of Jameson's articulation of it, becomes progressively more elusive.

Jameson establishes a three-stage process of totalization designed to move from text to context.[16] The first step is to read the text as "a socially symbolic act," which means to read it as "an ideological act . . . with the function of inventing imaginary or formal 'solutions' to unresolvable social contradictions" (p. 79). In effect, the text is being defined here as a form of false consciousness, a means for evading the dilemmas of a rad-

---

15. Terry Eagleton, *Criticism and Ideology,* p. 74.

16. In the following discussion I have left out of account Jameson's other interpretive procedure for protecting the relative autonomy of the text while allowing the transcoding by which the text can be opened out to the *hors texte* of history. This is the application to the text of Greimas' "semiotic rectangle," represented as a grid capable of revealing that which has been suppressed: the presence of one narrative element will require the absence of another, an absence that Greimas' scheme will bring to light. The problem with this scheme is its vulnerability to the critique leveled at all forms of structuralist analysis. Narratology persistently claims the transhistorical ability to reveal the implicit structure of *all* narrative, a claim just as persistently discredited by the arbitrariness with which it constitutes the structures that are its object of study. Although it posits a wholly nonthematic structure capable of being described without the need to enter into the negotiations of interpretation, structure is in fact recognizable at all only by virtue of theme. And since structure is determined by meaning, narratology is as much subject to hermeneutic instability as less scientist methods.

ically unstable social existence. Yet this is not where Jameson wants to rest, with the text as a epiphenomenal instance of a more real history. Hence he insists that this type of interpretation "is more satisfactorily grasped as the rewriting of the literary text in such a way that the latter may itself be seen as the rewriting or restructuration of a prior historical or ideological *subtext,* it being always understood that that 'subtext' is not immediately present as such, not some commonsense external reality, nor even the conventional narratives of history manuals, but rather must itself always be (re)constructed after the fact" (p. 81). And Jameson goes on to offer a powerful but finally evasive account of what he rightly calls the paradox of textual-historical relations:

The symbolic act therefore begins by generating and producing its own context in the same moment of emergence in which it steps back from it, taking its measure with a view toward its own projects of transformation. The whole paradox of what we have here called the subtext may be summed up in this, that the literary work or cultural object, as though for the first time, brings into being that very situation to which it is also, at one and the same time, a reaction. (Pp. 81–82)

Ontologically the effect of the absent cause of history, the text enjoys a heuristic function that endows it with an anteriority that signals not causality itself but simply the illusion—"as though for the first time"—of causality.

Given Jameson's alertness to the dangers that beset his project, it is all the more telling that as his argument unfolds the text is not finally able to resist the totalizing pressures of a Marxist-defined history. This becomes unavoidably clear when he describes how the second and third stages of interpretation move out from the initial textual analysis into ever-widening horizons. The second stage locates the text within the binarism of class struggle, which requires the critic to determine whether the relation of the text to the hegemonic ideology of its historical moment is legitimizing or antagonistic. And the third stage locates both the text and the discursive formation of which it is a part on the diachronic axis of universal history as a sequence of modes of production (a static paradigm that Jameson seeks to enliven by substituting for its traditional economism the more inclusive notion of "perpetual cultural revolution" [p. 97]). In effect, both of these analyses are ways of passing Marxist judgment upon the text, of determining whether it contributes to the coming of Freedom or to the continued reign of Necessity.

The totalizing presumption that underwrites Jameson's theoretical project is, as he puts it with admirable clarity, that "no working model of the functioning of language, the nature of communication or of the speech act, and the dynamics of formal and stylistic change is conceivable which does not imply a whole philosophy of history" (p. 59). To understand anything presupposes an understanding of everything. And given the exhaustion of both Christian *Geschichtestheologie* and of the liberal progressivism of a heroic bourgeoisie, the only viable philosophy of history remains Marxism. "My position here," Jameson thus states, "is that only Marxism offers a philosophically coherent and ideologically compelling resolution to the dilemma of historicism" (p. 19). Only Marxism can provide interpretive categories able to reveal the coherence of past and present, to make visible the totality; hence it provides the "ultimate *semantic* precondition for the intelligibility of literary and cultural texts" (p. 75).

It is the word "ultimate" (rather than Jameson's emphasized *semantic*) that raises the crucial issue. The Marxist philosophy of history—as both a synchronic analysis of class struggle and a diachronic account of the sequence of modes of production—is not in fact where textual analysis arrives, despite Jameson's carefully articulated three stages; on the contrary, it is where it begins. In reality the lines of interpretive force run from the outside in, from the largest to the smallest; and this collapse of the three expanding horizons into one fatally compromises the effort at mediation. The result is a hermeneutic as relentlessly preemptive as Exegetics, a comparison that Jameson himself solicits with his respectful invocation of the medieval fourfold method as an analogue to Marxist interpretation (pp. 29–33). For him the Marxist hermeneutic is

a vast interpretive allegory in which a sequence of historical events or texts and artifacts is rewritten in terms of some deeper, underlying, and more "fundamental" narrative, or a hidden master narrative which is the allegorical key or figural content of the first sequence of empirical materials. (P. 28)[17]

Quite apart from the prescriptive quality of this hermeneutic, the insertion of individual items (whether "historical events or texts and artifacts") into the totality inevitably reduces them to simply instances of something far larger than themselves: this is a historicism that effaces the very object it seeks to recover. As Clifford Geertz puts it, "Either [man] dissolves, without residue, into his time and place, a child and a perfect captive of his age, or he becomes a conscripted soldier in a vast Tolstoian

---

17. Jameson offers this prescription as an account of the "expressive causality" or "historicism" rejected by Althusser, but it also well describes his own position. Significantly, at one point Jameson aligns himself, admittedly gingerly but nonetheless explicitly, with Hirsch's positivist methodology (p. 75 n. 56).

army, engulfed in one or another of the terrible historical determinisms with which we have been plagued from Hegel forward."[18]

The central, unconditional claim of Marxist thought is, in Marx's own famous words, that "the mode of production of material life conditions the social, political, and intellectual life process in general. It is not the consciousness of men that determines their being, but, on the contrary, their social being that determines their consciousness."[19] In the last analysis, this assertion must be decisive for all modes of thought that wish to designate themselves as Marxist. Yet the inescapable effect of thus privileging the material is to devalue the cultural: however finely reticulated the lines of force, they can ultimately run in only one direction, entailing both the subordination of the text to a historical context and its reduction to a mere attestation of the material forces that have brought it into being and shaped its nature.

3

If the root cause of this dilemma is the original and unequal distinction between material base and cultural superstructure, then a way out can be found only by its abolition. But then must not dialectical materialism itself be sacrificed, forcing us back into an idealist *Geistesgeschichte* that suppresses the political by ignoring the material conditions of life in favor of the priority of consciousness? Contemporary criticism has provided two responses to this question. One, the cultural materialism defined by Raymond Williams, explicitly affirms its Marxist affiliations, while the other, deriving ultimately from the discourse analysis of Michel Foucault and exemplified in the work of the self-designated New Historicists, veers away from Marxism while nonetheless locating political values at the center of its interpretive practice. What most powerfully enables these two revisionary movements is their common acceptance of the linguistic turn in contemporary thought. Alert to the gap between the verbal and the material that traditional Marxism finds itself unable to negotiate, these critical formations propose analogous but finally significantly different solutions to the paradox of textual-historical relations.

Williams starts by arguing that certain brands of Marxism wrongly hypostasize the capitalist distinction between mental and physical labor by designating only physical labor as material, and therefore belonging

18. Clifford Geertz, "The Impact of the Concept of Culture on the Concept of Man," *The Interpretation of Cultures* (New York: Basic Books, 1973), p. 37.

19. Karl Marx, Preface to *A Critique of Political Economy, Selected Writings,* ed. David McLellan (Oxford: Oxford University Press, 1977), p. 389.

to the economic base, with mental labor parasitically perched on that base as a manipulated superstructure.[20] The result of this error is

the projection (alienation) of a whole body of activities which have to be isolated as "the realm of art and ideas," as "aesthetics," as "ideology," or, less flatteringly, as "the superstructure." None of these can then be grasped as they are; as real practices, elements of a whole material social process; not a realm or a world or a superstructure, but many and variable productive practices, with specific conditions and intentions. (P. 94)

But, he continues, "the problem is different, from the beginning, if we see language and signification as indissoluble elements of the material social process itself, involved all the time both in production and reproduction" (p. 99). Art, and culture in general, are not merely superstructural consequences of the material processes by which man makes his world; on the contrary, they are themselves a form of praxis, a working upon the world in order to transform it. For Williams material production and the production of ideology, which includes the production of literature, are related not as base and superstructure but rather as two forms of cultural activity per se. Hence when he comes to talk about textual-historical relations, he argues that cultural practices should be seen not simply as reflected, displaced, or even mediated instances of the determinant social reality but rather as themselves constituents of that social reality.[21] The task of the critic is then not to compare a single practice with the real in order to understand it, but rather to use several practices as *examples* of the real, producing an account that will gain in persuasive force according to the number of examples he can muster.[22]

All of this is entirely to the good, not least because it reinstates the literary text as itself one of the cultural practices that constitutes reality. The gap between cultural practice and social reality is closed with the recognition that social reality is in effect constituted by cultural practice. But in what sense is this position specifically Marxist? Williams' answer depends upon his use of two crucial concepts of cultural analysis, ideol-

---

20. Williams (*Marxism and Literature*) argues that the crude distinction between material processes and acts of consciousness is simply idealism stood on its head: with this "mechanical materialist reversal of the idealist dualism" (p. 61), the subject-object problem remains in place, although with the lines of force now reversed.

21. This argument has also been launched from a Marxist perspective by Robert Weimann in *Structure and Society in Literary History,* Expanded Edition (Baltimore: Johns Hopkins University Press, 1984 [1976]): "Labor and art and consciousness all . . . are reflections of, and factors in, the never-ending endeavor of men to understand and control (and to affect by playing, and making images of) the destiny of their social existence" (p. 11).

22. Williams produces this account by way of discussing the method of "correspondences" pursued by Walter Benjamin; see pp. 103–5.

ogy and hegemony.[23] Ideology, Williams insists, cannot be adequately understood as simply false consciousness but must rather be defined as "the complicated process within which men 'become' (are) conscious of their interests and their conflicts. The categorical short-cut to an (abstract) distinction between 'true' and 'false' consciousness [must be] abandoned" (p. 68). Ideology is not merely a delusive structure of thought that serves to mystify the true nature of social being either in order to gain economic advantage or to provide a merely symbolic resolution of real contradictions; rather, it is the means by and through which man gives meaning to his social world and thereby makes it available to his practical activity.

As an agency of praxis, the symbolic actions of ideology in effect constitute culture, a position that brings Williams close to the semiotic conception of culture defined by functional anthropology that has proved (as we shall shortly see) so useful to New Historicism.[24] But while an-

---

23. Williams does offer another answer, whose unpersuasiveness leads me to consign it to a footnote. He insists upon what he calls "the material character of the production of a cultural order" (p. 93), by which he means both that the work of consciousness is inescapably social and that it is conducted by physical means. " 'Consciousness and its products' are always, though in variable forms, parts of the material social process itself: whether as what Marx called the necessary element of 'imagination' in the labour process; or as the necessary conditions of associated labour, in practical ideas of relationship; or, which is so often and significantly forgotten, in the real processes—all of them physical and material, most of them manifestly so—which are masked and idealized as 'consciousness and its products' but which, when seen without illusions, are themselves necessarily social material activities. . . . 'Thinking' and 'imagining' are from the beginning social processes (of course including that capacity for 'internalization' which is a necessary part of any social process between actual individuals) and . . . they become accessible only in unarguably physical and material ways: in voices, in sounds made by instruments, in penned or printed writing, in arranged pigments on canvas or plaster, in worked marble or stone" (pp. 61–62). But this claim is largely unpersuasive. For one thing, to insist upon the social nature of consciousness is hardly specific to Marxism, but characterizes virtually all anthropologically oriented understandings of culture. Indeed, the only target of such a claim is the radically ahistoricist individualism of various forms of Romantic and post-Romantic thought—including, to be sure, New Criticism. But it is hard to imagine any historicism worth the name that would attempt to explain the process of cultural reproduction in terms of an autonomous individualism. Second, while the invocation of the physical conditions necessary for cultural work has a certain force in a world in which access to means of artistic expression is restricted, this is not in fact the direction in which Williams chooses to develop his argument. On the contrary, his point is not historical but theoretical, which renders it both inconsequential in itself (i.e., Williams himself would not want to claim that it is the physical nature of language that renders it available to a Marxist analysis) and vulnerable to the charge of vulgar materialism because it seeks to submerge the acts of consciousness in materiality.

24. In "Ideology as a Cultural System," in *The Interpretation of Cultures,* Clifford Geertz argues that an ideological statement is not simply a misconceived understanding but a rhetorical act that draws "its power from its capacity to grasp, formulate, and communicate

thropology offers a merely descriptive and generally benign account, Williams insists that culture is organized in terms of inequality. Hence in order to disclose how a society's way of being serves the interests of its dominant members, he supplements ideology with the Gramscian term *hegemony*.[25] While ideology refers to a systematically articulated complex of beliefs, it ignores the actual social practices—the lived experience— that comprise the individual life; indeed, as a mentalistic term, it silently reinstitutes the base-superstructure model. Hegemony, on the other hand,

> is . . . not only the articulate upper level of "ideology," nor are its forms of control only those ordinarily seen as "manipulation" or "indoctrination." It is a whole body of practices and expectations, over the whole of living: our senses and assignments of energy, our shaping perceptions of ourselves and our world. It is a lived system of meanings and values—constitutive and constituting— which as they are experienced as practices appear as reciprocally confirming. It thus constitutes a sense of reality for most people in the society, a sense of abso- lute because experienced reality beyond which it is very difficult for most mem- bers of the society to move, in most areas of their lives. It is, that is to say, in the strongest sense a "culture," but a culture which has also to be seen as the lived dominance and subordination of particular classes. (P. 110)

Hegemony is thus a far more inclusive concept than ideology: it refers not just to what people think and believe but to the full spectrum of social practices in terms of which they live their lives, social practices that articulate at every turn social inequality. Nevertheless—and here is the central issue—Williams wants also to insist that for all its appropria- tive power, hegemony is never monolithically all-inclusive. On the con-

---

social realities that elude the tempered language of science" (p. 210). Ideology is symbolic action that functions as a means of giving meaning to the world. "The agent of his own realization, [man] creates out of his general capacity for the construction of symbolic mod- els the specific capabilities that define him. Or . . . it is through the construction of ideol- ogies, schematic images of social order, that man makes himself for better or worse a political animal" (p. 218). "The function of ideology is to make an autonomous politics possible by providing the authoritative concepts that render it meaningful, the suasive im- ages by means of which it can be sensibly grasped" (p. 218). For Geertz, however, ideology is a term that should be restricted to the description of specifically political structures of thought and should not be identified with culture per se, which includes and subsumes the political instead of (as for Marxism) being identical with it. As a systematic mode of polit- ical symbolization, an ideology typically arises in times of strain when other cultural re- sources are unable to deal with the changing events, e.g., the French Revolution. Further- more, while Geertz insists that the ideological and the scientific are two different kinds of symbolic representation of political reality, he nonetheless grants to the scientific a certain cognitive authority over the ideological (see pp. 232–33).

25. On Gramsci's concept of hegemony, and the crucial role of the intellectual in main- taining its coercive persuasiveness, see Anne Showstock Sassoon, *Gramsci's Politics* (New York: St. Martin's Press, 1980), pp. 109–46.

trary, it "does not just passively exist as a form of dominance. It has continually to be renewed, recreated, defended, and modified. It is also continually resisted, limited, altered, challenged by pressures not at all its own. We have then to add to the concept of hegemony the concepts of counter-hegemony and alternative hegemony, which are real and persistent elements of practice" (pp. 112–13). Hegemony may equal culture, but there remains, somehow, a possibility of standing outside culture, of being counterhegemonic, of seeking to install an alternative hegemony. Hegemony is lived reality "for most people"; it prescribes a circle of understanding beyond which "most members of the society" find it difficult to move. But some apparently can; these are people who see the way in which what appears to be simply and self-evidently the-way-things-are is in fact hegemonic, a form of dominance that can be imagined as undone and replaced with an alternative.

But where do these people stand when they come to this understanding? From what materials do they fashion an alternative? At issue here is a paradox that is peculiarly intense for Marxism—committed as it is to revolutionary action—but that in fact inhabits all efforts to conceptualize historical self-understanding.[26] In Marx's famous words, "Men make their own history, but they do not make it just as they please; they do not make it under circumstances chosen by themselves, but under circumstances directly encountered, given, and transmitted from the past. The tradition of all the dead generations weighs like a nightmare on the brain of the living."[27] As the agent of history, man is both subject and object, both the creator of and created by history, both free and determined. The more densely the web of historical determinants is woven (and Marxism has an interest in weaving it very tightly indeed), the less possible does it become to achieve an extrahistorical perspective that might allow for the understanding of the totality. If man is defined historically ("Man is not an abstract being squatting outside the world," to cite Marx again), then by what transcendent means can he pass judgment upon the history within which he moves and from which he takes his being? Put more simply, in what consists the knowledge of the Real that allows us to see hegemony for what it is?

26. The issue of historical self-understanding is most tellingly raised in Marxist analysis in discussions of the agency of historical change. If the proletariat is the revolutionary subject, then it must be endowed with the knowledge of totality that makes revolution possible. Yet it is empirically obvious that this knowledge is possessed not by the proletariat but by socialist intellectuals. Therefore, it must be—in Lukács' notorious term—"imputed" by them to the proletariat, an act that is historically carried out by the Party, which is empowered by its possession of correct theory to exercise political leadership in the name of the proletariat. The historical consequences of this argument provide a sufficiently vivid commentary.

27. Karl Marx, *The Eighteenth Brumaire of Louis Napoleon, Selected Writings,* p. 300.

On this point Williams is admirably straightforward:

> There is of course the difficulty that domination and subordination, as effective descriptions of cultural formation, will, by many, be refused; that the alternative language of co-operative shaping, of common contribution, which the traditional concept of "culture" so notably expressed, will be found preferable. In this fundamental choice there is no alternative, from any socialist position, to recognition and emphasis of the massive historical and immediate experience of class domination and subordination, in all their different forms. (P. 112)

There is no alternative: one either recognizes class domination as the central fact of historical life or one does not. That social inequality is at the center of all historical formations is the foundational conviction that enables Williams' Marxism: in effect, social inequality is the Real, and its truth is not to be controverted. But what is really at issue here, and what forecloses further argument, is not so much the fact of social inequality as its intolerability. Its presence is so overwhelming and so offensive that it forces itself upon Williams as the a priori condition that determines his critical activity: it is nonnegotiable. Williams is not invoking, it must be stressed, a transhistorical, axiomatic truth by which to enforce agreement on matters of critical methodology, a norm of theoretical correctness intrinsic to historical study; on the contrary, he is presenting a particular understanding of history that is itself historically contingent. The bottom line is a political commitment that is understood not as a transhistorical imperative but as a "massive historical and immediate *experience.*"[28]

4

Both contemporary thought, with its relentless relativizing of value, and the still-potent objectivism of traditional historicism, have taught us to mistrust all forms of explicit political commitment, seeing them not as enabling assumptions but as constraining dogmatisms. But before allowing skepticism to do its subversive work, we would do well to explore a critical formation that is both drawn to political ways of thinking and yet sensitive, perhaps even to the point of paralysis, to the dangers of foundationalism. While the term New Historicism designates neither a single methodology nor a monolithic critical group, it has nonetheless come to characterize a recognizable critical orientation shared by a num-

---

28. Williams' reliance upon experience rather than theory has been criticized by Eagleton; see the discussion by John Higgins, "Raymond Williams and the Problem of Ideology," in Jonathan Arac, ed., *Postmodernism and Politics* (Minneapolis: University of Minnesota Press, 1986), pp. 112–22.

ber of scholars working in the Renaissance.[29] It represents the coalescence of several by no means congruent developments in contemporary critical thought. One is the deconstructive attack upon representation. For deconstruction the paradox of textual-historical relations—the text as at once constituted by and constituting history—can be resolved by collapsing both elements into textuality. While objectivist historicism (which would include the traditional Marxism espoused by Jameson) grants priority to history and so designates the text as dependent, a mere supplement, the deconstructionist argues that if history admits supplementation at all—and the fact that it can be known only textually shows that it does—then it must be incomplete in itself. According to the logic of supplementarity, history is a secondary entity that suffers from an originary lack, an absence that writing simultaneously conceals and reveals. As Derrida concludes,

Through this sequence of supplements a necessity is announced: that of an infinite chain, ineluctably multiplying the supplementary mediations that produce the sense of the very thing they defer: the mirage of the thing itself, of immediate presence, of originary perception. Immediacy is derived.[30]

---

29. The central figure in the New Historicism, and its christener, is Stephen Greenblatt; other prominent practitioners are Louis Adrian Montrose, Jonathan Goldberg, Steven Mullaney, Don Wayne, Leonard Tennenhouse, Arthur Marotti, and Frank Whigham. General comments on the movement are offered by Greenblatt in his introduction to a collection of essays he edited, *The Power of Forms in the English Renaissance* (Norman: Pilgrim Books, 1982), pp. 3–6; by Jonathan Goldberg, "The Politics of Renaissance Literature: A Review Essay," *ELH* 49 (1982), 514–42; by David Norbrook, *Poetry and Politics in the English Renaissance* (London: Routledge and Kegan Paul, 1984), pp. 1–17; by Herbert Lindenberger, "Toward a New History in Literary Study," in Richard Brod and Phyllis Franklin, eds., *Profession 84,* pp. 16–23; by Louis Montrose, "Renaissance Studies and the Subject of History," *English Literary Renaissance* 16 (1986), 5–12; and by Jean E. Howard, "The New Historicism in Renaissance Studies," *English Literary Renaissance* 16 (1986), 13–43. I have also benefited from an unpublished paper by Walter Cohen, "Shakespeare and the Politics of Criticism." It would be quite wrong to assume that only the self-designated New Historicists are opening up new initiatives in the historical criticism of the Renaissance; in fact, as I shall argue, there are alternative kinds of historical and specifically political criticism being done in Renaissance studies that offer importantly revisionary perspectives on New Historicism. Scholars one might cite here are the feminists Lisa Jardine, Madelon Gohlke, and Coppélia Kahn; the Marxists Robert Weimann and Walter Cohen, the Marxist-influenced Gunther Kress, Robert Hodge, and David Aers (on whom see the fine review article by Richard Helgerson, *Comparative Literature* 35 [1983], 362–73), and Jonathan Dollimore, who promotes a Raymond Williams-inspired cultural materialism; and a group of scholars who continue to insist on the priority of local intentions and topical circumstances, such as David Norbrook, Annabel Patterson, and Leah Marcus. One might note that New Historicist self-presentation occasionally includes a totalizing impulse—historicism, *c'est nous*—that is unhappily consistent with the totalizing Foucauldianism that has so influenced it. This is a quality painfully in evidence, for instance, in Goldberg's *ELH* essay.

30. Jacques Derrida, *Of Grammatology,* trans. Gayatri Chakravorty Spivak (Baltimore: Johns Hopkins University Press, 1976), p. 157.

Historical being is always deferred: it is not a presence but an *effect* of presence created by textuality. There is no *hors texte,* and in trying to discover the historically real we enter into a labyrinthine world that not only forecloses access to history in its original form but calls into question its very existence as an object of knowledge. Writing absorbs the social context into a textuality that is wholly alienated from the real, "even if," as Paul de Man notoriously said, "these texts masquerade in the guise of wars or revolutions."[31]

For Marxism deconstruction is to be rejected out of hand as an empty idealism motivated by the irresponsible desire to escape from history.[32] But the New Historicists, unconstrained by Marxist loyalties, are not as willing to abandon the powerful interpretive techniques made available by deconstruction; indeed, while deconstruction remains a largely unacknowledged influence on their writing, it is everywhere in evidence in their often dazzling interpretive subtlety, their ideological skepticism, and their reticence about the constraints implied by their own social situations and political commitments. It must be insisted, of course, that deconstruction is by no means per se apolitical. Derrida has himself forcefully made this point:

[Deconstruction is], at the very least, a way of taking a position, in its work of analysis, concerning the political and institutional structures that make possible and govern our practices, our competencies, our performances. . . . Deconstruction is neither a methodological reform that should reassure the organization in place nor a flourish of irresponsible and irresponsible-making destruction, whose most certain effect would be to leave everything as it is and to consolidate the most immobile forces within the university.[33]

31. Paul de Man, "Literary History and Literary Modernity," *Blindness and Insight,* 2d ed. (Minneapolis: University of Minnesota Press, 1983 [1971]), p. 165.

32. For a characteristic Marxist dismissal of deconstruction, see Eagleton, *Literary Theory,* pp. 144–45. A more generous, and in my view more accurate, political understanding of deconstruction is offered by Robert Weimann in *Structure and Society in Literary History.* Weimann argues, in a way reminiscent of Theodor Adorno's meditations on the role of the intellectual in society, that the theoretical crisis of representation is determined by a social crisis of representativity: far from being himself a "representative man," a title Emerson was able to claim for the poet, "the avant-garde literary intellectual finds himself at . . . an exorbitant distance from both the centers of political and economic power and the ordinary pursuits of the huge majority of the population" (p. 290). The poststructuralist turn away from history is not simply a desire for escape but rather "the determination of the individual not to lend his voice to invisible arrangements of mute power" (p. 291)—in short, an act of negativity consistent with the negativity that characterizes art from the beginning of high modernism. Put succinctly, Weimann sees "the argument against representation as a deliberate self-destruction of cultural identity through the preclusion of unwelcome relationships" (p. 292).

33. "The Conflict of Faculties," cited by Jonathan Culler, *On Deconstruction: Theory*

It must nonetheless be acknowledged that in its transatlantic form deconstruction has often been reduced to an ahistorical formalism, and its privileging of the sophisticated interpretive maneuvers that support its hermeneutics of suspicion encourages it in this tendency. But the New Historicists do not wish "to stand convicted of formalism," in Terry Eagleton's threatening phrase, and the focus of their attention remains on what they might call (albeit with a distinctively non-Marxist accent) the social text.[34]

In order to support this attention, they have turned to what functional anthropologists like Clifford Geertz and Marshall Sahlins have called a "semiotic concept of culture" as an "interworked system of construable signs."[35] Culture is "the kingdom of symbolic order," in Sahlins' phrase, and—the crucial point—it is only within and by means of this kingdom that material interests take shape: "it is culture which constitutes utility" and not vice versa.[36] Far from being that through which the material interests that organize society are mediated and made visible, i.e., a secondary effect determined by a materialist base, culture is itself the primary agency of the social constitution of the real. In the debate between utility and meaning, Sahlins insists that priority resides with meaning.

The unity of the cultural order is constituted by . . . meaning. And it is this meaningful system that defines all functionality; that is, according to the particular structure and finalities of the cultural order. It follows that no functional explanation is ever sufficient by itself; for functional value is always relative to the given cultural scheme. . . . Material effects depend on their cultural encompassment. . . . The practical interest of men in production is symbolically constituted. The finalities as well as the modalities of production come from the cultural side: the material means of the cultural organization as well as the organization of the material means. (Pp. 206–7)

Man's primary activities are not material but symbolic: he is a creature who is constituted by his own constitution of the symbolic activity that is culture.[37]

This definition of the priority of the symbolic—of man as a being who above all makes meaning—underwrites Stephen Greenblatt's influ-

---

and Criticism after Structuralism (Ithaca: Cornell University Press, 1982), p. 156. For Derrida's forceful self-defense on a specific issue—apartheid—see "But, beyond . . . Open Letter to Anne McClintock and Rob Nixon," *Critical Inquiry* 13 (1986), 155–70.

34. For Eagleton's phrase, see *Criticism and Ideology,* p. 83.

35. Clifford Geertz, "Thick Description: Toward an Interpretive Theory of Culture," *Interpretation of Cultures,* p. 14.

36. Marshall Sahlins, *Culture and Practical Reason* (Chicago: University of Chicago Press, 1976), p. viii; further references will be included within the text.

37. On this conception of man as culturally constituted, see Geertz, "The Impact of the Concept of Culture on the Concept of Man," *Interpretation of Cultures,* pp. 33–54.

ential notion of "cultural poesis": not only must all of culture be read as an act of symbolic making, but such making is itself the primary category of historical action. The strength of this notion, like Williams' cultural materialism, is that not only does it render so-called literary texts agents of práxis, but it extends this legitimizing capacity to other texts: by erasing the difference between the historical and the textual it establishes the critic's field of interpretation as all-inclusive. Yet unlike Williams, who insists upon the historical primacy of class struggle, this enabling is here accomplished by accepting the deconstructive absorption of the historical by the textual. The symbolic constitutes the real; in a phrase from Geertz's *Negara: The Theatre State in Nineteenth-Century Bali* that Jonathan Goldberg uses to sum up his own understanding of Jacobean statecraft, "The real is as imagined as the imaginary."[38] Given that interchangeability, what difference between them could there be? If social reality is inherently and inescapably theatrical, then the distinction between the real and the fictive (*lege* history and text) need not be sustained.

Hence, for example, when in a recent essay Stephen Greenblatt takes as his example of cultural poesis the Renaissance effort to establish a sharp demarcation between the theatrical and the real on the topic of exorcism, we should hardly be surprised (nor is he) that each is seen as having blended insensibly and dizzyingly into the other. Not even death is free of the taint of theatricality: "Indeed, there is no more theatrical event in the Renaissance than a public execution."[39] In short, "the prospect opens to an infinite regress of disclosure and uncertainty" (p. 337), and Greenblatt cannot push his analysis beyond "the maddening doubleness implicit in the theatricality of exorcism" (p. 339). So too, Goldberg's reading of Jacobean politics establishes as its final term an aporetic impasse familiar to deconstruction:

Power—the ruler's, the poet's—styles itself in denial: the poet points to the ruler, the ruler to the abstract principles. Denying itself, contradiction defines the essence of the discourse of power. To voice sovereign power is to enter into duplicities, now twice removed. How then can the text be read? How is the truth to be found? . . . Contradictions govern politics and poetics at once. (Pp. 7, 11)

---

38. Clifford Geertz, *Negara: The Theatre State in Nineteenth-Century Bali* (Princeton: Princeton University Press, 1980), p. 136; cited by Jonathan Goldberg, *James I and the Politics of Literature* (Baltimore: Johns Hopkins University Press, 1983), p. 33. Goldberg later adds: "Style here, as in Geertz's Java, is content" (p. 47). The New Historicist conception of Renaissance culture (and, indeed, all culture) as essentially theatrical finds one of its sources in Stephen Orgel, *The Illusion of Power* (Berkeley: University of California Press, 1975).

39. Stephen Greenblatt, "Loudun and London," *Critical Inquiry* 12 (1986), 331–32.

To take a final example, Louis Montrose's dazzling explication of the conjunction of gender and politics in *A Midsummer Night's Dream* reads the play as finally arriving at an irresolvable contradiction: "the ostensible project of elaborating Queen Elizabeth's personal mythology inexorably subverts itself—generates ironies, contradictions, resistances which undo the royal magic. . . . Thus, the structure of Shakespeare's comedy symbolically neutralizes the forms of royal power to which it ostensibly pays homage."[40] Indeed, the argumentative structure of New Historicist writing as a whole tends to be incorporative rather than differentiating, both/and rather than either/or: neither element of the cultural oppositions that New Historicism so skillfully analyzes can finally be excluded from or subjugated to the other, but both remain suspended together in an uneasy solution "in which," to cite Greenblatt, "risks and advantages, pressure and protection, are continually renegotiated."[41]

By treating cultural history as a text, New Historicism is able to bring to bear the formidable techniques of interpretation that literary criticism has been developing for the past fifty years or so. The result is a series of readings of great subtlety and power, readings that anatomize the shifting imperatives and ambitions of Renaissance culture without subjecting them to easy—or indeed any—resolution: history is finally as undecidable as poetry, as of course it must be when read as a poem. Absorbing the historical into the textual, New Historicism endows it with the irresolution that, for deconstruction, characterizes textuality per se. But there is a price to pay for this absorption. To adopt an interpretive method that assumes that history is not merely known through but constituted by language is to act as if there are no acts other than speech acts. But while we can all agree that language cannot be prised off the world, that whatever nonverbal, nonsymbolic reality exists can be known only by means of linguistic mediation, this does not allow us to abandon the category of the historically real entirely. History is impelled by consequential and determinative acts of material production: building cities, making wars, collecting wealth, imposing discipline, seizing and denying freedom—these are material processes that, while enacted in terms of and made known by symbolic forms, possess a palpable force and an intentional purposiveness, however we may finally come to understand them, that stand against the irresolutions and undecidabilities valued by contemporary techniques of interpretation. It is true that the literary historian must perforce operate within the closed world of textuality, and

---

40. Louis Montrose, " 'Shaping Fantasies': Figurations of Gender and Power in Elizabethan Culture," *Representations* 2 (1983), 84–85.
41. Greenblatt, "Loudun and London," p. 343.

that he must not hypostasize a part of his evidence as the historically real. But our experience also teaches us that the historically real—as economic, political, social, and material reality—does indeed exist, and that action in the world has a presence and consequentiality that cannot be evaded. To apply the conditions of our scholarship to life is an almost inevitable transaction, but it in fact denatures, because it dematerializes, our historical existence. Indeed, the lines of influence ought really to run the other way, from our lives to our scholarship: in dealing with the textuality by which the historical makes itself known, we must not merely acknowledge but seek to accommodate, in however inevitably partial a fashion, something of the palpability and unavoidability of historical action.

My concern that the skeptical self-cancellations of contemporary textuality should not subvert the category of the historically real is derived not from some notion of philosophical correctness: indeed, since the historically real cannot exist apart from the textuality by which it is made known, deconstruction is surely right to insist that the priority of neither element can ever finally be demonstrated. Rather, it is the political consequences entailed by such a subversion that seem to me particularly persuasive. For in foregrounding the self-contradictions that haunt historical action, New Historicism discloses a world strangely drained of dynamism, in which every effort to enact change issues in a reaffirmation of the status quo, and where the continually renegotiated antagonisms of Renaissance culture are always already inscribed within a space of stasis. It arrives, in fact, at a paradox: on the one hand Renaissance culture is an arena of social contradictions engaged in ceaseless strife, and yet on the other hand, nothing happens. On the one hand, New Historicism sets itself against the monologic idealism of traditional *Geistesgeschichte,* with its insistence upon cultural homogeneity, and yet on the other ends up presenting a Renaissance as synchronically isolated and politically uniform as anything we find in Tillyard's *Elizabethan World Picture.*[42] The terms with which Greenblatt designates this condition are containment and subversion: Renaissance discourses *contain* subversion, in the double sense that they simultaneously elicit and control it, grant it a space for its enactment but finally encompass and disarm it.[43] Cultural oppositions may require continual renegotiation, but the results are always the same.

---

42. The term "monologic" is used by Greenblatt to characterize the old historicism over against which the New Historicism is to be defined; see his Introduction to *The Power of Forms in the English Renaissance,* pp. 3–6.

43. Stephen Greenblatt, "Invisible Bullets: Renaissance Authority and Its Subversion," *Glyph* 8 (1981), 40–61; in "The Politics of Renaissance Literature," Goldberg has shrewdly noted that "there is in Greenblatt's work too great a need not to express the possibility that

An illuminating instance of this process is offered by Greenblatt in "Loudun and London," where he describes how the attempt "to exorcise the theatricality of exorcism" through execution simply reinstated the theatrical. But the authorities did not stop there in their attempt to gain control. Rather, they instituted a public act of confessional guidance, in which the priestly exorcist would whisper in the ear of the possessed: "In effect, the theatre of possession and exorcism is made to cede place to a mute public spectacle and an inaudible, private discourse of spiritual interiority" (p. 332). What Greenblatt traces here is an early stage in the "negotiation of cultural power" by which public display gives way to private manipulation. The end of this story is not only easy to imagine but has in fact already been written, in Foucault's *Discipline and Punish*. There Foucault argues that in the late eighteenth century the dangers of execution as a display of power were fully recognized, so that the public enactment of authority was replaced with the secret, inward manipulation of the subject—a process that has now reached its fulfillment in the monolithic carceral society of the modern world, with its inescapable reproduction of itself within each individual.

The underwriting presence of Foucault in Greenblatt's account is symptomatic of his pervasive influence throughout New Historicism generally. For one thing, Foucault's argument that culture can be best understood through the analysis of the discursive practices that constitute its reality is another, and less depoliticized, way to bridge the gap between history and textuality than the solution offered by deconstruction. And for another, the central, almost obsessive focus of New Historicist attention is upon Foucault's own topic—power—and power understood in a specifically Foucauldian rather than Marxist way. That is, for Foucault power is not a capacity possessed by one group in society that advantageously deploys it against another, as the Marxist account of class struggle would have it, but rather a capacity that inhabits the very sinews and nerves of the body politic. To imagine that power is possessed or controlled by someone would be to imagine a space outside power, a wholly free and autonomous place from which power issues but which is itself uncontrolled. But to imagine such a place is to fall prey to the central cunning by which power enforces itself, that is, to imagine that

---

what he calls containment may not in fact have been absolute, a need related to the desire of his project to contain all in a controlling frame" (p. 533). And Goldberg adds, in commenting on Montrose's work, "Change needs to be accounted for; the possibility that change can occur must be read into texts that appear to confirm power, and into the institutions—court, theatre—that appear to preserve power" (p. 528). It is sometimes difficult to remember, in reading New Historicist accounts, that the English Renaissance reached its culmination in 1642 with a revolution.

one is somehow autonomous, a pure subjectivity from which unconditioned actions can issue, an individual. As Frank Lentricchia has cogently
argued, for Foucault power is virtually a metaphysical principle:

> In his social theory power tends to occupy the "anonymous" place which classi-
> cal treatises in metaphysics reserved for substance: without location, identity, or
> boundaries, it is everywhere and nowhere at the same time. . . . To put it as
> Foucault puts it is to suggest that power has no predominant direction, no pre-
> dominant point of departure, no predominant point of terminus. Like the God
> of theism, it is ubiquitous; unlike God it has no intention.[44]

And unlike God, its effects are malevolent. Foucault provides the ultimate fulfillment of a nightmare vision of a world so perfectly adminis-
tered (Adorno), so thoroughly bureaucratized (Weber), that reality itself
is constituted through the insidious, invisible workings of power. "The
exercise of power," says Foucault, "is a total structure of actions brought
to bear upon possible actions; it incites, it induces, it seduces, it makes
easier or more difficult; in the extreme it constrains or forbids absolutely;
it is nevertheless always a way of acting upon an acting subject or acting
subjects *by virtue of their acting or being capable of action.*"[45] The very entrance upon a field of action implicates the agent in a web of power relations that predetermines the scope and direction of his action. Power
may presuppose freedom, but it remains itself the primary term: freedom
is simply that which power requires for its actions, and is thus brought
into being in order to provide the necessary conditions for power's
enactment.

This totalizing vision of an entrapping world organized not primarily
but exclusively by structures of domination and submission, implicit in
much New Historicist work, becomes an explicit source of concern in
Greenblatt's *Renaissance Self-Fashioning*. Greenblatt rather ruefully acknowledges that although the topic of his book is the creation of the
Renaissance self, in the course of its writing "the human subject itself
began to seem remarkably unfree, the ideological product of the relations
of power in a particular society."[46] Similarly, in the struggle between con-

---

44. Frank Lentricchia, "Reading Foucault (Punishment, Labor, Resistance): Part Two,"
Raritan 2, 1 (Summer 1982), 50–51.
45. Michel Foucault, "The Subject and Power," in Herbert L. Dreyfus and Paul Rabi-
now, *Michel Foucault: Beyond Structuralism and Hermeneutics* (Chicago: University of Chicago
Press, 1982), p. 220 (my italics).
46. Stephen Greenblatt, *Renaissance Self-Fashioning* (Chicago: University of Chicago
Press, 1980), p. 256. Greenblatt continues: "Whenever I focused sharply upon a moment
of apparently autonomous self-fashioning, I found not an epiphany of identity freely chosen but a cultural artifact. If there remained traces of free choice, the choice was among
possibilities whose range was strictly delineated by the social and ideological systems in

tainment and subversion, containment remains the dominant mode, as in all logic it must since it has itself summoned up subversion in order to reconfirm, over and over, its dominance. Given this prescribed dynamic, individual and contingent political action is revealed as an illusion: whatever acts may be undertaken, they are instantly inscribed within already established structures. Hence the New Historicist refusal to specify authorial intention: the most that Greenblatt will say about Jacobean theatrical representations of exorcism is that "they do the state some service," as of course they inevitably must, since all cultural activity can serve only to confirm the authority always already in place; at one point in his essay on *A Midsummer Night's Dream* Montrose describes the play as attempting to assert royalist values that it then unwittingly undoes, but he later reverses the lines of force by presenting it as an attempt at subversion that is inevitably inscribed within an authoritative ideology.[47] More tendentiously, for Montrose Spenser's *Shepheardes Calender,* and indeed all Elizabethan pastoral, serves to legitimize hierarchical power structures by representing them as benign, a reading that ignores the fact that Spenser clearly intended his poem as an attack upon specific political practices supported by Elizabeth.[48] It is quite true that specific and explicit intention can never fully govern the meaning of a text, that literature serves to constitute cultural reality in ways it can never fully know and that may run counter to its own most insistent purposes. But simply to set aside these intentions and purposes as unworthy of discussion is effectively to silence dissent; and by raising analysis to a level at which individual actions and motives become submerged into a totalized vision of a monolithic culture is to beg the question by adopting a

---

force." This is a concern also voiced by the book's otherwise enthusiastic reviewers. See, for example, Louis Adrian Montrose, "A Poetics of Renaissance Culture," *Criticism* 23 (1981), 349–59; and Thomas M. Greene, *Comparative Literature* 34 (1982), 184–86. In his *ELH* Article, Goldberg describes the book as offering a "frighteningly totalistic and implicitly totalitarian vision" (p. 529).

47. Greenblatt, "Loudun and London," p. 341; Montrose, " 'Shaping Fantasies,' " pp. 74, 84–85.

48. Louis Montrose, " 'Eliza, Queene of Shepheardes,' and the Pastoral of Power," *English Literary Renaissance* 10 (1980), 153–82; see also "Gifts and Reasons: The Contexts of Peele's *Araygnement of Paris,*" *ELH* 47 (1980), 433–61, and " 'The perfecte paterne of a Poete': The Poetics of Courtship in *The Shepheardes Calender,*" *Texas Studies in Language and Literature* 21 (1979), 34–67. For the anti-Elizabethan politics of *The Shepheardes Calender,* see Norbrook, *Poetry and Politics in the English Renaissance,* pp. 59–90. Norbrook concludes: "In *The Shepheardes Calender* Spenser established a political rhetoric that was to remain popular until the Civil War. The figure of the shepherd poet became associated with the kind of policies adopted by Leicester and his political heir, the Earl of Essex: a militant foreign policy and at home a religious policy that was reasonably sympathetic to the more radical brethren, while not necessarily favouring all radical demands" (p. 89).

method that can prove only the hypothesis at issue.[49] The Foucauldian vision of a carceral society is dangerously self-confirming: the individual disappears because the historian stops looking for him, just as the nonpolitical yields wholly to a decoding that reveals it to have been political all along.[50] There is no space outside power because power is the only term in the analyst's arsenal.

While thus setting itself up as providing a dialogic alternative to the monologic idealism of traditional historicism, New Historicism finds itself in danger of falling into an analogous narrowness. The valence has been reversed but the condition remains the same: where old historicism saw Renaissance culture as conforming to the norm of Tillyard's benign *Elizabethan World Picture*, the New Historicists now see it as organized according to the malign principle of power. Quite against its explicit intentions, New Historicism effects a monolithic totalization, suppressing the individual in favor of the general and the disparate in favor of the homogenous. Similarly, while New Historicism seeks to promote the power of discourse—"The Power of Forms," to use Greenblatt's title—it ends up representing discourse as in fact impotent: language may constitute reality but is itself constrained by rules and procedures so intricately interwoven into its fabric as to be impervious to investigation and change.

Finally, New Historicist investigation is as relentlessly synchronic as any *Geistesgeschichte*. Sharing the current distrust of diachronic historicism, a distrust impelled by the discrediting of the concept of the origin, the collapse of the classic model of cause-and-effect causality, and the unpersuasiveness of evolutionary and teleological claims, New Historicism seeks instead to achieve what Geertz calls "thick description," an analysis of the conditions of cultural production. No longer believing that cultural phenomena can be usefully explained as effects of anterior causes, New Historicism is released from the narrow criterion of relevance that constrained older literary historians. The result is both an enlightening extension of the range of materials to be brought to bear upon a text—New Historicist essays typically begin with an apparently out of the way anecdote or event in order eventually to show how it too bespeaks the central problematic of the culture as a whole—and yet a weak-

---

49. As Norbrook trenchantly points out, "If, as so often in the Renaissance period, authorial intention has a substantial and under-acknowledged political element, to ignore the intention is effectively to depoliticize" (*Poetry and Politics in the English Renaissance*, p. 8).

50. For two instances of this decoding in contemporary Renaissance studies, see Arthur Marotti, " 'Love is not love': Elizabethan Sonnet Sequences and the Social Order," *ELH* 49 (1982), 396–428; and Frank Whigham, *Ambition and Privilege: The Social Tropes of Elizabethan Courtesy Theory* (Berkeley: University of California Press, 1984).

ening of explanatory force. For if the New Historicists rightly refuse to reduce the text to an effect of either a straightforward authorial intention or a determinant social context, they also decline to specify the ground of comparison—the historically real—that supports their analyses. Neither the period consciousness of *Geistesgeschichte* nor the class struggle of Marxism provides them with adequate explanatory categories for cultural production, with the result that the critic withdraws from the task of explanation entirely and settles for the less definitive act of interpretation. At issue here is the same question raised by Adorno in his debate with Benjamin over Benjamin's *Passagenarbeit*. For Adorno, Benjamin's juxtapositioning of disparate cultural elements could yield results only if grounded in a critical perspective secured by its political commitments. Otherwise his instances of nineteenth-century culture became images that simply instantiated contradictions and could not serve as materials for a historical understanding to be developed through critical analysis.[51] At heart, in other words, the question was—and remains—whether cultural analysis is possible without an explicit commitment to a specific philosophy of history, a specific definition of the real. Can history be written without causality? And if not, is causal explanation possible without a foundational commitment to some narrative of historical action, be it the fulfillment of the Spirit, the rise of a heroic bourgeoisie, or the class struggle entailed by social inequality?

This question presents itself with some urgency for the medievalist because New Historicism, despite its laudable self-consciousness, in fact operates largely according to a traditional historiographical scheme that not only sets the Renaissance over against the Middle Ages but understands the opposition in terms originally established by nineteenth-century liberal philology. That is, the crucial heuristic category for New Historicism remains the individual versus society, although with the valence of the opposition now reversed. For Burckhardt, the Renaissance was the time in which man asserted his individuality, as opposed to the corporatist, collectivist Middle Ages in which "man was conscious of himself only as a member of a race, people, party, family, or corporation—only through some general category."[52] For the New Historicists, on the other hand, the Renaissance is the time when man discovers that the individuality he is seeking to assert does not in fact exist, that selfhood is not atemporally given but socially constituted.[53] From this per-

51. A brief account of the debate is offered by Susan Buck-Morss, *The Origin of Negative Dialectics* (New York: Free Press, 1977), pp. 143–46.

52. Jacob Burckhardt, *The Civilization of the Renaissance in Italy* (London: Phaidon Books, 1965), p. 81.

53. In *Renaissance Self-Fashioning* Greenblatt argues that "there are always selves—a

spective, then, it is the Middle Ages that is the time of heroic individuality while the Renaissance emerges from feudalism into the reification and alienation entailed by capitalism.[54] Indeed, one might almost be back with Ruskin, for whom Gothic freedom of expression was destroyed by "the poison-tree of the Renaissance," initiating a decline that culminated in the monolithic regimentation and pervasive alienation of the nineteenth-century factory—the Foucauldian locus of the carceral society.

My point is not simply that New Historicism is perhaps not so new after all; indeed, since our entire cultural situation has not moved much beyond the nineteenth-century opposition of left and right wing, however these may be variously defined, we can hardly expect our literary criticism to do so either. The issue is not how to get beyond the opposition—which, if we grant the inescapability of the political, in practice means how to evade it—but rather how to locate one's scholarly work within it in a way consistent with what one takes one's political values to be. Hence my point here is that New Historicism (and probably this *is* an effect of its insistence on its novelty) has in ways perhaps unbeknownst to itself found itself in a conservative political posture. At the most basic level, the Foucauldian account of cultural formation that the New Historicists have adopted, by depoliticizing power, calls into question the

---

sense of personal order, a characteristic mode of address to the world, a structure of bounded desires—and always some sense of deliberate shaping in the formation and expression of identity. . . . Moreover, there is considerable empirical evidence that there may well have been less *autonomy* in self-fashioning in the sixteenth century than before, that family, state, and religious institutions impose a more rigid and far-reaching discipline upon their middle-class and aristocratic subjects. . . . What *is* essential is the perception—as old in academic writing as Burckhardt and Michelet—that there is in the early modern period a change in the intellectual, social, psychological, and aesthetic structures that govern the generation of identities. This change is difficult to characterize in our usual ways because it is not only complex but resolutely dialectical. If we say that there is a new stress on the executive power of the will, we must say that there is the most sustained and relentless assault upon the will; if we say that there is a new social mobility, we must say that there is a new assertion of power by both family and state to determine all movement within the society; if we say that there is a heightened awareness of the existence of alternative modes of social, theological, and psychological organization, we must say that there is a new dedication to the imposition of control upon those modes and ultimately to the destruction of alternatives" (pp. 1–2). In *Radical Tragedy: Religion, Ideology, and Power in the Drama of Shakespeare and His Contemporaries* (Chicago: University of Chicago Press, 1984), Jonathan Dollimore argues that the Jacobean period saw the emergence of "a conception of subjectivity legitimately identified in terms of materialist perspective rather than one of essentialist humanism" (p. 249)—i.e., subjectivity as a function of the reification of the self entailed by capitalist modes of production. See also Don E. Wayne, *Penshurst: The Semiotics of Place and the Poetics of History* (Madison: University of Wisconsin Press, 1984).

54. For a lucid description of the Marxist theory of the generation of the sense of autonomous individuality by capitalism, see István Mészáros, *Marx's Theory of Alienation* (London: Merlin Press, 1970), pp. 255–58.

efficacy of local and contingent political action: since all of life is always already inscribed within and predetermined by structures of dominance and subordination, the powers-that-be will always be the powers-that-be. At a more local level, New Historicism typically focuses its attention not on the subversive and suppressed elements of society but on the dominating structures—and largely without criticism: the court, the aristocracy, the upwardly mobile. Indeed, in its attentive recreation of the ways in which Elizabethan and Jacobean monarchs used cultural productions in order to sustain their dominance it too often displays an uncritical celebration of what Fernand Braudel once called "that *Adelswelt* to which [the historian] is secretly drawn."[55]

Given both its explicit polemic against a reactionarily "idealist" old historicism, and its own commitment not only to the priority of the social but to conceptualizing it in terms of instability and contradiction, the conservative drift of New Historicism is best understood as an unintended embarrassment. Indeed, this unintentionality shows in vivid terms how a prevailing ideology can come to dominate even antithetical theoretical formations, regardless of their sophistication. The late 1970s and 1980s are self-evidently a time of hegemonic conservatism, in which the privatization of value has reached new extremes and in which the cult of success has become an explicit and unashamed justification for the crudest forms of economic and social injustice. To think that the academy is somehow exempt from this process would be naive, and yet academic discourse still maintains an objectivist style that implicitly denies the relevance of the writer's own social situation to his work of investigation. My point is *not* that the New Historicists are grasping and materialist seekers after fame and fortune who are betraying the noble values of their humanist discipline; not only can I not exempt myself from exactly the same charge, since the writing of this book is undertaken within a system of punishments and rewards that has an unmistakably prescriptive force, but phrasing the issue in these terms both invokes a set of indefensible assumptions and obscures a more central if difficult point. For while we may agree that it is necessary to stand against the dominant ideology of our times, it is the immense difficulty of doing so that must be acknowledged. Indeed, perhaps the lesson that the unintended conservatism of New Historicism teaches is that if you do not have an explicit politics—an ideology—then one will certainly have you.

To assume that the social totality prescribes not only the terms of

55. Fernand Braudel, *On History*, trans. Sarah Matthews (Chicago: University of Chicago Press, 1980), p. 125. For instances of this attraction, see the works of Orgel, Goldberg, and Whigham cited above.

every local and contingent opposition but the course of their contestation—that the progressive and the reactionary are two sides of the same repressive coin, subversion a function of containment—is not only to foreclose the possibility of political progress but in effect to annul the local and the contingent entirely. This is a recipe for despair: human beings have no other arena for action than the here and now, make no decisions that are not local, assert no values that are not contingent. Our daily lives are the only lives we have: there is no escaping from the historically specific, and it is in terms of this specificity that we must decide what work to do and how to do it. Our scholarly activity, in other words, can never be guided by some impossible norm of correctness but only by the relation we want to establish to the social and political formations governing our own historical moment.

These formations are at the moment deeply antipathetic to just the kind of small-scale, tactical activity that is our most available way of interacting with the world and participating in its development. It is not just the academic who has his historical irrelevance forced upon him; it is everybody. The homogenization of value and the annulment of the individual have reached extraordinary lengths in contemporary America; the culture industry has achieved a virtually undisputed dominance over American consciousness; corporate, military, and institutional interests pursue their goals with little restraint; and the most vigorous political formation at work in the United States is a fundamentalist conservatism dedicated to the growth of state power and the further eradication of difference. But if indeed Foucault's dystopic vision of the carceral society is on the way to fulfillment, then surely our scholarly task should be to stand against it. There is, for instance, something scandalous in the fact that the current, virulent attacks on humanism issue from two diametrical points on the political compass, the religious right and the theoretical left. How is it that the academic intellectual has come to conspire in his own demise? Almost twenty years ago Adorno understood this process with prescient clarity: "The more individuals are really degraded to functions of the social totality, as it becomes more systematized, the more will man pure and simple, man as a principle with the attributes of creativity and absolute domination, be consoled by exaltation of his mind."[56] The contemporary theoretical effort to subvert the false stability of the ideology of the subject is best understood not as a simple emancipation from reified bourgeois categories but rather as a totalizing intellectualism correlative to the hegemonic homogenization that character-

---

56. Theodor Adorno, "Subject and Object" (1969), in Andrew Arato and Eike Gebhardt, eds., *The Essential Frankfurt School Reader* (New York: Urizen Books, 1978), p. 500.

izes our time. Of course, to propose the recuperation of humanism will inevitably be seen by many as simply the reaction of an offended liberalism. But if we cannot return to the transhistorical bourgeois individual with his dominating ego and self-identical subjectivity, neither can we afford to dispense with the category of individualism altogether. To deprive the human agent of any purchase upon the social whole is to signal the end of a politics we desperately need.

But even if the force of these political considerations be granted, what is their relevance to the problems and procedures of literary historicism? To begin with, they entail a criticism that insists not only upon the dialectical nature of its relation to its own time but upon the negativity of that dialectic, upon adopting an antagonistic stance to the depersonalized, depoliticized, and tranquilized homogenization accomplished by modern American culture. Specifically, then, we must be alert at the level of critical method to the dangers of what the Frankfurt School thinkers called "identity theory," the underwriting assumption of those forms of historicism that would reduce difference and opposition to sameness by collapsing together subject and object, either through an idealist appropriation of the object world (as in *Geistesgeschichte*) or through a materialist economism (as in Marxism). On the contrary, our work should seek to preserve and understand threatened categories of difference, the imperative that Adorno called "the morality of thought":

The morality of thought lies in a procedure that is neither entrenched nor detached, neither blind nor empty, neither atomistic nor consequential. . . . Nothing less is asked of the thinker today than that he should be at every moment both within things and outside them—Münchhausen pulling himself out of the bog by his pig-tail becomes the pattern of knowledge which wishes to be more than either verification or speculation.[57]

Not the least of these categories of difference, and one with which medievalists are almost obsessively concerned, is that between the present-as-subject and the past-as-object. This is not, it must be insisted, a difference that can be theorized: the otherness of the past, and the demands of recognition and self-restraint it places upon us, can become the subject of homiletic urgings but not—as the failure of objectivism and the largely negative character of hermeneutics show—of theoretical prescriptions.[58] In attempting to understand the past, we inevitably enter into elaborate and endless negotiations, struggles between desire and

57. Theodor Adorno, *Minima Moralia: Reflections from Damaged Life,* trans. E. F. N. Jephcott (London: New Left Books, 1974), p. 74.

58. For comments on Hans Robert Jauss's most recent effort to theorize it in terms of Medieval Studies, see Chapter 1 n. 9.

knowledge that can never be granted closure. But negotiations can take place only between two equal and independent parties, and this fiction— a fiction because the past can never exist independently of our memory of it—must be consciously and painfully maintained. The paradox involved is again well illuminated by Adorno:

> The preponderant exertion of knowledge is destruction of its usual exertion, that of using violence against the object. Approaching knowledge of the object is the act in which the subject rends the veil it is weaving around the object. It can do this only where, fearlessly passive, it entrusts itself to its own experience. In places where subjective reason scents subjective contingency, the primacy of the object is shimmering through—whatever in the object is not a subjective admixture.[59]

The contradictions in this passage pile up because historical understanding is by definition a vacillation between contradictions that must not yield to closure.

Another antinomy whose irresolution must be respected is, as we have seen, that between the individual and the totality. In literary-historical terms this respect presents itself in the form of intention, an interpretive category that contemporary criticism has largely written off as a vestige of positivism. To be sure, there are constraints upon intention, and serious ones: writing comes into being within a socially determined context and by means of a socially constituted discourse, and it always makes meanings beyond and often other than those the author intended. Clearly the present is endowed with a capacity to understand the past in ways that it cannot understand itself: history takes place behind man's back as well as in front of his face. But a text is also a function of specific human intentions, in the sense both of self-consciously maintained purposes and of impulses that may be incapable of articulation but nonetheless issue from a historical intentionality, and it is a large part of our task to understand how these intentions went into its making. Much of what we come to know about texts was also available to their makers, albeit in a variety of unfamiliar cognitive forms, and to empower our

---

59. Adorno, "Subject and Object," p. 506. On this passage, see also Jay, *Adorno*, pp. 73–74. In *Minima Moralia* Adorno offers a similar account of the difficult reliability of aesthetic experience: "Anyone who, drawing on the strength of his precise reaction to a work of art, has ever subjected himself in earnest to its discipline, to its immanent formal law, the compulsion of its structure, will find that the objections to the merely subjective quality of his experience vanish like a pitiful illusion: and every step that he takes, by virtue of his highly subjective innervation, towards the heart of the matter, has incomparably greater force than the comprehensive and fully backed-up analyses of such things as 'style,' whose claims to scientific status are made at the expense of such experience. This is doubly true in the era of positivism and the culture industry, where objectivity is calculated by the subjects managing it" (p. 70).

critical abilities by devaluing theirs is to initiate an exchange that will ultimately rebound upon ourselves. To grant the social totality unfettered sway over the individual, who is then reduced to a helpless mediator of historical forces that can be fully understood only by the modern historian, is to invoke an "absolute historicism," in Gramsci's phrase, that entraps us all. Adorno's famous critique of Benjamin is relevant here:

Before his Medusan glance, man turns into a stage on which an objective process unfolds. For this reason Benjamin's philosophy is no less a source of terror than a promise of happiness.[60]

Whatever individualism we seek to sustain must, to be sure, insist upon its historicity: the idea of the individual arises at certain historical moments and becomes submerged at others. But it is clearly not an idea dependent simply upon capitalism (how then can we explain its twelfth-century presence?), and neither can it be read as simply a function of subjection. The self may be made, but it is also self-made.

Finally, a correlative historical category that literary scholars cannot really do without is that of literature itself. That this is a *historical* category is beyond dispute, and that its boundaries, definitions, and purposes change over time is also true. Contemporary criticism characteristically understands it as an agency for authoritarian and conservative forces: the canon of literary works is devised in order to enforce hegemonic interests. But this is not always true: in the Middle Ages many of the texts we now call literary carved out for themselves, without the benefit of a theory of the literary, a space of ideological opposition. It is, moreover, precisely their negtive relationship to the dominant formations of their time that make such texts as, for example, the Chartrian poems, the *Roman de la rose, Piers Plowman,* and the *Canterbury Tales* such accurate indices of the historical world from which they arise and upon which they reflect. This is not to say that they are not themselves conditioned by social forces that remain outside their own articulation, forces that the historian can recuperate; but it is to argue that they bear a privileged relation to their historical moment, and that we must respect and rely upon this privilege. These texts can hardly tell us everything we want or need to know about the past, but when securely located at the center of our investigations (as not objects but subjects) they can help us to negotiate an otherwise enigmatic terrain.

---

60. Theodor Adorno, *Prisms,* trans. Samuel Weber and Shierry Weber (Cambridge: MIT Press, 1981), p. 235.

II. INVENTING ORIGINALITY

3. The Logic of Textual Criticism and the Way of Genius: The Kane-Donaldson *Piers Plowman* in Historical Perspective

OF THE many methodological notions that have been advanced through-out the history of textual criticism, perhaps the oldest is the distinction between external and internal evidence. The external evidence has to do with the manuscripts in which a reading occurs and the frequency of its attestations; the internal evidence is the quality of a reading in relation to its variants. The first kind of evidence is documentary; it exists as man-uscripts (or prints) to be dated, counted, and assessed; the second kind of evidence is (apparently) judgmental: it exists as a distinction that must be drawn by the skill of the editor. The first kind of evidence is often considered authoritative, especially when it is absent, as in the familiar dismissal "th[is] emendation is without authority."[1] The second kind is often considered unreliable, especially when it is present, as in the equally familiar criticism that an editor, "having abandoned the evidence of the witnesses, . . . leaves textual judgments to the whims of the indi-

---

1. While the phrasing is ubiquitous, this particular example is taken from Archibald A. Hill, "Some Postulates for Distributional Study of Texts," *Studies in Bibliography* 3 (1950–51), 76. Hill is commenting on Theobald's " 'a babbled of green fields."

vidual practitioner."[2] In short, a method based on external evidence is usually thought to be objective, one based on internal evidence subjective. The distinction has been with us in theory since the humanists defined two kinds of *emendatio,* one *ope ingenii* and the other *ope codicum,* and in practice ever since documents were first transmitted, and the history of textual criticism can be and usually is written in terms of the shifting allegiances between the two methods. So that while this is a distinction that textual criticism apparently needs—the subject is hardly describable without it—it is also at the source of most of the issues that divide critics. This may be because the distinction itself has rarely received any sustained attention, simply because the problems arise not with making it but after it is already in place.[3]

A recent, and highly controversial, publication provides an ideal opportunity to ventilate this fundamental issue; the 1975 Athlone Press edition of the B-Text of Langland's *Piers Plowman,* edited by George Kane and E. Talbot Donaldson. Apart from the sheer magnitude of its achievement, the Kane-Donaldson edition is notable for its rigorous rethinking of the questions surrounding not only this work but textual criticism itself. Furthermore, the editors adopt a position that has been characterized by one reviewer as a "profoundly informed subjectivity," a description with which they would probably not quarrel.[4] At every turn in their 220-page introduction they stress the priority of internal over external evidence, a procedure that has led another, less friendly commentator to describe their method as "editorial free choice" and the edition as a whole as "radical, if not revolutionary."[5] In fact, what the edition represents is a profound reconceptualization of the whole question of what constitutes evidence, with results that show how characterizing terms like "subjective" and "objective" are profoundly misleading. This is a conclusion, however, that not even the editors make fully explicit, and for its force to be appreciated two kinds of exposition are necessary. One is to define

---

2. Gordon D. Fee, "Rigorous or Reasoned Eclecticism—Which?" in James K. Elliott, ed., *Studies in New Testament Language and Text,* Novum Testamentum Supplements 44 (Leiden: Brill, 1976), p. 177. Fee is arguing against George Kilpatrick's rigorous eclecticism and in favor of a return to Hort's conservatism.

3. An exception is Vinton A. Dearing, *Principles and Practices of Textual Analysis* (Berkeley: University of California Press, 1974).

4. Eric G. Stanley, "The B Version of 'Piers Plowman': A New Edition," *Notes and Queries* 221 (1976), 436. Other important reviews are by Derek Pearsall, *Medium Aevum* 46 (1977), 278–85; Manfred Görlach, *Archiv* 213 (1976), 396–99; J. A. W. Bennett, *Review of English Studies* n.s. 28 (1977), 323–26; and, most extensively and critically, David C. Fowler, *Yearbook of English Studies* 7 (1977), 23–42.

5. Anne Hudson, "Middle English," in A. G. Rigg, ed., *Editing Medieval Texts* (New York: Garland Press, 1977), pp. 44 and 42.

the thoroughly systematic nature of the editors' procedures and methodology; the other is to locate the edition within the history of textual criticism. The first is necessary to counter the editors' own, I think misplaced, resistance to codifying their procedures into a generally applicable system. So concerned are they to dispute the claims of a mechanistic stemmatics, with its assumptions of objectivity and certainty, that they devalue—in exposition although not in practice—system per se, and specifically the powerful logic of their own procedure. Second, by locating the edition historically we will be able to see that the values at issue in textual criticism derive from the same historical matrix as those being debated in the larger world of literary theory.

The Kane-Donaldson text is underwritten by a powerful set of humanist assumptions, assumptions that are now under attack from a number of quarters. As always, there is the tenacious opposition of a positivist historicism for which the specificity of the past forecloses the possibility of transhistorical recuperation; in editorial terms, this means that the bewildering corpus of textual variants is thought to overwhelm editorial ministrations that would seek to rescue from them an original text.[6] Similarly, for an avant-garde deconstruction the very notion of originality is suspect, and recent developments in textual criticism that have decomposed previously unified texts into a series of variant versions is the triumphant enactment at the level of editorial practice of what deconstruction has been doing all along at the level of interpretation.[7] Finally, there is a politically motivated critique that sees the attempt to establish an original text as denying the "fundamentally social" nature of authorship by promoting a singular authorial intention, a critique that in its strongest form sees the Kane-Donaldson *Piers Plowman* as produced by a "low profile subjectivism" and representing a pure instance of bourgeois liberalism and individualism.[8] All of these criticisms draw upon strong traditions of thought, and in specific instances they carry an un-

6. These are the doubts expressed by most of the edition's reviewers (see above, note 4), and it continues to be a widely shared opinion among medievalists. For an especially egregious and ill-informed instance, see John Norton-Smith, *William Langland* (Leiden: Brill, 1983), on which see the telling review by John Alford, *Speculum* 61 (1986), 192–95.

7. This activity is especially satisfying when it attacks that bastion of patriarchal values, Shakespeare studies; see, for instance, Jonathan Goldberg's argument in "Textual Properties," *Shakespeare Quarterly* 37 (1986), that "post-structuralism and the new textual criticism coincide, historically—and theoretically. Both have called the criterion of authorial intention into question, thereby detaching the supposed sovereign author from texts open to and constituted by a variety of interventions" (p. 213).

8. For the "fundamentally social" nature of authorship, see Jerome J. McGann, *A Critique of Modern Textual Criticism* (Chicago: University of Chicago Press, 1983), p. 8; for the explicitly Marxist designation of Kane-Donaldson as bourgeois liberalism, see Stephen Knight, "Textual Variants: Textual Variance," *Southern Review* 16 (1983), 44–54.

deniable force: one axiom of textual criticism is that each instance must be assessed in its own terms, and certainly the crucial distinction between manuscript and print cultures inevitably limits the relevance of whatever lessons we might seek to draw from the Kane-Donaldson edition. But what is striking is how inadequately the edition has been understood, both as a project in its own right and in terms of its ideological valence. Lurking within the criticisms is the implicit if vague notion that somehow the edition displays on its face the bankruptcy of the entire humanist project, that its "subjectivism" impeaches its integrity and reveals a guilty—and even unrecognized—ideological motivation. But as I hope to show, not only is this criticism radically misplaced, but when the edition is properly understood it stands as a powerfully self-consistent instance and proponent of the humanism that is under attack. Moreover, it argues both explicitly and by implication that the alternatives are far less attractive than they might seem in prospect. Indeed, perhaps the most powerful lesson the edition teaches is that we had better keep what we have—and learn to use it properly—before handing ourselves over to something that is not clearly better.

I

At heart external evidence is nothing other than the fact that a particular reading occurs in one or more manuscripts, i.e., attestation; internal evidence is nothing other than the fact that there is on many occasions more than one reading, i.e., variation. Both internal and external evidence are evidence of originality; both are, in and of themselves, equally factual, equally objective, equally historical. Both are used for the same purpose, which is to discover the history of transmission, on the presumption that once this history is known the editor will be able to reverse it, to run the process backward until the original comes into view. With internal evidence the history of transmission is discovered by determining the direction of the variation, that is, which of the variants is the source of the others. This is accomplished, as we shall see, by an elaborate process of interpretation. It is often assumed, however, that external evidence enters into the editorial process in a direct and wholly "objective" form, untainted by interpretive activity. That this is not the case can be demonstrated by a brief look at the fate of stemmatics.

External evidence has traditionally been used by editors to discover the history of transmission by constructing a genealogy or stemma of the surviving manuscripts, a stemma that then determines both the relative value of the manuscripts and the nature of the missing ancestors, especially the founding father. The initial step in constructing this stemma is to classify the manuscripts into families, a procedure that can be accomplished in two ways. One is by means of shared paleographical characteristics such as format and mutilation. A spectacular example is found in the manuscripts of Epictetus, where one manuscript has been defaced with a large greasy stain and all the others are lacking just the obliterated passage.[9] But this example is very much an exception, and despite recent advances paleography has not yet managed to provide evidence about the relationship among documents that is unambiguous.[10] The other method of classification is by shared error, a procedure that is now in disrepute for two reasons. The first is that it is considered to be historically inaccurate, for it depends upon a number of doubtful assumptions: that scribes made the same error only when they were copying from each other and not independently; that errors traveled only down the family tree and not across it, through a process of contamination; and that among the variants only one is correct and all the rest are errors.[11] The second reason, and the one that most concerns us here, is that the procedure is theoretically absurd. It designates its first step as classification by shared error whereas in fact it is with the very *identification* of error that the process actually begins. If this act is indeed so self-evident as to require no methodological discussion, then so too, it would seem, is the whole process of editing, which is after all concerned with nothing other than the identification of error. Consequently, by basing its conclusions on the compilation of what it takes to be "raw" data, the external method renders itself unable to understand the interpretive processes by which it produced those data in the first place. It is, in short, subject to the charge of bad faith because it has hidden from itself the means by which it produced its results.

In his well-known rejection of stemmatics, Joseph Bédier focused on

---

9. This example is offered by Hill, "Some Postulates for Distributional Study of Texts," p. 82.

10. For instance, the important article by A. I. Doyle and M. B. Parkes, "The Production of Copies of the *Canterbury Tales* and the *Confessio Amantis* in the Early Fifteenth Century," in M. B. Parkes and Andrew G. Watson, eds., *Medieval Scribes, Manuscripts and Libraries* (London: Scolar Press, 1978), pp. 163–210, provides much useful information in regard to the early Chaucer manuscripts, especially Ellesmere and Hengwrt, as well as crucial information about reception and modes of reading, but it does not (nor is it meant to) advance our understanding of the genealogical relationships among these manuscripts. In short, while codicology is certainly one of the richest areas of new research in medieval literary studies, its relevance to textual criticism has not yet become clear.

11. Perhaps the most damaging attack on stemmatics was launched by Giorgio Pasquali, first in his review of Paul Maas's *Textkritik* (Leipzig and Berlin: Teubner, 1927) in *Gnomon* 5 (1929), 417–35, 498–521, then in the vastly expanded *Storia della tradizione e critica del testo* (Florence: Le Monnier, 1934; 2d ed., 1962). For the famous rejection of stemmatics by Joseph Bédier, see the next note.

just this methodological bad faith, and in terms that are relevant both to this discussion and to our later account of the history of textual criticism.[12] Bédier's point was not simply (as it is sometimes taken to be) that editors produce bifid stemmata in order to avoid a mechanical triage of two against one that would preempt their judgment, but rather that the initial stage of discrimination upon which the stemma was based was itself uncontrolled by any methodological limitations that might restrain its reductions. In other words, once an editor had divided his manuscripts into families, his powers of textual analysis would continue to work upon the variants until, by discovering certain family resemblances among members of the stemma, it had inevitably reduced the families to only two. As Bédier eloquently put it, the stemmaticist is possessed by an "inquiétude persistante, si loin qu'il ait poussé la critique des variantes, de ne l'avoir pas poussée encore assez loin" (p. 175). "Une sorte de nécessité morale" obliges the editor to consider the possibility that two of his three families may be only one in disguise: "c'est un scrupule qui l'obsède. . . . La force dichotomique, une fois déchaînée, agit jusqu'au bout. Le système lachmannien l'a lancé dans la chasse aux fautes communes, mais sans lui donner aucun moyen de savoir à quel moment il a le devoir de s'arrêter" (p. 176). It is this *force dichotomique* that is at the heart of every editorial procedure: the desire, that is, to distinguish originality from the unoriginal. But by refusing to acknowledge its workings, stemmatics is unable to subject it to methodological constraints and so becomes victimized by the very libido that motivates it in the first place.

This hidden first step of stemmatics is in fact nothing more (nor less) than the interpretation of variation by which internal evidence is evaluated. If it is true, as the editorial dictum asserts, that manuscripts must be weighed (i.e., interpreted) and not merely counted, then the process of interpretation can begin only with the attempt to identify which of the variants are scribal. The principles upon which this is to be done have received a good deal of attention, although much less than that accorded to the necessarily secondary step of manuscript classification.[13] Two of these principles are the famous rules *difficilior* (or *durior*) and *brevior lectio potior*. Others are procedures that in their details vary with the kind of

---

12. In the most fully articulated account of his rejection of stemmatics, Joseph Bédier, "La tradition manuscrite du *Lai de l'ombre:* Réflexions sur l'art d'éditer les anciens textes," *Romania* 54 (1928), 161–96, 321–56. Subsequent references are cited within the text.

13. Most systematically by J. J. Griesbach, *Novum Testamentum Graece,* vol. 1 (London and Halle, 1796). On Griesbach's contribution to textual criticism, and his continuing relevance, see Bernard Orchard and Thomas R. W. Longstaff, eds., *J. J. Griesbach: Synoptic and Text-Critical Studies, 1776–1976* (Cambridge: Cambridge University Press, 1978).

text at issue but are, as procedures, universally applicable. These consist in the discovery of norms of meter, grammar, and usage, specific both to the writer's culture and to him individually, that can together serve to define an authorial *usus scribendi*. Armed with these tools, the textual critic is now able to begin to distinguish between an authorial and a scribal reading, in short, to edit. It is by means of these principles of discrimination that the evaluation of all the evidence, whether external or internal, is begun. This does not mean that the external is set aside as somehow irrelevant or by nature impenetrable: on the contrary, the specific manuscript in which a reading is attested and the frequency of its attestation are important pieces of evidence for the originality of a reading and must be evaluated. But the mere fact of attestation and its frequency can by themselves provide no guidance to the editor until he has begun to understand something of the nature of attestation per se in the particular manuscript tradition at issue.

The Kane-Donaldson edition of the B-Text is volume 2 of the total *Piers Plowman* project, and it is in volume 1, edited by George Kane alone, that these issues begin to be discussed.[14] The process by which any edited text is achieved is inevitably and appropriately circular, in which early hypothetical reconstructions are subjected to a series of testings against various kinds of evidence until a final version that most persuasively and efficiently answers the evidential questions is achieved.[15] Nonetheless, Kane's editorial method can be staged as four consecutive procedures. The first was to test all the readings offered by the manuscripts according to the internal criteria defined above, and by this means to arrive at a preliminary version of the original text. The second stage was to use this text to identify the errors in each individual manuscript and so to make possible a classification of the manuscripts according to shared error. Classification may seem superfluous but it is in fact essential; the degree of frequency with which a reading appears is a fact that any hypothesis about these manuscripts—and an edition is such a hypothesis—must explain.[16] In collating the manuscripts against his text

14. William Langland, *Piers Plowman: The A Version,* ed. George Kane (London: Athlone Press, 1960), pp. 1–172.

15. It must be admitted that both Kane and, later, Kane and Donaldson phrase the hypothetical nature of their initial findings less tentatively than might have been expected. For a discussion of a very similar procedure, that does stress the preliminary nature of the initial findings, see the account of their editorial practice offered by B. F. Westcott and F. J. A. Hort, *New Testament in the Original Greek* (Cambridge and New York: Macmillan, 1881; rev. ed., 1891), 1:541–62.

16. Kane presents his classification as having been undertaken primarily if not solely to test the genealogy put forward by Thomas A. Knott and David C. Fowler, *Piers the Plowman: A Critical Edition of the A-Version* (Baltimore: Johns Hopkins University Press,

and then classifying them not (as is usually the case) according merely to "significant" error but *all* error, Kane discovered that although he could identify a number of variational groups the evidence was too contradictory to allow him to establish any genetic relationships among these groups. But the true value of the attempt at classification was that it revealed the degree to which certain manuscripts agreed in error when, because of their agreement with other manuscripts, they could not possibly share a genetic relationship.[17] The presence of this "convergent variation," as Kane (following Greg) calls it,[18] was so overwhelming that it could not be explained simply by contamination; on the contrary, it indicated that scribes habitually made the same mistakes independently. As mentioned before, stemmatics necessarily assumes that a large proportion of errors are inherited and so can be used to trace descent; but the thoroughness of Kane's collation revealed that the truth was, at least for this poem, exactly the opposite. Moreover, an analysis of the variants revealed that the principle of coincidence extended not only to mechanical errors but to deliberate scribal substitutions as well. In short, it became clear that there was operating throughout the processes of transmission a logic of error, and that by making this logic explicit an editor could reconstruct the history of that transmission. Having rejected Lachmann's famous dictum *recensio sine interpretatione,* Kane was now able to establish the counter principle of *recensio per interpretationem* on a wholly new footing.

The third stage in the editorial process, then, was to refine and make explicit this logic of error. Operating on the principle that scribal substi-

---

1952), but while this may have been the initial motive it hardly proved to be the only purpose served. Similarly, Kane and Donaldson present their classification of the manuscripts of the B-Text as a response to the account offered by E. Chick in an unpublished University of London M.A. thesis (1914) and subsequently published by E. Blackman, "Notes on the B-Text MSS. of *Piers Plowman," Journal of English and Germanic Philology* 17 (1918), 498–518. But these explanations are somewhat disingenuous; the effort at classification is a crucial part of the assessment of the documentary evidence, and any editorial project that failed to attempt such a classification would be seriously deficient. In their exposition here we perhaps glimpse an effect of the editors' antistemmaticist prejudice.

17. On the rationale of this mutual exclusiveness, see below, pp. 85–86.

18. W. W. Greg, *The Calculus of Variants* (Oxford: Clarendon Press, 1927), p. 11. Greg's book seems to have exerted a powerful influence on the editors, along with the writings of A. E. Housman. An instructive comparison, for example, can be made between Housman's "The Application of Thought to Textual Criticism" (1921), reprinted in *Selected Prose* (Cambridge: Cambridge University Press, 1961), pp. 131–50, and Donaldson's "The Psychology of Editors of Middle English Texts" (1966), reprinted in *Speaking of Chaucer* (New York: Norton, 1970), pp. 102–18. Interestingly enough, Housman's first student at University College, London, was R. W. Chambers, who initiated the edition of *Piers Plowman* that Kane (who also taught for a time at University College, London) and Donaldson have now begun to bring to completion.

tution was on the whole less likely than retention of the original reading, Kane examined with particular attention those variants where, on the basis primarily of attestation, originality was not seriously in doubt. Armed with this data, he was then able to define scribal habits of substitution and especially the various forms of trivialization by which scribes dealt with a poem of evidently immense technical and thematic difficulty. This scribal *usus scribendi* could then be used to refine its authorial counterpart, and together these two norms could provide a double test; on the one hand, the original reading must conform to the authorial *usus scribendi,* and on the other, the scribal variants must conform to known habits of scribal substitution, that is, to the scribal *usus scribendi.* The fourth and final stage of editing, then, was to extrapolate these norms from the known to the unknown, from those heavily attested examples where originality was clear to others where the original reading was weakly attested or even where the unanimously attested reading appeared to be scribal. Far from being a bold maneuver, this extrapolation is not only possible but obligatory: if a certain kind of reading is demonstrably scribal where it is weakly attested then it must be just as scribal where it is strongly and even unanimously attested. The descent of error from the archetype to all extant manuscripts is not merely likely but inevitable, especially where that reading is *facilior,* and to preserve a reading that is prima facie scribal simply because in one context it is unanimously attested is a violation of the entire editorial project. In short, to preserve such a manuscript reading is to fly in the face of the evidence.

The editing of the B-Text follows the same procedures, although now applied (as the editors stress) in a more "rigorously logical" fashion.[19] In part this renewed emphasis is simply a recognition that logic by definition always operates at a maximum level of rigor; in part it is required by the nature of the evidence, which is both superabundant and precarious. For here the attempt at classification reveals a degree of convergent variation that is virtually epidemic. This point is worth illustrating in some detail. For example, the editors establish three manuscripts, Bm, Bo and Cot, as a variational group that is almost certainly genetic because these manuscripts share over 800 unique variants or common errors; furthermore, there are another 250 variants that these three manuscripts share with a fourth manuscript, C. These facts would yield the diagram shown on the following page. The editors then point out, however, that a fifth manuscript, F, shares over 80 unique variants with

---

19. George Kane and E. Talbot Donaldson, eds., *Piers Plowman: The B Version* (London: Athlone Press, 1975), p. 159 n. 78. See also, for example, pp. 129–30; and for recantations by Kane of decisions taken in the course of editing the A-Text while still "deluded by the 'ideal' of conservative editing," see pp. 205 n. 154; 129 nn. 1 and 2; 75 n. 15.

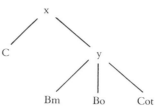

BmBoCot, errors that C does not have. There is no place for F in this stemma: lacking the 800 errors that identify the descendents of y, it cannot be placed in that branch of the family; and lacking the 250 errors that identify the descendents of x, it has in fact no place in the family at all. Therefore, the 80 unique variants that it shares with BmBoCot are evidence not of genetic relationship but of convergent variation. As the editors say:

In designating BmBoCotF a random group we propose that rather more than once in 100 lines scribal variation in the exclusive common ancestor of BmBoCot and in F or an immediate ancestor took the same form at the same point. No other conclusion seems logically possible; further, the convergent variation was, specifically, coincident. (P. 48)

And they generalize their findings as follows:

The logic of convergent variation is harsh: whether or not any of our genetic identifications is accepted the variant groups of the B manuscripts proclaim its occurrence. These manuscripts are necessarily in some vertical genetic relation; where they form many variant groups in the nature of things only a few of these can be genetic. The rest—identified or not—must have originated in convergent variation. . . . The reader who finds convergent variation a difficult explanation . . . is invited to reflect on the character of any other. (Pp. 37–38 n. 47, p. 58)

I have dwelt on this point for reasons both specific and general. Specifically, the demonstrated fact of this degree of convergent variation both impeaches stemmatics and, more usefully, accredits the logic of error, for it shows that scribal substitution was often identical and was therefore undertaken under the guidance of certain principles. Generally, as the editors point out, these facts urge upon us "the importance of accepting this phenomenon in the editing of Middle English texts" (p. 47)—and, one might suggest, all vernacular texts. All one need do is to read through Manly and Rickert's tortuous attempts to explain their classification of the manuscripts of the *Canterbury Tales* by multiple changes of exemplar to realize how fruitful this procedure might be in the reediting of even so carefully edited a poet as Chaucer.

Kane and Donaldson's analysis of the external evidence, then, uncovers the ubiquity of convergent variation and so seriously undermines the bare fact of attestation as a criterion for originality.[20] However, because this poem exists in two other versions (A and C), the B-Text manuscripts are not the only source of attestation. For about 35 percent of its length the poem is attested by two other manuscript traditions, and for another 45 percent by one other tradition (usually C, but in the first eleven passus occasionally A).[21] That this attestation is complicated by the fact of revision is of course true; but as the editors point out, there is one case in which the evidence is unequivocal and provides conclusions that can be relied upon in more ambiguous circumstances: when AC agree against B, and especially when internal criteria mark B as scribal.[22] In the approximately 1,800 lines that are doubly attested there are almost 150 cases of this, an impressive body of data from which to draw conclusions; as the editors say, in these circumstances A and C "afford a rigorous check upon the originality of readings in the exclusive common ancestor of the B manuscripts" (p. 83).[23] It should also be noted that here as elsewhere two processes are applied to the attested readings in order to assess originality: consistency with authorial *usus scribendi* and, for the variants, production by known means of scribal substitution, i.e., scribal *usus scribendi*.

---

20. As Kane and Donaldson say, "This situation brings home to the editor the relative unimportance of strength of attestation as evidence of originality, and directs his attention to the readings" (p. 63); and they add in a note, "The old maxim 'manuscripts must be weighed, not counted' should be revised to run 'readings should be weighed, not manuscripts counted.' But to the inexperienced in textual criticism an array of sigils after a variant is bound to seem impressive" (p. 63 n. 100).

21. These figures can be only approximate because Kane and Donaldson do not in fact provide the reader with precise information on this point, and they can be ascertained only by comparing the edited A and C texts (the latter not yet available to the reader, but consulted by Kane and Donaldson) on a line-by-line basis. The point is important because there are in some cases sharply differing rates of originality depending on the kind of comparison that is being made, at least to judge by necessarily approximate figures; see below, n. 55.

22. "These agreements between the texts of A and C against the archetypal text of B amount to a compelling assessment of the quality of this archetypal text; they are, in fact, the determinant circumstance in the editing of the B version of *Piers Plowman*" (p. 76), because, presumably, they show both the extent and the nature of the corruption to which the archetype was subject. So far as I have been able to determine, Kane and Donaldson do not cite a single instance where B disagrees with AC but can be thought to be, on internal grounds, original.

23. The use of the symbols A and C should not be allowed to mask the fact that what are being invoked as norms of comparison are not simply data but reconstructed original texts that are themselves the product of precisely the same editorial process that is here being enacted. While not yet printed, the C-Text was far enough along for its editor, G. A. Russell, to provide Kane and Donaldson with readings; see above, n. 21.

As well as this initial, crucial comparison there are three other relevant comparisons that can be made among these three versions, and the editors avail themselves of all three: B - A alone, where C does not correspond; B - C, both where B is and is not revised; and A - BC, again both where A is and is not revised.[24] The effect of these comparisons is to reveal the corruption of the B-Text archetype and the only slightly less serious corruption of the manuscript from which Langland worked in composing the C-Text. For our purposes what is important is the editors' consistent assertion of the priority of internal over external criteria of judgment, both here and throughout the editorial process. As they say, it should be clear to a reader of their introduction how far they have "set the reliability of discrimination [between scribal and authorial readings] as a determinant of originality in various editorial situations above that of attestation" (p. 163). This is a carefully qualified statement, but it can be qualified even further by stressing the degree to which attestation itself figures in this process of discrimination. For example, when the archetypal B-Text is compared to the A-Text it is revealed to have "some 100" (p. 98) readings that the editors regard as scribal by the standards of authorial and scribal *usus*. But attestation figures as a crucial element not only in the definition of these standards, but specifically as well in the identification of the scribal nature of these particular readings. For more than half of the 100 already appear, the editors point out, "as scribal variants of original A readings in the post-archetypal tradition of A, that is in surviving A manuscripts" (pp. 101–2). In other words, the possibility that the readings the editors choose as the B original could have been corrupted into the variant that appears, often unanimously attested, in the B manuscripts has already been demonstrated in the textual history of the A manuscripts. It is of course true that this evidence could be interpreted in such a way as to arrive at precisely the opposite conclusion: we could choose as the A original the variant that is most heavily attested in the B manuscripts. But to arrive at this conclusion we would have to demonstrate that the editors have misconceived the direction of variation among the A readings, which would then require us to explain apparently identical directions of variation in other cases where attestation is equivalently supportive of the same kind of originality that we wish to dispute here. In short, the choice is not between frequency of attestation

---

24. Why the two remaining comparisons, AB - C and A - C, are not performed is not explained, although in the case of A - C the reason must be both lack of opportunity and irrelevance to the question of the originality of B. AB - C certainly *is* relevant, but there are perhaps no cases in which AB stand against an unrevised C in a way that reveals anything other than the originality of C. Nonetheless, this is an omission that violates the systematic nature of the edition.

and editorial judgment among variants but between two different hypotheses by which to explain all the evidence. Hence while it remains correct to say that methodological priority is given to internal criteria, in that the choice between original and unoriginal readings starts from and must accord with the definitions of authorial and scribal *usus,* it would be entirely wrong to say that the external evidence is somehow ignored or overridden. On the contrary, each editorial decision must accord precisely with that evidence—with the fact and frequency of attestation—as well as with principles derived from the most careful scrutiny of rival readings.

My second qualifying example has to do with the editors' habit of emending the B-Text archetype on the basis of metrical deficiency, a procedure that has come under sharp criticism.[25] In fact their procedure here is an epitome of their methodology throughout and so invites particular attention. Specifically at issue are some 350 lines in the archetypal B-Text that contain fewer than three alliterating staves: is this metrical peculiarity a sign of scribal substitution or is it part of Langland's technical repertoire? To answer this question the editors examine some 800 lines that are, by the standards of both attestation and authorial *usus,* demonstrably scribal and that alliterate in only two staves. Of the twelve possible alliterative patterns in two staves these lines in fact make use of only five, and these five are not only "precisely the alliterative patterns of the two-stave lines in the archetypal B text" (p. 137) but moreover occur there "in approximately similar proportions" to their appearance in the lines that are unambiguously scribal (p. 137 n. 29). In short, a scribal alliterative *usus* in two staves is thus established; the rest of the poem has established an authorial *usus* against alliterating in less than three staves; and these 350 lines may now safely be identified as unoriginal and in need of emendation.[26] Indeed, to print them as original (regardless of their attestation) would be in gross violation of the evidence.

The methodological conclusion to which the practice of this edition directs us should by now be clear. It is that we cannot align the distinction between internal and external evidence with the distinction between

---

25. See especially Fowler's review, cited in n. 4 above. The validity of metrical regularity as a ground for emendation in poets other than Langland has recently been greatly advanced by the important work of Hoyt N. Duggan, "Alliterative Patterning as a Basis for Emendation in Middle English Alliterative Poetry," *Studies in the Age of Chaucer* 8 (1986), 73–104, and "The Shape of the B-Verse in Middle English Alliterative Poetry," *Speculum* 61 (1986), 564–92.

26. The editors use an identical procedure to identify forty-six lines that alliterate on the penultimate or final stave as scribal. The fact that, given four stresses, there are only twelve possible alliternative patterns in two staves is my observation, not the editors', but it does seem to strengthen their point.

subjective and objective methodologies. Neither internal nor external evidence is more objective than the other; they are both facts that can be verified by reading the manuscripts. Moreover, and crucially, both kinds of facts have value within the editorial process only when they have been subjected to interpretation, when, that is, their place within the total body of all of the evidence has been defined. As Kane and Donaldson definitively demonstrate, the appearance of a reading in any or all of the manuscripts (i.e., attestation) does not in and of itself endow that reading with any authority. Put more boldly, they demonstrate that neither attestation (nor, for that matter, variation) has any real evidential value until it has been interpreted; prior to being taken up into the editorial process the presence of a specific reading in a specific manuscript or manuscripts is of no more weight in editorial decisions than the quality of the parchment or the color of the ink. In fact, the weight that it does eventually come to have derives not largely but entirely from the interpretive process that has transformed it from a piece of raw data into evidence. To castigate an editorial choice, therefore, because it lacks the "authority" of attestation and is therefore "subjective" is to believe that somewhere there exists a set of textual facts whose meaning is self-evident. Conversely, to claim that mere attestation is a piece of "external evidence" and that one is being "objective" in relying upon it to establish a text is to take comfort in a set of dangerously unexamined assumptions. My purpose here is in no sense to attack the idea of objectivity in favor of subjectivity, nor is it to disparage the editorial requisite of detailed and accurate scholarship. On the contrary, an uncritical reliance upon external evidence is itself a failure of scholarship. The basic problem is that the very distinction between objective and subjective is itself untenable. Just as there is no objective evidence whose significance is unambiguously and self-evidently clear—and least of all the evidence offered by attestation—so too is there nothing in the editorial process that we can without qualification label subjective. Every editorial decision is a function of precisely the same process: the application of the interpretive capacities of the observer to a set of facts. The success of this process will naturally depend on any number of variables, including the editor's diligence, the sophistication of his interpretive procedures and the logic and comprehensiveness of their application, and the accuracy and completeness of his facts. But the facts themselves, whether external or internal, are ontologically identical and cannot in and of themselves validate any editorial method. It is an unfortunate fact in the history of textual criticism that attestation has been designated "external" evidence while variation has been held to be somehow "internal." Indeed, the very terminology "internal"/"external" is misleading: it would probably be useful if neutral terms like "lectional" and "documentary" could be used instead. Internal evidence has to do with the nature of the readings or lections, external with the nature of the documents in which the lections appear. And it is even more unfortunate that those who have based their editorial decisions upon documentary evidence have been thought to be operating in a peculiarly "objective" way, while those who have resisted the claims of the objectivists have, defiantly but misguidedly, embraced the cause of the subjective, which they usually elevate by using the term "judgment." There are important historical and theoretical reasons for this, to which I shall shortly turn, but it should by now be clear that both of these positions are theoretically inadequate.

One of the dicta regularly invoked by objectivists is F. J. A. Hort's injunction that "knowledge of documents should precede final judgment upon readings."[27] Despite the uses to which the statement has been put by editors, including Hort himself, it urges not a reliance upon mere frequency of attestation but rather the inclusion within the editorial process of the full body of documentary evidence. This evidence includes the fact and frequency of attestation, but it also includes the nature of the manuscripts in which a specific reading appears, their date, condition, and relation to other manuscripts. Even when the frequency of attestation proves to be of little use as a guide to originality—and in *Piers Plowman,* because of convergent variation, "the significance of numerical support for readings is both essentially obscure and potentially misleading" (p. 164)—the documentary evidence may not be set aside as irrelevant. On the contrary, it is precisely the uselessness of numerical support that is significant, revealing as it does both the corruption of the B-Text archetype and the ubiquity of convergent variation, a fact that reveals in turn the logic of error that is the main editorial instrument. Moreover, documentary evidence that supports an editorial decision made on other grounds must not be simply invoked in support but explained. When, therefore, the editors find some 100 original readings in a manuscript that is otherwise notoriously unreliable, they do not simply congratulate themselves on their good fortune but carefully (and, to my mind, convincingly) explain how those readings came about.[28]

---

27. Hort, *New Testament in the Original Greek,* p. 543.

28. This manuscript is Corpus Christi Oxford 201 (F), which is "in the old sense, a thoroughly unreliable manuscript": it has 700 errors inherited from the archetypal B tradition, 500 more that it shares with its genetic pair R and that therefore come from a common ancestor at some remove from the B archetype, "hundreds more" it shares with a wide range of other manuscripts, and more than 1,000 unique to itself (p. 166). Nonetheless, it alone has "about 100" readings that the editors deem to be original, more than 70 of which are also attested by AC or A or C. The problem that the editors face is to account

An edition is finally, as the editors point out, "a theoretical structure, a complex hypothesis designed to account for a body of phenomena in the light of knowledge about the circumstances which generate them" (p. 212). I hope to have shown how Kane and Donaldson have confronted these phenomena—i.e., the evidence both documentary and lectional—with exemplary rigor and comprehensiveness, and how the evidence finds its rightful place in the total system that is their edition. As a system, the edition attempts to fit each individual reading into a coherent and self-consistent whole. What is perhaps most disappointing about the unfavorable reception the edition has received is that this systematic nature has been either ignored or devalued, with virtually all criticism being directed at the fitness of individual readings. But no specific criticism, however trenchant, can have relevance beyond its own singularity. As a system, this edition validates each individual reading in terms of every other reading, which means that if some of the readings are correct, then—unless the editorial principles have in an individual instance been misapplied—they must all be correct. This is not to say that the edition is invulnerable, only that criticism at the level of counterexample, no matter how often made, is necessarily inconsequential as a criticism of the edition as a whole. Moreover, if these criticisms derive from editorial principles sharply different from those which govern the readings in question, and especially from the perspective of an editorial tradition that overvalues attestation as evidence of originality, then the criticisms are necessarily irrelevant. Indeed, the only way such criticisms could be effective would be if they were part of a sustained effort to provide a contrary hypothesis by which to explain the phenomena—to provide, in other words, another edition. Again, this is not to say that if the principles upon which Kane and Donaldson base their edition are to be questioned the poem must be reedited. But it is to claim that criticism at the level of counterexample, which is virtually the only criticism that this edition has received, is in itself futile. In the last analysis, Kane and Don-

---

for this originality. After a detailed discussion (pp. 165–73) that applies each of three possible explanations—correction, fortuitous restoration of originality by convergent variation, or survival of originality here and its effacement by convergent variation in all other manuscripts—to each of the 70 readings attested by the manuscript traditions of the other versions, the editors settle upon correction from a prearchetypal manuscript as their solution. Again we see at work their habitual testing of hypotheses within a context where both *usus scribendi* and attestation support originality in order to arrive at a credible explanation of the evidence. As they say in another context, "to explain textual phenomena as random is (we believe) permissable only when there is no reasonable alternative, that is when other explanations in terms of *established processes of cause and effect* are not acceptable" (p. 103, my italics). With this examination, then, they designate correction from a prearchetypal manuscript as an established process of cause and effect.

aldson's systematic interpretation of the data can be effectively challenged only by another, better system. The methodology of the natural sciences teaches us that a theory can be disproven only by a better theory. Until one appears, then, the Kane-Donaldson edition must stand as not only the best *Piers Plowman* but as the correct one.

2

What is the significance of this edition for literary criticism? It will be many years before its impact on the practical criticism of the poem will be known, and while forecasts are obviously possible my interest here is rather in its significance for literary criticism per se. Methodologically, the edition stands squarely within the tradition of Anglo-American empiricism, although largely purged of its prejudice against system: the editors subscribe to what they call "that article of faith by which all students of literature validate their preoccupation with it: that the intellective and critical processes, when applied to literary works of art, can produce accurate results" (p. 77). Their method depends "on the enabling proposition of textual criticism, that it is possible in a sufficiently large number of cases to distinguish original from unoriginal readings," and as a method, "it is almost wholly empirical" (p. 123). In this commitment the editors align themselves with the main tradition of textual criticism, a tradition that embraces methodologies as disparate as stemmatics on the one hand and "eclecticism" on the other.[29] Yet there is also a persistent strain in our literary culture that is unsympathetic to empirical procedures, in part because of the excessive claims toward certainty that are made when empiricism becomes positivism, in part because of the belief that literary objects cannot be understood in the same terms as other cultural products. For our purposes we can call this attitude "intuitionism" and locate its defining characteristic in the conviction that literary works of art are essentially symbolic, manifestations of a

---

29. "Eclecticism" can mean at least two and possibly three things: (1) "free choice among readings": Ernest C. Colwell, *Studies in Methodology in Textual Criticism of the New Testament,* New Testament Tools and Studies 9 (Leiden: Brill, 1969), p. 154; (2) a choice among readings taken not from individual manuscripts but from different genealogical traditions, i.e., from what are called in biblical criticism "text types": see Carlo M. Martini, "Eclecticism and Atticism in the Textual Criticism of the Greek New Testament," in Matthew Black and William A. Smalley, eds., *On Language, Culture, and Religion: Essays in Honor of Eugene A. Nida* (The Hague: Mouton, 1974), pp. 149–56; and (3) "eclecticism, that is, no shutting up of the different branches of the science into water-tight compartments; verbal criticism, external and internal criticism, all have their parts to play": Leon Vaganay, *An Introduction to the Textual Criticism of the New Testament,* trans. B. V. Miller (London: Sands, 1937), p. 91; cited by Colwell, p. 154 n. 2. Also, see above, n. 2.

higher reality to which they witness and which can be fully apprehended only by an understanding that is able to transcend the empirical evidence. In due course a fuller account will be given of this essentially Romantic attitude, but for the moment let us note only that it too is a familiar presence in textual criticism in general and in this edition in particular, and that it inevitably exerts a pervasive pressure upon both the recovery of the text and the way it is delivered to its audience.

We can begin our approach to this issue by examining the criteria by which the editors judge lectional evidence. The errors by which a reading reveals its scribal nature are of four kinds: mechanical (e.g., eye skip), metrical, stylistic, and semantic, that is, a violation of the poem's meaning. The criteria for the first two kinds of error are perfectly straightforward; for the third the editors invoke several traditional norms (*difficilior, brevior*) plus several that are specific to this poem (e.g., more emphatic readings, bowdlerization, and sophistication—procedures that stem from what the editors call scribal participation in the poem); and for the fourth, which is necessarily ad hoc, the standard of appropriateness of meaning, which in practice means consistency. Now the correctness of these criteria, either in theory or in the process of editing can be assessed only by examining both the evidence from which they are derived and that to which they are applied, and such an assessment is not my purpose here. Rather I wish to suggest that these criteria must inevitably work in some situations at cross-purposes, and that this inherent contradiction reflects the two very different views of poetry that are implicit within the traditions of textual and literary criticism.

In discussing the means for determining semantic error, Kane and Donaldson produce a foursquare account of the qualifications required to define a criterion of appropriateness of meaning. These qualifications are "familiarity with the content of the poem, and a historically correct understanding of its whole structure of meaning," an understanding that at least approximates if it can never equal that of the poet himself: "because it is presumable that the poet understood his poem any reading repugnant to its meaning must have originated in scribal miscomprehension of this" (p. 131). Setting aside the practical questions of applicability (to which the editors are fully alert), we should note that the criterion of appropriateness of meaning implies an essentially rhetorical view of poetry. It presumes that meaning is possessed by the poet and then expressed by him in suitable language, that the *res* of significance is bodied forth in carefully chosen *verba*. As a criterion by which correctness is to be assessed, meaning must necessarily be conceived of as standing apart from language, a "whole structure" of significance that can be applied in any given case to individual passages. In practice, the application of this standard must inevitably result in a certain smoothing out of anomalies in favor of analogies, an unavoidable effect of any procedure in which consistency is the standard of judgment.

On the other hand, in assessing stylistic errors the editors invoke (among other criteria) the traditional canon of difficulty: *difficilior lectio potior,* on the grounds that scribes habitually trivialize their texts. This principle is of special importance in the editing of *Piers Plowman,* however, because not only is the poem lexically difficult, thanks to the esoteric nature of the alliterative style, but because Langland's characteristic locutions require of the reader an unremitting attention. Throughout the introduction the editors stress the challenge of Langland's *usus scribendi,* as in this description of scribal and authorial styles:

Just as scribal variants tend to flat statement or crude overemphasis, diffuseness in denotation and loss of connotation, dilution of meaning and absence of tension, in general a bald, colourless and prosy expression, so the style of the poet is vigorous, nervous, flexible and relatively compressed, made distinctive by characteristic mannerisms and figures. (P. 130)[30]

Given this kind of poem, and scribal habits of trivialization, one of the editors' constant preoccupations is with the restoration of meaning where scribal substitution has weakened it. Now when a scribe substitutes an easy reading for a hard one he is performing an interpretation: confronted with a line that he either does not understand himself or fears that his readers will not, he provides an interpretive gloss in place of the text. He transmits, in other words, a text that has been preread, smoothing the way for the reader but denying him the opportunity to arrive at his own meaning. The task of the editors, then, is to reverse this process, to return the text to a readable but as yet unread condition. The assumption that governs this procedure is that the poem aspires to a condition of maximum meaningfulness; hence the editors, for example, can designate a reading as scribal because it is "uncharacteristic (because not meaningful)" (p. 113). Hence, too, ambiguity or polysemy is a source of difficulty for the scribes, who offer a substitution that expresses one meaning but effaces the others.[31] The task of the editors, in sum, is to

---

30. For similar descriptions, see pp. 82, 84, and passim.

31. An already notorious example of an editorial emendation that turns on ambiguity is B.7.123, where the B-Text archetype reads "bely ioye" and the editors emend to the A-Text "belyue" or (in the spelling of their MS) "bilyue." This later word means *sustenance*—14 of the A-Text manuscripts read the lexically easier "liflode"—but it can also, as Anne Hudson points out, be construed as "bileue" or *faith, belief* ("Middle English," pp. 43–44). In the context this would appear to be a very awkward meaning: Piers has just torn the pardon given him by Truth and declares angrily that he will no longer "aboute my *bely ioye? bilyue?* so bisy be na moore." Hudson speculates that if Langland did write "belyue"/

recover the most difficult meaning possible—short, that is, of nonsense: as Wallace Stevens said, "The poem must resist the intelligence / *Almost* successfully."[32]

The theoretical assumptions that govern the editors' recovery of meaning are those not of a rhetorical but of a symbolist poetics, in which poetic language is not transparent but dense and even opaque, by definition overdetermined and furnishing an abundance of signification. Here meaning is not a given with which the poet governs the details of his poem throughout but rather a characteristic of the language with which the poem is constructed and so continually capable of forming its own configurations. A poet is a speaker who always means more than he says, perhaps even unwittingly. The conflict, then, between the more appropriate and the more difficult reading is not simply between two criteria of textual originality but between two ways of editing and two views of poetry.[33] The first is rhetorical and empirical; it assumes that literature is a means of conveying truth and that that truth can be apprehended by the same methods as are applied to other cultural objects. The second is symbolist and intuitional; it assumes that literature is a special kind of linguistic object that proceeds from mysterious sources (in the past designated as Genius, but more recently called Language) and that offers meanings that can be understood only by special faculties. The first attitude is classical; the second Romantic. Both are persistent elements in our literary culture and both are present in Kane and Donaldson's edition of *Piers Plowman*.

The editors' commitment to empiricism is both explicitly stated and methodologically enacted in their systematic and comprehensive assessment of the evidence. But other aspects of the edition, to which I have given less attention, presume certain characteristically Romantic attitudes. Throughout their introduction, for example, Kane and Donald-

---

"bilyue" in A, "is it not likely that he realised its unfortunate similarity in spelling with the inappropriate noun *bileue*, 'faith,' a potential confusion that he sought to avoid by altering the word to a stronger synonym?" (pp. 43–44) But it is just this ambiguity that marks "bilyue" as *difficilior* and therefore more likely to be original than the unambiguous "bely ioye," despite the fact that (as Hudson also points out) "bely ioye" is lexically rare (p. 55 n. 41). Moreover, according to the editors there is at 11.301–2 of the B-Text a complex series of corruptions that arise precisely because of the ambiguity of *bilyue*, a corruption so debilitating that the entire passage is omitted from the C-Text (p. 114). This passage, and several others in C, would support the use of *bilyue*, even when ambiguous, as an authorial *usus scribendi*, and its corruption would serve to define a scribal *usus* in relation to the same word.

32. Wallace Stevens, "Man Carrying Thing," *Collected Poems* (New York: Knopf, 1968), p. 350; my italics.

33. This discussion would suggest, then, that the editors' designation of a reading as original because it bears a "better, because somehow demonstrably more appropriate (and therefore also a harder) meaning" (p. 145) is implicitly self-contradictory.

son establish as one of the principles of their editing their belief in Langland's preeminence as a poet, in his poetic genius, in effect. By no means thoughtless bardolatry, this assertion is in fact the foundation of their distinction between authorial and scribal *usus scribendi*. Editors have traditionally made this distinction on the basis of chronology, the lapse of time between the original and the manuscripts in which it has survived. In the case of the classics this lapse amounts usually to some six or seven centuries; in the case of the New Testament, to some four centuries. But with Langland the gap is at most a century and in some instances only a couple of decades.[34] What distinguishes Langland from his scribes, then, is not time but talent, variously designated by the editors as "Langland's quality as a poet" (p. 101), "the excellence of Langland's poem" (p. 213), and so forth.[35] As they say, their edition is "governed by a presumption of the quality of Langland's art" (p. 212). This does not mean, however, that the terms by which that quality is to be defined are presumed. On the contrary, the laborious process of comparing authorial and scribal readings in cases where originality is not seriously in doubt is undertaken precisely in order to discover those terms, to define if not to codify just the ways in which Langland differs from his scribes. But what *is* presumed is that this difference is absolute. The scribes are many, the poet unique; the scribes write the language of common men, the poet composes a language of his own. The poet traces no conventional path but marks out for himself the way of genius, and it is the task of his editors to rediscover that way from among the ruins of the manuscripts. "On the whole," said Carlyle, "Genius has privileges of its own; it selects an orbit for itself; and be this never so eccentric, if it is indeed a celestial orbit, we mere star-gazers must at last compose ourselves; must cease to cavil at it, and begin to observe it, and calculate its laws."[36] This edition is, among many other things, a calculation of the laws of genius.

The methodological counterpart to poetic genius is critical intuitionism, and while there is in fact—as we have seen—nothing ad hoc or instinctive about the editors' procedures they occasionally describe them as if there were. They speak of their "sense of Langland's highly individual ways of writing" and define their understanding as "aesthetic, subjec-

---

34. The range of dates assigned to the manuscripts extends from the late fourteenth–early fifteenth centuries to the middle of the sixteenth century; there are no manuscripts that can be unambiguously dated in the fourteenth century. Naturally there are many chronological variants, but they represent on the editors' showing a very small proportion of the total.

35. See also, for example, the comments on pp. 73, 75, 77, 83 and passim.

36. Thomas Carlyle, "Jean Paul Friedrich Richter" (1827), quoted by Meyer Abrams, *The Mirror and the Lamp* (New York: Oxford University Press, 1953), p. 26.

tive" (pp. 130–31); and they describe how "the editor's subconscious mind," stored with documentary data, will at length provide for him "some accuracy of feeling for the turns of speech and even of thought respectively characteristic of the poet and his scribes" (p. 213). In adopting this language the editors are forestalling any claim that textual criticism in general and their edition in particular should be measured by positivistic canons of accuracy. But are they not conceding too much? Obviously their edition is neither predictive nor verifiable, but these are by no means the only criteria by which the validity of an intellectual procedure should be judged. Their editing is empirical, which means that it is neither certain in its conclusions nor strictly replicable in its procedures; it relies on judgment, which is both subjective and fallible; its canons of taste are aesthetic, which means that they have to do with art. But what it is not is ad hoc, capricious, arbitrary, or intuitional; it does not proceed from an instinctive blending of souls that o'erleaps time—this is no disguised collaboration between editor and author. Our methodological choices, in short, are not merely between scientific certainty (i.e., objective truth) and intuitional surmise (i.e., subjective taste) but include a *tertium quid,* careful empirical investigation that produces results that are probable, an activity that Kane and Donaldson rightly describe as (in speaking of conjectural emandation) "a real process of inference from available data" (p. 210).

The editors' rhetorical flirtation with intuitionism doubtless derives from a number of motives, among them resistance to the excessive claims put forward by other editorial theorists and a humanistic overvaluation of the degree of certainty obtainable by other kinds of inquiry. But even granting the mitigating pressure of these polemical interests, the claim if not the practice of intuitionism bespeaks ideological commitments that are central to the whole enterprise of textual criticism. To be sure, it would be easy enough to impeach these commitments by compiling a rogue's gallery of editions conceived under the sign of genius, perhaps with Bentley's *Paradise Lost* as the prime exhibit. But Bentley's indiscretion is less a denial of his critical principles than their enactment in an aberrant form; in an important sense his construction of *Paradise Lost* complements his deconstruction of the Letters of Phalaris. Or take the example of Housman, a man hardly given to aberrations. In the preface to the first volume of Manilius he comments on his predecessors by noting that Scaliger, Manilius' first editor, was indeed a man of "genius" and so equal to his poet. And yet "at the side of Bentley [he] is no more than a marvellous boy," a Chatterton to Bentley's Wordsworth. "*Lucida tela diei:* these are the words that come into one's mind when one has halted at some stubborn perplexity of reading or interpretation, has witnessed Scaliger . . . fumble at it . . . , and then turns to Bentley and sees Bentley strike his finger on the place and say *thou ailest here, and here*."[37] Like Christ the Physician, Housman's Bentley sees the corruption in the flesh that has infected the spirit, and with a laying on of hands he makes the corpus of Manilius whole again. Nor is the bond of genius confined to the relation of editor to poet. It unites as well editor and editor, joined together in their common understanding. If we should ask, for example, why a man of Housman's extraordinary gifts should have devoted so much of his talent to so obscure a poet, we need only read the closing lines to the preface of the final volume of Manilius. "Perhaps," he concludes, "there will be no long posterity for learning; but the reader whose good opinion I desire and have done my best to secure is the next Bentley or Scaliger who may chance to occupy himself with Manilius."[38] Here, indeed, is the visionary company. It is a group to which Kane and Donaldson also belong, and they too conclude their preface with a challenging invitation: "Whether we have carried out our task efficiently," they say, with threatening modesty, "must be assessed by reenacting it" (p. 220).

The persistence of the way of genius in textual criticism, as in literary criticism, bespeaks not a desire to avoid the careful appraisal of difficult historical documents, as some strictures might imply, but rather the conviction that these documents cannot contain the whole truth. It derives from an assumption that literary value must be transhistorical, rising above and even annulling the conditions of its historical existence. In textual criticism this attitude is implicit in the very strategy that distinguishes a text from the manuscripts in which it is, imperfectly, embodied; in contemporary literary criticism it is expressed by the privileging of interpretation, that act that discovers in the poem a meaning that transcends both the words in which it is expressed and the historical context of its enunciation. It is an attitude that has traditionally undergirded the entire literary enterprise and that has been an element of literary culture since the time of Plato. But it is also quintessentially Romantic, and certainly it is as enunciated by Wordsworth and especially Coleridge that it has entered into contemporary Anglo-American thinking in the form of New Criticism. Its most immediate impact on textual criticism can also be traced back to the Romantic period, and it is to a necessarily brief survey of this context, and of its relevance to this edition, that I wish now to turn.

37. A. E. Housman, ed., *M. Manilii Astronomicon Liber Primus* (London: Richards Press, 1903), pp. xvi–xvii.

38. A. E. Housman, ed., *M. Manilii Astronomicon Liber Quintus* (London: Richards Press, 1930), pp. xxxvi–xxxvii.

In the field of textual criticism the analytic dissections of the Enlightenment took a particularly threatening form. The editorial equivalents to Hume's empiricism and Hartley's associationism were the textual studies produced in Germany in the latter years of the eighteenth century. Of particular importance was J. G. Eichhorn's *Introduction to the Old Testament* (1780–83) in which he analyzed the scholia (or Masorah) of the early Hebrew grammarians and with the results constructed a *Textgeschichte* that not only revealed the Old Testament to be a historical document composed of varying strata but, in its original form, irrecoverable.[39] It was from this work, and from similar textual analyses, that issued the skepticism about scriptural authority as a whole that was to become known as the Higher Criticism, in distinction to this, the Lower or textual Criticism. A direct and deliberate parallel in classical studies is provided by F. A. Wolf's analysis of the Homeric scholia in his famous *Prolegomena ad Homerum* (1795). Modeling his work on Eichhorn's volumes, Wolf set out to discover the *vera forma* of the *Iliad* but arrived at the conclusion that the poem had neither a form nor an author.[40] This was not a happy development; as Wolf ruefully admitted, "No one can be as angry with me as I am with myself."[41] Attempting to remove the encrustation of the ages from the monuments upon which their culture was founded, these textual critics applied a corrosive so powerful that it dissolved the monuments themselves. The subsequent history of textual criticism may be seen as a search for some ingredient that would either dilute the aquafortis of critical analysis or else render it error specific. For in its pure form it was all too clearly a dangerous weapon, destroying that which it sought to restore.[42]

The critical analyses performed by men like Wolf and Eichhorn did not merely historicize the classic texts of Western culture but splintered them, scattering the fragments across the whole of the first millennium before Christ. These scholars were victims of the painful irony that the very means by which historicism recovers the past all too often renders

---

39. On Eichhorn, see Elinor S. Shaffer, *"Kubla Khan" and the Fall of Jerusalem* (Cambridge: Cambridge University Press, 1975), pp. 21–24; and the next note.

40. See Michael Murrin, *The Allegorical Epic* (Chicago: University of Chicago Press, 1980), p. 191; Wolf's reliance on Eichhorn's *Introduction* has been demonstrated by Anthony Grafton, "Prolegomena to Friedrich August Wolf," *Journal of the Warburg and Courtauld Institutes* 44 (1981), 101–29.

41. Quoted by R. C. Jebb, *Homer: An Introduction to the Iliad and the Odyssey,* 2d ed. (Glasgow: J. Maclehose and Sons, 1887), p. 110: "vix mihi quisquam irasci et succensere gravius poterit, quam ipse facio mihi." This translation is given by Howard Clarke, *Homer's Readers: A Historical Introduction to the Iliad and the Odyssey* (Newark: University of Delaware Press, 1981), p. 159.

42. As Bédier, alert to the *force dichotomique* that motivates textual criticism, fully understood; see above, p. 82.

it unusable. Nor was it only in the field of textual criticism that this principle was at work, for it also proved to apply to the larger enterprise of literary studies as a whole. Literary historicism is necessarily predicated on the assumed coherence of all historical periods and the correlative belief that a text can yield up its significance only when its affiliations with its historical moment are laid bare. Unhappily, the enactment of this program in the nineteenth and early twentieth centuries served to ground the text so securely in its historical context that its status as a value was scarcely visible, with effects upon the text that were strikingly similar to those of runaway textual criticism. Operating according to a positivist scheme of cause and effect, the historicist sought to explain the text by reference to any number of influences from without. The author's biography, his political and social condition, the intellectual and religious interests of the time, the literary models at hand, and the expectations of his audience—all this information and more provide the literary historian with explanatory categories by which to account for the text. Since historicism necessarily regarded all information as at least potentially relevant, and since it resisted designating the literary text as a special kind of document among other kinds, it was left with no principle of discrimination by which to judge relevance. As Roman Jakobson put it as early as 1921, literary historians are like "police who are supposed to arrest a certain person, arrest everybody and carry off everything they find in the house and all the people who pass by chance in the street. Thus the historians of literature appropriate everything—the social setting, psychology, politics, philosophy."[43] The net result of applying this indiscriminately assembled mix of causes to the text was to reduce it to a comparably disparate collection of effects. As a unified locus of meaning the literary work was effectively undone, and with it went the *mission civilisatrice* that literary culture had always been thought to fulfill. This was a deconstruction that presented the champions of literary culture with two choices: either to reformulate the atemporality of their classics in terms that would resist the acid of historicism; or to deploy the methods of historicism itself in such a way that they could not dissolve the values they were employed to discover. In the analogous realms of literary and textual criticism both of these procedures were used simultaneously, and it is in tracing out these analogies that we can situate the Kane-Donaldson edition and textual criticism in general in relation to larger theoretical and methodological issues.

At the level of literary criticism, the reaction to the analytic dissolu-

---

43. Cited by René Wellek, "The Fall of Literary History," in Michel Cadot et al., eds., *Actes du VIe Congrès de l'Association Internationale de Littérature Comparée* (Stuttgart: Erich Bieber, 1975), p. 29.

tions of historicism was on the one hand the Romantic hermeneutics of
German transcendentalism, mediated to England by the enthusiastic
Coleridge, and on the other the severe yet nonetheless carefully humanistic historicism of *Altertumswissenschaft.* Romantic hermeneutics established a link between past and present that, thanks to the mediation of
Geist, did not depend upon specific documents. Poems, like mountains,
are "Characters of the great Apocalypse, / The types and symbols of
Eternity."[44] They are less bearers of meaning than occasions for the discovery of a transcendent meaning to which they witness, and their frag-
mentariness is to be welcomed precisely because it requires of the reader
an act of going beyond, a movement toward that "something evermore
about to be" that can never be historicized. Hence for Coleridge the fact
that Homer was but "a mere concrete name for the rhapsodies of the
Iliad" was no cause for concern since even a complete *Iliad* was itself
merely a fragment and a symptom of the great I AM.[45]

As chroniclers of more recent critical history have pointed out, this
Romantic hermeneutics has continued to play a central part in literary
criticism. The Romantics insisted that not just the historically distant
culture object but *all* literary works partake of this mediatory role—that
they are essentially agents of something greater than themselves that is
itself uncircumscribed by historical context. The theory of poetic reception enunciated in Wordworth's Preface to the *Lyrical Ballads,* for instance, defines the poem as the means by which the alienated reader is
brought back into communion with nature and his fellow man, while
for Coleridge the poem is a mediating instrument in the triangular *cir-
cuitus spiritualis* that binds together God, Nature, and the Poet. In this
scheme the poem offers the reader both a symbolic representation of the
concrete universal and a specific instance of the process by which transcendent values are rendered immanent.[46] This strain of literary thinking
is also present, in a necessarily uncritical form, in Arnold's touchstone
theory and Housman's physiological test of poetic excellence, both of
which seek to subtend a culture that has lost its religious legitimization
with literary values that must consequently be protected from empirical
definition. It is by means of New Criticism, however, that these Romantic notions have had their greatest impact upon modern literary criticism.

New Criticism is a libertarian creed, in its theoretical ambitions as in

---

44. William Wordsworth, *The Prelude* (1805), 6.570–71.
45. S. T. Coleridge, *Table Talk* (1830), cited by Abrams, *Mirror and the Lamp,* p. 257.
46. See M. H. Abrams, *Natural Supernaturalism* (New York: Norton, 1971) and Coleridge's *Biographia Literaria,* ed. J. Shawcross, 2 vols. (Oxford: Clarendon Press, 1907). Especially pertinent to this topic are two of Coleridge's essays included in Shawcross' edition
of the *Biographia,* "On Poesy or Art" and "On the Principles of Genial Criticism."

its programmatic efforts to free literature from what it sees as the dead hand of an institutionalized historicist orthodoxy. Its most direct theoretical polemic was the double attack upon intentionalism and affectivism, a project motivated by a desire to assert the independence of the literary work from a confining historicity. The historical moment of neither the author (purportedly controlling the text in the form of a stated intention) nor reader (articulated as affect) is to be allowed to supervene upon the transhistorical object that is the poem. So too is the literary text exempted from the demands of representational accuracy expected of other modes of discourse. Poetic language is granted a special status, and literary discourse is to be understood contextually, as a self-referential, autotelic system, rather than in terms of its correspondence to a historical world that it has never sought to mime. A literary work is never true to life, only to itself. Correlatively, New Criticism insists that literature is unconstrained by ideological commitments. The true poetic aptitude is at heart one of Kantian disinterestedness that remains at a distance from dogma and subordinates the gratifications of faith to the severer demands of understanding. Hence poetry is not rhetorical but dramatic, aspiring not to enforce claims of belief but rather to act out their implications.

Moreover, the New Critical attack upon historicism shared with Romantic idealism a commitment to literature's cultural role. For all its celebration of the work of art as a value in and of itself, New Criticism was opposed as much to hedonistic aestheticism as to narrow moralism. It never abandoned the Romantic and Arnoldian claim that literature offers the alienated reader a saving knowledge, although it sometimes expressed this claim in terms that resisted easy codification (e.g., Ransom's "world's body," Wimsatt's "concrete universal") and that consequently gave rise to charges of mystification and irrationalism.[47] But in fact New Criticism always insisted that the task of the reader was not to appreciate but to understand, and to articulate that understanding in the form of *readings,* interpretations that converted the poem into a language that made explicit the moral vision the work mutely but eloquently bodied forth. This practice of interpretation was underwritten by a "common humanism" that was articulated by what R. S. Crane astutely recognized as "a set of reduction terms": "life and death, . . . good and evil, love and hate, harmony and strife, order and disorder, eternity and time, reality and appearance, truth and falsity . . . emotion and reason, complexity and simplicity, nature and art."[48] Establishing interpretation as not

---

47. E.g., Gerald Graff, *Literature against Itself* (Chicago: University of Chicago Press, 1979).

48. R. S. Crane, *The Languages of Criticism and the Structures of Poetry* (Toronto: Uni-

merely the privileged but the only legitimate form of literary study, New Criticism insisted that the function of poetry is to lead us beyond its own constricting historicity to those permanent truths that legitimize not merely literary study but the enterprise of cultural understanding as a whole.

In sum, then, the project of literary criticism from the Romantics through New Criticism can be appropriately read as an attempt to counter a voracious historicism that threatened to disable the very cultural recovery it meant to accomplish. As the only means of access to either the transcendental values of Romantic idealism or the common humanism of New Critical pragmatism, the literary work could not be allowed to leak away into a historical context that threatened to absorb it piecemeal. On the contrary, the text had to be established as a stable, self-sufficient artifact that owed no ultimate allegiance to its historical moment but spoke rather to a realm of universal value. A similar effort at countering the devaluations of positivistic historicism was also at work within the bastion of *Altertumswissenschaft* itself, in the development of cultural history. In part, cultural history was simply an effort to emend the apparent incompleteness of the literary object by relocating it within a fully reconstructed context. If the *Iliad* appeared fragmentary to modern readers it was only because they failed to apprehend the wholeness of the Hellenic culture of which it was but a part. And it is also true that some historians saw the cultural unity of each period as foreclosing the possibility of historical understanding per se: for Oswald Spengler, to take the most extreme instance, the notion that we can understand the past is merely sentimental humanitarianism. But the philosophical hermeneutics developed by Schleiermacher and Dilthey argued not only that full knowledge of the cultural objects of another period is possible but that it is made possible by a common *humanitas* that undergirds both past and present. Erich Auerbach, perhaps one of the last scholars fully capable of participating in this project, summed up its basic premise in an essay on Vico, the man who was in many respects its unacknowledged founder:

The entire development of human history, as made by men, is potentially contained in the human mind, and may therefore, by a process of research and re-evocation, be understood by men. The re-evocation is not only analytic; it has to be synthetic, as an understanding of every historical stage as an integral whole, of its genius (its *Geist,* as the German romantics would have said), a genius pervading all human activities and expressions of the period concerned.[49]

---

versity of Toronto Press, 1953), pp. 123–24; cited by Jonathan Culler, *The Pursuit of Signs* (Ithaca: Cornell University Press, 1981), p. 5.

    49. Erich Auerbach, "Vico and Aesthetic Historism," *Scenes from the Drama of European*

In effect, *Altertumswissenschaft* becomes *Geistesgeschichte,* a spiritualized historicism in which historical analysis is at once justified and contained by the discovery of the genius that is at the heart of history.

While New Criticism and *Geistesgeschichte* are united in their resistance to the fragmentation of the aesthetic object unwittingly perpetrated by historicism, they are in other ways sharply at odds. New Criticism seeks to liberate the literary work from history per se, while it is precisely within the very heart of history that *Geistesgeschichte* finds a saving permanence. What makes this opposition noteworthy for our purposes is its presence within the single discipline of textual criticism. For in its effort to mitigate the depredations of historical analysis, textual criticism has habitually made use of both of these procedures despite their implicit opposition. This is a paradox that is strikingly illustrated in the work of the leading nineteenth-century textual critic, Karl Lachmann (d. 1851). Moreover, the literary values that guided this great "Held der Wissenschaft," as one of his eulogists called him,[50] provide an illuminating parallel to those which motivate the Kane-Donaldson *Piers Plowman.* On the one hand, Lachmann's classical and biblical editing was severely conservative. His goal here was not to recover the original text but rather simply to return to the earliest manuscript. In his earliest edition, of Propertius in 1816, he produced a work that was, in Timpinaro's phrase, "rigorously diplomatic," and even his most mature—and dazzling— achievement, the 1850 edition of Lucretius, was notable far less for its textual discoveries than because Lachmann claimed to be able to reconstruct the format of the very manuscript that was the archetype of all surviving witnesses. Similarly, while his edition of the New Testament was the first to go behind the *textus receptus* to the manuscripts, it stopped short of attempting to recover originality. Unwilling to risk defacing the *sacra pagina* itself, he ignored his own genealogical imperatives and reverted to the diplomaticism of the Propertius; according to Scrivener's analysis, "Lachmann's text seldom rests on more than four Greek codices, very often on three, not infrequently on two; [and in some passages] on but one."[51] In effect, then, not only is the return to originality dis-

---

Literature (New York: Meridian, 1959), p. 197. Also relevant is Auerbach's preface to his *Literary Language and Its Public in Late Latin Antiquity and in the Middle Ages* (New York: Pantheon, 1965), pp. 5–24.

50. So described by Friedrich Leo, "Rede zur Säcularfeier Karl Lachmanns am 4. März 1893," *Ausgewählte Kleine Schriften,* ed. Eduard Fraenkel (Rome: Edizioni di Storia e Letteratura, 1960), p. 416. The essential book on Lachmann is Sebastiano Timpanaro, *La genesi del metodo del Lachmann* (Florence: Le Monnier, 1963), upon which I have drawn throughout my discussion.

51. Cited by Bruce M. Metzger, *The Text of the New Testament,* 2d ed. (New York: Oxford University Press, 1968), p. 125.

missed as impossible, but the physical document becomes not merely the foundation but the goal of textual criticism; the fragment and the original have become the same thing.

Lachmann's work as a Germanist, however, moves in a very different direction, perhaps best exemplified in his edition of the *Nibelungenlied*.[52] In an 1817 review of F. H. von der Hagen's edition Lachmann pointed out that the relationship among the manuscripts made it possible to reconstruct one of the two hyparchetypes by genealogical recension. But when in 1826 Lachmann came himself to edit the poem he declined to follow his own advice. This was not because he mistrusted its accuracy but because he was no longer prepared to settle for only the hyparchetype, or even the archetype. On the contrary, under the spell of the primitivist theories of authorship to which Wolf's dismemberment of the *Iliad* had in part given rise, and eager to demonstrate that the author of the *Nibelungenlied* was not a thirteenth-century poet as von der Hagen had proposed but *das Volk,* Lachmann was now engaged in a quest for origins that were by definition incapable of documentation.[53] Hence in his edition he printed what he took to be the poem's *ursprüngliche Aufzeichnung* as it appeared in one of the manuscripts, but then designated in his edition the original twenty *Lieder* from which this later redaction had been constructed. He identified these *Lieder* by means of internal criteria that he had defined with the help of a repertoire of tools he had himself painstakingly prepared: a Middle High German lexicon, a rhyming dictionary, and a grammar. Armed with the instruments of analysis already available to the classical and biblical scholar, Lachmann established a Middle High German *usus scribendi* by which to test originality; where grammar and, especially, meter fell below the defined standard of correctness he detected corruption. The true poems then emerged from the detritus of history, and in his 1840 edition of *Zwanzig alte Lieder von der Nibelungen* he finally presented them in their pure form.

Lachmann's first imperative as an editor, then, was not methodological but cultural: his goal was to establish a text that was, above all else, stable. In the case of classical and biblical texts this meant tying them securely to some documentary form, even if, as in the case of the New Testament and Lucretius, this form was clearly at some steps away from

---

52. Timpanaro discusses Lachmann as a Germanist only briefly, but a more detailed account is offered by Peter F. Ganz, "Lachmann as an Editor of Middle High German Texts," in Peter F. Ganz and Werner Schröder, eds., *Probleme Mittelalterlicher Überlieferung und Textkritik* (Berlin: Erich Schmidt, 1968), pp. 12–30. I have also benefited from an unpublished paper by Dr. Stephanie van d' Elden.

53. See the passage cited by Mary Thorp, *The Study of the Nibelungenlied* (Oxford: Clarendon Press, 1940), p. 27 n. 4.

the original. In this context Lachmann appears to modern eyes excessively conservative: his attempt to reidentify text and manuscript forces him to deny the workings of the critical judgment even when it is most at work; and consequently he has been accused of having fostered such deleterious habits as the cult of the best manuscript and a mechanistic system that promises an objectivity and certainty it cannot deliver. But with vernacular texts his strategy is wholly different. Here his safeguard against disintegration is a *usus scribendi* that returns a wayward text to an ordered wholeness and clarity. Perhaps most in evidence in his projected edition of *Das Minnesangs Frühling,* completed after his death by Moriz Haupt (1857), it operates as we have seen even in the case of an "author-less" poem like the *Nibelungenlied.* And while its initial effect may be disintegrating, the final result is to arrive at a bedrock of originality, in this case the *Zwanzig Lieder* from which the *ursprüngliche Aufzeichnung* developed. Far from disappearing into the dark backward and abysm of time, the poem's origins are clearly fixed and its development is charted as a number of clearly delineated stages, all except the first being correlated with a specific manuscript. Interestingly enough, while Wolf was careful not to designate which parts of the received text of the *Iliad* either witnessed to or actually represented the original lays, Lachmann resolved this dangerous uncertainty by designating eighteen specific passages as original. That no manuscript existed that contained only these 18 passages, in a doubtless yet more primitive form, could be seen less as an argument against Lachmann's designation than as a historical accident that time might yet remedy. Once again a physical document, whether hypothesized or actually recovered, stands at the beginning and end of the entire process, the legitimating authority that functions as the ultimate specific against the acid of textual criticism.

That the highest priority of Lachmann's editorial projects is textual stability is suggested as well by the format of his editions. Even when the texts are heavily annotated—and the overwhelming impact of the edition of Lucretius derived as much from the range and profundity of the learning embedded in the commentary as from the reconstruction of the archetypal manuscript—Lachmann's editorial pronouncements remain terse and (an oft-repeated description) oracular. The printed text stands as the product of the editor's lucubrations, the result of archeological procedures of enormous delicacy and complexity that nonetheless remain, despite their abundance, resolutely invisible. The reader's attention is directed not to the process but to the product, the poem that has now emerged from the ruins of the manuscripts and has at last been fixed into typographical immutability. Lachmann's commitment is finally to the poetic text itself; as Peter Ganz has said, "He was not interested in the problems of textual criticism for their own sakes: his aim was always to make great poetry of the past accessible to his contemporaries,"[54] and he was himself both a poet and a translator of Shakespeare. His reluctance to expatiate on his editorial procedures, in short, may be a function of his notorious arrogance, but it is also strategic, in two senses: one, it implicitly asserts that no one can understand these issues unless he has repeated them himself, while explanations to the truly initiated are unnecessary; and two, more generously, it assumes that the editor's task is to deliver up the text in a form in which it can become part of the cultural foundations of his society.

Clearly Kane and Donaldson are heirs to the complex tradition to which Lachmann is a prime witness, and their edition inevitably reflects this mixed inheritance. At times the tensions show through: the editors' empirical desire to make their data available, for example, is in sharp contrast to their unwillingness to provide cross-references that would make the data available in individual instances. The result is a visual text that is curiously at odds with itself. On the one hand, the plethora of brackets and the thick band of variants at the foot of the page continually remind the reader that he is dealing with an *edited* text: the false security of unmarred print, such as we find in virtually every edition of Chaucer, for instance, is here denied us. No longer can the interpreter in the executive suite blandly assume that his job starts when the editors in the basement have finished theirs. On the other hand, the data on which the text is based are resolutely hidden away in an introduction that is arranged not as a scientific exposition but as an elegantly written narrative. Moreover, there is a considerable amount of data that we are not given, especially those having to do with rates of originality in various situations.[55] The editors' purpose, I think, is not to protect themselves from

---

54. Ganz, "Lachmann as an Editor of Middle High German Texts," p. 13.

55. Because of the editors' mode of exposition, it is often extremely difficult to grasp the total effect of the comparisons that are being made among the three versions. The following example illustrates both the methodological problem and the practical fact that a preponderant degree of originality is vested in the A-Text. In the absence of specific figures, I have estimated that A corresponds to BC for some 1,900 lines, and to B alone (C absent) for some 400 lines: A contains a total of 2,441 lines, and the corresponding portions of B and C, 3,669 and 3,660 lines respectively, so I am estimating that 2,300 of A's 2,441 lines are retained in B and 1,900 in C. Now the editors assert that when A is compared with BC, there are 135 original readings in A that are scribally corrupted in BC (pp. 98, 102, 111): this is a rate of originality of 1 per 14 lines. However, when A is compared with B alone, there are "more than 300" (p. 83) original readings in A: this is a rate of originality of 1 per 1.3 lines. This is not, to be sure, the whole story: when AC are compared with B they reveal 140 original readings in AC, which demonstrates that the C tradition is less corrupt than the B (and here the rate of originality is again about 1 per 14 lines). But is it more than 10 times less corrupt? When C is compared directly with B (A absent) over the

scrutiny but to accommodate two finally irreconcilable imperatives: to offer, on the one hand, a text that is marked as a reconstruction and that therefore requires of the reader not merely an awareness of but an assent to the fact of editorial intervention; and on the other hand, to offer a text that is fully available to the institutions of literary consumption.

The unresolved interests whose clash disturbs the decorum of the text's presentation derive from the disparate traditions of literary study that we have surveyed. On the one hand is a positivist historicism that requires a scrupulous attention to the facts, however divisive or inscrutable they may be; that privileges literalistic explanation based on cause and effect over interpretive procedures that rely on notions of symbolic representation; and that, apparently unconcerned with the cultural mission of literary studies, accepts with equanimity the limitations of its own method and declines to engage those less-determinate literary and editorial problems, such as the establishment of meaning or originality, whose solution remains always unverifiable. On the other hand is a humanist belief that even amid the welter of fragmentary details that history has left us there abides a transhistorical value, a meaning that we can grasp and make our own. For *Geistesgeschichte* this value is diffused throughout the particulars of a historical period and can be crystallized as a *Weltanschauung* or *mentalité*. For New Criticism, by contrast, this value is fully represented by and embodied in the literary text, an artifact that triumphantly resists historical contextualization.

In claiming to be able to discover an original text from the fragments and vestiges that history has left us, textual criticism subscribes to this general humanist assumption. Steeped as it is in historical knowledge of the most precise and demanding sort, textual criticism nonetheless deploys its erudition in a struggle to wrest from the past an originality that time threatens to efface, an originality it designates as the text. In this effort, then, textual criticism is not merely a humanist enterprise but aligns itself more closely than might be expected with New Criticism. To be sure, just as textual criticism reconstitutes the text from the context of scribalisms in which it is submerged, so does New Criticism proclaim the text's transcendence of historical forces. But more tellingly,

---

approximately 3,760 lines where they correspond (pp. 89–96), C is reckoned to have an original reading only some 150 times (1 per 25 lines). On the face of it, not only is A granted a quite remarkable degree of originality (which is of course in part—but only in part—a function of Kane's editorial reconstruction), but the rate at which B is corrupt (or, conversely, A preserves originality) varies dramatically from one context to another. My purpose is not to cast doubt upon the editorial procedures (although these findings are, at least at first sight, disquieting), but to suggest that a more systematic form of exposition would have both made these (and other) disparities explicit and allowed for the development of appropriate explanations.

the procedures developed by textual criticism to establish the text in an edition are based on essentially the same literary values that New Criticism uses to legitimize the text as a cultural authority. We have already seen that the basic activity of textual criticism is perforce the evaluation of lectional evidence, i.e., the variant readings, and as the example of Kane and Donaldson's *Piers Plowman* suggests, this examination is characteristically governed by two potentially contradictory criteria. One is *difficilior lectio potior,* a principle that assumes that the poetic language of the author is qualitatively different from the prosaic language of the scribes. The other is appropriateness of meaning, which assumes that the poem embodies a "whole structure of meaning" (p. 131) that can be made explicit by interpretation. These two criteria correspond in more than a rough way to the two principles by which New Criticism sought to validate the poem as a cultural authority: its radical difference from other discursive forms, and yet its availability to interpretation. In other words, the task of the editor confronted with the mass of lectional evidence is to "read" the evidence as a New Critic would read a poem, and to produce as a result of his labors an interpretation that is, in fact, the poem itself.

3

In its final movement, the argument I have been prosecuting issues not in a programmatic conclusion but in a dilemma. In tracing the lines of affiliation between New Criticism and the Kane-Donaldson *Piers Plowman,* I might seem to be impeaching their edition by designating it as the product of a single critical school. But to draw this conclusion would be, I think, to misapprehend the force of the argument. For as I have tried to show, New Criticism—like *Geistesgeschichte*—is part of a larger effort within literary studies to protect literature from the fragmentations and reductions of a positivist historicism. It is not merely an interlude in the history of criticism but an expression of a profound strain of humanist thought that found its most powerful instance in Romanticism and has come, until very recently, to dominate the entire field of literary studies. Its commitments, as my comments on Lachmann were designed to show, are central to the project of textual criticism as a whole, which has continually sought for a way to stabilize the text by foreclosing the process of historical analysis. The point, then, is not that Kane and Donaldson have manipulated the evidence before them in order to produce a poem that accords with the canons of literature as defined by a Romantic and New Critical aesthetic. Rather, it is that the means for establishing a text that literary culture has developed over some five

centuries—and that is itself founded on values that are virtually coexten-
sive with Western civilization itself—allows for no other result. As Kane
and Donaldson demonstrate, the editorial process is enabled by three
assumptions: that there is an original; that the original is qualitatively
different from an unoriginality in which it is submerged; and that it has
a meaning that is enacted in the language at every point. If these assumptions are accepted, then the rest follows.

Yet most varieties of contemporary critical thought do not in fact
accept these assumptions. On the contrary, for poststructuralism, the
presumption of an origin is a delusive strategy by which a logocentric
culture seeks to mask the absence of a legitimizing transcendence. For
the postmodern critic the text is either a *bricolage,* a mosaic of citations
that is constituted by and transforms other texts, or a discursive instance
that derives from a larger formation that itself serves particular ideological interests. By its very nature unstable, the text is thus peculiarly vulnerable to a hermeneutics of suspicion able to foreground unacknowledged significances that upset its equilibrium and reveal disquieting
depths. From this perspective, then, the "establishment of a text" is
a theoretically untenable project. Indeed, for the strongest versions
of poststructuralism there is little to choose between a holograph and a
scribal copy: insofar as the subject is constituted by its enunciation rather
than vice versa, the very concept of a holograph as a text inscribed by its
author becomes problematic, and the concept of authorship, defined as
an act by which the sovereign subject sets itself over against an encom-
passing totality, must be rejected as a humanist delusion.

Since the effect of this radical critique is to foreclose the very possibility of textual criticism, then the response it entails is not to revise our
editorial techniques but to abandon them entirely. Hence the dilemma.
There are, it must be insisted, any number of instances in which not
editing is the appropriate response to the conditions of literary production, and in which the current task of textual criticism is to undo that
which was wrongly done in the name of nineteenth-century philology.
These are the instances (*King Lear* being the most prominent) that enforce the arguments of recent skeptical theorists of textual criticism,
theorists who concern themselves virtually without exception with
printed documents.[56] But the real claim of the critique is, after all, theoretical: it is directed not toward particular instances but toward the project as a whole. And before medievalists commit themselves to this po-

---

56. See, for the argument of undoing past errors, Randall McLeod, "Unediting Shakespeare," *Sub-Stance* 33–34 (1982), 26–55; and for the skeptical argument in general, Mc-
Gann, *Critique of Modern Textual Criticism.*

sition—or, more likely, draw upon it to ratify other kinds of interests—they would do well to consider the implications. For textual criticism is motivated by the desire to recover the past as a value, and its methodological enshrining of humanist values—specifically, its assumption that authorial *usus scribendi* can be determined by the application of certain interpretive principles—is at once entailed by and constitutive of the desire to find in the past a humanness that is correlative to our own. To be sure, its privileging of authorship, of the category of the literary, and of the unity and self-identity of the text defines that humanness in terms that are historically contingent and ideologically specific—as, of course, are all definitions of value. But given the massive evidence assembled by Kane and Donaldson, are we really prepared to say that their understanding of *Piers Plowman* is *merely* ideological? And more important, are we prepared to abandon their commitment to historical understanding per se and accept *Piers Plowman*—and medieval literature in general—as by definition incapable of yielding to editorial ministrations?

It is this last possibility that seems to me the most dismaying prospect, because the refusal to edit—which is part of the larger refusal to interpret—is an all too tenacious tradition within medieval studies. Not editing has, to be sure, many different degrees, ranging from a diplomatic printing that candidly offers little more than the transcription of a single manuscript to the traditional "conservative" edition that qualifies its critical commitments by privileging a single manuscript as its copy-text. By conceiving of his editorial project as the emendation of an imperfect document, rather than as the establishment of a text to which the manuscripts witness but which they do not themselves embody, an editor is able to ensure that the text will not disappear in the process of being recovered. The effect of this circumscription, however, as the previous discussion has shown, is to undermine both the rigor and the inclusiveness of the interpretive activity that is at the heart of textual criticism. And ironically, what justifies such a refusal is not an inordinate faith in documentary evidence but precisely the opposite, a skepticism that the documents can be made to yield meaning (i.e., originality). Doubting that the distinction between scribal and authorial can be accurately or consistently drawn, the conservative editor invests a single manuscript with the authority he declines to exercise himself. But when properly read, the Kane-Donaldson *Piers Plowman* shows that such methodological skepticism is unwarranted. Given sufficient evidence, the discrimination between authorial and scribal can indeed be made on empirical rather than intuitional grounds, with results that are of course not verifiable, in the sense of being measurable by some standard that itself stands apart from any interpretive process whatsoever, but are nonetheless secure enough to counter a disabling skepticism. And again, the alternative—at least for the medievalist—is not some other mode of interpretation, or some other kind of edition, but the refusal of interpretation entirely and an edition that, for all its conservative claims to soundness and reliability, in fact represents an arbitrarily foreclosed act of historical understanding.

Perhaps, then, the present dilemma of medieval textual criticism can be formulated as a set of questions. Most pressingly, if the humanist premises that have underwritten textual criticism in the past are now to be dismissed, what is to take their place? The force of this question derives from the fact that there is and will always be a positivist historicism ready to rush into any methodological vacuum with a preclusive interdiction against detailed and penetrating interpretation. Again, while any usable past must be based upon enabling assumptions of some kind, do these assumptions in fact prescribe the use to which the past will be put? Specifically, it is by no means clear that the idealist transcendentalism that has typically characterized humanism forecloses more historically determined interpretive possibilities. If we want to insist upon the priority of the political, and upon the historically contingent nature of value, must we (and should we) jettison the humanist methodology that has made our field of understanding available? At any rate, while I ask these questions in a genuinely interrogative voice, I also raise them here in the conviction that it is these questions, and others like them, that must be answered by those who would reject, by whatever rationale, the Kane-Donaldson *Piers Plowman* and the kind of historical understanding to which it so splendidly witnesses.

4. Ambiguity and Interpretation: A Fifteenth-Century Reading of *Troilus and Criseyde*

How DID medieval readers read medieval poetry? Middle English poems that are now encrusted with glosses and surrounded with commentary were once, we surmise, immediately accessible to similarly prelapsarian readers. Of course this assumption is as backward-looking as most Edenic fantasies, but it does witness to our sense of distance from the original response. In a sense, the question is at the center of the entire historicist project, acknowledging as it does that literary meaning is not an atemporal constant but a historical variable. Of the various critical activities currently in force, it is Exegetics that has most explicitly insisted upon the historicity of interpretation: in its strongest and most defensible form, Exegetics seeks to recuperate less the meaning of the poem per se than the medieval understanding of that meaning. To then reject its readings—as New Criticism habitually did—by reference either to "the poetry itself" or to transhistorical canons of interpretation is both polemically evasive and theoretically indefensible. The point is that the Exegetical challenge can be met only on its own, historicist grounds—specifically, in terms of the history of reading.

There are a number of ways to reconstruct this history. The institutions of literary learning, for one thing, provide a set of protocols and assumptions that governed the reception of texts other than the Bible, and in reconstructing these institutions we can gain valuable insights into the categories of understanding by which texts were received.[1] For another thing, later poets can be read in terms of their readings of their predecessors, an intertextuality underwritten by interpretive assumptions that can presumably be made visible. But in both cases we are dealing with a specialized audience, a fact that while in no sense impeaching the results of these investigations must nonetheless narrow their relevance: unless we accept the notion of a culturally monolithic Middle Ages, we cannot assume that the habits of one group of readers can simply be extended across the cultural field as a whole. Similarly, while there are a number of fictional representations of the act of reading—the case of Paolo and Francesca is the best known—historical instances are very rare. The common reader (if the category may be admitted) was content to leave at most a list of likes and dislikes, evidence that is not much more specific than that provided by library catalogues or manuscript censuses.[2]

In this chapter I shall offer evidence from a little known and perhaps unlikely source that can help us to reconstruct something like at least one medieval experience of reading Chaucer's *Troilus and Criseyde*. In a fifteenth-century treatise for women religious there appears an extended discussion that is explicit in its reference to the poem (a key stanza is quoted) and that provides the foundation for a coherent interpretation. My purpose here is to offer an edition of this hitherto unprinted discussion and, more extensively, to supply the multiple contexts, both literary and social, that will allow us to grasp its import. What is special about this material is that it allows us to reconstruct an inescapably individual moment of literary reception, a moment whose specificity is palpable and whose significance, while necessarily open to debate, raises questions that have an immediacy that the modern reader cannot evade. And what is methodologically interesting, I think, is precisely the amount of interpretation that is required to recover the act of interpretation itself: far from bearing its meaning on its face, this instance of medieval reading requires extensive and careful ministrations to reveal its significance.[3]

---

1. The most notable efforts along these lines are by Alastair J. Minnis, *Medieval Theory of Authorship* (London: Scolar Press, 1984), and Judson Boyce Allen, *The Ethical Poetic of the Later Middle Ages* (Toronto: University of Toronto Press, 1982).

2. For the (minimal) evidence of the response of Chaucer's medieval readers to his poetry, see Caroline F. Spurgeon, *Five Hundred Years of Chaucer Criticism and Allusion,* 3 vols. (Cambridge: Cambridge University Press, 1925), 1.1–63, 3.1–8; Paul Strohm, "Jean of Angoulême: A Fifteenth-Century Reader of Chaucer," *Neuphilologische Mitteilungen* 72 (1971), 69–76.

3. This passage has been discussed only by Willis Wager, "'Fleshly Love' in Chaucer's 'Troilus,'" *Modern Language Review* 34 (1939), 62–66; the allusion escaped both Spurgeon

The treatise is called by its compiler *Disce mori*. It survives in two closely related manuscripts, Oxford, Jesus 39 (J), written in the mid-fifteenth century, and Oxford, Bodleian, Laud misc. 99 (L), written about 1500.[4] Internal evidence suggests that this "compendie," as it calls itself, was compiled in the 1450s: at one point the compiler describes his foppish contemporaries as "all effeminat herte and body, as the losying of France and Guienne shewe at eygh" (p. 88),[5] doubtless a reference to the defeat of 1453 that concluded the Hundred Years' War. The work is

---

and William L. Alderson, "A Check-List of Supplements to Spurgeon's Chaucer Allusions," *Philological Quarterly* 32 (1953), 418–27. Wager unfortunately worked not from the manuscripts but from notes made by Carleton Brown, and his account is both incomplete and misleading. The only reference in Chaucer criticism to Wager's article that I have found is Donald Howard, *The Three Temptations: Medieval Man in Search of the World* (Princeton: Princeton University Press, 1966), p. 124 n. 74, who is misled by Wager into believing that the commentary presents *Troilus and Criseyde* simply as a condemnation of fleshly love, which is not, I think, the case. That the matter remains arguable is well shown by the comment of Chauncey Wood about an earlier version of the present chapter: "One recent critic, having discovered a fifteenth-century text in which a verse of the *Troilus* is used as part of a condemnation of romantic love outside of marriage, prefers his own interpretation to the earlier one . . ." (*The Elements of Chaucer's Troilus* [Durham: Duke University Press, 1984], p. 167). Wood's admittedly passing comment seems to assume that reading is a matter of choosing between a meaning that is really there (however distasteful) or one's self-indulgent (mis)interpretation. But of course reading is always a matter of choosing among interpretations—a fact that is well illustrated by Wood's own invocation of marriage as the topic of this discussion. Since it in fact never mentions marriage, and is located within a conventual context in which marriage is out of the question, Wood's interpretation of the discussion as about marriage is presumably guided by an unspoken assumption.

The appearance of the *Troilus* stanza in this treatise is recorded in Carleton Brown and Rossell Hope Robbins, *The Index of Middle English Verse* (New York: Columbia University Press, 1943), item 3327; George B. Pace, "Cotton Otho A. XVIII," *Speculum* 26 (1951), 306–8; Anne Hudson, "A Chapter from Walter Hilton in Two Middle English Compilations," *Neophilologus* 52 (1968), 419 n. 28.

4. Eric Colledge and Joyce Bazire, *The Chastising of God's Children and the Treatise of Perfection of the Sons of God* (Oxford: Blackwell, 1957), date J in the second half of the fifteenth century and L about 1500 on paleographical grounds; see also Hudson, "Chapter from Walter Hilton in Two Middle English Compilations," pp. 416–17.

A later-fifteenth-century compilation, the so-called *Ignorancia sacerdotum* (MS Bodleian eng. th. c. 57), is composed entirely of sections of the *Disce mori*. Colledge and Bazire compare the texts and define their relation to *The Chastising of God's Children,* showing both that J is the earlier and superior of the two MSS of the *Disce mori* and that the *Ignorancia* is derived from *Disce mori* rather than vice versa (pp. 26–28). In fact, the *Ignorancia* appears to be drawn from J rather than L: *Ignorancia,* fols. 119v–120r, matches J, pp. 297–98, but the corresponding passage is missing in L.

In an M.A. dissertation (Liverpool, 1966), N. A. Chadwick edited the Introduction and the section on the sins. An apparently original Latin poem embedded in the *remedium* for lechery has been edited by A. G. Rigg, "'Jam nunc in Proximo': A Latin Mortality Poem," *Medium Aevum* 36 (1967), 249–52.

5. Unless otherwise noted, all references are to the page number in MS J. This passage is absent in the *Ignorancia sacerdotum.*

addressed in three rhyme-royal stanzas to a woman religious, probably a nun, "my best-beloved Suster dame Alice, / Whiche that for Jesus' love have hool forsake / The world, the flessh, and the fende's malice" (L. fol. 1r).[6] J was almost certainly owned by Syon Abbey, and the work as a whole may even have been compiled there. On p. iii is written, in a sixteenth-century hand, the name "Dorothy Slyght." At the time of the dissolution of Syon in 1539, "Dorothye Slyghte" is listed as a sister, returning upon the restoration of the abbey in 1557; the Syon Martyrology lists "Dorothea Slithe" as deceased before 1576.[7] As to its place of compilation, the evidence also favors Syon. In the fifteenth century and later Syon was a center for the production of devotional texts, and as we shall see, several of these Syon treatises deal with the same topic (*amor* vs. *amicitia*) as our passage in *Disce mori,* and in very similar ways.[8] Furthermore, the topic itself, and the contents of *Disce mori* as a whole, are directed not only to a feminine and conventual audience but to one subject to the particular temptations offered by a foundation, such as Syon, in which both men and women were in residence.[9] Finally, although the sources of the *Disce mori* are known only in small part, those that are— including in particular the source for our passage—are from books that were available in the Syon Abbey library.[10]

The *Disce mori* is divided into five parts and a concluding "exhortation to the persone that hit was written to." The standard catechetical material is disposed throughout these five parts but, with the exception

---

6. In J the name "Alice" has been erased and "Lennox" written in the margin.

7. G. J. Aungier, *The History and Antiquities of Syon Monastery* (London: J. B. Nichols, 1840), p. 89; the Syon Martyrology is in British Library MS Add. 22285. See also Colledge and Bazire, *Chastising of God's Children,* p. 6 n. 1. The Martyrology lists some twelve Alicias who died in the fifteenth or early sixteenth century.

8. An up-to-date discussion of Syon Abbey, with bibliography, is provided by F. R. Johnston, "Syon Abbey," in J. S. Cockburn, H. P. F. King, and K. G. T. McDonnell, eds., *A History of the County of Middlesex* (Oxford: Oxford University Press, 1969), 1.182–91. Johnston provides a useful survey of the very considerable output of devotional texts accomplished by the brethren of Syon in the late fifteenth and early sixteenth centuries (pp. 186–87); see also A. I. Doyle, "Thomas Betson of Syon Abbey," *The Library,* 5th ser., 11 (1956), 115–18. Syon is better known to literary historians as an early center of humanist learning: see Denys Hay, "England and the Humanities in the Fifteenth Century," in Heiko A. Obermann and Thomas A. Brady, Jr., eds., *Itinerarium Italicum,* Studies in Medieval and Renaissance Thought 14 (Leiden: Brill, 1975), pp. 350–51, 365.

9. See below, pp. 000–000.

10. The known sources of the *Disce mori* include *The Chastising of God's Children* and various treatises by Hilton and Rolle: see Colledge and Bazire, *Chastising of God's Children,* pp. 26–28, and Hudson, "Chapter from Walter Hilton in Two Middle English Compilations," passim. The catalogue of the library has been published by Mary Bateson, *Syon Monastery: Library Catalogue* (Cambridge: Cambridge University Press, 1898). For the source of our passage, see below, p. 119, and for its availability at Syon, n. 14.

of the accounts of the sins (part 2), is presented with an emphasis upon
its appropriateness to the religious life.[11] Part 1 begins with *ars moriendi*
material, but expands it to include both general homiletic instruction (the
goods of fortune, nature, and grace) and specific topics appropriate for
conventual reading (the vanity of the world, the nature of true *franchise*);
part 2 discusses the sins; part 3 discusses temptations and tribulations and
includes such topics as visions and tears; part 4 includes a discussion of
penance that focuses upon satisfaction and especially prayer; and part 5
has an elaborate exposition of the Pater Noster designed for meditative
reading.

The concluding Exhortation of eighteen chapters is specifically addressed to Sister Alice and is concerned with "þe love of God and of þe
lyf had in contemplacion, to þ'ende to sture þe reders unto þat lyf,
whiche is þe surest and joyfullest lyf in erthe" (p. 627). Chapter 17 of the
Exhortation opens by discussing obstructions that hinder the full enjoy-
ment of the contemplative life and then turns to an account of how
"flesshly love" (*amor*) undermines "love spiritual" (*amicitia*). The burden
of this discussion is to define seven tokens by which the two loves can be
distinguished. It is at the beginning of this account that the stanza from
Troilus and Criseyde is quoted and at the end the interested reader is referred to the poem itself.

Fortunately for the archeologist of reading, the situation is usefully
complicated by another text. Like probably everything else in the *Disce
mori*, the account of the seven tokens is not original with our compiler.
It is a translation of a chapter and a half from a mid-thirteenth-century
handbook for nuns by David of Augsburg, *De exterioris et interioris hominis compositione*, also known as the *Formula novitiorum*.[12] A Franciscan,
David based the structure of his book on the *Epistola ad fratres de Monte
Dei* by William of St. Thierry, but unlike William he provides not so
much guidance for spiritual questers as sensible advice about the practicalities of the conventual life.[13] As a result, the treatise was enormously
popular throughout the later Middle Ages: the modern editors list over

---

11. The section on the sins is drawn from the tradition of the *Miroir du monde* (M. C.
O'Connor, *The Art of Dying Well* [New York: Columbia University Press, 1942], p. 18 n.
35; Hudson, "Chapter from Walter Hilton in Two Middle English Compilations," p. 417),
and is unadapted to its new audience: the account of lechery, for instance, is virulently
antifeminist.

12. There is a modern edition (Quaracchi: Collegius Sanctae Bonaventurae, 1899) and
a modern English translation by D. Devas (London: Burns, Oates and Washburn, 1937).
David wrote his work c. 1250; he died in 1272.

13. P. Jacques Heerinckx, "Influence de l'*Epistola ad Fratres de Monte Dei* sur la composition de *L'homme extérieur et intérieur* de David d'Augsburg," *Etudes franciscaines* 45
(1933), 330–47.

370 surviving manuscripts. The chapters included in the *Disce mori* appear in the third and final part of David's treatise (3.34–35), and have important filiations with their own thirteenth-century literary context. That the compiler of *Disce mori* should have chosen to apply this account to *Troilus and Criseyde* is by no means accidental, for as we shall see David addresses himself to precisely the literary tradition from which Chaucer's poem emerges.

Before we turn to the text of *Disce mori,* however, one more minor complication must be mentioned. David's account of the seven tokens also appears in three other fifteenth-century Middle English translations. Two are in complete translations of the *De exterioris;*[14] the other is in a text called *A Litill Tretise ayence flesshly affecciouns and all unþrifty loves.*[15] While the ambiguous relationship between these texts and the *Disce mori* can be at least tentatively sorted out, it need not in fact detain us here.[16]

---

14. University Library Cambridge MS Dd.ii.33 and Queen's College Cambridge MS 31; these treatises are discussed by P. S. Jolliffe, "Middle English Translations of the *De Exterioris et Interioris Hominis Compositione," Mediaeval Studies* 36 (1974), 259–77. As Jolliffe demonstrates, these two manuscripts represent independent translations of the *De exterioris.* Jolliffe also discusses several other fragmentary translations and "abstracts" of the *De exterioris,* but not the chapter in *Disce mori* nor *A Litill Tretise* (n. 15, below). U.L.C. MS Dd.ii.33 was written (and translated?) by Thomas Prestius, a brother of Syon (fol. 193v); Prestius was pensioned in 1539 and died in 1544; Johnston, "Syon Abbey," p. 186. For the availability of David's original at Syon, see in Bateson, *Library Catalogue,* items M24, M57, and M78. Bateson suggests that the *Formula novitorum* referred to in these listings is the *De institutione novitiorum* by Hugh of St. Victor (*PL* 176:925–52), but the listings do not name the author.

15. Bodleian MS Rawlinson C.894, fols. 97v–108v; British Library MS Royal 17.c.xviii, fols. 121r–132v. This very interesting treatise was brought to my attention by Dr. Anne Hudson, who also mentions it in "Chapter from Walter Hilton in Two Middle English Compilations," p. 421 n. 28. On the possible, although by no means certain, Syon provenance of these MSS, see A. I. Doyle, "A Survey of the Origins and Circulation of Theological Writings in English in the Fourteenth, Fifteenth, and Early Sixteenth Centuries," Cambridge Ph.D. Diss. 2301–2302, 2 vols. 2.215–21.

16. Although the vast field of Middle English devotional treatises is at present only imperfectly mapped, a preliminary account of the relationships among the texts can be offered. The two complete translations of the *De exterioris* seem to be independent of each other, of the *Disce mori,* and of *A Litill Tretise.* As Jolliffe points out, Q.C.C. MS 31 is an unusually faithful translation, literal to the point of creating errors in both English grammar and sense; U.L.C. Dd.ii.33 appears to be a more finished product, but remains little more than a translation. Neither treatise offers any parallels in phrasing or emphasis that would argue for a relationship with the *Disce mori* or *A Litill Tretise;* and both were probably written later anyway. The situation with the *Disce mori* and *A Litill Tretise* is more ambiguous. Phrasings in both texts suggest direct access to the Latin original; but there is at least one passage that argues for a relationship between the texts themselves (see below, p. 000, lines 88–93, and note). But even assuming a relationship, which text has priority? In the absence of documentary evidence, our best guide is the difference in character of the two texts themselves. The translation in the *Disce mori* is a self-contained and sharply limited

For our purposes, only two facts need to be insisted upon: that the *De exterioris* is the ultimate source of the chapter in the *Disce mori;* and that the compiler of the *Disce mori* understood its discussion of the seven tokens of love as peculiarly appropriate to *Troilus and Criseyde.* Since our goal is to understand why he thought it appropriate, it is the *De exterioris, Troilus and Criseyde,* and the *Disce mori* that should be the focus of our attention. For it is from the alignment of these three texts, and from the delineation of their shared literary heritage and disparate historical contexts, that our most useful conclusions will emerge.

I. THE SEVEN TOKENS OF CARNAL LOVE

I print here the whole of the discussion of fleshly and spiritual love from *Disce mori.* The text is J, and variants from L in wording but not orthography have been noted. For this portion of the text J and L used the same exemplar (for shared errors, see lines 16, 17, 18, 100, 103, and 108). Both J and L have been corrected, although apparently by different correctors (see lines 18, 30, 54, 69, 103, 122, and 145). Editorial emendations are enclosed within brackets, emendations by the correctors (J1, L1) in single quotation marks. Scribal *u/v* and *i/j* have been modernized, abbreviations have been expanded, and modern punctuation introduced (editorial conventions I have also applied to manuscript quotations throughout my text). In the notes I have recorded only the most important of the translator's deviations from his source.[17]

> (p. 629) But for it is ofte seen anenst suche as can not discerne
> bitwix goode love and bad þat flesshly love hideth and coloureth
> him undre love spirituel, and groweth as cokel amonge þe whete, we shal
> declare here somme of þe spices of flesshly love, to þ'ende þat, þei
> 5   knowen, spirituel lovers may eschewe hem, lest and þei taste oones of

account of fleshly and spiritual love inserted in the midst of a vastly larger, heterogenous whole. *A Litill Tretise,* on the other hand, is devoted wholly to an account of the differences between the two loves, but the account itself is far longer than in *Disce mori*—about four times as long, in fact. *A Litill Tretise* accomplishes this more extensive treatment not primarily by the addition of new material but by interweaving and dilating upon the topics of the original account itself: it presents the seven tokens embedded in a larger context elaborated from the seven tokens themselves. Given the different models of composition implied by the difference between the texts, priority would seem to belong to the *Disce mori* and probably the best hypothesis is common authorship. Fortunately, however, these uncertainties can remain unresolved and embedded in a footnote. Regardless of where the compiler of *Disce mori* found the account of the seven tokens, the fact remains that he thought it relevant to *Troilus and Criseyde.* Our task is to find out why.

17. I should like to thank Professor George Rigg for guidance on editorial matters.

5–27. Not in the source, David of Augsburg, *De exterioris et interioris hominis compositione* (Quaracchi: Collegius Sanctae Bonaventurae, 1899).

þat swete poison þei cache þerby dethe or a sieknesse incurable. Þou
shalt furst undrestand þat goostly love is, as it is above ceriously
recited, þe noblest vertu þat is, whiche allone maketh a man parfit. For
as Seint Gregore seith, a grete wille to God is called love, and whan it
10   is fed with grace it is deleccion, and whan it is unit to God and useth
him as is possible to a viator it is charite. And he þat hath þis vertu
hath alle vertues, but for divers effectes it taketh divers names. For
whan it is dressed al to God it is called love of God, and whan it is set
on oure neghbore it is called þe love of oure neghbore, and whan we have
15   pitie of oure neghburs miserie it is þan called mercy, and 'whan' we
joie of his proufit it is called congratulacioun, and 'whan' it suffreth
adverside and grucheth not it is called pacience, and 'whan' it is not
veinly lifte up in high't' above resoun it is called humilite, and whan
it dooth goode ayenst evel it is called benignite, whan it hateth al
20   unclennesse it is called chastite, whan it forsaketh richesses it is
called of spirit þe poverte, and whan it departeth with þe pouere aftre his
power it is called largesse, whan it discerneth bitwix goode and better
and evel and wers it is called prudence, whan it yeveth to every man þat
is his it is called justice, whan it is not broken with delectacions
25   þan is it temperance, and whan it (p. 630) is not aferde to entre grete

---

6. *swete poison.* This oxymoron probably derives from Ovid. *Amores* 1.8.104 describes
feminine wiles with similar language: "inpia sub dulci melle venena latent"; in *Amores*
2.9.26, a variant form refers to women: "usque adeo dulce puella malum est." For medieval
examples of *dulce venenum,* see John of Garland, *Poetria Parisiana* 1.251–52 (ed. Traugott
Lawler [New Haven: Yale University Press, 1974], p. 16): "Qui luxuriam amplecitur ve-
neno dulcedinis inquinatur"; Robert Holcot, *Super librum sapientiae* 3.38 ([Basel, 1586], p.
134): "Foemina fax Sathanae, foetus, dulce venenum / Semper prona rei quae prohibetur
ei." The more common phrase is *dulce malum,* as in the oft-repeated definitions by Alan of
Lille and John of Garland: see below, footnote 60. Both of these phrases are adapted
throughout medieval vernacular literature: to give just one example, in *Decameron* 2.7 Boccaccio speaks "dell'amoroso veleno che egli con gli occhi bevea" (ed. Aldo Rossi [Bologna:
Capelli, 1977], p. 112). An important extension of the phrase's meaning is achieved by
Boethius, who uses *dulce venenum* to describe the deadly medicine the Muses are adminis-
tering to him when Lady Philosophy interrupts them: 1, prosa 1 (translated by Chaucer as
"sweete venym"). This phrase, along with the Boethian scene as a whole, contributed to
the rhetoric of condemnation applied to poetry throughout the Middle Ages, as Boccaccio
witnesses by his defense: *Genealogia deorum gentilium* 14.20; and see the note by Charles G.
Osgood, *Boccaccio on Poetry* (Indianapolis: Bobbs-Merrill, 1956), p. 183 n. 1. In the *Canterbury Tales* the Merchant refers to the gifts of Fortune as "sweete venym queynte" (IV, 206L).

8. *maketh a man* J: *a man makith* L.

8–11. I have not located this comment in Gregory's works, but for an analogous discussion of charity as the mother and custodian of the virtues, see *Moralia* 10.6.8ff. (*PL*
75:922–26).

12. *effectes it* J: *effectes 'hit' in marg.* L1.

15. *þan* J: *om.L. 'whan' suppl.* J1, L1 *in marg.*

16. *'whan' suppl.* J1 *in marg.,* L1 *sup. lin.*

17. *'whan' suppl.* J1 *in marg.,* L1 *sup. lin.*

18. *'t' suppl.* J1: *hegh* L.

25. *is it* J: *it is* L.

þingis þan it is strength. And so of feith, hoope and alle oþer vertues
oonly þis vertu, love spirituel, bereth þeire names and enbraceth hem.
And þerfore lest it were in any wise medled with flessly love, as
baume rial sophisticat is medled with oþer baume, it is in alle wises
30 necessarie to be advertised to þee of þe saiynge of Ysaie, *primo capitulo:*
Vinum tuum mixtum est aqua, þat is to undrestande, "Þi goostly love is
viciat and terned in to carnel." For þe subtiltee of þ'enemye at þe be-
gynnyng hideth þe lace of temptation undre coloure of goode unto þe love
encreste carnaly litel and litel unto it wex tough as lyme wiþ whiche
35 men taken birdes. So þat whan he and she, þat þus by flesshly love be
lymed, be wounded in þe eigh and þe herte with þe swerd of carnal affec-
cioun and suche concupiscens, þat þei wolde never bi þeire wille departe
a sondre ner it þat Malebouche and Jalousie ofte causeth hem to departe,
þe whiche ofte þei doo with grete hevynesse of herte and anoye. So grete
40 is 'þe' brennyng of love bitwix hem, for what so ever þat oon wol þat
oþer wol þe same. And in wise as foloweth carnal love shal be aspied.
    Þe furst token of carnal love is þat lyke as a goostly 'love is
acustumed to be fed with goostly' communycacioun and doctrines spirituel entendynge to þ'edificacioun of mannes soule, and to have in abhomi-
45 nacioun al ydel and unclene langage inpertinent, so in þe contrarie wise
flessly lovers oute of mesure desiren to commune no þinge of goostly
edificacion nor of þe spirit but of þeire love: how she loveth hym, and
he hir, and what he wol doo and suffre for hir and she for hym, and what
þei wissh and desire eche to other of wele and plesance it can not be
50 here expressed, for an houre suffiseth not to hem, ne a day, ne dayes,
ne no tyme to open þeire herte oon to oþer. For þenn þenketh þei
shal never have spoken ynough to geders ne be saciat of þe unleful
desires of þeire hertes. Þe whiche love, as seith þe philisophre, in
yonge men is called rage and in olde men it is called dotage. Here (p.

---

29. *oþer baume* J: *other baumes* L.
30. *to þee of* J: *to the 'entente' of* L1.
31. Isaiah 1:22.
34. *wex* J: *were* L.
35. *taken* J: *take* L.
36–37. A reader of J has drawn a crude sword in the margin.
37. *evill speking of people* in marg. L1.
38. *Malebouche and Jalousie:* see *Roman de la rose,* passim; the phrase does not occur in
De exterioris, which instead invokes the story of Samson and Dalila (pp. 235–36).
40. 'þe' suppl. J1 in marg.: *the* L.
42–43. 'love is acustumed to be fed with goostly' suppl. J1 in marg.
45. For "ydel and unclene langage impertinent" *De exterioris* reads "nugae et otiosae
fabulae" (p. 236), translated in U.L.C. MS Dd.ii.33 as "japys, trifulles and ydyl talys" and
in *A Litill Tretise* as "trifullis and idill tales" (Royal 17.c.xviii, fol. 124v). Given our author's
interest in *fabulae,* his (mis)translation is telling.
51. *herte* J: *hertes* L.
52–73. Not in *De exterioris.*
53–54. The philosopher is probably Seneca: see Hans Walther, *Lateinische Sprichwörter,*

55 631) accordeth þe poete Ovide, *De arte amandi,* saiyng þus:
    Nescio quid sit amor nec amoris cencio nodum,
    Set scio si quis amat nescit habere modum.
Þat is:
    I wote not what is love,
60   Ne I feele not þe knot,
    But I wote þat who so loveth
    Kepeth no more manere þan dooth a sotte.
And a noþer poete seith:
    If no love is O god what fele I so
65   And if love is what þinge and whiche is he
    If love be goode from whens cometh my woo
    If it be wykke a wondre þenketh me
    Sith every turment and adversite
    That from it cometh may be savoury þenke
70   For ay thrust I þe more þat I it drynke
    'And þe proverbe in Frenssh seith,

Vol. 1 (Göttingen: Vandenhoeck und Ruprecht, 1963), no. 919. But the English phrasing is also found in John Clanvowe, *The Boke of Cupid,* ll.168–69, and is probably itself proverbial, although unrecorded: "For loving is in yonge folke but rage, / And in old hit is a grete dotage" (ed. V. J. Scattergood, *English Philological Studies* 9 [1965]). For love as *rage,* see *Roman de la rose,* ed. Félix Lecoy, CFMA 95 (Paris: Champion, 1966), lines 10215–218, and the treatise on love included within *Li Hystore de Julius Cesar* (ed. A. Långfors, *Romania* 56 [1930], p. 367): "Volentei d'amer ki en vilain se met estriner le fait ausi comme une beste salvage, ne il ne poet son corage aploiier a nule cortoisie ne a nule bonté, ains aime folement et sans coverture. Et che n'est mie amours, ains est ensi comme rage, quant vilains s'entremet d'amer."

54. *it* J: *'h'it* L1.

55. *accordeth* J: *to accordeth* L.

56–57. This distich does not appear in Ovid but is a common medieval proverb: see Walther, *Sprichwörter,* Vol. 3 (Göttingen: Vandenhoeck und Ruprecht, 1965), nos. 16532 and 16531; Hans Walther, *Initia Carminum ac Versum Medii Aevi Posterioris Latinorum* (Göttingen: Vandenhoeck und Ruprecht, 1959), no. 11741; and Willis Wager, "'Fleshly Love' in Chaucer's 'Troilus,'" *Modern Language Review* 34 (1939), 66 n. 1. These lines are not written as verse in the MSS. This translation appears to be original with our author, but is not the first into English: G. R. Owst, *Literature and Pulpit in Medieval England* (Cambridge: Cambridge University Press, 1933), p. 21, prints a fourteenth-century translation in two four-line stanzas from Advocates' Library MS 18.7.21; see also Francis L. Utley, *The Crooked Rib* (Columbus: Ohio State University Press, 1944), pp. 150–51. For a Middle French translation, see *La fontaine d'amours et sa description,* in Anatole de Montaiglon, *Recueil de poésies françoises des XVe et XVIe siècles,* Vol. 4 (Paris: P. Jonnet, 1856), ll.18–23.

59–62. Not written as verse in the MSS.

64–70. *Troilus and Criseyde* 1.400–6. This stanza is printed here exactly as written in J. This one stanza also appears in U.L.C. MS Gg.iv.12, fol. 105v, and in British Library MS Cotton Otho A. XVIII (see George B. Pace, "Cotton Otho A. XVIII," *Speculum* 26 [1951], 306–8).

67. *wykke* J: *wikked* L.

69. *may* JL: *maketh* L1 suppl. in marg. *þenke* JL: corr. *þynke* L1.

71–73. om. JL: suppl. in marg. J1. For further citations of this proverb, see Jean Rych-

De chiens, d'oseaux, d'armes, d'amours,
Pour un plaisir quatre dolours.'
   The seconde token is þis, þat whan þees lovers desirously beholde
75 þat oon þat oþer and approche nygh to geders in secret places,
þei joyne þeire handes and mouthes and straitly clippe and handle brestes
and oþer parties naked to lecherously, and stele many a savoures double-
kosse. And in þe contrarie manere love spirituel kepeth rule and disci-
plyne in secrete suche as it kepeth openly. For it secheth no hirnes
80 but rather fleeth, but yf it be oonly þerby þe more commodiously to
entende to contemplacion or prayer. And whan suche a spirituel lovynge
womman speketh with a man, or suche a man with a womman, he or she
demeneth so þeire contenances, speche and mocions as þough al þe worlde
were þere present and herde hem, so ferforth þat Jalousie or Malebouche
85 shal not fynde in hem no þinge to reprove or chalenge.
   The thrid token is þe inquietude þat þees flesshly lovynge
hertes suffre, þat oon for þat oþer, whan þei may not come at þeire
wille to giders, þenkyng or saiynge eche to him self of othre: "A! where
is now my deere love? What ever he do now, wheþer he þenke now on me
90 as I now do on hym? Whan wol he come? Me þenke to longe sith I sawe
him. A! what meeneth (p. 632) it þat he sendeth me no writynges nor
toknes? I drede me sore þat his love wexeth colde. Ha! goode God! whan
shal I have message from him?" Þis is þeire hooly contemplacioun and
compleynt, oon for þat oþer, so þat þei mowe not have þeire mynde on
95 God, ne praye, ne no þinge doo for þe heele of her soules. So be þei
distracte in þeire wittes and occupied in þis blynde love þat noon oþer
þinge may delite hem or please hem, save whan þat oon hereth of þe wele-
fare and þe prosperite of þat oþer. Spirituel love þenketh of no suche
vanite but oonly hath his herte set to God and in his prayers comendeth
100 devoutly his lovers to Goddes kepyng. And if his lover happe to suffre
disease or have need, withoute distraccioun of herte he hath pitie on
his lovere and aftre his might releveth hym as reason axeth.

---

ner and Albert Henry, *Le testament Villon,* Vol. 2: *Commentaire* (Geneva: Droz, 1974), pp.
91–92 (notes to lines 622 and 624).
   84–85. Instead of Malebouche and Jalousie, *De exterioris* refers only to a *studiosus obser-
vator* (p. 237).
   88–93. In the original, this outburst is restrained within the confines of the third person: "ubi iam sit ille dilectus, quid agat, quando veniat, quamdiu defuerit, si de se cogitet,
si ex absentia amor eius circa se forte in aliquo tepuerit, quam longo tempore iam nihil ei
demandaverit, et quid in causa esse possit, quomodo valeat in corpore" (p. 237). In *A Litill
Tretise* the passage is both in direct speech and adds, as does *Disce mori,* the suggestive
reference to tokens and love letters: "Wher is now my well beloved frende? What doth he?
Wold God I wer now with hym. Whan shall he com hedir? Me thynke right longe sithen I
spake with hym. It is longe sith he sent any tokynne to me or writynge. I am aferde he
luffith me nott, or he is seke" (Royal 17.c.xviii, fol. 125r). In U.L.C. MS Dd.ii.33 the
passage is transposed into direct speech but is otherwise faithful to the original (fol. 125r).
   90. *now do* J: *do now* L.
   100. *lover* ed.: *lovers* JL.

The iiii'the' tokene of flesshly love is hasty ire and in-
pacience þat þat oon lover conceyveth anoon in herte if he fynde eny

105 poynte of unlove or straungenesse inconsuete in þat oþer, as if she
ymagyne þat he loveth a noþer with hir, or sende eny tokenes to oþer,
or kest his eigh goodly upon an oþer. For whiche she dredeth þat þat
oþer shulde be preferred 'befor' hir in 't'his love, for whiche she is
gretely replete with hevynesse. But spirituel love is joyful whan alle

110 oþer be loved even with him or better in God. For charite is com[un]icatif
to alle, and þe ferther þat it is spred þe more it loveth and þe gladder
it is of goode encrece, as dooth fyre, þe more matere it resceyveth
þe more encresceth and faster brenneth.

The v'the' tokene of flesshly love is þat þat oon lovere sendeth

115 to þat oþer lettres of love, tokenes and yiftes, which be worshipped,
kissed, used and kept as reliques; and maken either to oþer diners, sopers
and feestes, and þere either kerveth and leieth to oþer þe swettest
morsels, and eithre trede prively on oþers foote undre þe table, and many
an oþer amourous looke þei ween þei stele oon of þat oþer and suche oþer

120 observances, to longe to write here, þei use. Þei suppose unaspied to
kyndel with more and more (p. 633) þe fire of þeire seide flesshly love.
Þe whiche observances ne noon oþer lyke þerto, as Seint Jerome in a pistel
reherceth, holy love forsaketh pleynly, but rather resceyveth goode instruc-
cions edificatif for þe soule, and devoute prayers, and almesdede, whiche

125 be yiftes plesyng to God and conservatives of his love and his grace, and
loveth abstine'n'ce þere as þees oþer of carnalite do þe contrarie.

Þe vi'the' tokene of suche flesshly love is þat ofte for a litel
cause, or no cause but for suspecioun, falleth bitwix þe lovers wrath and
turbacion, causying þe excesse of magnitude of þeire love. For like as

130 þeire veine love ofte excedith þe bondes of resoun and kepeth no mesure
in blandisshynge, as is above, so in þe contrarie wise it kepeth no mesure
in ire and trouble. If þat oon happe in a litel þinge to offende þat
oþer, as not grauntyng his desires, or cherisshinge, o'r' yevynge his
yiftes to an oþer, for þe gretter þat þe love is bitwix hem þe gretter

135 hem þenke þ'offence or þe unkyndenesse shewde. Of þis þei reisen quarels
and inproperies of love and kyndnesses shewde afore, and yiftes and

---

103. *'the'* suppl. J1: om. L.

104. *impacience* J: *impaciece* L.

108. *'befor'* om. JL: suppl. J1 sup. lin. and L1 in marg. *'t'his t* suppl. J1: *this* L1.

110. *comicatif* J: *comunicatif* L.

111. *ferther þat* J: *ferther* L.

114–44. In *Disce mori* the fifth and sixth tokens are reversed from their normal order
in *De exterioris* and in the other ME translations.

114. *'the'* suppl. J1.

116–121. Not in *De exterioris*.

122. *ne noon* JL: *and all* suppl. L1.

122–23. Epistola 52 (*PL* 22:532).

126. *abstinece* JL: *'n'* suppl. J1.

133. *of* J, corr. to *or* J1.

135. *reisen* J: *reise* L.

136. *inproperies* glossed *reproves* in marg. L1.

trust whiche be lost, and þan þei avowe and swere þat þei shal never
trust ne love oþer aftre þat, so yeldyng eiþer to oþer hate for dilec-
cioun and evel for goode. And aftre þat eche sclaundre oþer and telleth
140 þe secrete and consailles þat were between hem, and many oþer
inconvenientes ensue of suche love. But goostly love is ever resonable,
modest, tretable and pesible, lightly foryevyng alle manere offenses, kepyng
quyete contynuely in his spirit, ever lovynge his lover and not passionat as is
þis oþer.
145 The vii^the tokene of flesshly love is inordinate dissimula-
cion of vices bitwix þees lovers, þe whiche þei favoure and excuse þat
oon þat oþer obstinatly ayenst alle oþer þat speke þer of or wolde amende
hem. So be þei confedered in ille as a þeef to a þeef and dronken of þis
sweet poison:
150 'Of which poison if ye lust more to rede,
Seeþ þe storie of Troilus, Creseide and Dyomede.'
Spirituel love, whiche hateth oones to taste þe swettenesse of 'suche
poison and' synne, of whiche þees oþer be so inebriat þat reson is clene
(p. 634) exiled from hem, dooth even þe contrarie. For þe more it is affec-
155 cionat to a creature þe hevyer it is to see vices in þat persone, as þe fadre
is sorier to wete a lak in his son þan in an oþer, and God punyssheth
sharplyer synne in suche as he loveth and be predestinat þan in oþer þat be
prescite and lakke his grace, as he shewd in Job, Tobie, David and oþer lyke,
as he seide him self: *Quos amo arguo et castigo.*
160 Now I takyng my leeve of þis matere of love, in whiche for it
is so swete I have so longe abiden, recite here aftre þe hooly man Bonaven-
ture hou a man may moste profit for hym self and plese God.

2. THE LITERARY CONTEXT OF THE *DE EXTERIORIS*

Many men, as we know from the testimony of the poets, have misused, by a literal
interpretation, the terms applied to Venus.
—Alan of Lille, *The Plaint of Nature*

What were the interpretive assumptions and procedures that led our
fifteenth-century reader to apply David of Augsburg's account of the
seven tokens of love to *Troilus and Criseyde?* This is our ultimate question,

138. *trust ne love* J: *love ne trust* L.
145. '*the*' suppl. J1: om. L.
147. *oon* J: *oon in* L.
150–51. om. J, suppl. in bottom marg. J1: *of which poison more to rede, Se of Troilus Creseid* L, in a gap.
152–153. '*suche poison and*' suppl. J1 sup. lin.
157. *prescite*, from *praecitus*, condemned.
159. Apoc. 3.19.
160–162. This is the beginning of the next (and final) chapter of the treatise.

but it must be approached through a prior one: what led David to include this account in his manual in the first place? Its presence in the *De exterioris* provides, after all, the crucial precedent for the compiler of *Disce mori*. The relevance of the account to the conditions of conventual life, and specifically to those at a double abbey like Syon, will be in due course the focus of our attention. But of more immediate significance is the fact that a suggestively *literary* relevance can be disclosed by reconstructing the cultural context in which David's account was written.

When William of St. Thierry composed his treatise on love in the early decades of the twelfth century he presented himself as a pious alternative to Ovid, the corrupt and corrupting *doctor artis amatoriae*.[18] David of Augsburg, in discriminating between true and false loves, is adopting the same role as his literary model, and doubtless with an even greater sense of urgency. Writing over a century later, in the very midst of the literary *aetas Ovidiana,* David is directing his attack against the licentiousness of both life and literature, against both illicit lovers and the vulgar amorists who urge them on. The literary aspect of his enterprise is declared by the very form of his analysis. The rhetoric of moral theology made available to David two major forms in which a condemnation of illicit sexuality could be disposed. One was the analysis of lechery as a typological enactment of the stages of sin—suggestion, delectation, and consent; the other was the *quinque lineae amoris,* the five fingers of the devil's hand, as Chaucer's Parson (among many others) puts it: looking, talking, touching, kissing, and "the stynkyng dede" itself.[19] David rejects both of these topoi in favor of the *signa* or *indicia amoris,* a project that derives from Ovid and is given in medieval form by Andreas Capellanus.[20] In the thirteenth century it becomes a common topos in Ovidian and pseudo-Ovidian writing. *La puissance d'amour* by Richard of Fournival, for instance, concludes with the "signes d'amor"; his follower Bernier of Chartres begins *La vraie médecine d'amour* by describing "quels coze est amors et quel sunt li signe"; and Enanchet supplements his version of Andreas' *De amore* with an elaborate expansion of the topos.[21]

---

18. William of St. Thierry, *De natura et dignitate amoris,* in M.-M. Davy, ed., *Deux traités de l'amour de Dieu* (Paris: J. Vrin, 1953), chap. 3, p. 72.

19. On lechery as a typology of sin, see the discussion in D. W. Robertson, Jr., *A Preface to Chaucer* (Princeton: Princeton University Press, 1963), pp. 94 ff.; on the *quinque lineae amoris,* see E. R. Curtius, *European Literature and the Latin Middle Ages* (New York: Harper, 1953), pp. 512–14; Peter Dronke, *Medieval Latin and the Rise of the European Love Lyric,* 2d ed., 2 vols. (Oxford: Clarendon Press, 1968), 2.488–89; Lionel Friedman, "Gradus Amoris," *Romance Philology* 19 (1965), 167–77; Geoffrey Chaucer, Parson's Tale, X.852–64, in *Works,* ed. F. N. Robinson, 2d ed. (Boston: Houghton Mifflin, 1957).

20. Ovid, *Ars amatoria* 1.723–38; Andreas Capellanus, *De amore,* ed. and trans. P. G. Walsh (London: Duckworth, 1982), 2.5 (pp. 236–37).

21. For *La puissance d'amour* and *La vraie médecine d'amour,* see Ferdinand Wolf, "Über

Having once adopted this Ovidian form, David then disposes a content that cites several of the traditional motifs of erotic writing. The first sign describes what the *Gawain* poet calls "luf-talkyng" (here rather brutally labeled "inutiles confabulationes"),[22] and includes a brief but unmistakable gesture toward the courtly love-duet: "the carnal lover is insatiable in whispering about the shared love, repeating how he loves her, how she loves him, so that hours do not suffice for this converse, nor days, nor any time whatsoever: when they come together they always have copious matter for an unending dialogue."[23] We are offered here literary judgment as well as moral instruction, a double target that is made explicit in the opening description of the first sign: spiritual love feeds itself with learned and edifying discourse while carnal love is solaced with "nugae et otiosae *fabulae*," a phrase that condemns at one stroke both courtly conversation and courtly literature.[24] The description of the third token also invokes a courtly convention, this time the Ovidian *complainte d'amour*, and here the citation moves toward direct quotation: "The separated lovers think always of each other: Where is he? what is he doing? is he coming now? how long will he stay away? is he thinking of her? does absence cool his love? what a long time since he has been heard from! is he ill? Held thus in suspense, the lovers are not free to pray, to meditate on God, or to do anything of value."[25] Again both life and literature, behavior and language, are invoked and judged together. David's text is thus commentary and metacommentary, providing both a guide to life and a purchase upon the ambiguities of erotic literature.

---

einige altfranzosische Doctrinen und Allegorien von der Minne," *Denkschriften der Kaiserlichen Akademie der Wissenschaften,* Philosophisch-Historische Classe 13 (Vienna, 1864), pp. 135–92; for Enanchet, see Werner Fiebig, ed., *Das 'Livre d'Enanchet,'* Berliner Beitrage zur romanischen Philologie 8, 3–4 (Jena: W. Gronau, 1938), pp. 59–61. The *indicia* or *signa amoris* have an elaborate and important history in the Middle Ages. The Ovidian *indicia* (leanness, blushing), although evidence simply of erotic interest, become part of the medical symptomology of *amor hereos* and figure throughout courtly literature: see below, n. 32.

If David is criticizing Ovidian rhetoric he also exploits it: Cicero claimed that there were no outward signs by which the quality of friendship could be judged, which means that David is stealing a page from Ovid's book in order to revise the theory of friendship—showing, in effect, that *amicitia* need not lag behind *amor* in the completeness of its doctrine.

22. All quotations are from the Quarrachi edition of *De exterioris et interioris hominis compositione* (see above, n. 12).

23. "Maxime de mutua dilectione insatiabiliter ruminat, quantum ipse eam et illa illum diligat, ita quod ad huiusmodi colloquia non sufficiant horae, non dies nec quaelibet tempora, sed semper, cum convenire possunt, copiosam habent loquendi materiam indeficienter" (p. 236).

24. For the *Disce mori's* mistranslation of this phrase, see note to line 45.

25. "Tertium est inquietudo cordis, quando sunt absentes cogitando de invicem, ubi iam sit ille dilectus, quid agat, quando veniat, quamdiu defuerit, si de se cogitet, si ex absentia amor eius circa se forte in aliquo tepuerit, quam longo tempore iam nihil ei demandaverit, et quid in causa esse possit, quomodo valeat in corpore; et ita, suspenso corde, nec orare libere possunt nec de Deo quiete meditari vel aliud agere" (p. 237).

But exactly what kind of erotic literature? Although we may not be able to specify particular texts, a survey of the relevant genres can define a precise literary context for David's account. One kind of writing that is surely at the forefront of his attention consists of those texts for women religious that allow their pious message to be infected and even corrupted by the forms of secular literature. These are texts in which the intensity and fastidiousness of *fine amor* are used to figure the devoted heart and scrupulous conscience of the bride of Christ.[26] A typical example is *La regle des fins amans,* a mid-thirteenth-century rule for beguines, which enumerates its doctrine according to a scheme that hovers uncertainly between catechetical and courtly meanings. "Par xii signes connoist on les fin amans," signs that are, to be sure, to be understood "esperituement" but that bear an all too obvious literal meaning as well.[27] The same topos appears in a less controversial context, a manuscript of about 1300 that was at one time in the library of the abbey of St. Arnould at Metz. This manuscript brings together straightforward didactic treatises like *Le livre du palmier* and the *Doctrinal sauvage,* love lyrics that are unadapted to a religious audience but could be read spiritually, a brief treatise on friendship, and an account of the "x signes qui sont en vraie

26. "Spiritual 'courtesy' was seized on as especially appropriate for the nun. . . . Latin and Old French poems about nuns' lovers . . . may concentrate on the sexual longings of nuns, but they also envisage the favoured suitor as a *courtly* lover, and it is assumed that he must possess qualities of virtue, wealth and breeding. . . . The nun [is seen] not just as the bride of Christ, but as his *courtly* mistress. [These poems] attempt to turn aristocratic fastidiousness into spiritual scruple, and not to discourage a girl from romantic dreams, but to attach them to a new hero." Jill Mann, *Chaucer and Medieval Estates Satire* (Cambridge: Cambridge University Press, 1973), pp. 134–37. Among the poems discussed by Mann, the most relevant to our inquiry is Gauthier de Coincy, "La chastée as nonnains" (c. 1223–27, and dedicated to the abbesses of Notre-Dame de Soissons and of Fontevrault); see also Baudouin de Condé, *Li contes d'amours* (c. 1300).

27. "Li premiers est de haïr ce que ses amis het: c'est pechiés. Li secons est garder les commandemens son ami. Li tiers est regehir et descouvrir souvent son cuer a son ami. Li quars est amer loiaument. Li quins est penser souvent et ententivement a son ami. Li vi est oïr volentiers la parole de son ami. Li vii est demander soinguesement noveles de son ami. Li viii est aler souvent et volentiers ou liu ou ses amis est. Li ix est envoier souvent joiaux et biaux dons a son ami. Li x est recevoir devotement les joiaux que ses amis envoie, qui son povretés, mesaises, maladies et tribulations. Li xi est avoir dolour del damaige son ami. Li xii est estre apareilliés de faire cuer et de cors et d'avoir quanque ses amis veut et commande. Cist xii signe sont tous jours en vraie amor et en fins amans. Les beguines les ont plus vraiement que les autres gens. Car eles les ont esperituement." "*La Regle des Fins Amans:* Eine Beginenregel aus dem Ende des XIII. Jahrhunderts," ed. Karl Christ, in B. Schadel and W. Mulertt, eds., *Philologische Studien* (Karl Voretzsch Festschrift) (Halle: M. Niemeyer, 1927), pp. 192–93. For a selection of beguine poetry that adopts similar tropes, see Alfons Hilka, "Mystik und Beginentum," *Zeitschrift für romanische Philologie* 47 (1927), 126–42; and for a secular parallel, see the twelve *signa amoris* in "Hec sunt duodecim signa," ed. J. Thomas, "Un art d'aimer du XIIIe siècle," *Revue belge de philologie et d'histoire* 36 (1958), 795–96.

enmour."[28] But the example of this appropriation of secular topoi by religious writers that bears the most remarkable relevance to David's chapter occurs in the *De doctrina cordis* by Gerard of Liège.[29]

The *De doctrina* is a treatise very like David's own: composed probably in the first half of the thirteenth century, and probably for the nuns of the aristocratic double abbey at Fontevrault, it too was a popular work (surviving in over fifty manuscripts) and was translated into English in the fifteenth century.[30] In the final section of his treatise Gerard offers an analysis of what a Middle English translation calls "extatik love," the *amor ecstaticus* discussed by Dionysius in the *De divinis nominibus:* "such love þe which bryngeth a lover al hool in to þe use and profite of þat þyng þat is lovyd—with such love our Lord lovyd us." But "extatik love also is take in a noþer wise. It is take oþer while for alienacion of þe meynde bi love, as ben al suche fleshly loveres þat wexyn mad for love." Naturally Gerard condemns this fleshly love out of hand. "Neverþeles," he continues, and the change of direction here is crucial, "for to prove gostli extatik love bi þe condicion of fleshly extatik love, þu shalt undirstonde þat þer ben many tokenes to know whan extatik fleshli love worchith in amourous fleshly creatures. Among al, seven þer ben, þe which I shall declare to þe, þat apperyn most in such amourous loveris."[31] Then fol-

---

28. Paul Meyer, "Notice du MS. 535 de la Bibliothèque Municipale de Metz," *Bulletin de la Société des Anciens Textes Français* 12 (1886), 41–76.

29. The ascription of this treatise to Gerard is argued by André Wilmart in his introduction to an edition of another treatise by Gerard: "Gérard de Liège: Un traité inédit de l'amour de Dieu," *Revue d'ascétique et de mystique* 12 (1931), 349–430. While there is no modern edition, the treatise has been twice printed: Paris, 1506, and Naples, 1607.

30. This translation survives in four manuscripts: see P. S. Jolliffe, *Check-List of Middle English Prose Writings,* item H1 (p. 91). The translation has been edited by Sister Mary Patrick Candon (Ph.D. Diss., Fordham, 1963); the relevant chapters are modernized by Clare Kirchberger, *The Coasts of the Country* (Chicago: Henry Regnery, 1952). All quotations in the text are from the ME translation in Trinity College, Cambridge, MS B.14.15.

31. T.C.C. MS B.14.15, fol. 70r. The relevant passage from the original is as follows: "Iste autem affectus multus, et inusitatus comparatur amori ecstatico, qui amare per amores vulgariter appellatur. Ecstaticus enim ab ecstasi: unde amor ecstaticus dicitur, qui mentem alienat, qui non sivit cor aliud cogitare, nisi circa rem dilectam. Sumitur tamen amor ecstaticus in bono, aliquando secundum quod de eo loquitur Dionysius, qui appellat amorem ecstaticum illum amorem, qui totaliter transfert amantem in usum, et profectum amati. Tali amore (sicut idem dicit) nos Deus dilexit, se totum in usum nostrum, et profectum totaliter transferens, dicens de tali amore: Est amor ecstaticus, qui non sivit suos esse amantes, sed amatorum. Sumitur etiam aliter ecstaticus, pro amore mentem alienante, secundum quod ecstasis dicitur alienatio: qui, scilicet amor apud Graecos ἔϱος appellatur. Est autem amor, ἔϱος, magnum desiderium, cum magna concupiscentia, et afflictione cogitationum. Heri dicuntur viri nobiles, qui semper mollitiem, et delitias vitae quaerunt, et subiecti sunt huiusmodi passioni. Licet autem amor iste valde sit reprehensibilis; tamen humanum animum valde reprehendit, et confugit in hoc, quod creaturae tam miserabiliter inhaeret, qui suo creatori, a quo, et ad quem factus, et posset, et deberet tam feliciter

lows an enumeration of the seven signs, which are closely related to the *signa* listed in the medical accounts of *amor hereos:* broken speech, dry skin, sunken eye sockets, dry and tearless eyes, unstable pulse, obsessive pensiveness and, finally, an abstraction of mind that amounts to insanity. These signs of course figure over and over again in erotic literature: Chaucer's well-known reference in the Knight's Tale to "the loveris maladye / Of Hereos" is only the most explicit instance of a ubiquitous topos.[32] The important point for our purposes is that, far from discriminating between rhetorics, Gerard deliberately conflates and confuses them. *Amor ecstaticus* is a very different *res* from *amor hereos,* but the *verba* in which both are described are identical. Hence, Gerard undertakes "to *prove* [comprobo] gostli extatik love bi þe condicion of fleshly extatik love" rather than to distinguish them. These texts both devalue religious feelings and enhance secular ones, and so stir crucial medieval doubts about the status and nature of the human affections. They also encourage the unwary to misread frankly erotic texts *spiritualiter,* allowing an entrance to all too fleshly love under a ghostly masquerade. It is to doubts and to texts like these that David in part addresses his analysis.

   The role of *amor* and *amicitia* in the secular literature of the thirteenth century defines the other area of David's concern. Here the process of appropriation is reversed, and high-minded language veils what prove to be biological pursuits. Again the particular problem of interpretation with which David's chapter is concerned can be specifically defined, but we need first to survey the larger area of ambiguity, rhetorical and ideological, which resulted from the interpenetration of *amor* and *amicitia.* That medieval erotic theorists supplemented their basic Ovidianism with

---

inhaerere. Ut ergo comprobemus, et cognoscamus unum amorem per alium. Notandum, quod huiusmodi amoris ecstatici multa sunt signa, inter quae septem tangemus, quae plus videntur amantibus inhaerere." F. Gerardus Leodiensi, *Speculum concionatorum* (Naples, 1607), pp. 278–79.

   Gerard's interest in vernacular love literature is also demonstrated in his *Septem remedia contra amorem illicitum valde utile,* ed. André Wilmart, *Analecta Reginensia,* Studi e Testi 59 (1933), 183–205. In speaking of the dangers of female companions, he lapses from Latin into French in order to describe "*les affectueus parlemens, les dous regars e les dous ris et les salus et les douces lettres et les guiaus,* quia omnia ista sunt rediviva, occasiones et materia carnalis amoris, et via ad casum et destructionem tocius religionis et tocius sanctitatis" (p. 196).

   32. The classic discussion is by John Livingstone Lowes, "The Loveres Maladye of Hereos," *Modern Philology* 11 (1913–14), 491–546; the *signa* from Arnold of Villanova are reprinted on p. 500 of his article. For Chaucer, see now Stephan Kohl, *Wissenschaft und Dichtung bei Chaucer* (Frankfurt: Akademische Verlagsanstalt, 1973), pp. 218–308; see also Massimo Ciavolella, "La tradizione dell'*aegritudo amoris* nel *Decameron,*" *Giornale storico della letteratura italiana* 147 (1970), 498–517 (on *Decameron* 2.8), and Bruno Nardi, "L'amore e i medici medievale," in *Studi in onore di A. Monteverdi* (Modena: Società Tipographia Editrice Modenese, 1959), 2.517–42.

large doses of (sometimes Christianized) Ciceronianism is generally recognized, but the thoroughness of the appropriation is rarely appreciated. As even a brief and generalized survey will show, virtually every item of the medieval theory of friendship finds an amorous correspondence.[33] Starting at the superficial level of manners, for example, the four impediments to friendship (*iracundia, instabilitas, suspicio,* and *garrulitas*) are all grounds for the dismissal of a *fin amant.*[34] Testing a friend for fidelity, good intent, discretion, and patience corresponds to the lover's test that provides the plot or occasion for most courtly literature, and the *suavitas* that makes a man amiable is the equivalent of the lover's *gentilesse.*[35] At a deeper level, the Ciceronian dictum that friendship must be disinterested matches the Ovidian tenet that love and riches are antipathetic;[36] the fidelity of lovers is equally required of friends;[37] and the most basic condition of friendship, a reciprocal and mutually enhancing goodness, appears in courtly contexts as the lover's *noblesse.* It is precisely this analogous idealism that makes the confusion between *amor* and *amicitia* so dangerous: lovers can feel thoroughly noble while doing exactly what they most desire, persuading themselves that they are idealistically as-

33. For a general introduction to the theory of Christian friendship, see G. Vansteenberghe, "Amitié," *Dictionnaire de spiritualité,* Vol. 1 (Paris: G. Beauchesne, 1933), cols. 500–29; Adele Fiske, "Paradisus Homo Amicus," *Speculum* 40 (1965), 436–59, and references cited there. I have illustrated my discussion largely by reference to Peter of Blois's *De amicitia christiana* (*PL* 207:871–96). Peter's treatise is little more than an undeviating exposition of the doctrine that Aelred of Rievaulx developed in an exploratory style in the *De spirituali amicitia* and the *Speculum caritatis*—hence it is usefully flatfooted and unoriginal: see G. Vansteenberghe, "Deux théoriciens de l'amitié au XII siècle: Pierre de Blois et Aelred de Riéval," *Revue des sciences religieuses* 12 (1932), 572–88. References to Peter's *De amicitia christiana* are to chapter and column in the *Patrologia Latina;* the treatise is also edited by M.-M. Davy, *Un traité d'amour du XIIe siècle* (Paris: E. de Boccard, 1932).

34. Peter's account of *suspicio* and *garrulitas* are particularly suggestive of the courtly Jalousie and Malebouche; see especially 13.884.

35. Peter prescribes "in nostro sermone jucunditas, hilaritas in vultu, suavitas in moribus, et ipso aspectu quaedam oculorum favorabilis et grata jucunditas (18.887).

36. Ovid, *Ars amatoria* 2.161–66; medieval erotic theorists virtually always include this kind of attack upon mercenary love—in the *Roman de la rose* it is one of the few things about which Raison and Amis agree.

37. "Nihil in amicitia fide praestantius, quae ipsius nutrix videtur et custos" (Pseudo-Augustine, *De amicitia* 19 [*PL* 40:840]—another twelfth-century summary of Aelred). Peter applies the phrase "nutrix et custos" to patience (14.884); and see Andreas Capellanus, *De amore,* 2.2, where *vera zelotypia* is designated the *nutrix amoris* (p. 228). Even when a friendship must be brought to an end because our friend has proved himself unworthy, we should never stop loving him: "The graciousness of past familiarity should remain in our memory, and no supervening ill-will should abolish it" (Peter, 24.894). Another aspect of the requirement of fidelity, however, suggests that all disappointments will not be so easily absorbed: "Amicitia quae desinere potest, nunquam vera fuit" is an oft-quoted dictum from Jerome's letter to his sometime friend Ruffinus (Ep. 41; see Peter, 1.873), and it prescribes a recognition that is sure to poison all but the noblest of memories.

cending from carnal to spiritual while they in fact decline in the other direction.

This last point requires some expansion, for this is the crucial area of lexical ambiguity. Both classical and medieval writers define the idealism of friendship in terms that find persuasive if misleading counterparts in less disinterested texts. "Virtus," says Cicero, "et conciliat amicitias et conservat. In ea est enim convenientia rerum, in ea stabilitas, in ea constantia."[38] Attracted to the virtue of another, the friend loves that which is most truly himself (i.e., an *alter ego*). Together the friends become superior moral beings. In the Christianization of this scheme, virtue is replaced by God himself. "Here we are, you and I," writes Aelred of Rievaulx to his friend, "and Christ is, I hope, the third between us."[39] Human friendship is both a model of and a way to divine love, an early stage of the ascent and an encouraging prefiguration of the goal. Hence Aelred makes so bold as to revise St. John's text to read, "Qui manet in *amicitia,* in Deo manet et Deus in eo."[40] To love a friend is to obey the *lex amicitiae* by which God ordains the harmony of all creation "in ipsius ordinis tranquillitate." But it is also to find a perfect and narrower harmony. "A man has well said of his friend," writes Augustine, rehearsing several important classical tropes, "that he is half his soul. For I thought that my soul and his soul were but one soul in two bodies."[41] Peter of Blois invokes another central norm when he defines the *forma amicitiae* as opening one's heart to the friend and doing his will.[42] Both the ideology and the rhetoric of this powerful complex of ideas have easily recogniz-

---

38. Cicero, *De amicitia* 27.100 (Loeb ed., p. 206).

39. Quoted by Adele Fiske, "Aelred's of Rievaulx Idea of Friendship and Love," *Cîteaux, Commentarii Cistercienses* 13 (1962), 114.

40. Aelred is here (*De spirituali amicitia* 1 [*PL* 195:670]) expanding upon a suggestion by Cassian: see Fiske, "Paradisus Homo Amicus," pp. 437, 451. Fiske, "Aelred's of Rievaulx Idea of Friendship and Love" rightly stresses Aelred's important assertion of the continuity between human and divine friendship, and the anticipation of beatitude that friendship can provide: see especially pp. 14–15, 124–25, 130–32; and Fiske, "Paradisus Homo Amicus," passim. See also Peter, 3.875: "Amicitia quidam gradus est hominibus ad Deum. Dilectione enim mediante, homo Deo approximat, dum ex hominis amico Dei amicus efficitur"; and 10.880–81, where he explains that the mutual virtuousness of *amicitia* reforms the *imago Dei* within to its original condition.

41. For the *lex amicitiae,* see the *Speculum caritatis* 1.21 (*PL* 195:524), and Fiske, "Aelred's of Rievaulx Idea of Friendship and Love," p. 103; in the *De planctu naturae,* Alan of Lille describes the harmony of creation as a *pax amicitiae* (ed. Nikolaus M. Häring, *Studi medievali,* ser. 3, 19[1978], 811). For the locus classicus, see Cicero, *De amicitia* 7.24; and for Augustine, *Confessions* 4.6.

42. "In his verbis, sicut ait B. Ambrosius, dedit nobis formam amicitiae, quam sequamur, ut secreta nostra revelemus invicem, et amicorum voluntatem alterutram faciamus" (18.887). Both Migne and Davy gloss Peter's reference to Ambrose as *De officiis* 3.13 (*PL* 16:178–79), but the passage is hardly relevant (Davy's *PL* 16:182–83 seems to be an error).

able courtly parallels. The *virtus* of the friend is the *cor gentil* of the lover; the ascent to God is an enlargement in noble manners; *lex amicitiae* is "Amors, qui toz les cuers justise";[43] and the unification of souls and singleness of will are anything from openheartedness and the sharing of secrets to single-minded fornication. Friendship is a paradisal garden, filled with flowers, streams, and poetry; it is joyful, gay, and above all sweet (*suavis, dulcis*); in their desire to attain the highest reaches of virtue, friends inflict precious *vulnera amici* upon each other; friendship can be likened to a tree (see *Li arbres d'amours*), to a cement that binds friends together (see *Li chiment d'amours*).[44] And so on: virtually every trope of the rhetoric of friendship has a secular counterpart in courtly poetry.[45]

Sanctioned by impeccable authority, the extraordinary language of friendship makes its way into medieval literary culture and becomes (the last thing the authors could have wanted) lexically indistinguishable from the language of *fine amor*. There are, of course, crucial differences beneath the verbal similarities, and writers on friendship were careful to point them out. Spiritual friendship arises from the perception of an inner beauty, while *amor carnalis* is aroused by images "pulchorum corporum vel rerum voluptuosarum."[46] Friends rebuke each other when they fall short of their increasingly high standards, but lovers are bound together in a conspiracy of mutual indulgence, a *consensus vitiorum*.[47] Above all, "a

---

43. Chrétien de Troyes, *Le chevalier de la charrete,* ed. Mario Roques, Les classiques français du moyen âge, 86 (Paris: Champion, 1963), line 1233.

44. Fiske, "Paradisus Homo Amicus," provides a particularly full and valuable conspectus of the rhetoric of friendship.

45. For a general discussion of this interpenetration of rhetorics, see especially Leo Pollmann, *Die Liebe in der hochmittelalterlichen Literatur Frankreichs,* Analecta Romanica 18 (Frankfurt: Klostermann, 1966). It should be emphasized that my purpose here is not to trace origins and so sort out the genuine from the fraudulent: not only does the currency of the phrasing make any such attempt impractical, but the very problem David is confronting arises precisely because language can never be tethered to its origins.

46. Pseudo-Augustine, *De amicitia* 3 (*PL* 40:833).

47. Aelred, *De spirituali amicitia* 1 (*PL* 195:665). This crucial concept of mutual reprehension in the name of virtue has a Ciceronian source (*De am.* 22.83: friendship is the *adiutrix virtutum* not a *comes vitiorum*) but is extended and enhanced in medieval discussions. See, for instance, Peter's discussion (again authorized by a reference to Ambrose): "Si quid vitiosum deprehendis in amico, illum prius occulte corripe; si te non audierit, corripe eum palam; si vero se laedi putat, tu tamen eum corripe; et si animum ejus vulneret amara correptio, tu tamen corripe. Tolerabilia enim magis sunt amici vulnera quam adulantium oscula [Prov. 27:6]" (22.892). Peter comments on the negative aspect in discussing *amor carnalis:* "Sicque animus aspectibus impudicis, verbis et nutibus, et obsequiis illectus et attractus, in malum miserabiliter captivatur; dumque duae mentes quodam foedere foedo in una voluntate conflantur, quod odibilius est Deo et animae perniciosius operantes, se infelices omnia lege amicitiae facere arbitrantur. Porro haec amicitia nec ex deliberatione initur, nec probatur judicio, nec ratione regitur; sed sequens vagae affectionis impetum, per illicita indiscrete raptatur: nimirum nec modum tenens, nec serviens honestati, nec inter

friend is *pax, concordia dulcis;* his words calm the storm within one's heart;
. . . a friend, like heaven itself, is *requies mentis,*"[48] while carnal love, in
contrast, is led by the *spiritus vertiginis* and marked by suspicion, anxiety,
and irascibility.[49] The differences are in theory clear, but practice is another matter. Clasped in Troilus' arms, Criseyde "opened hir herte,
and tolde hym hire entent" (3.1239). And if both the lovers were misled by the nature of their affection, was the medieval reader altogether
invulnerable?

David of Augsburg's enumeration of the seven tokens by which *amor*
and *amicitia* can be distinguished draws upon and even summarizes these
earlier attempts at discrimination.[50] But as I have suggested, the literary
nature of David's discussion suggests that his target is reading as well as
doing, texts as well as deeds. Hence we should ask ourselves how the
language of *amor* and *amicitia* was disposed in the sentimental literature
of the later Middle Ages. On these grounds we can divide the relevant
texts into three broad categories. First, there are those that are explicitly
Ovidian in attitude. It was of course Ovid who advised the would-be
lover to mask his intentions under the guise of Ciceronian friendship:
"Let love find entrance in friendship's name. I have seen an unwilling
mistress deluded by this approach. . . . *Amicitia* is but a name."[51] Several
Ovidian poems of the Middle Ages show this strategy at work. In the
anonymous *Pamphilus,* the eponymous hero begins his seduction by beg-
ging Galathea to allow him to show her that he is her true "amicus" (line
232), and Galathea tells the old woman that a "vera amicitia" has joined
them together (line 434), a touching innocence that is shattered by the
climactic rape.[52] In the *Roman de la rose* Amis advises the lover to present
himself as impelled "par amor leal et fine / de nete pensee" (lines 7565–
66), although he in fact wants only to pluck the rose, even though the

---

commoda et damnossa discernens" (6.877). Hence Aelred prefers Cicero's definition of
amicitia as "rerum humanorum et divinarum cum benevolentia et caritate consensio" (*De
am.* 20) to Sallust's ("idem velle et idem nolle"): *De sp. am.* 2 (*PL* 195:673); see Fiske,
"Aelred's of Rievaulx Idea of Friendship and Love," pp. 5–6. We might note here that in
his first conversation with Troilus Pandarus undermines this central virtue by assuring Troilus that "myn entencioun / Nis nat to yow of reprehencioun" (1.683–84).

48. Fiske, "Paradisus Homo Amicus," pp. 448–49.

49. Peter of Blois, 2.877.

50. As, for instance, by Aelred in *De spirituali amicitia* 1 (*PL* 195:665–66); see also Peter
of Blois, 2:876–77, and Fiske, "Aelred's of Rievaulx Idea of Friendship and Love," pp. 119–
20. While I have not discovered a specific source for David's trope of the seven *signa*, it may
of course exist; but the major conclusions of our argument should not be affected in any
case.

51. Ovid, *Ars am.* 1.719–22, 740.

52. Eugène Evesque, ed. and trans., *Pamphilus,* in Gustave Cohen, ed., *La comédie
latine en France au XIIe siècle,* 2 vols. (Paris: Les Belles Lettres, 1931), 2.169–223.

distinction between "fole amor" (line 4563) and "amistiez" (line 4655) has previously been established by Raison.[53] Most pertinent to our inquiry, however, is the scene in book 2 of *Troilus and Criseyde*. Pandarus, trying to persuade Criseyde of Troilus' good intentions, tells her that all Troilus wants is "love of frendes" (2.379). Later he informs Troilus that Criseyde had agreed to grant him "hire love of frendshipe" (2.962). We can now recognize Pandarus' Ovidian intent to deceive, that he is in fact advising Criseyde to hide *amor* under *amicitia,* when we hear him say "Swych love of frendes regneth al this town, / And wry you in that mantel evere moo" (2.379–80); but is the same recognition available to Criseyde, or to all the poem's medieval readers?

By using *amicitia* as a standard to condemn the behavior they elsewhere display, these multivalent texts seem finally to settle on an attitude that is anti-Ovidian. But even so hesitant an account reduces their multiple ironies: Raison promotes *amistiez* in a context in which its rejection is inevitable and even, given the nature of the psychological condition in which generation must take place, necessary. Given this (Ovidian) complexity of form, we should not be surprised to find an alternative tradition of consistent anti-Ovidianism in a group of texts that offer an unmistakable condemnation of *fole amor* in favor of marital *amicitia.*[54] These are texts in which Cupid wears a wedding ring, chastity is one of the virtues of the *fin amant,* true love is always reasonable, and salacious readers are told to go elsewhere: "Ki bosdie quiert en amours, / Si quire autres conseillours."[55] The best known of these poems is the *Traité selonc*

---

53. For *amicitia* in the *Roman,* see Lionel J. Friedman, "Jean de Meun and Ethelred of Rievaulx," *Esprit créateur* 2 (1962), 135–41. Andreas Capellanus also invokes *amicitia* as a legitimate alternative to the now-rejected *amor* in the palinode to the third book; and even in book 1 the values of *amicitia* are invoked by a lady in order to deflate an eager lover: "the man who neglects the interests of a comrade, and seeks only what is advantageous to his own designs, is not accounted a true friend. One must not accede to the will of the kind of friend who seeks merely his own advantage" (*De amore,* p. 179). See Douglas Kelly, "Courtly Love in Perspective: The Hierarchy of Love in Andreas Capellanus," *Traditio* 24 (1968), 119–47.

54. On marital *amicitia,* see Henry A. Kelly, *Love and Marriage in the Age of Chaucer* (Ithaca: Cornell University Press, 1975), and references cited there. For the classical world, *amicitia* between men and women was impossible: friends had to be equals. Aquinas explains that although the husband has sovereignty over his wife, they are equal in their mutual submission to the laws of marriage: *Summa contra Gentiles* 3.2.123–24.

55. See, for instance, the Anglo-Norman poem of c. 1300 printed by O. Sodegard, "Un art d'aimer anglo-normand," *Romania* 77 (1956), 289–330; the small treatise on love included within *Li Hystore de Julius Cesar* by Jehan de Turm (ed. A. Långfors, *Romania* 56 [1930], 362–73; and see L. F. Flutre, *Romania* 59 [1933], 270–76); Robert of Blois, "Chanson d'Amors," in *Sämmtliche Werke,* ed. Jacob Ulrich (Berlin: Mayer and Müller, 1891), 2.103–43. The quotation is from *Li Arbres d'amours,* ed. A. Långfors, *Romania* 56 (1930), 377–88, lines 581–82. See C. B. West, *Courtoisie in Anglo-Norman Literature,* Medium Ae-

les auctours pour essampler les amantz marietz that Gower appends to the *Confessio amantis,* a praise of married love set against the *Confessio's* exposure of "la sotie de cellui qui par amours aime par especial."[56] . The straightforward moralism of these texts makes explicit the anti-Ovidianism that remains only an implication in more subtly wrought (and interesting) poems, but the differences in method cannot disguise the basic similarity of attitude.

But there is a third kind of treatise, and it is the kind particularly relevant to our inquiry. These are works in which the final attitude remains genuinely uncertain despite a straightforward rhetorical strategy. These texts simply juxtapose the rival vocabularies and values of Ovidian *amor* and Ciceronian *amicitia,* not only without offering the reader an unequivocal moral prospect but without even marking the separate elements as deriving from separate ideologies and traditions. I shall offer just one analysis, but it could be multiplied.[57] *Li Consaus d'amours* is a mid-thirteenth-century prose treatise almost certainly written by Richard of Fournival.[58] Although addressed to his sister, who has a "grant desirrier d'amer par amours," Richard presents his treatise as a serious philosophical analysis of *amor* in its largest sense, as in effect a vernacular analogue to Aelred's *De spirituali amicitia* or William of St. Thierry's *De natura et dignitate amoris.* He proceeds "par ordene" (p. 244) in establishing a scholastic stemma for "amour par amour" that will locate it within the genus of "amours en general." With every division one of the alter-

---

vum Monographs 3 (Oxford: Blackwell, 1938), pp. 144–50; and Gervase Mathew, "Ideals of Friendship," in John Lawlor, ed., *Patterns of Love and Courtesy* (London: Edward Arnold, 1966), pp. 45–53. In the *Roman de la rose* Raison concludes her analysis of *amicitia* with a similar definition of reasonable love: "Ceste amor que ci te propos / n'est pas contraire a mon propos . . ./. . ./C'est a toute vertu s'amort, / mes l'autre met les genz a mort" (lines 4733–34, 4737–38).

56. *Traité selonc les auctours pour essampler les amantz marietz, The Complete Works of John Gower,* ed. G. C. Macaulay, Vol. 1 (Oxford: Clarendon Press, 1899), pp. 379–92.

57. Other salient examples are the so-called *L'Amistiés de vraie amour,* ed. J. Thomas, *Revue belge de philologie et d'histoire* 36 (1958), 786–811, and ed. Cedric E. Pickford, *Bulletin of the John Rylands Library* 34 (1951–52), 333–65; "La Diffinission de Amurs," ed. Paul Studer, in *Mélanges de philologie et d'histoire offerts à M. Antoine Thomas* (Paris: Champion, 1927), pp. 433–36; [Richard of Fournival?], *Li Commens d'amours,* ed. Antoinette Saly, *Travaux de linguistique et littérature* 10 (1972), 21–55. For a typical, smaller instance, see the lyric "La Lescun as Lëaus amaunz," ed. E. Stengel, *Zeitschrift für französische Sprache und Literatur* 14 (1892), 158–59.

58. [Richard of Fournival?], *Li Consaus d'amours,* ed. Gian Battista Speroni, *Medioevo romanzo* 1 (1974), 217–78, replacing the edition by William M. McLeod, *Studies in Philology* 32 (1935), 1–21. For Richard of Fournival, see the introduction by Cesare Segre to his edition of the *Bestiaires d'amours* (Milan and Naples: Ricciardi, 1957), pp. xxix–xxx, and, especially, A. Birkenmajer, *Etudes d'histoire des sciences et de la philosophie du moyen âge,* Studia Copernicana 1 (Wroclaw, Warsaw, and Cracow: Ossolinskich, 1970).

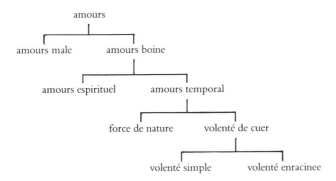

natives is excluded: "amours male" is not really love and so is a contradiction in terms; "amours espirituel" is Ciceronian *amicitia* and not Richard's present subject (although he urges his sister to maintain this love "tous jours en vostre cuer" [p. 247]); love motivated by the "force de nature" is the affection we feel for kin; and "volenté simple" is an impersonal charity that extends to all people. "Amour par amour" derives, then, from "boine volentés ki vient soudainement de la racine du cuer" (p. 255). That this analysis imitates the careful discriminations drawn by theorists like Aelred and William is clear,[59] but that it is a wholly superficial imitation is disclosed only when Richard finally arrives at his subject matter. For despite the subordination accomplished by his own analysis, Richard now claims that "toutes les autres amours naissent de ceste amour: car c'est li estos dont les fleurs et li fruit des autres amours naissent, et est la droite racine de toutes vertus, et matere de tous biens" (p. 248).

It is apparent, then, that moral theology has contributed not a controlling intellectual structure to Richard's treatise but merely a rhetorical effect. It provides an entry into the subject that multiplies distinctions in order to avoid differences and that exploits the theory of spiritual friendship to enhance a familiar encomium to *fine amor.* The body of the treatise provides comparable conflations, perhaps nowhere more strikingly than in his two definitions of what *aimer par amour* means. One is from John of Garland's familiar oxymorons, here given a careful *expositio* (pp. 250–42);[60] the other is a startling adaptation of a key Ciceronian phrase:

---

59. Discriminations that are also, and correctly, drawn by David of Augsburg in the chapter that precedes his account of the seven tokens (3.34).

60. From the *Epithalamium Beate Marie Virginis,* in L. J. Paetow, *The Morale scolarium of John of Garland,* Memoirs of the University of California 4.2 (Berkeley: University of California Press, 1927), pp. 113–14; see also Alan of Lille's similar definition in the *De planctu naturae* (pp. 842–43), translated by Jean de Meun at the beginning of his *ars amatoria* (lines 4263–4310).

"Tulles dist, . . . 'Amer par amours n'est autre cose k'amer celi c'on aime sans regarder nul pourfit'" (p. 256)[61]—a definition that would have out-raged moral Gower with his condemnation of "la sotie de cellui qui par amours aime par especial."[62] Again, Richard rehearses the standard courtly motif that love enters at the eyes, but then manages an exposition that disarms the criticism that carnal love is based on mere images. "La droite voie d'amours sont li oeul, car ce sont les fenestres dou cuer et ont lor racines u cuer, ne li oeul ne pueent pas si mentir con fait li bouce" (p. 261): in providing an unmediated access to the heart the eyes allow love to pass from one person to another without distortion.[63] But although he has evaded the epistemological challenge, Richard then discards his advantage with a list of the varieties of love sickness (*blanc fievre, li maus sans repos, li mals deguises*) that makes it clear that love is just as dangerous as the moralists say.

One obvious way to deal with this baffling text is to mark it as ironic, but Richard's high-minded analysis of the *noblece* a *fin amant* must pos-sess, and his sensible advice about *prolongance* (i.e., courtship), will hardly support a consistently ironic reading. The moral valence of his text, whether deliberately or by inadvertence, is genuinely ambiguous, an ambiguity that can be resolved only by a reader with a preemptive hermeneutic. The implications of this fact will be discussed more fully in relation to *Troilus and Criseyde*. But for the moment an interesting comment made by John Benton in the course of his debunking of "courtly love" will serve, by contrast, to indicate the direction of the argument:

While some authors wrote ambiguously about love, the literature I have read does not convince me that medieval people themselves inadvertently confused the categories and could not tell the difference between love which was concu-piscent and that which was not. It seems to me that medieval authors and audi-

---

61. Cicero, *De am.* 27.100: "Amare autem nihil est aliud nisi eum ipsum diligere quem ames, nulla indigentia, nulla utilitate quaesita." The *Amistiés de vraie amour* also sets Ovidian and Ciceronian definitions side by side, and (despite the assertions by the editors) shows no preference, nor even an awareness of opposition.

62. Nor would Jean de Meun's Raison have been much impressed with Richard's de-fense of *amour par amour:* "c'est une cose que jounece escuse, ne 'Nostre Sires ne met pas si a remenbrance' si con l'Escriture dist, 'les trespassemens de jounece con il fait les autres' [see Psalm 24:7]. Et on set bien que jus, soulas et joie sont coses que nature aime mout, et mout confortent le nature; et nature n'a besoigne d'estre destrainte en se jounece" (p. 254). Raison, on the other hand, launches a powerful attack on the folly of youth (lines 4392–4597), citing the *De senectute* as her authority; and the effect of Nature on the action of the poem is of course extensive and by no means entirely rational. Besides this passage, much of the *Consaus* offers striking parallels to the *Roman*.

63. For this trope, see Ruth Cline, "Heart and Eyes," *Romance Philology* 25 (1971–72), 263–97.

ences enjoyed ambiguity in literature, not because they felt it reflected a basic ambiguity in the universe or the heart of man, but because their natural tendency was to think in very rigid categories.[64]

Benton's point is both important and, I think, in the final analysis misleading. In its claim that the ambiguity of medieval literature is a function of the spiritual self-confidence of its readers, it assumes, correctly, that ambiguity is resolved not by literary techniques but by prior moral commitments and habits. But it is unpersuasive in assuming that "medieval authors and audiences" were uniformly endowed with a clear and unruffled grasp of the "very rigid categories" of the medieval moral universe. Categories such as *amor* and *amicitia* are as prescriptive as other cultural forms and, like them, must be learned. David's chapter is just such a pedagogy, teaching the reader how to decode amorous rhetoric and behavior with the key of the seven signs.

This decoding is also a demystification. If medieval readers were capable of anticipating the modern taste for ambiguity, the temptation of misreading was also available to them. And as we might expect of a culture of the book, medieval misprision brought with it little but anxiety. Far from freeing readers from the burden of the past, it delivered them into the hands of the enemy: witness the two most famous of all medieval misreaders, Paolo and Francesca.[65] Hence David's chapter invokes the tropes of erotic writing not to appreciate but to denounce, to disclose the immorality that marks them as unfit for the pious reader. His businesslike Latinity betrays no interest in the courtly conventions it picks up and puts down: the "nugae et otiosae fabulae" are rejected at the outset. Nor is this kind of critique swayed by the intention of the author, even if it is known, even if it is unequivocal. Andreas Capellanus may have meant his treatise ironically, but Bishop Tempier missed the point or feared others would, and so condemned it. And he was right to do so: the thirteenth-century translation by Drouart la Vache suppresses Andreas' ironies and renders the treatise an unambiguous handbook of *fine amor*.[66] Given such puckish, or ill-informed, or careless, or even wicked writers, medieval reading is clearly a dangerous enterprise.

---

64. John Benton, "Clio and Venus: An Historical View of Medieval Love," in F. X. Newman, ed., *The Meaning of Courtly Love* (Albany: SUNY Press, 1968), p. 31.

65. And they are significantly compared to other exemplary readers, Augustine reading the Scriptures in his garden and Abelard and Heloise reading the *auctores* together: see Robert B. Hollander, *Allegory in Dante's Commedia* (Princeton: Princeton University Press, 1969), pp. 106–14, and Peter Dronke, "Francesca and Heloise," *Comparative Literature* 27 (1975), 113–35.

66. Barbara Nelson Sargent, "A Medieval Commentary on Andreas Capellanus," *Romania* 94 (1973), 528–41.

3. *TROILUS AND CRISEYDE* IN THE NUNNERY

> Pero ti prego, dolce caro padre,
>   che mi dimostri amore.
>
> —Dante, *Purgatorio*, 18.13–14

The context of *Disce mori* is pretty clearly indicated by its address to Sister Alice, but further evidence can both deepen and make more precise our sense of the appropriateness of including an account of *amor* and *amicitia* in a handbook for nuns. From the beginnings of Christian literature this kind of warning was addressed above all to women religious. If Ovid advises the lover to use *amicitia* as a cover, St. Jerome warns the pious woman to avoid just such a subterfuge. Writing to a Roman nun, he cautions her that spiritual love is easily perverted into lust and that the "sweet and death-dealing song of the sirens" must not lead her astray.[67] Letters of friendship sent between men and women religious are filled not only with the extravagant rhetoric of friendship but with assurances (or warnings) that they should not be construed as letters of love.[68] In the *Speculum caritatis* Aelred comments on just this possibility:

---

67. *Epistola* 22.18 (*PL* 22:405); *The Letters of St. Jerome*, trans. C. C. Mierow (Westminister, Md.: Newman Press, 1963), p. 150.

68. An example of such a warning may be found in one of the letters written by Constance, a nun of Le Ronceray, to her monastic friend Baudri of Bourgueil: *Les oeuvres poétiques de Baudri de Bourgueil*, ed. Phyllis Abrahams (Paris: Champion, 1926), p. 347 (lines 110–25). This correspondence, the genre of letters of friendship, and other relevant matters, are discussed by Dronke, *Medieval Latin and the Rise of the European Love Lyric*, 1.192–263; the classic article on the subject is by Jean Leclercq, "L'amitié dans les lettres au moyen âge," *Revue du moyen âge latin* 1 (1945), 391–410. The rhetoric of these letters poses an interesting problem for the interpreter. While Dronke rightly warns us against sentimental overreadings of conventional language, to the reader innocent of historical method and interested mainly in the moral valence of a given text (surely the situation of a medieval reader), these letters offer their rhetoric unmarked by any clear moral value. Such a reader could learn from David's handbook that one of the signs of carnal love is the cherishing of letters, "tenderly worded love-letters . . . that are kissed and clasped . . . and venerated as relics" (pp. 238–39). How then would he have interpreted this passage from one of Isidore's letters? "Dearest son, when you receive letters from a friend, do not delay to embrace them in behalf of your friend. This is the second consolation among those absent: that if he who is loved is not present, then his letters may be embraced in his stead" (*Epistola* 2 [*PL* 83:898]; quoted by F. C. Gardiner, *The Pilgrimage of Desire* [Leiden: Brill, 1971], p. 61). This kind of advice is matched by a comparable extremity of language. Anselm writes to his two younger friends, "They now desire, most beloved sons, my eyes desire your faces, my arms extend themselves in your embraces, my mouth pants for your kisses" (*Epistola* 2.28 [*PL* 158:1180]; quoted by Gardiner, p. 59). Examples could easily be multiplied: in passage after passage these letters demand of the reader a discretion that is able to hold literary taste firmly within the controlling context of moral judgment. While sophisticated writers were doubtless able to sustain this subordination, other texts show less mature correspondents allowing the tropes of *amicitia* to serve as camouflage for a flirtatious if

Friendship can in time change into something really dangerous, if it becomes familiar and tender and sought after for its own sake. I myself have known good and holy men who have had an extreme horror of anything unclean, being most chaste and continent, yet they have fallen in love with young nuns to whom they had originally been attracted because of their virtues. . . . Friendship can easily degenerate, unfortunately, into carnal lust. . . . Endearments and tokens of love must not be indulged in, unless we really know what we are doing, and do it with moderation and prudence, in order that the virtues we love and praise in others may be the more encouraged.[69]

The English treatises for women religious pay a persistent attention to this theme—witness the well-known discussion in the *Ancrene Riwle*.[70] Even when, in its original form, the advice is not intended specifically for women, the relevant passages were often excerpted and included in compilations assembled for nuns. The best example is Walter Hilton's *Eight Chapters of Perfection*. It contains an account of how "bi litil and litil goostli love falliþ and dieþ and fleischli love wexiþ and qwikeneþ," misleading spiritual friends into thinking "þat þei may use siche spekyngis, lokyngis, touchyngis, handlyngis, kissyngis and siche tokenes of fleschli love withoute perel."[71] One manuscript written for women religious that excerpts the relevant chapters is Univ. Lib. Camb. Hh.i.12 (chapters 1, 5, and 8).[72] Moreover, three of the ten surviving manuscripts of the *Eight Chapters* not only were written for women religious but were perhaps even owned by Syon Abbey itself: Harley 993, Bodleian Rawl. C. 894, and British Library Royal 17.c.xviii.[73] The latter two manuscripts are

---

(more or less) innocent *amor*. Dronke draws our attention to an eleventh-century manuscript, having as its provenance an aristocratic nunnery like Regensburg or Le Ronceray, that includes a collection of verse letters sent by the nuns to their *magister*, a scholar from Liège. While "such verses were simply part of one's education, and sending them was a custom hallowed by the Christian tradition of *amicitia*," a reading of the letters leads Dronke to conclude that "at least several of his pupils seem to have fallen in love with [their teacher] and become jealous of one another"—an all too apt precedent for David's warnings (1.221–29).

69. Aelred of Rievaulx, *Speculum caritatis* 3.28 (*PL* 195:601–2), trans. Geoffrey Webb and Adrian Walker (London: A. R. Mowbray, 1962), p. 120.

70. *Ancrene Riwle*, trans. M. B. Salu (Notre Dame: University of Notre Dame Press, 1956), p. 42.

71. Walter Hilton, *Eight Chapters of Perfection*, ed. Fumio Kuriyagawa (Tokyo: Keio Institute of Cultural and Linguistic Studies, 1967), pp. 30–31.

72. On the provenance of Hh.i.12, see Doyle, "Survey of the Origins and Circulation of Theological Writings in English," 2.111.

73. To the eight manuscripts listed by Kuriyagawa should be added the two mentioned by Hudson, "Chapter from Walter Hilton in Two Middle English Compilations," p. 421 n. 20. On the possible Syon provenance of Harley 993, Rawl. C. 894, and Royal 17.c.xviii, see Doyle, "Survey of the Origins and Circulation of Theological Writings in English," 2.210, 215–21.

notable for another reason: they both contain *A Litill Tretise ayence flesshly affecciouns and all unþrifty loves,* the previously discussed translation and expansion of the same chapters of David's *De exterioris* translated in the *Disce mori.*[74] Nor is the *Disce mori* itself content with only a single treatment of the theme. In addition to its translation of David's chapter, it includes a rewriting of Hilton's chapter 8 (pp. 175–77) and, for good measure, a translation of Aelred's discussion taken from *The Chastising of God's Children* (pp. 284–88).[75]

The attention paid to this theme in these texts is striking, especially in the context of Syon Abbey, where both men and women were in residence. They were, to be sure, rigidly separated, and even at the time of the dissolution Syon was acknowledged to be an exemplary establishment.[76] But there was one occasion for extended familiarity between men and women: before her enclosure each young woman would spend a year receiving instruction. Two of the texts surviving from Syon contain what may be precious remembrances of this period. In the last half of the fifteenth century a novice named Joanna Sewell (d. 1532) went through this process under the direction of James Greenhalgh, a Carthusian recluse at Sheen. Among the books they read together were Richard Rolle's *Incendium amoris* (which itself contains a full discussion of *amor* and *amicitia*)[77] and Walter Hilton's *Scala perfectionis.* The texts which they read survive, and in the margins of both are found inscribed James's and Joanna's eloquently overlapping initials.[78]

While tentative, this description of the kind of audience for which the *Disce mori* was probably compiled does serve to give it a human resonance and a local habitation. It also reinvokes the anxiety of medieval reading, and makes us ask why the compiler of the treatise should have thought that *Troilus and Criseyde* was appropriate reading for Sister Alice. One part of the answer must surely be that he saw *Troilus and Criseyde* as in fact fulfilling the monastic requirements for spiritual reading. At first glance, admittedly, this seems improbable, for contemporary prescriptions for "vertuus redinge" are severely restrictive: "Rede þe livis of sentis and þe[r] doctrine, þat bi þe exampul of þe[r] holy levyng þu may be . . . illumyned in þi undrestandynge to knowe and to undrestande trwe

---

74. See above, p. 120 and note 16.

75. See Hudson, "Chapter from Walter Hilton in Two Middle English Compilations," passim, and Colledge and Bazire, *Chastising of God's Children,* pp. 193–98.

76. Enclosure at Syon was permanent, and according to the *Orders and Constitutions of the Nuns of Syon* sisters and brothers communicated only through the wheel set into the wall (British Library MS Arundel 146, fols. 96r–v).

77. Richard Rolle, *Incendium amoris,* ed. Margaret Deanesly (Manchester: University of Manchester Press, 1915), pp. 261–66.

78. The evidence is fully presented, without comment, by Deanesly, ibid., pp. 79–83.

fro false, gode fro eville, vice fro vertu and þe remedies ageniste vices and temptacions."[79] But if *Troilus and Criseyde* is not about saints and their doctrine, it does aim to distinguish true from false, good from evil, vice from virtue. If placed in this severely moralistic context, Chaucer's poem can provide moral discriminations that are at least comparable to those drawn by David of Augsburg. The difference between David's absolutes and Chaucer's nuances is of course obvious, but it derives less from a difference in moral attitude than from different generic choices that prescribe different rhetorical strategies. David provides the diagnosis of moral theology (each sign is a symptom that signifies a moral condition or *habitus*), while Chaucer offers the gradual revelations of narrative romance (the conclusion makes explicit an *entente* that was at the beginning only a latent possibility). To ignore these rhetorical differences would be to misread both texts, and there is evidence that the compiler of *Disce mori* did not; but to use them to dismiss the similarities is to narrow the full range of the compiler's response. By applying David's categories to Chaucer's poem the compiler allows the reader to moralize *Troilus and Criseyde,* to render it not only harmless but instructive.

But this conclusion, although comfortable, is only part of the story: it suggests how David of Augsburg would have read the poem (had he allowed himself to read it at all) but not how our fifteenth-century reader actually did read it. That there is a difference is suggested by the alterations and additions to the source that appear in the translation. These changes disclose a warm understanding of values that are, as we have seen, foreign to David's attitude. Our reader begins his condemnation of love by quoting one of the most beautiful stanzas of love poetry in the language, and despite its new context the stanza remains to an important degree what it is in *Troilus and Criseyde*—a celebration of and submission to the god of love. That he appreciates Chaucer's prosodic genius is clear from the not unskillful rhyme royal of his dedication, and even the doggerel he scatters through his text shows a kind of wit.[80] But perhaps most

---

79. MS Arundel 197, fol. 52v (from "An abstracte owte of a boke þat is callid formula noviciorum," a selection from David's *De exterioris*). See also MS Harley 494, fols. 14r–v, where specific chapters from "the lyf of Jesus after Bonaventura" are assigned to each day of the week. Doyle, "Survey of the Origins and Circulation of Theological Writings in English," 2.216, points out that in the margin of MS Royal 17.c.xviii, fol. 23v, the word "Thorsday" (?) is written, "possibly a mark of daily reading (as it is found in the Orchard of Syon, St. John's C. 25, almost exactly)."

That other Chaucerian poetry found its way into Syon is shown by MS Laud misc. 416, a mid-fifteenth-century manuscript owned by two Syon nuns (Anne Colyvylle and Clemencia Thaseburght): among other didactic and poetic pieces (*Cursor Mundi, Siege of Thebes*) it contains the *Parlement of Foules* (Doyle, 2.44).

80. The compiler's literary tastes are also disclosed by his familiarity with the *Roman*

revealing is the grasp of the conventions of love poetry that he displays in his translation, a grasp that far exceeds his original. The amorous complaint of the third token is invigorated by being cast in direct speech and pointed with apostrophes, and the love duet of the first token employs a subtly mimetic syntax, the appositional phrases extending the sentence just as the lovers prolong their discourse: "it can not be here expressed—for an houre suffiseth not to hem—ne a day—ne dayes—ne no tyme to open þeire herte oon to oþer."[81]

Our reader's attention to and regard for the forms of vernacular love poetry provide one answer to the question why, in reading David's chapter, he thought of Chaucer's poem. Recognizing the literary character of David's analysis, he naturally turned to literature for illustration. But there is another answer as well: our reader's comparable attention to the *content* of Chaucer's poem. This attention is so persistent that the action of the *Troilus* exerts a visible pressure upon the translation. There are, to be sure, astonishing and fortuitous parallels between the seven tokens and the behavior of Chaucer's lovers: the first token describes how lovers talk endlessly about their love and open their hearts to one another, as do Troilus and Criseyde in book 3; the lover suffers deeply when the beloved is absent and wonders if he will ever return, as does Troilus in book 5; lovers exchange love letters that are worshiped and kept as relics, which describes Troilus in books 2 and 5; disappointed lovers deny their love altogether and return hate for love, and if this does not describe Troilus it certainly fits Pandarus, who tells Troilus that he hates Criseyde and always will; and then there is Troilus' final reluctance to admit the truth about Criseyde, which the translator invokes to illustrate the seventh token. That this parallelism between David's tokens and the action of Chaucer's poem also struck our fifteenth-century reader is shown by a telling alteration in his translation. Writing for a woman, he naturally makes his despairing lover feminine: "A! what meeneth it þat he sendeth me no writynges nor toknes? . . . Ha! goode God! whan shal I have message from him?" But later not even a change of gender stands between the fleshly lover and Troilus. In a change unique to this translation, the disillusioned lover of the sixth token is not a woman but a man: "If þat oon happe in a litel þinge to offende þat oþer, as not grauntyng his

---

de la rose, or at least the ME *Romaunt:* Malebouche and Jalousie are mentioned in our chapter, and Constraint Abstinence and Fals Semblant in the account of hypocrisy in part 2 (Laud, fol. 217v); also relevant is the Latin poem edited by Rigg (above, n. 4).

81. Wager also discusses this passage, and comments on the "representational quality of the fifteenth-century writer's prose. . . . It is easy to see that he has read widely. He has a poet's power of representing his feelings vividly" ("'Fleshly Love' in Chaucer's 'Troilus,'" pp. 65–66).

desires, or cherisshinge, *or yevynge his yiftes to an oþer,* for þe gretter þat þe love is bitwix hem þe gretter hem þenke þ'offence or þe unkyndenesse shewde." Moreover, not only is there a change in gender but the key, italicized phrase, which recalls so sharply Troilus' discovery of his brooch on Diomede's armor, is added by the translator to the original.

Although themselves diminutive, these details point to a large conclusion, for they suggest the kind of reading our author gave the poem and the kind for which he is offering guidance. The action of the poem is felt by him as fully *real,* as an accurate (and dangerously imitable) depiction of human conduct. The details of the poem can be smoothly accommodated to what purports to be an account of contemporary behavior—indeed, were we missing David's original we might well think the *Disce mori* chapter a prose summary of the *Troilus.* That all three accounts are largely if not wholly literary does not, of course, mean that our fifteenth-century reader is mistaken in the immediacy of his response. On the contrary, this evidence means that our reader categorized *Troilus and Criseyde* as a text to be read literally, i.e., as an exemplary instance. Hence his analysis avoids any search for an allegorical subtext. Troilus' Petrarchan song is read not as signifying a blasphemous homage to Cupid but as describing a psychological reality, the conflict and bewilderment brought on by love. So too the reading of Criseyde's infidelity avoids such obvious exegetical keys as the fallibility of women or the Boethian vanity of human wishes; it focuses instead upon a psychological process, the moral blindness that progressively afflicts the lovers. Of course his interpretations attach ideas to the narrative structure, and to that extent they are, like all interpretation, allegorical.[82] But they display an attention to the texture of the poem and a respect for the psychological reality of the characters that sharply mark them off from fully fledged spiritualizations.

Our argument has apparently reached a familiar impasse in an opposition of the aesthetic and the didactic, *dulce* set against *utile.* The literary sensibility displayed throughout the chapter seems to undermine its ostensible subject: can our reader be both fully sensitive to the beauties of *Troilus and Criseyde* and still stretch it on the procrustean bed of the seven tokens? It is tempting to conclude the argument with this question, leaving our reader in a tension that suggestively matches that which more recent readers have perceived in Chaucer's poetry.[83] But this irresolution

---

82. On this too often overlooked point, see Northrop Frye, *An Anatomy of Criticism* (Princeton: Princeton University Press, 1957), p. 89.

83. This is the classic New Critical reading of the poem, recently and thoroughly articulated by Alfred David, *The Strumpet Muse: Art and Morals in Chaucer's Poetry* (Bloomington: Indiana University Press, 1976).

is finally, I think, too simple for both parties. I should like to enter two qualifications, one practical and one theoretical.

The practical one has to do with the mechanics of moralization: what does this reader recognize in *Troilus and Criseyde* that leads him to apply the topos of *amor* and *amicitia?* The answer is, of course, the topos of *amor* and *amicitia.* The apparent circularity of this process should not disguise its importance. For in this act of recognition our reader accomplishes no mean feat of literary historicism, one that no modern scholar (to my knowledge) has quite duplicated. That *amicitia* is an important element of the moral structure of the poem is, to be sure, well known: it is a standard that can be applied to Pandarus, to the courtly world of Trojan society, and to the lovers themselves.[84] But what is not well known is that Chaucer's use of the topos to define the love relationship is almost entirely his addition to Boccaccio's narrative.[85] We have already mentioned perhaps the most important Chaucerian addition, Pandarus' use of the Ovidian strategy of concealing the urgings of *amor* with the disinterested affection of *amicitia* ("love of frendes"). In case we might have missed this motif in its first appearance, Chaucer repeats it in the later description of Diomede's courtship. At first Diomede comforts Criseyde by offering "to ben youre frend" (5.128)—"taketh naught my frendshipe in despite," he advises her (5.135)—but all too soon he is assuring her that he loves her "as paramours."[86] With this reenactment of the first wooing, Chaucer allows a coarseness that was originally, between Troilus and Criseyde (and Pandarus), only an awkward possibility to become now harshly realized. The largest movements of his poem are toward just such retrospective revelation, toward the gradual enactment of the implications of *entente* into the inarguable explicitness of destiny. And in this process *amor* and *amicitia* play crucial roles.

---

84. The basic article is by Alan Gaylord, "Friendship in Chaucer's *Troilus,*" *Chaucer Review* 3 (1968–69), 239–64; see also Leah Rieber Freiwald, "Swych Love of Frendes: Pandarus and Troilus," *Chaucer Review* 6 (1971–72), 120–29, and Robert G. Cook, "Chaucer's Pandarus and the Medieval Ideal of Friendship," *Journal of English and Germanic Philology* 69 (1970), 407–24.

85. Not that Boccaccio's poem is entirely free of the topos, but it occurs largely in the predictable context of the friendship of Troilo and Pandaro, which each refers to as "la nostra amistade" (2.2, 2.4). That the values of *amicitia* are relevant to Troilo and Criseida is, however, briefly suggested: in thinking about whether to yield, Criseida contrasts the equality of "si fatta amistade" to the subjection of marriage (2.73), and in trying to lure her back to Troy toward the end of the poem, Troilo writes Criseida about their "amor, qual tiene ed ha tenuta / Nostra amista congiunta" (7.53). But these brief gestures hardly constitute a coherent motif, unlike Chaucer's uses. Quotations are from *Il Filostrato,* ed. and trans. N. E. Griffin and A. B. Myrick (Philadelphia: University of Pennsylvania Press, 1929).

86. Gaylord, "Friendship in Chaucer's *Troilus,*" pp. 262–63.

One of Chaucer's most significant alterations in the quality of Boccaccio's poem is his enhancement of his hero's moral stature: however
deluded, Troilus achieves even if he does not sustain a nobility of spirit
and a capacity for philosophical aspiration that are never available to
Boccaccio's Troilo. As disquieting possibilities, earlier suppressed in the
interests of idealism and intensity, become all too actual, we are shown
that Troilus' most tenacious (and most commendable) illusion is that
fleshly lovers can sustain the values of spiritual friendship. Hence his insistence that Criseyde is a fully moral being, displayed most clearly in his
rejection of Pandarus' plan to carry her off rather than let her go to the
Greek camp: the choice must remain with her. That we are to read this
self-restraint as a sign of Troilus' capacity for *amicitia* is shown by what
is surely Chaucer's most telling revision. As Boccaccio's lovers bid farewell, Troilo offers Criseida a description of herself as the quintessential
courtly lady, doubtless hoping that this model will urge virtuous behavior upon her.[87] Chaucer, on the other hand, has Criseyde speak an appreciative encomium to Troilus:

> For trusteth wel, that youre estat roial,
> Ne veyn delit, nor only worthinesse
> Of yow in werre or torney marcial,
> Ne pompe, array, nobleye, or ek richesse
> Ne made me to rewe on youre destresse;
> But moral vertu, grounded upon trouthe,
> That was the cause I first hadde on yow routhe!
>
> (4.1667–73)

Criseyde says this about Troilus because Troilus cannot say it about her,
and that he cannot accounts for both his fate and hers: alone capable of
the "moral vertu, grounded upon trouthe" that is the essence of *amicitia,*
Troilus has bound himself to an *alter ego* who can never enact the virtues
of his own best self.

In order to shore up the uncertain moral structure of Boccaccio's
poem Chaucer reached into the amorous literature we earlier surveyed
for his organizing topos of *amor* and *amicitia,* the very literature to which
David of Augsburg directed *his* commentary on the same topos. By ap-

---

87. "Beauty, which is often wont to take others in its net, drew me not to love thee,
nor did gentle birth, which is ever like to catch the desire of the noble, draw me to love
thee, nor yet did ornaments nor riches, in all of which thou art more abundant than was
ever amorous lady, make me feel love for thee in my heart. But thy noble and princely
manners, thy excellence and thy courtly speech, thy ways more high-bred than those of
any other lady, and thy graceful ladylike disdain, whereby every low-born desire and action
seemeth base to thee—such art thou to me, O sovereign lady mine—have enthroned thee
in my mind with love" (4.164–65; Griffin and Myrick, p. 367).

plying David's treatise to Chaucer's poem, our fifteenth-century reader allows us to recognise this fact of literary history. He also defines, by the very literariness of his reading, an important principle of Chaucerian interpretation. He proceeds, as we have seen, not by allegorical exegesis but by what we might call rhetorical or even topical recognition. The act our reader performs is in essence an exercise in literary identification: he surveys the available topoi and aligns the matching pair. This self-reflexive literariness is both characteristically medieval (the best gloss on a text is always another text) and appreciative in a way that matches our reader's appreciation of more obviously literary values. Moral interpretation, in other words, comes in the form of literary appreciation. There is no sharp distinction between a moral and a rhetorical reading, and if the didactic and the aesthetic responses are simultaneous, they are doubtless felt as synonymous. Horace taught that *utile* and *dulce* should come together, and it seems that for this medieval reader they do. What this also implies for a Chaucerian poetics is that we should perhaps reinstate an approach to his poetry that has recently become unfashionable. This fifteenth-century reader acted on the assumption that Chaucer's thematic imperatives were enacted through choices of and between conventions. His procedure for reading, in other words, argues that the systematic and self-reflexive quality of medieval writing was an assumption shared by poet and reader alike, and that we can define as one of the crucial protocols of Chaucerian reception the awareness that the poem stands within and reflects upon a system of literary conventions and traditions. This suggests, then, that a priority for our own reading should be to prepare an inventory of this system, a lexicon of the topoi available to the poet. As a final implication, we might even be led to argue that late-medieval literary creation operates, deliberately and even enthusiastically, at the level of form, and that the poet understands his immediate task as being to dispose and vary a range of inherited tropes. Chaucerian writing, in other words, is always a rewriting; and so must our reading be a rereading.

My theoretical point is an extension of these practicalities and returns us to our earlier discussion of ambiguity. Ambiguity is usually recognized as a characteristic possessed by the text, an uncertainty of meaning in fact present in discourse itself. But like other kinds of verbal meaning, whether fixed or indeterminate, ambiguity is also a function of reading: a text is ambiguous only to someone. As recent medieval criticism witnesses, there are many readers to whom no poem is ambiguous. Nor are these readers wrong in ascribing the meanings they do to the poems they interpret: indeed, correctness is clearly a misleading criterion to apply to criticism. Disambiguating is always, and properly, a process of deciding not what a text means but what we want it to mean. We do this, basically, by locating the text in an interpretive context, such as an authorial intention or a genre (e.g., Christian instruction, courtly lyric), that organizes meanings into primary and secondary. Put simply, by privileging one context at the expense of others we decide how the text's ironies should be read, whence they derive their authority, and against whom they are directed.[88] One of the great achievements of Augustinian hermeneutics is to make the preemptive nature of interpretation explicit. The Christian reader comes to the text (Scripture) already possessed of its message (the double law of charity), and his task is to understand not its meaning but its way of signifying that meaning.[89] One purpose of this preemptive hermeneutic is to inoculate the reader against the sweetness of the letter by endowing him with the strength of moral interpretation—with, in effect, the spirit. Reading with the *oculus amoris,* he may entertain the solicitations of the text without anxiety. Possessing the authority of the *signifié,* he is able to enjoy the delectation of the *signifiant,* "le plaisir du texte," as Roland Barthes calls it, "la valeur passée au rang somptueux de signifiant."[90]

To imply that Augustine prefigures Barthes is a mischievousness that most medievalists will doubtless be unwilling to tolerate. But the point is not meant frivolously. While a full-scale survey of medieval interpretive strategies is impossible on this occasion, we can at least define one line of development as it unfolds from Augustine to Boccaccio. For Augustine, pagan fable can never be justified by allegorical moralization: "This husk shakes sounding pebbles inside its sweet shell, but it is not food for men but for swine."[91] The severity of Augustine's dismissal was of course qualified throughout the Middle Ages, and Boccaccio's defense of his mythological encyclopedia, the *Genealogia deorum gentilium,* draws in part upon a post-Augustinian tradition of allegorical moralization. But Boccaccio's crucial argument is not that the text can be rendered harmless by interpretation but that the truly pious reader comes to it already

---

88. Of the many recent discussions of the problematics of verbal meaning, perhaps the most relevant to my argument here is that by Stanley Fish, "Normal Circumstances . . . and Other Special Cases," *Critical Inquiry* 4 (1977–78), 625–44.

89. The preemptiveness of Augustine's hermeneutic is best expressed in the following passage from the *De doctrina christiana:* "Whoever, therefore, thinks that he understands the divine Scriptures or any part of them so that it does not build the double love of God and of our neighbor does not understand it at all. Whoever finds a lesson there useful to the building of charity, even though he has not said what the author may be shown to have intended in that place, has not been deceived, nor is he lying in any way" (1.36; trans. D. W. Robertson, Jr. [Indianapolis: Bobbs-Merrill, 1953], p. 30).

90. Roland Barthes, *Le plaisir du texte* (Paris: Editions du Seuil, 1973), p. 103.

91. Augustine, *De doctrina* 3.7; Robertson, p. 85.

immune to its temptations. However seductive its sweet letter or hereti-
cal its alien spirit, the text can be read with impunity by a reader endowed with "a pure and steadfast mind."[92] Hence when Boccaccio turns
to the defense of his personal commitment to the pagan authors, he argues not their virtuousness but his own: "I have armed my breast with
the truth of the Gospel, the holy doctrine of Paul, and with the commands, advice, and admonitions of Augustine and many other very rev-
erend Fathers. Wherefore little have I to fear from the weapons of paganism, . . . for their power is disarmed by many a true reason familiar to
me, and with their force thus spent and routed the fight is easy."[93] Once
the reader has secured himself within the orthodoxy of faith—and Boccaccio carefully and elaborately recites an extensive *credo* (15.9)—then all
literature, regardless of its moral valence, is available to him.

By locating *Troilus and Criseyde* within the context of *amor* and *amicitia*
our fifteenth-century reader provides a stance from which disambiguating can take place. But as his affectionate regard for the poem's texture
shows, the inevitable reductions of interpretation are not for him a primary task. They are instead a potentiality that enables a fully responsive
reading. Medieval discussions of literature habitually draw an analogy
between literary and sexual seduction, and our reader invokes the analogy in his elliptical—and deeply allusive—phrase "sweet poison," which
refers to the double temptation of sweethearts and Muses.[94] Chaucer exploits this analogy throughout his poem, and nowhere more explicitly
than in the description of Troilus' (mis)reading of Criseyde's eyes:

> This Troilus ful ofte hire eyen two
> Gan for to kisse, and seyde, "O eyen clere,
> It weren ye that wroughte me swich wo,
> Ye humble nettes of my lady deere!
> Though ther be mercy writen in youre cheere,
> God woot, the text ful hard is, soth, to fynde!
> How koude ye withouten bond me bynde?"
>
> (3.1352–58)[95]

---

92. Boccaccio, *Genealogia deorum gentilium* 14.18, *Boccaccio on Poetry,* trans. Charles G.
Osgood (Indianapolis: Bobbs-Merrill, 1956), p. 84.
93. Ibid., 15.9; Osgood, pp. 128–29.
94. For the allusions, see the edition above, note to line 6.
95. The seductiveness of *Troilus and Criseyde* is marked at the beginning of the poem
by the narrator's definition of his audience as "loveres," whether already bathing in the
"gladnesse" of their mistress' love or still aspiring to it. There is, apparently, no third
position, and it is within this wholly amorous context that we are asked to place the poem.
This is what the narrator means when he asks us to "herk[en] with a good entencioun"
(1.52). Perhaps the clearest Chaucerian expression of the seductiveness of literature is provided in book 1 of the *House of Fame.* There the narrator's reading of the *Aeneid* in the

As every reader knows, the poem solicits an equally delicate implication, inviting us to participate in its actions and taste its pleasures. Nor does this fifteenth-century reader refuse the invitation, invoking the action throughout and quoting some of the poem's most beautiful verses. That he does so in order to condemn love means not that his response is inconsistent but that his hermeneutic is sophisticated. For (unlike David of Augsburg) he seeks not to disarm the text but to arm the reader, and he accomplishes this by locating the poem in a context that allows its reading to be at once safe and loving.

Temple of Venus is fatally compromised by the urgency of his response to Dido. In falling prey to her attractions the Chaucerian reader reenacts the experience of Virgil's hero, and he too emerges from the experience to find himself, like Aeneas, "in the desert of Lybye" (line 488) and in need of rescue (cf. *Aeneid* 4.257). As in *Troilus and Criseyde,* the relationship between Virgil's lovers figures the relationship between the reader and Virgil's text.

III. MEDIEVAL
HISTORICISM

5. Virgil and the Historical Consciousness of the Twelfth Century: The *Roman d'Eneas* and *Erec et Enide*

"IT WAS not the least splendid achievement of Latin Christendom in the twelfth century to awaken in men's minds an active awareness of human history." Thus Father Chenu, who further argues that the twelfth century was not simply a great age of historiography, but one that saw the recuperation of historicity itself, a *prise de conscience* that, for all its qualifications, stands as a decisive moment in the development of the West.[1] The assertion that this century was (to cite another authority, Georges Duby) "a crucial time for the history of history" has become one of the fixed points in our modern understanding of the past.[2] Twelfth-century historicism marks not only the transition from Marc Bloch's First Feudal Age to the Second; it also stands as a decisive break with the archaic ontology of traditional culture, a break that issues in the "crisis of historicism" that has come to characterize modernity.[3] Whether we choose to ratify

---

1. M.-D. Chenu "Theology and the New Awareness of History," *Nature, Man, and Society in the Twelfth Century,* trans. Jerome Taylor and Lester K. Little (Chicago: University of Chicago Press, 1968), p. 162.

2. Georges Duby, *The Chivalrous Society,* trans. Cynthia Postan (Berkeley: University of California Press, 1977), p. 155.

3. Marc Bloch, *Feudal Society,* trans. L. A. Manyon (Chicago: University of Chicago Press, 1961), pp. 105–6. The central documents of the modern "crisis of historicism" are

or dispute this historiographical scheme it remains inescapable, a structure of understanding that is itself a key constitutive element of the very modernity it seeks to explain. Yet the relentless progressivism of this interpretation, its commitment to an undeviating linearity, invites reconsideration. As we know, history rarely proceeds in a straight line, and here as elsewhere the historian is confronted with processes that are as wayward in their individual movements as they are determinative in their overall effect. By focusing on one small instance, I want here to trace some paths in the waywardness of the European historical consciousness, the fitfulness of its workings, and the complexity of its articulation.

My exhibits are two twelfth-century narratives in French verse, the anonymous *Roman d'Eneas* and the first of the romances written by Chrétien de Troyes, *Erec et Enide*. These texts are linked by chronology and provenance: the *Eneas* was almost certainly written shortly after the coronation of England's Henry II in 1154 and within the context of royal legitimization, while *Erec et Enide* includes what seem to be allusions to the *Eneas* and has itself important thematic affiliations with Angevin ambitions.[4] Both these texts stand as well near the beginnings of vernacular literature itself, at an originary moment that blurs our modern distinction between history and fiction; both, moreover, celebrate secular values that stand over against the pervasive spiritualism of most contemporary Latin narratives. They serve, in other words, as initiatory agents in the process by which medieval writing was gradually laicized, a process in the service of an ideology that sought to reestablish the historical world as itself a locus of value.[5] Equally committed, then, to the recuperation of historicity as both present worldliness and past greatness, these two

---

Friedrich Nietzsche's *Vom Nutzen und Nachteil der Historie für das Leben* (1874) and Ernst Troeltsche's *Der Historismus und seine Probleme* (1922).

4. The Angevin provenance of the *Eneas* has been persuasively argued by Giovanna Angeli, *L'"Eneas" e i primi romanzi volgari* (Milan: Riccardo Ricciardi, 1971); for Chrétien's connection with Angevin ambitions, see in general Erich Köhler, *Ideal und Wirklichkeit in der höfischen Epik* (Tübingen: M. Niemeyer, 1956); and for specific indications, Beate Schmolke-Hasselmann, "Henry II Plantagenêt, roi d'Angleterre, et la genèse d'*Erec et Enide*," *Cahiers de civilisation médiévale* 24 (1981), 241–46 (who dates the poem c. 1169); and Constance Bullock-Davies, "Chrétien de Troyes and England," in Richard Barber, ed., *Arthurian Literature* 1 (1981), 1–61. The indebtedness of *Erec et Enide* to the *Eneas* has been argued by Angeli, pp. 178–86; Raymond J. Cormier, "Remarques sur le *Roman d'Eneas* et l'*Erec et Enide* de Chrétien de Troyes," *Revue des langues romanes* 82 (1976), 85–97; and Joseph S. Wittig, "The Aeneas-Dido Allusion in Chrétien's *Erec et Enide*," *Comparative Literature* 22 (1970), 237–53.

5. See the comment on the *romans d'antiquité* in general and Alberic's *Roman d'Alexandre* in particular made by Guy Raynaud de Lage in "Les romans antiques et la représentation de l'antiquité," *Le moyen âge* 67 (1961): "la place faite à l'inspiration 'antique,' quoi qu'il en soit de cette 'Antiquité,' a determiné ou favorisé la laïcisation de la littérature; c'est le roman qui a contribué à 'désacraliser' la chanson de geste" (pp. 250–51).

works are further and most profoundly linked by their shared, if divergent, reliance upon a common ancestor, Virgil's *Aeneid*. Themselves quasi-historical narratives aligned with secularity and even imperialism, both the *Eneas* and *Erec et Enide* seek to institute their values through the recovery of an antique text that itself confronts the dilemmas of the historical consciousness. If in both cases the recovery is inescapably partial, this should be understood as a function neither of ignorance nor of ineptitude but of the protocols and imperatives of the poem's cultural moment, and specifically, as we shall see, of their concern to establish a realm of privatized and subjective value. Moreover, while both poems deliberately evade the full challenge of Virgilian historiography, they nonetheless also articulate in their separate ways elements of Virgil's text that the confidently historicized readings of post-Renaissance criticism have continually slighted. The past they recover, in other words, and by means of which they define their own present values, may be sharply different from that now taken as authentic by modern historicism, but it has a nonetheless inescapable perspicuity and persuasiveness.

The problematic that governs the reception of the *Aeneid* conditions as well, as I shall argue in the next chapter, the nature of the central documents of the legendary historiography by which the Middle Ages imagined its origins. It is a problematic that is at the heart of the historical consciousness per se, and so necessarily finds an articulation within the *Aeneid* itself. When Aeneas enters Dido's palace in book 1, he discovers among her queenly possessions golden plates "engraved with the heroic deeds of the Carthaginian forefathers, a long lineage of glory traced through many heroes right from its earliest source" (1.641–42).[6] It is just such a *series longissima rerum* that Virgil's poem seeks to provide for Rome, a historical plot capable of joining past and future into a seamless linearity, a continuous and purposive narrative that will issue in the *imperium sine fine* of Rome. For such a project to succeed, however, the discontinuities and disasters that mark that past must be annulled through the intervention of an extrahistorical source of legitimization. Just such a source is thus invoked at the outset of the poem in the Jovian *sententia* that makes manifest the decrees of *fatum* (1.257–96), a transcendent assertion that the origin of Rome is not derived from within the historical world but has instead a divine source that accords with the eternality of the Roman Empire itself. Yet, despite this assurance, much of the greatness of Virgilian poetry derives from its refusal to evade a

---

6. *The Aeneid of Virgil,* ed. R. D. Williams, 2 vols. (London: Macmillan, 1972–73): "series longissima rerum / per tot ducta viros antiqua ab origine gentis." For my translations I have largely relied upon Allen Mandelbaum (Berkeley: University of California Press, 1971) and upon Williams' notes, but I have upon occasion offered my own rendering.

confrontation with the body of history itself. Indeed, that the project is first imaged in the form not of Roman history itself but of the history of the Roman nemesis Carthage suggests at the outset something of the instabilities that are involved, and Virgil's poem as a whole witnesses to a persistent ambivalence that also comes to define, with surprising aptness, the terms by which his twelfth-century inheritors enacted a similarly indecisive dynamic of historical understanding.

It was, after all, by means of the Virgilian model, transmitted through the topoi of Trojan foundation and *translatio imperii,* that the notion of a secular, purposive, linear historicity was made available to the Middle Ages. To be sure, Virgilianism was never able to achieve an unambiguous authority within medieval thought because it was subject to pressure from a variety of sources, including the Augustinian and Boethian dismissals of historicity *per se,* the tenacious dream of a prophetic *Geschichtestheologie,* and the dubious historiographical status of many of its crucial legitimizing texts (Geoffrey of Monmouth, the Arthurian romances, and the Trojan legendary). But it also contained, as an inheritance from Virgil himself, an inherent instability that rendered its project uncertain. Put simply, the tension that at once animates and inhibits the *Aeneid* is a struggle between, on the one hand, a linear purposiveness that sees the past as a moment of failure to be redeemed by a magnificent future and, on the other, a commemorative idealism that sees it as instead a heroic origin to be emulated, a period of gigantic achievement that a belated future can never hope to replicate. Thus the past is endowed with a double, contradictory value: it is at once a guilty if potent origin to be suppressed and forgotten, and a heroic precedent to be reinvoked and reenacted. And so too the medieval rewriting of Virgil becomes itself—as we shall see—a site of both emulation and exorcism, of slavish imitation coupled with decisive rejection.

I

It is of course true that the premise upon which the *Aeneid* is founded is that the present can serve as the agency by which past and future can be brought together into a coherent linearity. In the narrative it is Aeneas who must perform this act of temporal affiliation: a semidivine, semihuman protagonist, he stoically bears the burden of both past (his father) and future (his shield). Moreover, as Aeneas is in quest of an Italy that is to be his fatherland, and of a promised patrimony or *genus* descended "ab Iove summo" (1.380, 6.123), so Virgil is describing in his poem a past that, when fully discovered, will prove to have been already known. As deeply inscribed with the signs of Augustan times as Aeneas' shield, the

Aeneid offers a representation of the past as present and the present as past, a double perspective that serves not to impeach but to validate its historiography. The more strikingly Aeneas prefigures Augustus, the more authoritive is his story, especially in a historiographical discourse that habitually conflates the authoritative and the authorized.[7] The ties that bind past to present are warrants of legitimacy, validating both the heroic history that is being displayed and the Augustans who are its inheritors, themselves members of a *genus ab Iove summo.* Nowhere is this etiological impulse more profoundly or more serenely at work than in the account of Anchises' funeral games in book 5, an account that rewrites the Homeric original of *Iliad* 23 to match the forms of contemporary festivals, both the athletic contests (re)instituted by Augustus and the commemorative ritual of the Parentalia performed by Romans on the anniversary of a father's death.[8] The games are at once a farewell to the past and a prefiguration of the future: Aeneas divests himself of a Trojan father prior to his entrance into his own Italian paternity, a disavowal that allows Anchises to reappear in the underworld as a guide to the imperial future. Similarly, the labyrinthine *lusus Troiae* performed by Ascanius and his youthful comrades at once commemorates a fallen city, prepares for the *labor et inextricabilis error* of the catabasis of book 6, in particular, and of the devastating Italian war, in general, and yet promises that in the fullness of time the *pax Augusta* will transfigure martial suffering into boyish playfulness. In this book, in sum, both in these details and throughout, the past is a secure foundation upon which the future can be built, a glorious and heroic time that the present simultaneously reconstitutes and passes on.

Yet book 5 is itself a moment out of time, a narrative pause that is the temporal equivalent of its spatial location in the geographically and ideologically marginal Sicily. Similarly unavailing is the poise it achieves between past and future, for in the body of the *Aeneid* their transactions are rarely so benevolent. Indeed, the very project itself is shadowed with an authorial awareness of the poem's ambiguous value to a present it seeks to legitimize but comes to devalue and even indict. As a representation of a heroic past of mythological scope, the *Aeneid* is always in danger of dwarfing the very present it hopes to celebrate. This is a threat that the poem itself confronts and reflects upon. Consider, for instance, the scene in book 1 of Aeneas fixed fast in a trancelike gaze upon the

---

7. A suggestive survey of the analogies between the poem and Augustan history is offered by W. A. Camps, *An Introduction to Virgil's Aeneid* (London: Oxford University Press, 1969), pp. 11–20, 95–104, 137–43. The establishment of such analogies has of course been a staple of Virgilian criticism since at least the time of Servius.

8. See Williams' introductory note to book 5 and the notes to 5.42ff. and 5.59–60.

pictured representation of the Trojan War in Dido's Temple of Juno. Battered by disaster, bereft of his father and mocked by his mother, uncertain both of his identity and his future, Aeneas solaces himself with the past greatness inscribed on these walls. But the poem insists that nostalgia, here as elsewhere, offers dangerous solace. Aeneas "feeds his soul upon these empty pictures" (1.464), forgetting that they are a commemorative sign of Juno's triumph over Troy and hence evidence of the fact that Carthage is a place not of safety, as he had hoped (1.451, 463), but of danger. The pictures inscribe as well lessons about both the divine superintendence that doomed Troy in order to establish Rome and the relation of a divinely sanctioned *pietas* to the savagery of the successful warrior—lessons that the stupefied Aeneas is here incapable of learning.[9]

Nostalgia for a monumentalized past and the corresponding impotence of a present that feels itself hopelessly belated mark the poem throughout. Books 2 and 3 record the powerful lure of a past, both historical (for Aeneas) and literary (for Virgil), that must be subject to a continual if necessarily incomplete exorcism. In book 2 Aeneas is repeatedly drawn back into a burning Troy that a series of visionary revelations mark as doomed by divine decree. And in book 3 the wandering Trojans are tempted to cut short the "longus cursus" (3.430) of their journey, first at Aenos, then at Pergamum, then at Crete, and finally at Buthrotum, where Trojan survivors have constructed a "parva Troia" (3.349) which, by so pathetically reinvoking the lost original, shows how truly lost it now is. Correspondingly, in book 2 it is an Achillean heroic nihilism that tempts Aeneas and that Virgil embodies in the diminished and finally discredited figure of Pyrrhus, while in book 3 it is the *dirus* and *saevus* Ulysses who stands as the Homeric antitype to Aeneas' Roman heroism. As Aeneas seeks to alienate himself from Troy, in other words, so does Virgil rewrite his Greek pre-texts so as to inscribe a redemptive Roman difference. This is a distancing that continues in book 4, which allows the language and values of Greek tragedy to coalesce about the figure of Dido, a conjunction that solicits a mutual impeachment. But while this process persists throughout the poem, it never achieves a resolution, whether a final exorcism of discredited Homeric values or a fully achieved appropriation of Homeric heroism. On the contrary, the *Aeneid* is a *series* or *narratio* that is shadowed by the specter of repetition. Unable fully to divest themselves of their past, both protagonist and poem plot a narrative course that gradually but unavoidably bends itself into a circle.

---

9. I have discussed this scene in more detail in "'Rapt with Pleasaunce': Vision and Narration in the Epic," *ELH* 48 (1981), 455–75.

This circularity is implicit, if submerged, in the very form of Virgil's narrative. Book 5, we remember, reenacts the funeral games of *Iliad* 23. This is an imitation that reminds us that for Homer a narrative of war issued first in the pause that is here remembered, and then, in the twenty-fourth and final book, in a scene of final reconciliation, Achilles' reconciliation both with the paternal Priam and, more profoundly, with the mortality that is his filial inheritance.[10] But Virgil shapes his narrative to the opposite effect: his book 5 is indeed a pause in the struggle, and it too leads to the reconciliation of book 6, in which the hero confronts and accepts, paradoxically, his own *im*mortality. But what follows is precisely the war that in the *Iliad* had been put behind, and the civilization that Homer allowed to be reaffirmed is now, in Virgil's rewriting, put all the more deeply into question. Nor is this a questioning that Virgil evades or even disguises. The final six books of the *Aeneid* return with progressive insistence to the Homeric prototype, and the assertion of Roman difference—and with it of the linearity of historical development—becomes all the more difficult to sustain. Bound by her implacable hatred of the Trojans to a fixity of purpose that preempts the possibility of change, Juno defines the war she initiates as a recapitulation of the first Trojan War: Aeneas will prove to be an *alter Paris* who will, she hopes, destroy again a "recurrent Troy" or "recidiva Pergama" (7.319–22). Conversely, Venus fears that this "recidiva Pergama" (10.58) will never attain completion, and urges Juno to allow the Trojans at least to return to "soil that once was Troy," if it is to be their fate here in Italy to reenact again ("iterum revolvere") the fall of their city (10.60–62).

That the Trojans are in this instance victorious would seem to be a definitive statement of the power of the present to redeem the past, yet the terms in which victory is represented reinvoke that tenacious past in all its horror. To be sure, the configuration of the final battle conforms to the imperial prescriptions of the Jovian *sententia*. Driven mad by Allecto, Turnus comes to embody the chthonic and savage "furor impius" (1.294) that it is the Roman mission to extirpate. Himself expressing his desire to "rage out [*furere*] this rage [*furorem*] before the end" (12.680), he is not only compared in significant detail with Achilles throughout his *aristeia* but makes the comparison himself (e.g., 9.742). Yet in fact his defeat expresses not a Roman transcendence of the Greek past but rather a recapitulation of its darkest moment, the slaughter of Hector by the implacable Achilles. Turnus may have come to stand for all those forces

---

10. On Priam as a surrogate for Achilles' father Peleus, see *Iliad* 24.507–12. As Thomas M. Greene rightly says in *The Descent from Heaven* (New Haven: Yale University Press, 1963), "The most important recognition scenes in epic are not between two people but between the hero and his mortality" (p. 15).

that must be suppressed if the "dirae portae" of war are to be forever closed (1.293–94),[11] but his slayer becomes possessed by them as well. Compared to Achilles at crucial points throughout the narrative (e.g., 10.270–75), Aeneas then exhibits a truly Achillean savagery when he rejects Turnus' supplication and strikes the final blow while "inflamed with fury and wrath" ("furiis accensus et ira" [12.946]). This complicity is made all the more disturbingly insistent by the occasion that Virgil posits for Aeneas' violence. Swayed for a moment by Turnus' plea, Aeneas hesitates until he catches sight of the "infelix balteus" (12.941–42), the sword-belt of Pallas that gleams on Turnus' shoulder, and then, "fervidus" (12.951), he strikes home. The sword-belt is here described as a "saevi monimenta doloris" (12.945)—a monument to and commemoration of a savage sorrow. The phrase is elliptical, referring in the first instance to the brutality and pain with which Pallas was both killed and avenged—the savagery, that is, of Turnus and Aeneas, the sorrow endured by (among others) Aeneas and Turnus—but invoking as well the mythological "scene of crime" (10.497) with which it is engraved, the murder of the fifty sons of Aegyptus by the fifty daughters of his brother Danaus on their wedding night. It is this hideous crime, a violation of the family bond in virtually all its forms, that serves as bitter commentary on the heroic confrontation of Aeneas and Turnus. Akin in their ferocity as in their intransigence, Turnus and Aeneas are driven by imperatives derived from an inexorable Homeric paternity. In denying mercy to Turnus, Aeneas is motivated by both the memory of Pallas and, more profoundly, by the *saevi monimenta doloris* of Homeric heroism. No less than the sons of Aegyptus and the daughters of Danaus, Turnus and Aeneas are sacrificed to a primitive vengefulness that underwrites the protocols and rituals of civilization with violence.[12]

The regressive pull of a primitive and barbaric past is felt frequently throughout the *Aeneid*. A particularly telling instance, and one that contributes to a thematic pattern repeated throughout the poem, occurs in book 10, when Aeneas "savages" (10.569) the field of battle and is compared to the Titan Briareus, whose hundred hands and fifty mouths and chests prefigure the fifty sons and fifty daughters of the criminal brothers

---

11. Turnus' victimization, and the role of the *Dira* or Fury in his destruction, are discussed by W. R. Johnson, *Darkness Visible: A Study of Vergil's Aeneid* (Berkeley: University of California Press, 1976), pp. 114–34.

12. The orthodox reading of this final scene proceeds by impeaching Turnus' character in order to recuperate Aeneas'; it enters Virgil criticism as early as Servius' commentary, which argues that Aeneas' actions throughout the scene are a perfect demonstration of *pietas*—first he considers Turnus' plea but then rejects it in favor of his obligation to Evander to avenge Pallas. See Williams' note to 12.938–39.

engraved on Pallas' sword-belt (10.565–70). For it is just such a Titan—
in this case, Atlas—who stands as the common ancestor of the Trojans
and the Arcadians, a primitive "unus sanguis" (8.142) that paradoxically
unites the pastoral world with the imperial race that will prove to be its
undoing (8.134–42). For the point is not simply that pastoralism is vulnerable to military violence, as Silvia's stag is vulnerable to the shafts of
the ambitious Ascanius, but that the pastoral world is itself posited upon
just such a primitive and barely suppressed violence. This subversive
foundation is acknowledged in a number of tacit but unmistakable details: the horns ("cornus") of Silvia's stag (7.483, 488) are cognate both
to the curving bow ("curvus cornus" [7.497]) by which it is killed and
the shepherd's horn ("cornus recurvus" [7.513]) that signals the start of
war; when the Trojans arrive, the Arcardians are celebrating the festival
of Hercules, an irreducibly ambiguous figure of semidivine capacities
who is virtually indistinguishable from the "semihomo" Cacus (8.194),
a criminal whom Hercules was able to drag out of his house of darkness
(itself cognate to the Tartarean depths into which Aeneas enters in book
6) only by literally tearing apart the very pastoral landscape he had come
to cleanse; and finally, and most extensively, we are never allowed to
forget that the Saturnian golden age of the Arcadians survives only by
virtue of the harsh Jovian rule of order, a relationship that articulates in
historical form the most profound representation of paternal and filial
violence available to antique narrative and that in this instance prefigures
the ultimate transfer of hegemony from Arcadian pastoralism to Roman
imperium. In sum, at the origin of pastoralism as of imperialism is an
unthinking, chthonic violence that can be displaced but never exorcised.
And Virgilian historiography, it appears, records not the transcendence
of this origin, nor its domestication, but its repeated enactment.

My final instance of the power of the past in the *Aeneid* is the most
important, both for the poem and for the literary history we are here
concerned to trace. For it involves the inflammatory book 4 and its
haunting protagonist, Dido. A brooding presence in this book, as in
book 8, is the Titan Atlas, here placed in telling apposition to his grand-
son Mercury, who flies past him on his way to recommit Aeneas to his
imperial destiny:

> And now in flight, he sights
> the summit and high sides of hardy Atlas
> who props up heaven with his crest—Atlas,
> whose head is crowned with pines and battered by
> the wind and rain and always girdled by
> black clouds; his shoulders' cloak is falling snow;
> above the old man's chin the rivers rush;

his bristling beard is stiff with ice. Here first
Cyllene's god poised on his even wings
and halted; then he hurled himself headlong
and seaward with his body, like a bird
that, over shores and reefs where fishes throng,
swoops low along the surface of the waters.
Not unlike this, Cyllene's god between
the earth and heaven as he flies, cleaving
the sandy shore of Libya from the winds
that sweep from Atlas, father of his mother.

(4.246–58)[13]

As its most recent editor points out, this passage "has come in for harsh criticism from most commentators, mainly on the ground that a poet should know whether he is describing a mountain or a man."[14] But the ambiguity is the point: child of primal earth, Atlas has returned to his origins in a regression that bears witness not just to the failure of his rebellious assault on the Olympians, but more profoundly to the ineluctably material and chthonic forces that threaten to submerge Aeneas, forces against which Mercury has been dispatched—a Mercury who himself here pauses, as if in fascination before that which he so definitively is not, and yet that to which he nonetheless owes his very being.

But the menace of the chthonic is most fully expressed in this book in the form of Dido, herself modeled in part on the cavern goddess Kalypso, in part on such fury-driven women as Medea, Phaedra, Agave, and Clytemnestra.[15] It is of course in a cavern hollowed out of and hallowed by "primal Earth" (4.166) that Dido and Aeneas perform a "mixing" (4.112, 160–61) that would deny to the West its destined *imperium* by drawing the Trojans back into the Eastern world from which they are

---

13.   iamque volans apicem et latera ardua cernit
Atlantis duri caelum qui vertice fulcit,
Atlantis, cinctum adsidue cui nubibus atris
piniferum caput et vento pulsatur et imbri,
nix umeros infusa tegit, tum flumina mento
praecipitant senis, et glacie riget horrida barba.
hic primum paribus nitens Cyllenius alis
constitit; hinc toto praeceps se corpore ad undas
misit avi similis, quae circum litora, circum
piscosos scopulos humilis volat aequora iuxta.
haud aliter terras inter caelumque volabat
litus harenosum ad Libyae, ventosque secabat
materno veniens ab avo Cyllenia proles.
In the text I have used Mandelbaum's excellent translation.
14.   Williams, *Aeneid*, 1.353.
15.   For Kalypso as a cavern goddess, see *Odyssey* 5.55–58.

struggling to emerge. The immediate offspring of this illegitimate conjunction is the monstrous Fama, herself born of Terra and thus sister to the Titans (4.178–79).[16] That the mating is a regressive return to an absorptive origin is suggested as well by the details of the two famous similes that serve simultaneously to exalt and expose the lovers. In book 1 Dido is compared to Diana when, in Bacchic fashion, she leads forth her *chorus* and joy suffuses the breast of her mother, Latona (1.498–502); while in book 4 Aeneas is likened to Apollo when he too visits "maternal Delos, where he renews the dances" among his various ("mixti") band of followers (4.143–49). Both similes focus on moments of glad and even excessive riot set against the harsh and demanding winter that constrains the world of historical action. And both focus on the return to a maternal presence, a common source that taints the sexual conjunction of these Eastern lovers with the illegitimacy of incest.

This sense of the complicity of *infelix Dido* with primitive and chthonic forces is further enforced at crucial moments throughout book 4. Not only is she, in her rage, almost literally possessed by the infernal Furies, but she deliberately commits herself to magic arts derived from the "ultimus locus" of Ethiopia, home of "maximus Atlas" (4.481). Indeed, the very narrative of book 4 itself signals recursiveness: its opening phrase—"At regina"—appears three times (4.1, 296, 504), as if the narrative were three times retracing the same discursive ground, and there are significant thematic parallels among the three parts of the book thus demarcated. In fact, the book ends in a perverse mimicry of its opening event, with the sexual conjunction in the cave being horridly reenacted on the lovers' "customary couch" (4.648): reclining beside Aeneas' possessions and his effigy, Dido stabs herself with her lover's sword and surrenders her body to the flames that have been metaphorically consuming her throughout, thus consigning her soul to its inevitable locale, "sub terras" (4.654).

In this powerfully imagined and enormously influential account, Virgil is at pains to define eroticism not merely as hibernal irresponsibility but more powerfully as a regressive surrender to dark, chthonic forces, a reversionary impulse toward an obscure and unredeemed primitivism.[17] While this turn toward psychic primitivism—here located at the

---

16. There is an important connection between the barbaric cave dweller Polyphemus in *Odyssey* 9—who serves as an occasion for the self-promoting taunts by which Odysseus makes himself both known and vulnerable to Poseidon—and the Fama which arouses the barbaric Iarbas to ask Jupiter for vengeance: Polyphemus' name points to his role in achieving renown for Odysseus (*poly* + *pheme* = many reports) and is cognate to the word (*fama*) by which Dido and Aeneas achieve a similar notoriety.

17. The *fortuna* of Dido in the Middle Ages is long and complex: she manages to

center of sexuality—may be adumbrated and presided over by the female, whether conceived as spousal or maternal, it calls to something
deeply responsive within the male. Aeneas and his Trojan companions
are themselves in quest of what the Apollonian prophecy of book 3 calls
the "antiquam matrem" of Italy (3.96), and Aeneas himself is deeply
marked as both subject to and invested with chthonic powers. The famous simile in book 4, comparing the steadfast Aeneas resisting Dido's
imprecations to an oak tree withstanding Alpine blasts, insists that lofty
eminence is a function of infernal depths: "as steeply as it thrusts its
crown into the upper air, so deep the roots it reaches down to Tartarus"
(4.445–46). Analogously, it is in order to affirm his divinely authorized
election that he descends, in book 6, into "dark Tartarus" (6.134–35).
Thus, when Dido accuses Aeneas of a chthonic or savage birth—"the
bristling Caucasus was father to you on his harsh crags; Hyrcanian ti-
gresses gave you their teats" (4.366–67)—she is in an important sense
correct. Her accusation reveals both the deep kinship between her lover
and herself and, more profoundly, her own fate as the stigmatized other
in the thematic economy of imperial historiography. She must be ban-
ished from Virgil's narrative because she too closely expresses those aspects of the hero's own personality that are discontinuous with the ideology of his mission.[18] In bespeaking values that both the poem and its
protagonist seek to impeach, but of which they cannot wholly divest
themselves, Dido thus functions as the female counterpart to Turnus. If
Turnus represents a lawless vengefulness and militarism that Aeneas simultaneously assumes and suppresses, Dido speaks to an instinctual and
primitive energy that is implicit in the very fabric of the heroic personality and that declares itself explicitly in the erotic transactions of
book 4.

   While seeking to provide its Augustan audience with an undeviating
and rectilinear myth of origin, then, Virgil's poem in fact finds itself
engaged in a profound meditation on the complex negotiations and sub-
versions that define the relation of the present to its imagined past. As
even this briefest of surveys suggests, the etiological project that is the
Aeneid discovers the past to be more threatening than supportive, more

---

encapsulate in one figure a very wide range of masculine attitudes toward the feminine,
including fascination (Dido as sexual object), guilt (Dido as victim), and admiration (Dido
as chaste heroine). The topic has not yet received its full treatment but for a useful preliminary account, see John Fyler, *Chaucer and Ovid* (New Haven: Yale University Press, 1979),
p. 34; see also Mary Louise Lord, "Dido as an Example of Chastity: The Influence of
Example Literature," *Harvard Library Bulletin* 17 (1969), 22–44, 216–32.

   18. The parallels between Dido and Aeneas are extensive, including their shared fate
as refugees from Asia Minor and their mutual commitment to erecting an imperial city that
will dominate the surrounding hinterland.

destabilizing than legitimizing. What was thought to be a narrative line of straightforward rectitude is revealed to harbor recursions and regressions that impeach the very idea of progress. The menace that the past poses for the present is articulated in the poem in two disparate and even contradictory forms. One is the power of a monumentalized past to unman the very present to which it is in service, a power that accrues both to the Homeric original in relation to its Virgilian imitation and to Virgil's own antiquarian representation of the empire's mythic past in relation to its Roman present. At a crucial moment in the poem Virgil gives expression to his own double implication in this process, as both victim and victimizer. Book 6 opens with an ecphrasis of the scenes carved by Daedalus on the gates of the temple of Apollo. Daedalus records the narrative of the Cretan labyrinth, from the death of Minos' son Androgeos with which it begins to the death of his own son Icarus with which it concludes. Yet Icarus himself remains unrepresented: "And Icarus, you also would have played a great part in such work, had his grief allowed; twice he had tried to represent your fall in gold, twice his father's hands dropped" (6.31–33).[19] Icarus is that too-familiar Virgilian figure, the son destroyed in the attempt to surpass his father, and he adumbrates here the doomed youths who people the *Aeneid*—Marcellus, Euryalus, Pallas, Camilla, and all the nameless others. Present here in his absence, Icarus serves to express the guilt of the scene of writing itself, a filial victim who cannot be inscribed by the grief-stricken paternal hand.

The other danger posed by the past is its harboring of a primitive energy that simultaneously empowers and possesses. Whether turning back to the savage heroism of Turnus or to the absorbing sexuality of Dido, Aeneas enacts a regressive movement that impeaches the very progressivism that the *Aeneid* seeks to celebrate. At the very heart of this great narrative in praise of the linearity of history resides the specter of repetition. The *Aeneid* provided the West with a definitive statement of history as progress, as a one-way development that emerges from the darkness and disaster of the East and issues in the edification and enlightenment of the West. And despite the overwhelming challenge that Augustinian spiritualism offered to this vision, both in the early Christian era and throughout the Middle Ages, it was never ultimately effaced.[20]

---

19. Partem opere in tanto, sineret dolor, Icare, haberes.
   bis conatus est casus effingere in auro,
   bis patriae cecidere manus. (6.31–33)

20. This complicated process, barely touched on here, is given more detailed treatment by Charles Norris Cochrane, *Christianity and Classical Culture* (Oxford: Clarendon Press, 1940), and R. A. Markus, *Saeculum: History and Society in the Theology of St. Augustine* (Cambridge: Cambridge University Press, 1970). See also Chapter 6, below.

From the twelfth century onward, indeed, it served as a central paradigm
for all who would protect secular history from apocalyptic judgment.
Hence the obsession with Trojan origins, from Geoffrey of Monmouth
on; hence Dante's recovery and respeaking of the Virgilian text in his
own complex replotting of the historical narrative.[21] Yet this effort had
to reckon with Virgil's own crucial ambivalence toward the very possibility of historical development, of the *translatio imperii* of which he was
simultaneously prophet and judge. The abiding interest of the *Roman
d'Eneas* and *Erec et Enide* is that they compute, with astonishing perspicuity, precisely this reckoning.

2

In the *Roman d'Eneas* the density of Virgilian style is sharply, almost
painfully, attenuated; as Erich Auerbach has shown, the sublimity of the
Aeneid is here rewritten into the *mediocritas* of a conversational and pleasing style.[22] For Auerbach this decline is the result of a failure of historical
understanding, an inability to conceive of the individual as a historical
being whose significance derives not from his relation to a timeless world
of spiritual values but instead from his place within an unfolding historical continuum that has its own legitimacy. This slighting of the historical also issues, for Auerbach, in an inattention to the tensions and contradictions that render history tragically in need of the redemption it
simultaneously solicits and defers—a dynamic he sees as the prerequisite
for sublimity.[23] At the level of style, the degree to which the *Eneas* falls
short of a full recuperation of historicity can be measured by noting the

---

21. Of course, the Trojan origin of the Western nations had been asserted before Geoffrey (by Nennius for England, for instance, and "Fredegar" for France), but it was Geoffrey's full-scale Virgilian vision of secular history that simultaneously displaced the Augustinian model (defined for England by Bede's *Historia ecclesiastica*) and provided a new,
secular paradigm.

22. Auerbach discusses the *Roman d'Eneas* in *Literary Language and Its Public in Late
Latin Antiquity and in the Middle Ages,* trans. Ralph Manheim (New York: Pantheon, 1965),
pp. 181–233. My discussion of his work draws as well upon the account of the development
of "realistic works of serious style and character"—i.e., of a sublime realism—that he offers
in *Mimesis: The Representation of Reality in Western Literature,* trans. Willard Trask (Princeton:
Princeton University Press, 1953); the citation is from p. 556.

23. Particularly relevant to this understanding of Auerbach is his treatment of Dante,
both in *Mimesis* and in the much earlier, and unfortunately now rarely read, *Dante: Poet of
the Secular World,* trans. Ralph Manheim (Chicago: University of Chicago Press, 1961). For
Auerbach Dante is the first and indeed only vernacular writer who recaptures the classical
sublime while locating it within a Christian context that endows it with a force that sur-
passes anything possible in the classical world. The most recent and detailed reassessment
of Auerbach's criticism is by Paul A. Bové, *Intellectuals in Power: A Genealogy of Critical
Humanism* (New York: Columbia University Press, 1986), pp. 79–208.

thinness of its texture of allusion. Compared with the *Aeneid,* which conducts a polyphonous and multivalent conversation among a variety of subtexts and contexts, the *Eneas* draws upon its classical models for narrative armature or rhetorical ornament, but rarely allows its allusions to articulate a fully historical meaning. A small but telling instance is the use made by the *Eneas* poet of the previously discussed Virgilian similes comparing Dido to Diana (1.498–502) and Aeneas to Apollo (4.143–49), similes that for Virgil express the paradoxical fact that Carthaginian love is simultaneously divinely authorized and dangerously regressive. Moreover, not only do Virgil's similes comment upon the event they describe, they resonate powerfully within the context of their models in the *Odyssey* and the *Argonautica,* an echoic sounding that analogizes the regressiveness they describe (Diana and Apollo returning to maternal Greece) to the allusive strategy they bespeak (Virgil returning to his Greek originals).[24] In the *Eneas* the similes are remembered together, as the lovers-to-be prepare for hunting, a sign that the *Eneas* poet recognized their mutuality. But they are reproduced in a sadly diminished form: Eneas sees Dido and "she seems to him like Diana herself, a most beautiful huntress, who in everything resembles indeed a goddess" (lines 1486–88: "ce li fu vis que fust Dïene: / molt i ot bele veneresse, / del tot resenblot bien deesse"), while Eneas "seemed not at all ignoble; it would have seemed to you as if he were Phoebus" (lines 1498–99: "ne sanbloit pas de rien vilain; / ce vos sanblast que fust Febus").[25] Compared with the richness of detail and complexity of reference of the original, these allusions provide little more than a perfunctory, hyperbolic ornament. For not only does the *Eneas* poet eschew the rich interpretive possibilities Virgil exploits, but his indifference discourages a recourse to the Virgilian original. Far from being inscribed within his text, the original stands behind and apart; rather than a living presence, it is at best an alienated and shadowy memory.

This process of diminishing and so suppressing an apparently too-powerful past is the central strategy that governs the whole of the *Eneas,* both in the story it tells and in its way of telling. To remain for the moment at the level of poetic procedure, the suppressive impulse also governs the larger mythographic allusions that the poet permits himself.

---

24. For the scholarly controversy about the relation of the Diana simile to its Homeric original, see Viktor Pöschl, *The Art of Vergil,* trans. Gerda Seligson (Ann Arbor: University of Michigan Press, 1962), pp. 60–65.

25. *Eneas: Roman de XIIe siècle,* ed. J.-J. Salverda de Grave, 2 vols., Les classiques français du moyen âge, 44, 62 (Paris: H. Champion, 1925–29); all translations are by John A. Yunck, *Eneas: A Twelfth-Century French Romance* (New York: Columbia University Press, 1974).

While he largely eliminates the divine machinery of the *Aeneid* in order both to legitimize his narrative as *historia* and to exculpate Eneas from the charge of being the agent of forces that some would designate as demonic, he does introduce into his account two extended mythographic digressions, the Judgment of Paris (lines 99–130) and the adultery of Mars and Venus (lines 4353–74). Both these Ovidian cameos are, as the poet takes pains to point out, digressions from the narrative rather than integral parts of the *histoire* that is being recounted. In both cases the poet pauses, and in virtually identical words draws attention to the pause: "I wish to recount very briefly the cause of this judgment" (lines 99–100: "L'acheison de cel jugemant / voil reconter asez briemant"); "I wish to explain very briefly the occasion for this hatred between Venus and Vulcan" (lines 4353–54: "l'acheïson de cel maltalant / voil demostrer asez briemant").[26] Yet despite the rhetoric of causality, these episodes are in fact related to the narrative analogically: they are metaphoric illustrations—thematic exemplifications—rather than historical sources. The theme they serve to exemplify is that illicit venerean passion must be set aside in favor of the virile and authentic love fostered by Cupid and enacted by Eneas and Lavine.[27] Indeed, this moralistic point is enforced later in the poem by two other, largely implicit, Ovidian allusions: Lavine's first sight of Eneas (lines 8047–72) recalls Scylla's sight of Minos in *Metamorphoses* 8, while her halting and broken pronunciation of her lover's name to her mother—"En-e-as" (lines 8537–64)—invokes Myrrha's similar hesitation in revealing her guilty love for her father, Biblis, in *Metamorphoses* 9.[28] In both cases the Ovidian subtext function as a thematic antitype for the love of Lavine and Eneas: as with the French poem's celebrated love casuistry, Ovid has provided a form that is here refilled with a new, and redeemed, content. In all four of these cases, then, Ovidian poetry provides exemplary instances that serve to articulate the poem's moral concerns, allusions that are relevant at the level of theme. But at the level of narrative causality these allusions have, despite appearances, virtually no relevance. We are told that the wrath of Juno and Pallas at the Judgment of Paris was the only cause for the fall of Troy, but far from locating this presumably crucial fact within his unfolding

---

26. The OF *acheison/achoison* can mean either "occasion" or "cause"; hence Yunck's varying translation, just as ModE "occasion" can mean "cause" ("I have given you no occasion to be angry").

27. For an initially parallel but finally divergent reading of these passages, see Daniel Poirion, "De l'*Enéide* à l'*Eneas:* mythologie et moralisation," *Cahiers de civilisation médiévale* 19 (1976), 213–29.

28. These parallels were first pointed out by Edmond Faral, *Recherches sur les sources latines des contes et romans courtois du moyen âge* (Paris: H. Champion, 1913).

narrative and making it part of the significance of Trojan history, the *Eneas* poet uses it simply to exculpate Eneas from responsibility for the disaster. So too with the adultery of Mars and Venus, which has causal relevance neither to the account of the forging of Eneas' shield nor to the hero's eventual triumph. And so too with the other Ovidian allusions, mythographic moments that are drained of historical significance by their irrelevance to the poem's literal narrative. On the contrary, they are meaningful solely with reference to a timeless world of moral value, a world that stands apart from, and at times even in opposition to, a specifiable and singular historicity.

The poem's lack of interest in historical particularity, its eagerness to move to a level of generalized moral values, is an aspect of its programmatic ambitions. So committed is it to its legitimizing function—to show, that is, how the Roman imperial past is not merely relevant to, but continuous with, the Angevin present—that it deprives the past of its very historicity, of the pastness that endows it with legitimizing value in the first place. This suppression of historicity is most visible in the poem's resolute anachronicity, evident in its refusal to read the *Aeneid* as an Augustan or even national poem, or in its rewriting of the Aeneas-Turnus conflict into the terms of feudal legalism.[29] But it is more powerfully and interestingly at work within the narrative itself, both in its suppression of Eneas' past and in its privileging of continuity through its insistence on lineage. Virgil's Aeneas is a man who must abandon one past in order to assume another: forced to leave behind the Troy that is (so he thinks) his *patria*, he is finally brought to acknowledge that his true home is the Italy from which Dardanus first set forth. If he is to locate himself in a lineage that is not merely national but Olympian, and so lay claim to an inheritance that extends back to the origin of all things and forward to the timelessness of the Roman Empire, Aeneas must divest himself of the merely personal past of Troy. In part, Virgil's poem is committed to measuring the cost of this disavowal, a cost articulated above all in the list of victims who must fall before the ineluctable march of history: Creusa, Anchises, Dido, Palinurus, Misenus, Marcellus, Camilla, and both Pallas and his slayer Turnus. In a sense, the most prominent victim is Aeneas himself. Like the golden bough that signals his election, he is eternal but finally lifeless, and having been reduced to a mere agent of historical process in the course of Anchises' pedagogy in

---

29. A discussion from the point of view of anachronism is offered by Albert Pauphilet, "L'antiquité et Eneas," in *Les legs du moyen âge* (Melun: Librairie d'Argences, 1950), pp. 91–106; the most detailed comparison of the French poem to its Latin original is provided by Raymond Cormier, *One Heart One Mind: The Rebirth of Virgil's Hero in Medieval French Romance* (University, Miss.: Romance Monographs, 1973).

book 6, it is perhaps inevitable that he should emerge from the under-world through the gates of ivory. But as we have seen, Virgil's poem also insists that finally the past can never be divested, that primitive forces draw the hero back into an original matrix, that a scandalous history of brutality and failure cannot be suppressed in favor of an unambiguously legitimizing origin. Hence the return of the repressed in the poem's last six books, as the protagonist repossesses a human identity fashioned from the dubious substance of Iliadic violence. While the negotiations between past and present may be endless, in other words, finality ulti-mately resides in an intransigent past—a recognition that necessarily comes to subvert the entire genealogical project.

The *Eneas* poet, conversely, radically revises the nature of the hero's relationship to the past, a redefinition analogous to his own relationship to Virgil. Here there is no question of a hero torn between a double past, one authentic but embarrassing, the other enabling but fabricated; nor is the past seen as possessing an ineluctable and dangerous power. On the contrary, the Trojan past that plays so large a part in Virgil's poem is in the *Eneas* largely suppressed, and the hero's grief and nostalgia quickly evaporate in the face of his ascending future. It is a future, moreover, conceived in terms above all of lineage—a value that is insisted upon almost obsessively throughout the poem.[30] In the underworld Anchises reveals to Eneas not the future of Rome, as in Virgil, but his *ligniee,* "all those who are to be born of you" (line 2881: "çaus qui a nestre sont de toi"). Furthermore, Eneas' vision of the future has redefined the shape of his personal history into a form that construes the fall of Troy as a merely local setback.[31] When he sees his descendents "tot an ordre" (line 2928), he "was most joyful about his line, which he saw would be so famous that the world would submit to it; it would rule without end. He felt such great joy of it in his heart that he forgot the sorrow of Troy."[32] The crucial point thus becomes his insistence that his line is grounded not in any merely historical past but in a divine origin: he is himself of a "celes-tial ligniee" (line 572; and see line 1286), a phrase that refers not simply

---

30. See, for example, lines 2189, 2813–14, 2817–30, 2879–82, 2928, 2968–90, 3074, 3202–6, 3242, 3298, 3349–50, 3849, 4152, 4160, 4193, 6307–14, 6557, 9343–66, 9394, 10141–56.

31. For a similar statement of how the understanding of the future revalues Eneas' sense of his past, see lines 3105–8.

32.   molt se fait liez de sa ligniee,
      qu'il voit qui tant ert esçauciee
      que li monz ert vers lui aclin;
      il regnera toz tens senz fin.
      Anz an son cuer an a grant joie,
      oblïé a le duel de Troie.   (Lines 2987–92)

to his filial relation to Venus but to the entire context of divine superintendence that marks the Trojans as elect.[33] And by finding its origin in a divinity that stands before and thus outside history, Eneas' lineage will rule "toz tens senz fin" (2990), the phrase which here corresponds to the *imperium sine fine* which in book 1 of the *Aeneid* Jupiter grants to the Roman people.[34] Eneas' *ligniee,* issuing from the gods and continuing in unbroken extension down through the ages, functions as a timeless continuity that binds together history itself. It is, as it were, the structure or form of history, a continuity that organizes the flux of temporality but remains itself unaffected by the disruptions of accident or event.

What is true of this ideal genealogy is true as well of Trojan history itself, which, when seen aright, articulates a corresponding linearity. The Trojan messenger Ilioneus explains to Latinus that in settling in Italy the Trojans are returning "here where our race had its beginning" (line 3206: "ça dont nostre linnages fu"), a claim that Amata seeks to counter with a flat denial: "I will never believe in their lineage" (line 3298: "Ge ne crerrai ja lor ligniee").[35] But events prove the Trojans right, and before the final battle Eneas, in a passage that has no Virgilian counterpart, proclaims in confident and unambiguous tones the genealogically uninterrupted, if geographically errant, line of Trojan descent:

"My lords," he said, "I wish to explain my right to you, so that you do not accuse me of wishing to conquer, out of pride, another domain or another land by force. My ancestor, who was called Dardanus, was born here [in Italy]. He left this land and established himself in ours [at Troy], where he was a very strong man, and conquered much. From his lineage issued Tros, who founded Troy and its fortress, and who gave it his name; my father was of his lineage. Troy lasted long, with great power, until the Greeks conquered her. The gods took me from there and sent me here to this country where my ancestor was born. They have granted me all Italy, which is at it were my grandmother and great-grandmother."[36]

---

33. For further instances of the divine origin of Eneas' lineage, see lines 1797, 2275–78, 3184–3206, 3242, 3337–50, 6553–58.

34. *Aeneid,* 1.279; Jupiter's grant is to the *gens* that Romulus will call "Romans."

35. For Ilioneus' speech the *Eneas* poet follows the *Aeneid* closely (7.212–48), but Virgil has the Fury-maddened Amata triumphantly proclaim not the fraudulence of Trojan genealogy but rather Turnus' Greek origins, a claim that—together with a reminder of Paris' abduction of Helen—raises the characteristically Virgilian specter of repetition (7.359–72).

36.   Seignor, mon droit mostrer vos voil
      que nel m'atornoiz a orgoil
      que par force voille conquerre
      autrui enor ne autrui terre.
      De ci fu mis ancestres nez,
      qui Dardanus fu apelez;

The turn to Italy is thus an unequivocal return to the true origin, and Trojan experience is reduced to an extended deflection from the linearity of historical inevitability, a deflection which is ameliorated and finally redeemed by the rectitude of lineage. In Virgil's poem, as we have seen, the rise of Rome from the ashes of Troy casts an inevitable shadow upon the fact of foundation per se, while the myth of Dardanus and the Delphic oracle's designation of Italy as the Trojan's *antiquam matrem* serves less to resolve the issue than to complicate it. In the French poem there is no such complication: Troy is no longer a city that stands as the first human foundation—the very basis of secular history itself—but merely one event in the protagonist's biography. And even the threatening maternal source is here disarmed by being projected into a now enfeebled past.

Hence the fact of Trojan failure is introduced into the poem in its most insistent form by the hero's detractors, who see it not as a historiographical question but as a challenge to Eneas' ethical fitness as founding father. Turnus, for example, sees Troy's fall as disqualifying Eneas as both an Italian and a warrior: he designates the Trojans "a conquered and fugitive people" (lines 3468–69: "tel gent, / qui sont veincu et *recreant*"), and sneeringly suggests that "since they were conquered once, it is only right that they remain at peace" (lines 3471–72: "puis que conquis sont une foiz, / si se reposent, ce est droit"). Similarly, it is the rejected Dido who first refers to Eneas' role in the fall of Troy: "Trojans keep bad faith," she says (line 1700: "Malvese foi ont Troïan!"), a charge that in Virgil derives from Laomedon's faithlessness in his contract with the gods who helped raise the walls of his city, but that here almost certainly refers to the supposed role of Eneas in the betrayal of the city—a late addition to Virgil's myth.[37] Amata repeats the same charge—Eneas is

---

de ceste terre s'an ala,
en la nostre s'edefia.
Molt fu forz hom et molt vesqui.
De son linage Tros issi,
qui fonda Troie et le donjon,
et qui li anposa son nom;
mes peres fu de son linage.
Molt dura Troie an grant barnage,
desi que li Greu la conquistrent.
Li damedeu d'iluec me pristrent,
ça m'envoierent el païs
dunt mes ancestres fu naïs;
otroiee m'ont tote Itaire,
qui fu mon aire et mon besaire.   (Lines 9347–66)

37. The corresponding comment in the *Aeneid* occurs later in the action, when Dido refers to the *periuria gentis Laomedonteae* (4.542). See also, however, Dido's repeated epithet

"one who stole forth from his city out of cowardice when it was captured" (lines 3365–66: "qui s'en enbla par coardise / de la cité, quant al fu prise")—and so does Pallas' mother, in a lament over her son's body (lines 6319–33). Moreover, the charge is given credence by Eneas himself in his visit to the underworld: in Virgil he engages in a passionate dialogue with the shade of his dead comrade Deiphobus (6.494–534), himself a victim of Helen's treachery; but here he turns away in shame from the shades of his Trojan companions (lines 2663–84). The Trojan failure, in sum, is relevant not to the historical vision that subtends the foundation of Rome, but rather to Eneas' suitability as protagonist. Whatever questions it raises need not vex the total historiographical scheme but can be answered by demonstrating Eneas' courage and fidelity. The complexities of Virgil's historical vision are thus redefined as complexities in the ethical life of the hero. This is a redefinition, be it noted, that is also a diminution: the broad patterns of the historical life are reduced and internalized into the individual life of Eneas, and what needs to be renewed is not the historical world per se but merely this specific hero.

This privatizing of historical value is accomplished by the *Eneas* poet's boldest act of revision, his grafting of Ovidian eroticism onto the body of Virgilian epic. As criticism has persuasively argued, it is through the love that Eneas comes to share with Lavine that his triumph over Turnus is fully legitimized.[38] For this love not only exculpates Eneas from the charge of Trojan infidelity (and—equally dangerous to the maintenance of lineage—homosexuality), but asserts by metaphoric extension the newness of the Roman foundation, its unprecedented originality. By focusing our attention upon the birth of the innocent Lavine's love and its subsequent effect upon the apparently more worldly Eneas, the poet establishes an analogy between the creation of a mutual love and the founding of an empire based upon that love. This analogy is strengthened by the poet's telling strategy of using Ovid's trope of coercive love as the psychological equivalent of the imperatives of Virgil's historical destiny. The demands of Virgilian *fatum,* in short, are here translated into the constraints of Ovidian *amor.* Indeed, Lavine herself recognizes that her love is the product of a divine intervention comparable to the providential guidance that has brought Eneas to Italy:

Is it not Cupid, the brother of Eneas and the god of love, who has conquered me? He has inflamed me much for his brother. What defense have I against

---

for Aeneas, *perfidus* (as in, e.g., 4.421). Aeneas' responsibility, with Antenor, for the fall of Troy was introduced into the myth by Dares: *The Trojan War,* trans. R. M. Frazer, Jr. (Bloomington: Indiana University Press, 1966), pp. 164–66.

38. See Cormier, *One Heart One Mind* and, especially, Alfred Adler, "Eneas and Lavine: *Puer et Puella Senes,*" *Romanische Froschungen* 71 (1959), 73–91.

Love? Neither castle nor tower avails at all against him, nor high wall, nor deep moat. There is no stronghold under the heavens that can hold against him or endure boldly his assault. . . . Love, I am in your power: you have placed me under your rule.[39]

These martial and political metaphors serve to express not merely the familiar dictum *amor est militia,* but a more profound bond between the inner world of erotic experience and the historical world of martial deeds. Similarly, the Virgilian pattern of joy after woe, of suffering that gives way to a hard-earned celebration—"forsan et haec olim meminisse iuvabit" (1.203), in Virgil's famous phrase—is here shifted from a historical and literal mode into the inner world of eroticism. Amata assures Lavine that if love is at first "fierce and bitter" (line 8004: "fier et amer") it will shortly yield "grant dolçor" (line 8005). When Lavine falls in love she consoles herself with the thought that "I will have no mortal sorrow which will not later be repaid by goodness and sweetness" (lines 8323– 25: "n'en ai eü dolor mortal, / ne me rende tot par igal / le bien aprés et la dolçor"). Finally, in his battle with Turnus, Eneas is inspired not by Virgilian *furor* but by Ovidian *amor:*

Love has given me four hands. Love makes a man very bold; Love inflames him most quickly. Love, you grant many feats of bravery! Love, you increase men's courage much! Love, you are very firm and strong! Love, you are of very great power![40]

---

39. —Nenil, par foi n'est mie gas;
　　　n'est Cupido frere Eneas,
　　　li deus d'amor qui m'a conquise?
　　　Vers son frere m'a molt esprise.
　　　Quel deffanse ai ancontre amor?
　　　N'i valt noiant chastel ne tor,
　　　ne halt paliz ne grant fossé;
　　　soz ciel n'a cele fermeté
　　　qui se puisse vers lui tenir,
　　　ne son asalt gramment sofrir;

　　　. . . . .

　　　Amors, ge sui en ta baillie,
　　　an ton demoinne m'as saisie.
　　　Amors, dos or me clain par toi,
　　　Amors, no fere tel desroi!
　　　Amors, soëf un po me moine!　(Lines 8629–38, 8655–59)

40. quatre mains m'a doné Amor.
　　　Amor molt fait ome hardi,
　　　Amors l'a molt tost anaspri.
　　　Amors, molt dones vasalages!
　　　amors, molt faiz croistre corages!
　　　Amors, molt es roides et forz!
　　　Amors, molt es de grant efforz!　(Lines 9060–66)

In refiguring Virgilian historiography as Ovidian erotics, then, the *Eneas* poet collapses the historical and the individual: the foundation of Rome and the establishment of a love affair are not merely simultaneous but synonymous. The effect of this elision is to translate Virgil's tragedy (as Dante, rightly, called it in *Inferno* 20.113) into a romantic comedy, and so to assure the audience that at the heart of empire is a stable marriage and a secure lineage, an origin that is truly original and unencumbered with awkward precedents.

If we relocate the *Eneas* within the context of the Anglo-Norman political and social world from which it almost certainly emerged, its ideological function begins to come clear. For one thing, it expresses a number of values that were central to the entire Norman project: imperial ambition, the cult of the spectacular leader, and the divinely authorized war—these are the values that animated the Norman expansions of the eleventh and twelfth centuries and that also provide the conceptual framework for the *Eneas*.[41] More important, the *Eneas* contributes both to the myth of continuity that the Anglo-Norman ruling class promoted and to the privileging of lineage, and of primogeniture, that was so crucial to the Norman social and economic structure. Anglo-Norman historians typically rewrote the English past so as to inscribe the Normans within it, as if a history that had been in fact marked with violent ruptures—with hegemony passing from Celts to Anglo-Saxons to Normans—could somehow be synthesized into a continuous line.[42] Similarly, as social historians have shown, for Norman and Anglo-Norman noble families lineage was the primary means of defining social legitimacy, and they relied upon primogeniture to ensure that property would not be dispersed in the course of its transmission down the family line.[43]

---

41. Norman values are well discussed by Ralph H. C. Davis, *The Normans and Their Myth* (London: Thames and Hudson, 1976); David C. Douglas, *The Norman Achievement, 1050–1100* (Berkeley: University of California Press, 1969), and *The Norman Fate, 1100–1154* (Berkeley: University of California Press, 1976); and John Le Patourel, *The Norman Empire* (Oxford: Clarendon Press, 1976).

42. The most explicit instances of the historiographical reconciliation of the English and Norman pasts can be found in Geffrey Gaimar's *Estoire des Engleis* (1135–40) and William of Malmesbury's *Gesta Regum* (1125); as Davis says, "The Normans had projected themselves into the past and identified themselves with the pre-Norman history of England. . . . They belonged to England as much as England belonged to them" (*Normans and Their Myth,* p. 131). On Geoffrey of Monmouth's ironic attitude toward the effort to render British history continuous, see Chapter 6, below.

43. The importance of lineage to twelfth-century society, and its connection with a writing of rectitude or linearity, have been powerfully demonstrated by R. Howard Bloch, *Etymologies and Genealogies: A Literary Anthropology of the French Middle Ages* (Chicago: University of Chicago Press, 1983); for an excellent summary of the social history involved, see pp. 64–91. My own thinking on these topics is much indebted to Bloch's ar-

It is just this ideology of continuous lineage—of genealogy—that the *Eneas* presents in an especially unproblematic form.

It is the unproblematic nature of its representation that is most worthy of note; clearly the text functions as a propagandistic resolution of social and political oppositions that were historically far less tractable. Henry II's own inheritance of the throne, after all—if, in fact, "inheritance" is the right word for so aggressive an act of appropriation—was hardly as rectilinear as the model of Roman foundation prescribed; indeed, if William the Conqueror had, like Eneas, been presented with his future lineage stretched out before him he would doubtless have been appalled by the contentious route that his endowment would trace before it was finally seized by Henry. Moreover, Anglo-Norman history was throughout disfigured by internecine and generational violence, a habit initiated by William's own son, Robert Courthose, and notoriously revived in Henry's later years by his son, Henry the Young King. This is not to say that the *Eneas* is simply escapist fiction, for in fact it serves an important ideological purpose. If the assigned date for the poem of 1155–60 be accepted, then it was written during the period when Henry was engaged in a process of pacification that no doubt aspired to (even if it could not attain) the success of the *pax Augusta;* indeed, one chronicler gratefully referred to him as *rex pacificus.*[44] Osbert of Clare, Prior of Westminster Abbey, had similarly compared Henry to Maecenas, and with the *Eneas* Henry was thus possessed of a celebratory epic that relentlessly suppressed, as he was himself literally suppressing, the very real disruptions that marked the reality of Anglo-Norman politics and society.[45]

Yet this is a celebration, however strategically motivated, that is achieved only at a cost. The *Eneas* is not, after all, an explicitly Anglo-Norman epic, and the optimism of its vision can be sustained only at a distance, removed in both space and time from the pressing exigencies

guments, and to those of Gabrielle M. Spiegel, "Genealogy: Form and Function in Medieval Historical Narrative," *History and Theory* 22 (1983), 43–53. For a fine discussion of lineage and inheritance in Anglo-Norman romance, see Susan Crane, *Insular Romance: Politics, Faith, and Culture in Anglo-Norman and Middle English Literature* (Berkeley: University of California Press, 1986), pp. 13–91.

44. W. L. Warren, *Henry II* (Berkeley: University of California Press, 1973), p. 63, citing the *Chronicon Monasterii de Bello.*

45. For Osbert's comparison of Henry to Maecenas, see Walter F. Schirmer and Ulrich Broich, *Studien zum literarischen Patronat im England des 12. Jahrhunderts* (Cologne: Westdeutscher Verlag, 1962), p. 42. In about 1180 Jean de Marmoutier would write a royal biography of Henry's father, Geoffrey of Anjou, inspired, according to Georges Duby, by Virgil: "it consisted of two parts, war and peace, *parcere subjectos, debellare superbos*" (*The Three Orders: Feudal Society Imagined,* trans. Arthur Goldhammer [Chicago: University of Chicago Press, 1980], p. 280).

of contemporary history. It is an optimism, indeed, that is in a certain sense enabled by a denial of historicity per se. To assert the possibility of a lineage *senz fin* is to assert, illogically, the possibility of a historical process that somehow transcends the temporality that defines history; to interiorize the forces that shape history is to domesticate the otherness of the historical world, its brutal facticity and intractable strangeness; and to posit a wholly unprecedented secular foundation that draws its legitimacy from a divine origin is, in effect, to theologize history itself. Furthermore, just as Eneas, possessed of his *celestial ligniee,* suppresses the discontinuities and errancies of his past, so too does the poet perform a homogenization of his own literary inheritance. Committed above all else to linearity, the poet accommodates even the errancy of Ovidian eroticism: while the past, whether literary or political, may harbor dangerous antagonisms and disquieting contradictions, the poem bespeaks a will to consistency that disarms all threats. In sum, just as Eneas the protagonist is divested of the tragic history (whether past or future) that burdens Aeneas, so the *Eneas* as a poem reduces the complexities of the *Aeneid* to manageable proportions.

Yet to characterize the *Eneas* as a mere simplification and diminution of the *Aeneid* would be to misrepresent it. For one thing, for all its commitment to the triumph of a historiography of continuity, and despite its claims that world-historical processes are fulfilled in concert with the movements of individual self-fulfillment, the *Eneas* is not immune to a counterawareness (expressed as well by the *Aeneid*) of the human cost of the historical life. This awareness is most visibly present in the poet's deployment of the topos of the marvellous. The salient examples are the gifts given to Dido by Aeneas (gifts that were originally given to Hecuba by Priam); Silvia's stag, with its branching antlers that serve as candelabra; Camilla, her steed, her cloak, her companions, and finally her tomb; and the tomb of Pallas. These marvels represent something of the otherness of the past, a grandeur and intricacy now lost beyond recovery. Hence the marvellous is conjoined throughout the poem to the mortal and the transitory, being represented either as a vulnerability that cannot withstand the march of historical inevitability (Silvia's stag, Camilla) or as a commemoration of something lost forever (Priam's gifts to Hecuba, the tombs of Pallas and Camilla). The figure of Dido also functions in something of the same way. While, as I shall later argue, she serves primarily as a foil to Lavine's redemptive eroticism, the poet cannot wholly withhold his sympathy from her. In the *Aeneid* her death, like her life, is located within the total historical vision of the poem, and thus it is she who, in the end, is made to invoke the avenger to come, a figure whom all Romans would have recognized as Hannibal (4.622–29). But in the

Eneas, in keeping with the privatization that governs the poem as a whole, this historical prophecy is suppressed, and Dido dies uttering a statement of forgiveness for Eneas. The total effect is one of pathos and victimization, an effect powerfully registered in the description of the funeral pyre, a pagan ritual foreign to the medieval Christian poet:

Dido is stricken to her death. Death presses hard upon her and torments her, and from one side the flame approaches, and engulfs and burns her whole body. She can speak neither loud nor soft, except when she whispers the name of Eneas. The flame has come so near her that her soul is separated from her body. She cannot protect her white and beautiful and tender flesh from the fire. She flames and burns and turns black, and in a very little time she is consumed.[46]

By focusing on the flesh that is given to the fire, the poet makes us feel that the justice enacted here is undermined by the horror of its enactment. For a moment, the poem pauses in its relentless progress: pathos overwhelms the narrative, and we attend to a single, unredeemed death and to the destruction of a body that will never be resurrected.

However gratifying to our modern sensibilities may be these signs of a complexity that is, at least in part, commensurate to an authentic Virgilianism, ultimately of far greater significance is the role played by the *Roman d'Eneas* in the formation of vernacular narrative literature. For not only did this poem serve as one of the preeminent means by which the achievements of the classical epic were transmitted to medieval French literature, but it mediated that achievement in a form that made it truly available to poets who lacked the kind of coherent literary tradition that empowered Virgil.[47] Ironically, the great service which the *Eneas* per-

---

46. Dido s'estoit a mort ferue,
   la mort l'apresse et argüe,
   et la flame de l'autre part,
   qui tot son cors esprant et art;
   ne puet parler ne halt ne bas,
   fors tant qu'ele nome Eneas.
   La flame l'a tant apressee
   l'arme li est del cors sevree,
   sa blanche char et bele et tendre
   contre lo feu ne puet deffandre;
   ele art et brulle et nercist,
   en molt po d'ore se desfist.   (Lines 2113–24)

47. Of the four *romans d'antiquité,* only the *Roman d'Eneas* and the *Roman de Thebes* rewrite classical pre-texts (the *Aeneid* and the *Thebaid*). Of these two, it is the *Eneas* that has had the far greater influence, as Angeli and others have shown. The reason is doubtless the political importance of the Trojan myth, although the fact that the *Eneas* is most interested in an authentic representation of antiquity, as Raynaud de Lage argues ("Romans antiques et la représentation de l'antiquité"), is probably a contributing factor. These texts achieved their greatest impact when they were prosed and included in the universal histories

formed for Virgil was to diminish and simplify his poem so it could be appropriated by a less richly endowed literary culture. In its resolute interiorization of the dynamic of Virgilian historiography, the *Eneas* foregrounds the individual, who will prove to be the focus of the romance genre that it serves, in large part, to inaugurate.[48] Moreover, while the *Eneas* largely elides the Virgilian opposition between the individual and his historical world, in later romances these oppositions are reinscribed within a psychologized narrative. Virgilian issues having been introjected into the self by the *Eneas,* as it were, they were now available to be projected back outward by a psychomachiac narrative able to thematize them in medieval terms. The ultimate effect of this process, as we shall now see in the case of Chrétien's *Erec et Enide,* is that the very diminishment which the *Eneas* works upon the *Aeneid* provides subsequent poets with access to the self-contradictory powers and tensions of the original.

3

If, as criticism has traditionally maintained, the central topic of the romances of Chrétien de Troyes is the realm of the self, we must also insist that this selfhood be understood not in terms of an autonomous individualism but rather as a subjectivity that embodies, in a psychologized form, the discontinuities and discordances of its historical world. In the case of *Erec et Enide,* the historical contradiction at issue derives from the opposition inherent in the chivalric ideology between individual prowess and social cohesion. The romance beings with an egregious instance, for the Arthurian hunt for the white stag is a custom that simultaneously constitutes and imperils the court. A ritual instituted by Uther Pendragon and reenacted every spring, the hunt produces a preeminent knight empowered to designate his lady the most beautiful damsel of the court, a designation that inevitably elicits challenges which threaten the social stability that has just been affirmed.[49] And while in

---

that circulated under the name of Orosius; see Paul Meyer, "Les premières compilations françaises d'histoire ancienne," *Romania* 14 (1885), 1–81; and two articles by Jacques Monfrin, "Humanisme et traductions au moyen âge," and "Les traducteurs et leur public en France au moyen âge," both in Anthime Fourrier, ed., *L'humanisme médiévale dans les littératures romanes du XII au XIV siècle* (Paris: C. Klincksieck, 1964), pp. 217–46, 247–62.

48. On this topic, see Robert W. Hanning, *The Individual in Twelfth-Century Romance* (New Haven: Yale University Press, 1977); the twelfth-century concern with individuality has been authoritatively discussed by John M. Benton, "Consciousness of Self and Perceptions of Individuality," in Robert L. Benson and Giles Constable, eds., *Renaissance and Renewal in the Twelfth Century* (Cambridge: Harvard University Press, 1982), pp. 263–95.

49. Erich Köhler, "Le rôle de la 'coutume' dans les romans de Chrétien de Troyes," *Romania* 81 (1960), 386–97.

this case the impasse is circumvented by its displacement into Erec's ac-
quisition of Enide in an analogous, but distant, competition for a sparrowhawk, the displacement in fact serves not to resolve these tensions
but to relocate them in the inner world of the lovers' marriage. It is
within this context, then, that the action of the poem takes place, a locus
temporally designated as the hiatus between their wedding and their coronation as king and queen of their own court, a ceremony that not only
removes them from the Arthurian court but necessarily sets them up as
an alternative. In effect, where the *Eneas* elides the Virgilian conflict
between the demands of the historical world and the desire for self-
fulfillment, *Erec et Enide* opens up a space between wedding and coronation, between their fulfillment as lovers and their assumption of the
burden of the historical world, in which to explore this quintessentially
Virgilian dilemma. Thus, while the interiorization and privatization that
were accomplished in the *Eneas* recur here as well, it is in the service not
of evading the terms of Virgilian historiography but rather of articulating
them, an articulation that takes the form of what will become a familiar
romance debate between *amour* and *chevalerie*.[50]

The analogy to the thematic economy of the *Aeneid* is neither arbitrary nor accidental. On the contrary, Chrétien's poem is itself a meditation on the problematic of *translatio studii,* with the *Aeneid* and the *Eneas*
as its crucial subtexts. Thematically, the poem recounts the transference
of value from an old and deeply flawed social order to a new, redeemed
one, a theme that rewrites the dynamic which the *Aeneid* both narrates
and describes. And it expresses this theme in terms of a protagonist who
is, like Aeneas, tempted by the *recréance* of an unbridled eroticism.[51]
Moreover, its lineage is explicitly hybrid, as the title suggests, yoking the
Celtic Erec to the Virgilian Enide.[52] It is also no coincidence that the
poem's opening premise—the instability of the Arthurian court—is expressed in terms of the killing of a stag, the very event that signals the
collapse into war in both the *Aeneid* and, in an elaborately amplified
form, the *Eneas*. At the poem's climax there are, as we shall see, several
specific and telling allusions that invoke both Virgil's poem and its
French translation.[53] Finally, and most sharply, Chrétien's narrative liter-

---

50. The centrality of the topic to this romance was first pointed out by Douglas Kelly,
"La forme et le sens de la quête dans l'*Erec et Enide* de Chrétien de Troyes," *Romania* 92
(1971), 326–58, although he argues that the romance seeks to demonstrate not the opposition between but compatability of love and chivalry.

51. For these analogies, see discussions by Angeli, *L'"Eneas" e i primi romanzi volgari,*
and Cormier, "Remarques sur le *Roman d'Eneas* et l'*Erec et Enide*."

52. Angeli, *L'"Eneas" e i primi romanzi volgari,* p. 178, plausibly suggests that the name
of Chrétien's heroine—"Enide"—derives from *Aeneid*.

53. Previous discussions of the affiliations among these three texts, in addition to those

alizes the central metaphor by which the twelfth century expressed its complicated historical consciousness—that of the dwarfs of the present astride the giants of the past. I give the metaphor here in the form ascribed to Bernard of Chartres by John of Salisbury:

We are like dwarfs sitting on the shoulders of giants: we can indeed see more and further than they, not because of the sharpness of our vision or the height of our bodies, but because we have been raised up on high and carried aloft by their gigantic size.[54]

Bernard's figure (if it was indeed Bernard's) became well known during the twelfth century and later, in part because of its rich ambiguity.[55] It expresses both humility and pride, submission and ascendency, just as it asserts both the discontinuities of history and its inevitable connectedness, permanence, and change. Further, it incorporates a shrewd judgment on the character of the two periods. The ancients are awesome in their magnitude but impaired by their very giantism: they are titanic overreachers, figures of earth whose size mirrors an overweening and finally hapless ambition. But the moderns are in their turn dwarfs, canny yet parasitic, alert but stunted, and it is typical of their elliptical, even elvish, wit to express itself in such a figure.

Chrétien's literalization of the metaphor in his narrative associates giantism with the chivalric aggressiveness and social instability of the old Arthurian court, while dwarfishness is linked to a set of new or modern values that Erec must learn to adopt. Despite the almost algebraic complexity of the narrative itself, its ethical and thematic center is a relatively straightforward confrontation between a chivalric ideology of knightly self-sufficiency and erotic possessiveness set in opposition to values that privilege self-consciousness, strategic circumspection, and a sense of

cited in n. 4, include W. Ziltener, *Chrétien und die Aeneis* (Graz: H. Böhlaus, 1957), H. C. R. Laurie, *Two Studies in Chrétien de Troyes* (Geneva: Droz, 1972).

54. John of Salisbury, *Metalogicon,* ed. C. C. J. Webb (Oxford: Clarendon Press, 1929): "Dicebat Bernardus Carnotensis nos esse quasi nanos gigantium humeris insidentes, ut possimus plura eis et remotiora videre, non utique proprii visus acumine aut eminentia corporis, sed quia in altum subvehimur et extollimur magnitudine gigantea" (p. 136).

55. Edouard Jeauneau, "'Nani gigantum humeris insidentes': Essai d'interprétation de Bernard de Chartres," *Vivarium* 5 (1967), 79–99. In *The Implications of Literacy* (Princeton: Princeton University Press, 1983), pp. 495–99, Brian Stock presents an interesting passage from Orderic Vitalis that seems to link the metaphor to folk materials, and that would thus provide a precedent for Chrétien's use. On giants and dwarfs in early romance, see Fritz Wohlgemuth, *Riesen und Zwerge in der altfranzösischen erzahlenden Dichtung* (Stuttgart: Druck von A. Bonz'erben, 1906). For a modern rewriting of the metaphor, see Nietzsche's *The Use and Abuse of History,* trans. Adrian Collins (New York: Liberal Arts Press, 1949): "One giant calls to the other across the waste space of time and the high spirit-talk goes on, undisturbed by the wanton noisy dwarfs who creep among them" (p. 66).

limitations. On the one hand stands a masculinity that perceives the female as but one among the many objects that in their richness and multiplicity ratify knightly prowess, while on the other is a feminine subjectivity that insists upon both the mutuality of erotic relations and the need to endow the object world with significance. The first of these attitudes is associated with the Arthurian court, with giantism and, unexpectedly but profoundly, with Lavinia; the second is associated with the new court of Erec and Enide, with dwarfism and, equally surprisingly, with Dido.

There are several giants in the narrative of *Erec et Enide,* but the two that matter for our argument are Yder and Maboagrains. Yder is a knight of apparently normal size who appears in the opening episode and serves to initiate Erec into the world of chivalric aggression, an initiation that results in Erec's coming to take his antagonist's place. While the other Arthurian knights are engaged in the hunt for the stag, Guenevere, her damsel, and Erec are accosted by Yder, his damsel, and a dwarf. When Guenevere sends first the damsel and then Erec to inquire after the identity of this unknown knight, the spiteful dwarf strikes first one and then the other with his whip. Unarmed, Erec can do no more than follow Yder and his company to their own court, and it is there that he engages in the tourney of the sparrowhawk, defeating Yder and replacing him as the knight with the most beautiful lady—in this case, Enide. Yder's giantism, significantly, is present in the narrative only allusively: he is compared to Morholt, the giant slain by Tristan, and his folkloric past also links him with the world of giants.[56] Similarly, it is through the malicious dwarf—"nains enuieus" (line 213), as Erec terms him—that his unmotivated and provocative violence is initially enacted. At this early stage in the narrative, then, both the fact and the meaning of Yder's giantism are disguised, while the dwarf functions not as an alternative to it but as a submissive surrogate.

It is in the confrontation with the second giant—who derives from the world of this initial adventure but appears only at the conclusion of Erec's quest—that the thematic value of this first encounter, and of the narrative as a whole, is made plain. As Erec and Enide make their way home after the course of their adventures together, they come upon a challenge enigmatically labeled the Joie de la Cort. It is embodied in a magic garden that apparently incorporates the most deeply desired values of courtly society. Filled with never-fading flowers and ever-ripening

---

56. All references are to Mario Roques, ed., *Erec et Enide,* Les classiques français du moyen âge, 80 (Paris: H. Champion, 1955); the translations are my own. For the allusion to Morholt, see line 1242, and for Yder's associations with giants, Joël Grisward, "Ider et le Tricephal," *Annales* 33 (1978), 279–93.

fruits, the garden contains at its center a damsel "endowed with every beauty" reclining upon a bed of silver (lines 5380–36). But, as with Enide at the tourney of the sparrowhawk, the love that the damsel solicits is inextricably involved with violence, and as Erec draws near he is accosted by a knight wearing blood-red arms. This knight's giantism is more explicit. He is "marvellously large" (line 5850: "granz a merevoilles"), a grossness that is explicitly stated to be disfiguring: "if he were not disturbingly large, there would have been no one under heaven more handsome than he; but he was more than a foot larger . . . than any knight one had ever seen."[57] In the course of events it is revealed that the lady on the couch is Enide's cousin, while the gigantic knight (Maboagrains) is her lover. When they were young—perhaps as young as Eric and Enide at the outset of the narrative—Maboagrains promised his lady to stay with her forever in the garden unless he were conquered by another knight. Thus he has been kept "an prison" (line 6047), captive to a chivalric ideology that has sentenced him to endless displays of prowess on behalf of a lady who is simultaneously passive possession and dominating jailer. In effect, the Joie de la Cort stands as an ideogram of the Arthurian court in particular, and of the erotic militarism of chivalry in general, for it discloses a prowess constrained to endless violence—the garden is ringed with stakes displaying the heads of Maboagrains' previous victims—and whose irrational will to power can be set aside only by defeat. Conquered by Erec, Maboagrains is at last able to lead his lady from the enchanted garden of chivalric perfection, just as Erec will shortly lead Enide from the Arthurian court to his own Breton kingdom.

The will to power that is figured by Maboagrains' giantism is connected, by a telling allusion, to the Virgilian *libido dominandi* (as Augustine described it) that is so ambivalently chronicled in the *Aeneid*. When Erec first comes upon the lady of the garden, alluringly displayed on her silver couch, she is favorably compared to "Lavine de Laurente" (line 5841), a comparison that links Virgilian imperialism with the erotic and martial obsessions of chivalry. Nor is this link wholly unexpected, since it is implicit in the Arthurian legend from its initial literary expression in Geoffrey of Monmouth's *Historia regum Britanniae,* where Arthurian preeminence is simultaneously asserted and undone by its own imperial challenge to Roman hegemony, a challenge that is undermined by the

---

57. s'il ne fust granz a enui
soz ciel n'eüst plus bel du lui,
mes il estoit un pié plus granz,
a tesmoing de totes les genz,
que chevaliers que l'an seüst. (Lines 5851–55)

internecine and generational violence generated within the Arthurian court itself.[58] In Chrétien's narrative this civil war is privatized, and is figured as the marital discord which the central portion of the romance chronicles. Having fallen into an amorous lethargy in the early days of his marriage, Erec is roused by the charge of *recréance* leveled against him by his knights and inadvertently transmitted by Enide in a *parole* which she tearfully speaks over his sleeping form (line 2519). It is in order to prove this *parole* false, both to himself and to the wife whom he supposes to have acted disloyally, that Erec goes off "en avanture" (line 2763), both scorning a knightly entourage and enjoining his too-talkative wife to a silent witnessing of his deeds. In effect, Erec hopes to demonstrate in these adventures the same kind of chivalric self-sufficiency that he initially displayed in winning Enide in the first place.

The course of Erec's adventures brings him to acknowledge the lesson of self-limitation that Maboagrains comes subsequently to exemplify, and as with Maboagrains, Erec's freedom from the burden of unconstrained chivalric ambition comes only through defeat. The narrative enactment of this defeat provides the mechanism both for the introduction of the dwarf and for his identification with Enide, in a complex of values that is subsequently linked with Dido and an anti-imperialist Virgilianism. Despite the injunction of silence, Enide continues to protect Erec with her *paroles:* she repeatedly warns him of antagonists who hope to catch him unawares, and twice she verbally manipulates would-be lovers who seek to kill her lord so that they might possess his wife. The second of these confrontations provides the narrative's climactic moment. Having grown progressively weaker in the course of his adventures, Erec is at last bathed in blood within his armor and falls into a deathlike trance. As Enide mourns his apparent death, she is accosted by Oringle, comte de Limors. Struck by her beauty, Oringle brings the "corpse" and widow to his palace where he prepares Erec for burial and Enide for remarriage. But Enide resists, and in his rage at her irrepressible loyalty and independence, Oringle strikes her, declaring to his scandalized retainers that "the lady is mine and I am hers: I will do with her what I please" (lines 4800–4801: "La dame est moie et je sui suens, / si ferai de li mon pleisir"). Enide's fiery speech of resistance provides the narrative with its peripeteia:

"Oh!" she cried, "it doesn't matter to me what you say nor what you do—I fear neither your blows nor your threats. Beat me, strike me—I will never find

---

58. The relevance of this message to Henry II was enhanced by Robert Wace's rewriting of Geoffrey of Monmouth in the *Roman de Brut,* a translation that Wace reputedly presented to Queen Eleanor. I discuss this issue further in Chapter 6, below.

you so manly that I would do either more or less for you, even if with your own hands you were now to pluck out my eyes or flay me alive!"[59]

The full significance of this outburst is explicated by its effect: Erec recovers from the death-in-life of his trance "like a man awakening" (line 4817: "ausi come hom qui s'esvoille"). As he rises from his bier, he recuperates and reintegrates the complex mix of militarism and eroticism that constitutes chivalric heroism, a mix that had been out of balance both in the *recréantise* of his amorous lethargy and in the overbearing tyranny and inhuman self-sufficiency of his adventures. "Anger and love for his wife gave him courage" (lines 4824–25: "ire li done hardemant, / et l'amors qu'an sa fame avoit"), and like a man possessed—the crowd gathered for the wedding thinks him a devil—he transforms the marriage feast into a scene of miraculous rebirth. "Run, run, here comes the dead man!" they cry (line 4840: "Fuiez! Fuiez! Veez le mort!"), but Erec is for the first time fully alive. As husband and wife make good their escape and dash rapidly through the moonlit landscape, Chrétien bathes them in a description that succeeds in capturing the almost magical sweetness of their reconciliation (and that must be cited in the original):

Par nuit s'an vont grant aleüre,
et ce lor fet grant soatume
que la nuit luisoit cler la lune.

(Lines 4898–4900)[60]

It is Enide, then, who by her opposition to Oringle's overbearing tyranny functions as the agent who releases Erec from his imprisonment within a masculinist ideology of erotic possessiveness and martial self-sufficiency.[61] This is a fact that will bear further explication, but for the

---

59.   Ahi! fet ele, ne me chaut
que tu me dïes ne ne faces:
ne criem tes cos ne tes menaces.
Asez me bat, asez me fier:
ja tant ne te troverai *fier*
que por toi face plus ne mains,
se tu or androit a tes mains
me devoies les ialz sachier
ou tote vive detranchier.   (Lines 4806–14)

I have translated the "fier" of line 4810 as "manly" in an effort to capture something of its ambiguous value: see A. J. Greimas, *Dictionnaire de l'ancien français* (Paris: Larousse, 1968), s.v.

60.   "They went rapidly through the night, and it gave them great comfort that the moon shone brightly."

61.   The way in which the Oringle episode functions to "caricatur[e] . . . the futility of a marriage based on nothing but the letter of the law," and thus the connection to Erec, was first demonstrated by Alfred Adler, "Sovereignty as the Principle of Unity in Chrétien's

moment let us follow Chrétien's narrative in order to discover the diminutive counterpart to the overgrown Maboagrains. For as Erec and Enide ride through the night, they encounter for the second time a knight called Guivret le Petit.[62] When Guivret first entered the romance he was described as endowed with "a very small body but with a large, bold heart" (lines 3665–66: "il estoit molt de cors petiz, / mes de grant cuer estoit / hardiz"), and this boldness expressed itself in a fierce battle with Erec that ended only with the breaking of Guivret's sword. While the description of that battle demonstrated that Erec and Guivret were in some sense equivalent, Guivret was also shown to be far more aware of his limitations than Erec. When his sword broke, he begged for mercy with a realistic candor quite foreign to Erec, and in pointing out to Erec that "we both have need of a physician" (line 3878: "Andui avons mestier de mire"), he offered him a succor that Erec unwisely declined. Now they meet again, and the narrator offers a mordant warning: "whoever wishes to do more than he can must either surrender or rest" (lines 4975–76: "qui plus vialt fere qu'il ne puet, / recroirre ou reposer l'estuet"). Failing to recognize each other, the two knights engage in combat and Erec is swiftly, and almost fatally, defeated. Only then does he accept the aid he earlier had declined, and when he is healed (through the ministrations of Guivret's sisters) and on his way home, Guivret joins his entourage.

Guivret le Petit represents a chivalric heroism that yields nothing in either aggression or, for that matter, feudal hegemony—he boasts of his control over his holdings (lines 3844–55)—but that is unencumbered by an erotically motivated need for unqualified dominance. Notably unaccompanied by a lady, Guivret presents a virility that is secure in its force but limited in its goals, a prowess that stands as a model for the overreaching Erec. Erec's other guide, who also accompanies him on the journey home, is of course Enide, and if Guivret is a valorized counterpart to Maboagrains, it is the Lavinia of the garden who is Enide's foil. As she and Erec prepare for their journey, Guivret gives her a palfrey bearing a symbolically ornamented saddle, a parting gift that will serve both to return her to the Arthurian world from which she first set out and yet to mark the difference that the estrangement of the quest has made—a difference that will be institutionalized in her coronation as queen of Brittany. The description of the palfrey is drawn from the account of the marvellous palfrey of Camilla in the *Roman d'Eneas;* and on

Erec," *PMLA* 50 (1945), 933, an unfortunately now largely unread article that still offers one of the best readings of the poem.

62. The figure of Guivret has been well discussed by Hanning, *The Individual in Twelfth-Century Romance,* pp. 71–80.

the saddle is engraved a version of the story of the *Aeneid,* telling "how Aeneas came from Troy, how at Carthage Dido received him into her city with great joy, how Aeneas deceived her, how she killed herself for him, how Aeneas then conquered Laurenteum and all Lombardy, of which he was king all of his life."[63] Missing from this retelling is the Lavine of the *Roman d'Eneas,* But Chrétien shortly makes good this omission by invoking her in the false paradise of Maboagrains' garden.

The linking of Enide with two rejected Virgilian women, the erotically dangerous Dido and the fiercely independent Camilla, can, in concert with the complementary analogy between Lavinia and the *belle dame sans merci* of the garden, illuminate for us Chrétien's understanding of the *Aeneid.* Moreover, both allusions show how Chrétien finds an access to Virgil's poem through the *Roman d'Eneas,* one that both makes use of and sets aside the French translation. In the *Eneas* the Virgilian Dido is reduced to an unqualifiedly negative foil to Lavine. The love she offers Eneas is both *soltaine* (which means, as Cormier has shown, solitary or unreciprocated) and *vieille,* the lustful obsession of a widow who betrays both the memory of her dead husband and her own people.[64] Moreover, her epitaph records a deeper, more profound self-betrayal: its last line reads, "her wisdom availed her nothing" (line 2144: "savior ne li valut noiant"). By "savoir" the French poet seems to be referring not only to Dido's previous capacities as a leader, but to a more general knowledgeability. As she herself says, "I was very noble and wise before love brought me to such madness" (lines 2057–58: "molt fui ançois et pros et sage, / que me donast amor tel rage"). In the *Eneas* this wisdom vanishes with the arrival of love, and she ends a hysterical woman, by turns dangerous and (as we have seen) pathetic. "What more shall I say?" the French poet has her conclude, "I am completely mad" (line 1814: "Que di ge mes? molt par sui fole").[65]

Virgil's Dido is also mad, of course, possessed by the *furor* that is the great antagonist of the new order that Aeneas has come to establish; but

---

63. comant Eneas vint de Troye,
     comant a Cartaige a grant joie
     Dido an son leu le reçut,
     comant Eneas la deçut,
     comant ele por lui s'ocist,
     comant Eneas puis conquist
     Laurente et tote Lonbardie,
     dom il fu rois tote sa vie.   (Lines 5291–98)
64. Cormier, *One Heart One Mind,* pp. 137–38.
65. Dido's madness and possession are stressed throughout the episode by the *Eneas* poet: see lines 1219–65, 1270'–71, 1302, 1391–92, 1796, 1814, 1882, 1968–70, 1990, 2015, 2027, 2107, 2144.

she is far from completely so, especially in her final ravings. On the contrary, in the three great speeches that precede her suicide, the Virgilian Dido moves progressively closer to an understanding of her fate. The crucial speeches are the second and third (both entirely omitted in the *Eneas*) in which she casts upon Rome the curses that Hannibal (and Cleopatra) will redeem, and in which she gropes toward a comprehension of what it means to be *infelix Dido,* at once a human being and yet a mere instrument of some larger fate. This process is brilliantly at work, for instance, in these two elliptical lines:

> quid loquor? aut ubi sum? quae mentem insania mutat?
> infelix Dido, nunc te facta impia tangunt?
>
> (4.595–96)

The first line is clear enough, and can be prosaically translated: "What am I saying? Where am I? What madness has transformed my mind?" But the second line is more uncertain, and two contemporary translations nicely illustrate the ambiguity. Allen Mandelbaum renders the line: "Poor Dido, does his foulness touch you now?" Construed in this way, the *facta impia* refer to Aeneas' disloyalty, a betrayal made ironically necessary by a *pietas* of which Dido can have no understanding (as she demonstrates, for example, in 4.496). From this perspective, she is *infelix* because she is a victim: infelicity is a condition imposed upon her. On the other hand, C. Day Lewis translates the second line self-referentially: "Poor Dido, *the wrong you have done*—is it only now coming home to you?"[66] Here the *facta impia* are deeds performed by Dido herself: probably the abandonment of her civic duty, certainly the violation of her oath to Sychaeus, but more generally and tellingly her unwitting attempt to thwart the destiny to which *pius Aeneas* so faithfully submits. In the second sense the epithet *infelix* construes not mere unluckiness but a complex mixture of guilt and adversity, the sense of having a role to play in the destined unfolding of events that can only be tragic. It is in acknowledgment of this largest apprehension that Virgil can refer to Dido as "haud ignara futuri" (4.508: "not ignorant of what is coming") and as calling upon the gods and stars "conscia fati" (4.519: "who know the fates"). This apprehension, moreover, subtends both Dido's curses and, more touchingly, her own just designation of herself as "magna" (4.654). As her life moves toward its close, in short, Dido comes to be not merely a hysterical woman, hellbent on destruction, but a tragic protagonist groping toward an understanding of her tragedy. The highly wrought

---

66. Mandelbaum, *Aeneid,* p. 101; C. Day Lewis, *The Aeneid of Virgil* (London: Oxford University Press, 1957), p. 99.

speeches of her closing moments are not merely rhetorical displays but instances of language deployed in the service of understanding, and she attempts to comprehend her fate to a degree that certainly rivals, if it does not surpass, that of Aeneas himself.

When we bring this perspective on Dido to bear on *Erec et Enide,* we see that the analogies between Virgil's heroine and Chrétien's are pervasive and profound. Like Dido, Enide is both an agent and a victim of sexual temptation, and she too attempts to understand her situation and to articulate that understanding in language. In large part, indeed, Enide serves as a consciousness that meditates upon the value of the events enacted in the narrative. For the first third of the poem, it is true, she is herself not merely a part of the object world of chivalry (the world, in Virgilian terms, of history) but the most valuable object of all, as the hyperbolic descriptions of her beauty continually remind us.[67] But as the rest of the romance insists, she is also a subject, and it is both her consciousness, rendered to us through elaborate interior monologues, and her language, her *parole,* that come to dominate the poem. This sense of the centrality of Enide's subjectivity, and its authority over otherwise-mute events, are rendered by a continually repeated scene of Enide watching over a sleeping, and finally unconscious, Erec. "Cil dormi et cele veilla," a phrase repeated throughout the first half of the quest (lines 2475, 3093; and see 3438–54) that describes the relationship between the spouses that persists until Erec is finally and definitively roused from his bier "like a man awakening" (line 4817). If Erec provides the force that motivates the quest, he is as inarticulate about its meaning and as obsessive in its enactment as Chrétien's other inadequate protagonists, the lovesick Lancelot, the half-crazed Yvain, and the childishly naive Perceval. It is, rather, Enide who guides the narrative toward its resolution, both by providing Erec with the visual alertness and verbal dexterity he

---

67. Enide's extraordinary beauty is stressed throughout the narrative, and it is made clear from the outset that the courtly society of the Arthurian world uses her as an opportunity for self-gratifying admiration:

> Que diroie de sa biauté?
> Ce fu cele por verité
> qui fu fete por esgarder,
> qu'an se poïst an li mirer
> ausi com an un mireor.   (Lines 437–41)

The reduction of Enide to an object is consistent with the Arthurian celebration of materiality, brought home to the reader with obsessive force in the nine hundred or so lines that extend from the dressing of Enide by Guenevere (1567ff.) to the lovers' installation in their marriage (c. 2429), lines that celebrate with loving detail the object world of chivalry. The counter to this materialism is found in the description of Erec's robe at his coronation, which is embroidered with representations of the quadrivium, those sciences by which the object world is subjected to the workings of the mind (lines 6674–6748).

needs to survive and, finally, in her rejection of Oringle, with its insistence upon her independence from a masculine domination that would once more reduce her to an object. It is through acknowledging this subjectivity, and the *parole* that renders it, that Erec is at last freed from his compulsions and able to direct his own course toward the new society envisaged at the poem's conclusion.

Chrétien's analogizing of Enide and Dido shows him returning not just to the *Aeneid* but to that aspect of the *Aeneid* which the simplifications of the *Eneas* had elided. It is not Virgilian imperialism that interests Chrétien, that assured linearity that the *Eneas* poet so assiduously retraced, but the other Virgilian voice that he hears, the Virgilian countertext that he rewrites.[68] For Chrétien invokes the chthonic and regressive Dido—the "old" Dido who is responsible for Eneas' *recréance*—only in order to reveal the redemptive power she possesses when rightly understood. It is in this sense that Chrétien returns to what is, for the modern reader, an authentic Virgilianism. But lest we once again too easily dismiss the *Eneas* as superficial and monochromatic, let us note in conclusion that the other Virgilian allusion applied to Enide—the modeling of the description of her palfrey upon that of Camilla—is derived from the *Eneas.* Chrétien's recourse in this instance to the French poem marks its difference from the *Aeneid,* and suggests that in its medievalism it speaks to concerns that are attenuated in the antique world but are powerfully at work in medieval Western culture. In the *Aeneid* Camilla represents a doomed youthfulness that is, as we have seen, embodied in a variety of figures (e.g., Misenus, Marcellus, Euryalus, Pallas, and so forth). That she is a woman is a cause for wonder, but only because of her ability to join martial sturdiness to feminine grace and beauty. In the *Eneas,* on the other hand, her gender is not only the most important of her characteristics, it is the very ground of her excellence. This is made clear in an exchange between the Trojan Tarcon and Camilla that the *Eneas* poet substitutes for Virgil's account of her childhood under Diana's care. In an effort to assert the Amazon's female inferiority before the terrified Trojan warriors, Tarcon launches a scurrilous antifeminist attack on Camilla. He offers her money for her sexual favors, and says he will share her with his squires, "but that will not suffice you at all, unless there are a hundred of us; you may become tired, but you will not be satisfied" (lines 7103–6). The offended Camilla strikes Tarcon down, and replies with a quiet nobility that affirms her virtue: "I do not come here to show myself off, or to indulge in debauchery, but to practice chivalry" (lines 7117–19). In adopting the language of antifeminism that has been used

68. Adam Parry, "The Two Voices of Virgil's *Aeneid,*" *Arion* 2.4 (1963), 66–80.

against her, she makes it clear that she embodies a female virtue that challenges the usual categories of masculine understanding: "I know better how to strike down a knight than to embrace him or make love to him; I do not know how to do battle on my back" (lines 7123–25).[69] Neither, of course, does Enide, and it is precisely to disentangle the martial and the erotic that Erec's adventures were undertaken. While Enide eschews Camilla's militarism, she shares her scorn for the easy assumptions of masculine superiority.

Surely it is this meaning, foreign to Virgil but becoming progressively more familiar to the medieval world, that Chrétien appropriates in his poem when he has Guivret le Petit endow Enide with a horse that recalls the *chevalerie* of Camilla. It is a meaning, finally, that is appropriate not only to a literary genre committed to an exploration of the feminine, but also to a cultural moment concerned about its ability to measure up to a powerful heritage. The conjunction of the diminutive Guivret and the womanly Enide under the sign of Dido and Camilla eloquently bespeaks an alliance of the culturally marginal. And by recuperating two of the victims of the imperialist project, as well as by anatomizing the inherent instabilities of the chivalric ideology, Chrétien comments trenchantly upon the role of the *Eneas* in legitimizing Anglo-Norman ambitions. If we are then prepared to locate Chrétien's early career within the context of the Angevin court, *Erec et Enide* reveals itself as a poem that not only meditates upon the problematic relation of the individual to historical action but serves itself as an act of historical intervention.[70]

---

69.   Mialz sai abatre un chevalier
    que acoler ne desnoier;
    ne me sai pas combatre anverse.   (Lines 7123–25).

70.   Attempts to link *Eric et Enide* with the early years of Henry II's reign must of course confront the problem of dating, a problem that has recently been given new life by Claude Luttrell's *The Creation of the First Arthurian Romance* (Evanston: Northwestern University Press, 1974), which dates *Erec et Enide* after 1184. Luttrell's arguments have been carefully and sympathetically reviewed by Tony Hunt, "Redating Chrestien de Troyes," *Bulletin bibliographique de la Société Internationale Arthurienne* 30 (1987), 209–37. Hunt does point out, however, that Luttrell's key argument—the dependence of *Erec et Enide* upon Alan of Lille's *De planctu naturae*—is in itself vulnerable since all of the elements that Luttrell claims Chrétien took from Alan can in fact be found elsewhere; and it should also be added that the latest discussion of the date of the *De planctu*, by James J. Sheridan in his translation (Toronto: Pontifical Institute of Mediaeval Studies, 1980), puts it in the period 1160–65. For evidence linking Chrétien to England, see above, note 4.

6. The Romance of History and the Alliterative *Morte Arthure*

SOMETIME ABOUT 1353, as French fortunes in the war with England were sinking toward their nadir, King John of France commissioned Pierre Bersuire to provide him with a translation of Livy's *History of Rome*. In his preface Bersuire disclosed John's motives in commissioning such a work. "It is indeed true," he said, "that excellent princes, the wiser they are the more they will want to learn about the virtuous deeds and remarkable works of the princes of antiquity, about the martial genius, the intelligence, and the industry with which these men conquered lands and territories, built empires and kingdoms, and founded, fostered, defended, and governed their empires, holding them through a grand succession that endured at length; so that modern princes can in the same way defend and govern their lands, defeat and dominate foreigners, discomfit enemies, defend their subjects, and aid their friends."[1] But despite Bersuire's rotund promises, Livy did King John little good. In 1356 he was captured by the English at the disastrous battle of Poitiers, spent the next four years a prisoner in England, and the following four ineffec-

---

1. While the whole text is unpublished, the preface is printed by Jacques Monfrin, "La traduction française de Tite-Live," *Histoire littéraire de la France* (Paris: Imprimerie Nationale, 1962), 39. 359–60; see also Jean Rychner, "Observations sur la traduction de Tite-Live par Pierre Bersuire (1354–56)," *Journal des savants* (Oct.–Dec. 1963), 242–67. A presentation picture from the fifteenth-century MS B.N. fr. 259 is reproduced in Millard Meiss, *French Painting in the Time of Jean de Berry: The Boucicault Master* (London: Phaidon, 1967), fig. 431 and p. 56.

tively searching for a way to act out his restless gallantry. Fortunately for France, he died in 1364 and left the kingdom in the capable hands of his son Charles the Wise.

In turning to Livy in his time of need, King John strikes the modern observer as hopelessly quixotic, but according to the standards of his day he was being both high-minded and sensible. Indeed, his remarkably successful son not only owned a copy of Bersuire's Livy but commissioned a steady stream of similar translations, in part for the same practical reasons as his father, in part for larger concerns both humanistic and political.[2] Any attempt to specify medieval historical interests must be alert both to this variety of motives, at work within individual projects as well as across the spectrum of historical writings, and to a common denominator of instinctive deference, even submissiveness, before the past. As has often been noted (but rarely explored), this is a deference that renders elusive what we would take to be a genuinely historical consciousness. Indeed, the most common of medieval historical writings, those that moralize the historical record into illustrative instances of success and failure, vice and virtue, are manifestly ahistorical: the past is rendered not as a process that has its own temporality but as a storehouse of disconnected and timeless *exempla* that assume authority precisely because they are no longer timebound. Nevertheless, we should remember that medieval writers also used the past historiographically—sometimes to delineate an instructive chronology of secular empire, more commonly to apprehend the plan of providential dispensation—and it would be a mistake to assent too quickly to the common proposition that the Middle Ages lacked a historical sense. Rather, we would do better to see the medieval historical consciousness as always at issue, at times emerging toward an authentic apprehension of temporality and periodization, at other times retreating under the pressure of various ideologies toward reification and idolization.[3]

---

2. Jacques Monfrin, "Les traducteurs et leur public en France au moyen âge," *Journal des savants* (Jan.–Mar. 1964), 5–20.

3. Among the many discussions of medieval historiography, those most useful to the argument presented in this chapter are R. W. Southern, "Aspects of the European Tradition of Historical Writing," *Transactions of the Royal Historical Society* 20 (1970), 173–96; 21 (1971), 159–79; 22 (1972), 159–80; M.-D. Chenu, "Conscience de l'histoire et théologie au XIIIᵉ siècle," *Archives d'histoire doctrinale et littéraire du moyen âge* 21 (1954), 107–33, appearing as chapter 5 of his *Nature, Man, and Society in the Twelfth Century*, trans. Jerome Taylor and Lester K. Little (Chicago: University of Chicago Press, 1968); Arnaldo Momigliano, *Essays in Ancient and Modern Historiography* (Middletown: Wesleyan University Press, 1977), especially chaps. 8 and 12; F. P. Pickering, *Augustinus oder Boethius? Geschichtsschreibung und epische Dichtung im Mittelalter—und in der Neuzeit* (Berlin: E. Schmidt, 1967), and chap. 3 of his *Literature and Art in the Middle Ages* (Coral Gables: University of Miami Press, 1970);

The most powerful of these ideologies, as I have suggested, was the fundamental definition of present legitimacy in terms of descent from an omnipotent past. *Verum quia vetus* is a medieval proverb that expresses a ubiquitous theology of origins in force across the whole range of medieval culture, and nowhere more visibly than in the political world. The disruptions of medieval political history were typically healed with the soothing continuities of a founding legend, and insecure rulers bolstered their regimes by invoking honorific if legendary precedents. The degree to which these political imperatives determined the kind of literature that was produced in the Middle Ages is not sufficiently appreciated; nor is the even more important fact that this literature continued throughout its medieval life to concern itself with essentially historiographical issues, issues such as the relation of individual action to historical process, or the use and abuse of historical precedent itself. My concern in this chapter is with just this self-reflexiveness, and specifically with the extent to which narratives that are now designated as romances (and hence as fictions largely unconcerned with historical reality) in fact meditate both upon the paradox of their own production—as historical fabrications designed to legitimize political power—and upon the problematic enterprise of reconstituting, from within history, a prehistorical origin. My particular focus here is upon the fifteenth-century Middle English poem, the Alliterative *Morte Arthure,* but I want to preface my discussion of that poem with more general and wide-ranging comments upon the historiographical issues that typically inhabit medieval romance.

I

As we have already seen in the previous chapter, the discontinuities of English political history foreclosed the attempt to trace a genuinely historical line of descent from a common origin. Anglo-Saxon hegemony was achieved by displacing Britain's original Celtic inhabitants and was itself sustained only by accommodating Scandinavian interlopers, and even this heavily qualified sovereignty was abrogated by the events of 1066. Furthermore, the subsequent Anglo-Norman supremacy was

---

Bernard Guenée, "Histoires, annales, chroniques: Essai sur les genres historiques au moyen âge," *Annales* 28 (1973), 997–1016, and his *Histoire et culture historique dans l'Occident médiéval* (Paris: Aubier, 1980); Roger D. Ray, "Medieval Historiography through the Twelfth Century: Problems and Progress of Research," *Viator* 5 (1974), 33–59; Ernst Briesach, ed., *Classical Rhetoric and Medieval Historiography,* Studies in Medieval Culture 19 (Kalamazoo: Medieval Institute Publications, 1985), and essays on historiography published in a special issue of *Medievalia et Humanistica* n.s. 5 (1974) by Amos Funkenstein, Marjorie Reeves, and Robert Hanning. It was Hanning's fine "*Beowulf* and Heroic History," pp. 77–102, that first provided me with a definition of my subject.

both challenged from below and, more seriously, subject to the fragmentations occasioned by its own inner dynamic.[4] Moreover, when Henry II ascended the disputed throne in 1154, he was as both duke of Normandy and king of England faced with a tangle of conflicting loyalties that required a firm assertion of royal sovereignty. Part of his effort at self-legitimization was literary. It is doubtless easy to overestimate Henry's role as a patron of letters, and Plantagenet patronage was by no means confined to the king.[5] But much of the court literature of the period shows patterns of interest that are consistent with Henry's political needs, most explicitly in the Latin and Anglo-Norman chronicles that recorded his *gestae* and those of his ancestors, works written in Latin by Aelred of Rievaulx and in the vernacular by Jordan Fantosme, Wace, and Benoît de Sainte-Maure.[6] But of more lasting importance were the legendary histories—or, as we now call them, romances—that, for all their undoubted reliance upon oral narratives, found both their literary inspiration and political purpose in Geoffrey of Monmouth's *Historia regum Britanniae*.[7]

---

4. See above, Chapter 5, p. 180.

5. On Henry II as a patron, see Walter F. Schirmer and Ulrich Broich, *Studien zum literarischen Patronat im England des 12. Jahrhunderts* (Cologne: Westdeutscher Verlag, 1962), pp. 27–203; Diana B. Tyson, "Patronage of French Vernacular History Writers in the Twelfth and Thirteenth Centuries," *Romania* 100 (1979), 180–222, 584; and Reto R. Bezzola, *Les origines et la formation de la littérature courtoise en Occident, 500–1200,* Vol. 3, pt. 1 (Paris: Champion, 1963).

6. Aelred wrote a *Genealogia regum* for Henry while he was still duke of Normandy but after he had been designated as Stephen's heir (1153–54) and a *Vita et miracula* for the translation of Edward the Confessor in 1163; Jordan Fantosme, *Histoire de la guerre d'Ecosse* (1174–75); Wace, *Roman de Rou* (1160–74); Benoît de Sainte-Maure, *Chronique des Ducs de Normandie* (c. 1174). That the author of the *Chronique* and the *Roman de Troie* (see below, p. 204) are the same Benoît is demonstrated by Carin Fahlin, *Etude sur le manuscrit de Tours de la Chronique Ducs de Normandie par Benoît* (Uppsala: Almqvist and Wiksells, 1937), pp. 141–72. There were, of course, many other historical works composed during Henry's reign (e.g., the *Gesta consulum Andegavorum* by Jean de Marmoutier, c. 1164–73), but it is doubtful that they should be ascribed to royal patronage; see Broich's survey, *Studien zum literarischen Patronat im England,* pp. 27–42, and Antonia Gransden, *Historical Writing in England c. 550 to c. 1307* (Ithaca: Cornell University Press, 1974), pp. 219–68. Broich also excludes Jordan of Fantosme's *Histoire* from the direct circle of patronized writings, but see Tyson, "Patronage of French Vernacular History Writers," pp. 193–201.

7. Despite the fact that throughout the Middle Ages the categories of what we have come to call "history" and "romance" blended insensibly into each other, it would be wrong to think that medieval writers had no awareness of or concern for the difference between the fictive and the factual. *Historia est narratio rei gestae:* Isidore of Seville's authoritative definition—derived from Cicero's *De inventione* 1.19.27 and endlessly repeated throughout the Middle Ages—accurately reflects the medieval view that history is an account of that which was done and is to be distinguished from fable. For a discussion of this important medieval awareness, see Guenée, *Histoire et culture historique dans l'Occident médiéval,* pp. 18–43, 77–128. In the present chapter I am concerned with texts that self-

The historiographical purpose of Geoffrey's project, to put a complex matter simply, was to replace the Augustinian dismissal of secular history that had inspired Bede's authoritative *Historia ecclesiastica* with a Virgilian narrative that located historical legitimacy not merely in terms of the development of the church but within the larger world of history itself.[8] Yet the claim of Geoffrey's *translatio imperii* was not only that legitimacy could be transferred through the long reaches of historical time without dilution, but that the legitimizing force at the origin was itself unproblematic. And as we have seen in the previous chapter, the Trojan story that Virgil passed on to the West, and that Geoffrey rewrote, called into question both the nature of that originating energy and the very linearity by which it was transmitted. This was a questioning that Geoffrey not only did not evade but that, in his often wildly parodic and ideologically unconstrained speculations, he eagerly exploited.[9] For Geoffrey's *Historia* tells of a refoundation that is accomplished only by the destruction of the very past it seeks to reenact: the founding father Brutus is himself a parricide, the preeminent Arthur is of dubious paternity and is supported by a prophet born of an incubus, the country's monarchical history is riven with generational violence, and its story as a whole consists of alternating periods of internecine self-destruction and imperial warfare directed against the Rome from which it took its origin. The *Historia*

---

consciously and deliberately override this basic distinction between the factual and the fabulous, history and romance, for their own strategic purposes.

On the meaning of the word and the genre *romance* in Middle English, see Paul Strohm, "The Origin and Meaning of Middle English *Romaunce*," *Genre* 10 (1977), 1–28; Kathryn Hume, "The Formal Nature of Middle English Romance," *Philological Quarterly* 53 (1974), 158–80; and John Finlayson, "Definitions of Middle English Romance," *Chaucer Review* 15 (1980–81), 44–62, 168–81. It is clear from these studies that the fictive nature of romance was always recognized, but that this did not necessarily disqualify such a work from entertaining historiographical interests.

8. Perhaps the clearest understanding of Geoffrey's historiographical purpose was offered at the end of the twelfth century by William of Newburgh, who bitterly attacked Geoffrey on three grounds: (1) that he substituted *conficta, fabula,* and *ridicula figmenta* for the *historica veritas* of *noster Beda;* (2) that he exalted the Britons to the level of the great civilizations of the classical past, as if Arthur were the equal of Alexander, Julius Caesar, and Caesar Augustus; and (3) that he presented the demonic Merlin as if he were another Isaiah. In sum, William saw that Geoffrey was replacing Bede's ecclesiastical history with a relentlessly secular narrative that claimed for itself the authority of the classical past, a claim that was enforced by invoking modes of narration (e.g., the legitimizing role of the prophet) derived from scriptural history. For William's comments, see the Preface to his *Historia Regum Anglicarum,* translated by Joseph Stevenson, *The Church Historians of England,* Vol. 4, pt. 2 (London: Seeleys, 1858), pp. 400–401.

9. While this is unfortunately not the place for a full discussion of Geoffrey's book, the view I am presenting of it here is consistent with that set forward by Valerie I. J. Flint, "The *Historia Regum Britanniae* of Geoffrey of Monmouth: Parody and Its Purpose. A Suggestion," *Speculum* 54 (1979), 447–68.

regum Britanniae, in sum, is a *Gründungsage* that undermines the very ground upon which it rests: when, in one of its most emblematic incidents, the foundations of Vortigern's tower give way, an excavation reveals a pool inhabited by two fighting dragons, symbols of the perpetual strife upon which history is founded and which it continually reenacts. In short, Geoffrey's seminal text is what Judith Shklar has called a "subversive genealogy," a "myth that expresses the outrage of those who know all the evils of the world and recognize their necessity." [10] It is a myth of origins that deconstructs the origin.

At about the time of Henry's uneasy accession to the throne Wace not only translated the *Historia* into Anglo-Norman but, according to Layamon, who later translated Wace's version into English, presented a copy to Queen Eleanor. [11] Moreover, the two great themes of Geoffrey's work—the Trojan foundation of Britain and the preeminence of Arthur—were not only immediately exploited for purposes of political legitimization but served throughout the later Middle Ages, as we shall see, as central sources for English monarchs eager to bolster their often unsteady hold upon the throne. And yet these rewritings of Geoffrey remained, despite their immediate ideological purpose, powerfully conditioned by the subversive impulses that had motivated Geoffrey in the first place. Appropriately enough, Geoffrey thus became a source who transmitted to his inheritors the very instability that he saw as haunting all merely historical origins.

The continued disruptions of English dynastic history—including the fourteenth-century depositions of Edward II and Richard II, and the chaos of the middle years of the fifteenth century—meant that the English monarchs who succeeded Henry, unlike the Capetian and Valois kings of France, looked back not upon an unruffled descent from a founding father (Charlemagne) but instead upon a political genealogy broken by violence and impeached by its own discontinuities. Hence it was in England that the historiography of legendary origins flourished with special vigor. To be sure, not just Britain but virtually every European nation claimed descent from a common origin at Troy: in his *Troy Book,* begun in 1412, Lydgate lists not just Britain as a Trojan foundation

---

10. Judith Shklar, "Subversive Genealogies," in Clifford Geertz, ed., *Myth, Symbol, and Culture* (New York: Norton, 1974), p. 141.

11. On the date and the relation of Wace's poem to Henry, see Broich, *Studien zum literarisch en Patronat im England,* pp. 65–77, Tyson, "Patronage of French Vernacular History Writers," pp. 193–96, and John S. P. Tatlock, *The Legendary History of Britain: Geoffrey of Monmouth's Historia Regum Britanniae and Its Early Vernacular Versions* (Berkeley: University of California Press, 1950), pp. 467–68; on the now lost translation by Geoffrey Gaimar, see Tatlock, pp. 452–56.

but also France (Francus), Venice (Antenor), Sicily (Sycanus), Naples (Aeneas), and Calabria (Diomedes), and throughout the Middle Ages other writers contributed many other instances—including Dudo of Saint-Quentin's early-eleventh-century assertion that Normandy had been founded by Antenor. But while on the Continent the claim to Trojan origin was asserted perfunctorily in the course of pursuing other interests, in England it remained a powerful instrument of royal propaganda. This is illustrated by Lydgate's own poem, for instance, which was commissioned by the future Henry V only a dozen or so years after his father had seized the crown—the same Henry who had earlier had made for himself a deluxe manuscript of the finest Trojan poem written in the Middle Ages, Chaucer's *Troilus and Criseyde*.[12] Even more telling is the fact that the authoritative version of the Troy story, and the ultimate source for Lydgate's poem, had also been commissioned by an English monarch: the *Roman de Troie* was written early in Henry II's reign by Benoît de Sainte-Maure, who was later to provide the king with a genealogical history in the *Chronique des Ducs de Normandie*.[13]

This correlation between political instability and Trojan historiography, while not prescriptive, does serve to indicate that the Trojan narrative served English monarchs as a legitimizing device. Yet it also never lost its capacity to call into question the very purpose for which it was designed. There are various ways in which this subversiveness becomes manifest in medieval Troy narratives. For one thing, virtually every version of the story opens with an attack upon the authenticity of the others, a self-justifying gesture that necessarily undermines the authority of the entire enterprise—especially given the fact that texts claiming to be Trojan histories ranged from the eyewitness reports of Dares and Dictys to the elaborate Silver Age *imitatio* of Joseph of Exeter's *Bellum Troianum* to the sober prose of Guido delle Colonne's *Historia destructionis Troiae,* not to mention the widely divergent vernacular versions. And for another, a continual theme of Trojan historiography is the inexplicable nature of the events themselves: as Guido says, "Even if these many woes were pleasing to the gods, still, the original cause of these things, as trifling as

---

12. This is the Campsall manuscript, described by R. K. Root, *The Textual Tradition of Chaucer's Troilus,* Chaucer Society, 1st ser., 99 (London: Kegan Paul, Trench, Trübner, 1916), p. 5. The *Troilus* also figures in another less likely, political context: despite the fact that English books hardly ever crossed the Channel, the ambitious dukes of Burgundy bolstered their substantial Trojan collection with at least one and perhaps two copies of Chaucer's poem. See Eleanor Hammond, "A Burgundian Copy of Chaucer's *Troilus,*" *Modern Language Notes* 26 (1911), 32; and for the literary milieu, Ruth Morse, "Historical Fiction in Fifteenth-Century Burgundy," *Modern Language Review* 75 (1980), 48–64.

13. See above, n. 6.

unimportant, rightly troubles human hearts."[14] But for our purposes, the most telling evidence of the instability of the Trojan story is the generic instability of its various instantiations. The literary history of Troy begins with the "diaries" or *ephemeroi* of Dares and Dictys, texts that unequivocally proclaim their historicity. But Benoît's 26,000-line rewriting elaborately amplifies these originating documents with the addition of extended amorous subplots, creating a generic instability that is then enacted throughout the subsequent history of the form. On the one hand, Guido delle Colonne not only translates the narrative into Latin prose but subordinates the romantic subplots to the martial exploits and political machinations that constitute the *narratio rei gestae* of medieval historiography. And yet on the other hand, Benoît's lovers were often detached from their historical context and used as instances of the erotic life, and nowhere more completely than in Boccaccio's *Filostrato,* where their significance derives not from their historical value but from the service they can render to the author's own courtly life. It is only, then, with Chaucer's *Troilus and Criseyde* that these conflicting registers are reunited in a complex balance, allowing the story to speak once more to historical concerns. And yet the uncertain status of the very narrative that medieval secular historiography invoked as its founding moment is implied by Chaucer in his designation of his source as "Lollius," by which he seems to have meant a mumbler (from the ME *lollen, lullen*) with classical pretensions (hence the Latinate suffix -*ius*).

Although necessarily brief, these comments on the medieval historiography of Troy mean to suggest that the various tensions and contradictions that inhabited medieval thinking about history per se were registered at the level of textuality as a generic vacillation between history and romance, an instability that itself put into question not merely the authenticity of a particular narrative, or even of historiography as a whole, but the legitimacy of the historical life itself. Very much the same problematic may be seen at work in the development and deployment of the Arthurian legend, and is articulated in all its complexity in the Alliterative *Morte Arthure.* Again, it is Henry II who first appropriated the Arthurian aura for political purposes, as Wace's translation of Geoffrey's *Historia* suggests. In fact, Henry's court was something of a center of Arthurian literature, much to the irritation of its more Latinate members.[15] The works of Thomas of Britain and Marie de France were prob-

---

14. Guido della Colonne, *Historia destructionis Troiae,* trans. Mary Elizabeth Meek (Bloomington: Indiana University Press, 1974), p. 9; see also pp. 10, 43, 114, 146–47.

15. In his *Speculum caritatis,* Aelred of Rievaulx has a monastic novice confess to being moved to tears by *fabulae* about "an Arthur of whom I know nothing" (ed. A. Hoste and C. Talbot, *CCM* 1 [Turnhout: Brepols, 1971], 2.17.51, p. 90), while his disciple Peter of

ably read in court circles, although probably not written there, and Chrétien de Troyes' first two romances, *Erec et Enide* and *Cligès,* have affiliations with Angevin interests that argue for an English provenance.[16] There is as well the fantastic *Draco Normannicus* (c. 1168) by Stephen of Rouen, a bizarre poetic composition that conflates Merlin's prophecies, Breton nationalism, romanticized French history, and Arthurian eschatology in order, apparently, both to exalt Henry and deflate Breton hopes for Arthur's return.[17]

Arthur's grip upon the medieval political imagination extended well past the twelfth century. In 1278 Edward I also had the tomb of his *quondam* predecessor opened and the remains transported to the high altar at Glastonbury, an event that was only the most dramatic of his many Arthurian observances.[18] So potent, apparently, was the Arthurian legitimization that it could be invoked in even the most illegitimate of contexts. When in 1321 Thomas of Lancaster was conspiring with the Scots to overthrow Edward II he went under the pseudonym "King Arthur,"[19] and when Roger Mortimer succeeded six years later in dethroning Edward he staged a "Round Table" tournament that invoked Arthurian pretensions that his family had had for three generations.[20] Given these strategies of division, it is clear why Edward III tried to reappropriate the Arthurian legend to the monarchy by founding the Order of the Garter

---

Blois, in a *Liber de confessione* intended for a more general audience, complains about the lachrymose effects of fables about Arthur, "Gangan" (Gawain?), and Tristan because they preempt emotions that should be directed to Christ (*PL* 207: 1088–89). Behind these complaints stands Augustine's guilty weeping for the death of Dido in *Confessions* 1.13.

16. On Marie de France, see Broich, *Studien zum literarischen Patronat im England,* p. 37 n. 50, and E. A. Francis, "Marie de France et son temps," *Romania* 72 (1951), 78–99; on Thomas of Britain, Bartina Wind, "Nos incertitudes au sujet du 'Tristan' de Thomas," in *Mélanges de langue et de littérature du moyen âge et de la Renaissance offerts à Jean Frappier* (Geneva: Droz, 1970), 2.1129–38; on Chrétien, see Constance Bullock-Davies, "Chrétien de Troyes and England," *Arthurian Literature* 1 (1981), 1–61; Anthime Fourrier, *Le courant réaliste dans le roman courtois* (Paris: A. G. Nizet, 1960), pp. 160–74, who reads *Cligès* as anti-Angevin, while Erich Köhler, *Ideal und Wirklichkeit in der höfischen Epik* (Tübingen: M. Niemeyer, 1956), trans. from the 2d ed. of 1970 by Eliane Kaufholz as *L'aventure chevaleresque* (Paris: Gallimard, 1974), sees Chrétien's oeuvre as promoting Angevin interests.

17. For a full summary, see Bezzola, *Origines et la formation de la littérature courtoise en Occident,* pp. 126–39; for commentary, Broich, *Studien zum literarischen Patronat im England,* pp. 88–92, and J. S. P. Tatlock, "Geoffrey and King Arthur in *Normannicus Draco,*" *Modern Philology* 31 (1933), 1–18, 113–25. On Arthur as an Angevin hero, see Gordon H. Gerould, "King Arthur and Politics," *Speculum* 2 (1927), 33–51.

18. Roger Sherman Loomis, "Edward I, Arthurian Enthusiast," *Speculum* 28 (1953), 114–27.

19. *Calendar of Close Rolls, 1318–23* (London: Longmans, 1895), pp. 525–26; May McKisack, *The Fourteenth Century* (Oxford: Clarendon Press, 1959), p. 68.

20. Mary Giffin, "Cadwalader, Arthur, and Brutus in the Wigmore Manuscript," *Speculum* 16 (1941), 109–20.

with its own Round Table.[21] But this repossession was necessarily temporary: at the end of the Middle Ages Henry Tudor encompassed himself with Arthuriana, including naming his eldest son "Arthur." When history is negotiable the future always has the last word.

Both in their first form and in their later versions, the Arthurian legends, like the Trojan, are persistently marked by the paradox of their origin. Fabrications used to affirm a historical past, their historical authenticity is from the beginning at issue: history, it seems, comes into existence and into question simultaneously. In his *Gesta regum Anglorum,* written in the early 1120s, William of Malmesbury had issued a call for a historian who would rescue "warlike Arthur" from the lying fables of the Britons and provide him with the truthful history he deserved.[22] Geoffrey's mockingly brilliant response aped the forms of historical accuracy that William and his fellow historian Henry of Huntingdon had established but placed them in the service of an elaborate and excessive counterfeit. Far from rescuing Arthur from factitiousness, Geoffrey's book served to ignite a controversy. William of Newburgh's commentary was the most explicit—and best informed—attack upon Geoffrey, but it was hardly the only one. Gerald of Wales, for instance, despite his heavy reliance on Geoffrey throughout his *Itinerarium Galliae,* (re)told a malicious story about the demonic properties of the *Historia,* and as late as the mid-fourteenth century Ranulph Higden cast doubt on the authenticity of Geoffrey's account.[23] But the most severe challenge to the historicity of the Arthurian story came not from historians—most of whom simply included an abbreviation of Geoffrey in their own accounts—but from the continued existence of the British fables that Geoffrey's work was supposed to repress. The Arthurian romances inevitably surrounded their chronicle cognates with an aura of fictiveness, casting upon historiography a shadow of incredibility. In the late-twelfth-century *Chanson des Saisnes* Jean Bodel had already chauvinistically devalued the matter of Britain as "vains et plaisants" (line 7) in comparison to the historically true matter of France, and Arthurian writing was never able to divest itself of this dubiousness.

---

21. For Edward III's Arthurian interests, as well as the assimilation of the king to the Arthurian model by his admirers, see William Matthews, *The Tragedy of Arthur: A Study of the Alliterative "Morte Arthure"* (Berkeley: University of California Press, 1960), pp. 187–90.

22. Erich Auerbach, *Literary Language and Its Public in Late Latin Antiquity and in the Middle Ages,* trans. Ralph Manheim (New York: Pantheon, 1965), p. 191.

23. For Gerald of Wales, see A. C. L. Brown in *Speculum* 2 (1927), 449–50, and E. K. Chambers, *Arthur of Britain* (London: Sidgwick and Jackson, 1927), pp. 268–76; for Ranulph Higden, see the *Polychronicon,* ed. C. Babington and J. R. Lumby, Rolls Series (London: Longmans, 1865–86), 5.337–39; John Trevisa, who translated the *Polychronicon* in the 1380s, attacks Higden for doubting Arthur's historicity.

The formal effect of this fact is that Arthurian romance, often used for purposes of political authentication, defines for itself a complicated relationship to the question of its own authenticity. Two brief examples, Chrétien's *Le chevalier au lion* and the Middle English *Sir Gawain and the Green Knight,* can prepare us for the more extended analysis of the Alliterative *Morte Arthure.* In the *Roman de Rou,* written before 1174, the Anglo-Norman historian Wace had recounted his journey to the forest of Brocéliande in quest of the marvels that were, he had been told, to be found there. But Wace found nothing but a forest, and he concluded bitterly,

> Merveilles quis, mes nes trovai,
> Fol m'en revinc, fol i alai,
> Fol i alai, fol m'en revinc.
> Folie quis, por fol me tinc.

> I sought marvels, but I didn't find any. A fool I returned from there, a fool I went there, a fool I went there, a fool I returned from there. I sought folly, I consider myself a fool.[24]

Now at the beginning of *Le chevalier au lion,* Chrétien has the Arthurian knight Calogrenant recount to his chivalric companions *his* visit to Brocéliande. Calogrenant did in fact discover a marvel, a fountain with dramatically magical properties and a huge knight who defended it from interlopers. Calogrenant enacted the fountain's magic—by pouring water on a stone he summoned up a violent storm—but was then humiliatingly outjousted by the fountain's defender. He concludes his account with a summarizing statement that alludes to Wace, although now the words have a very different meaning:

> Ensi alai, ensi reving,
> Au revenir por fol me ting.
> Si vos ai conté com fos
> Ce c'onques mes conter ne vos.

> Thus I went, thus I returned, and in returning I consider myself a fool. So I have told you, like a fool, that which I never before wished to tell.[25]

Both journeys were quests for validation and both ended in folly, but their terms are sharply at odds—a disparity that measures the difference between Wace's history and Chrétien's romance. Wace rebukes himself for having tried to validate a fable with the experience of the eyewitness,

---

24. Wace, *Roman de Rou,* ed. Hugo Andresen (Heilbron: Gebr. Henninger, 1879), 2.284, lines 6717–20.

25. Chrétien de Troyes, *Le chevalier au lion,* ed. Mario Roques (Paris: H. Champion, 1965), p. 18, lines 577–80.

but Calogrenant's self-rebuke is ethical: first he failed as a knight, and now he has brought shame upon himself by his admission of failure. Not that Calogrenant ignores the demands of historiographical authentication: on the contrary, he enjoins his audience by reminding them that he is himself the eyewitness to the events he recounts:

> Et qui or me voldra entandre,
> cuer et oroilles me doit randre,
> car ne vuel pas parler de songe,
> ne de fable, ne de mançonge.
> [Don maint autre vos ont servi,
> Ainz vos dirai ce que je vi.]

> And now whoever wishes to understand, he ought to yield me his heart and his ears, for I do not wish to speak of a dream, nor of a fable, nor of a lie. [Many others have offered you those, but I will tell you that which I saw.][26]

Moreover, throughout the romance Chrétien verifies Calogrenant's story by almost flippantly returning his heroes over and over again to the fountain that Wace could not find: it functions as the story's central locale, appearing no less than five times. By thus ostentatiously confecting the evidence that Wace labored so hard to discover, Chrétien is calling into question the historiographical mode of verification per se. But his purpose is not to dismiss it by implicitly charging it with a similar factitiousness—as if by fabricating evidence in his text he were suggesting that all forms of textual assertion were equally fabricated—but rather to set it aside as irrelevant to the deeper meanings at which his romance is aiming. For the verification to which both Calogrenant's tale and Chrétien's romance aspire, a passive witnessing is not satisfactory—just as Calogrenant's folly is more profound than Wace's. In fact, Calogrenant's words are made true or redeemed not by the mere existence of the fountain but by the heroism of Yvain, who avenges his comrade's defeat with his own victory over the fountain's defender. Yvain had vowed to return to the court with "true evidence" (line 899: "anseignes veraies") and a "witness" (lines 1348–49: "tesmoing") of his victory, and in marrying his enemy's widow and taking on the defense of the fountain he becomes himself the proof of his own success, living evidence that his words are true. It is, then, ethical verification that Chrétien's romance seeks to define: words, whether they be narratives or oaths, fables or personal accounts, are true not because they correspond to the historical world but

---

26. The first four lines are from Roques's edition, lines 169–72; the lines in brackets do not appear in the manuscript printed by Roques, but are correctly printed as authentic in the edition by Wendelin Foerster (Halle: Niemeyer, 1887), lines 169–74.

because they impose an imperative upon the man who speaks. Language is *made* true, in short, by the ethos of chivalry.

This principle is exemplified throughout Yvain's adventures, in which the greatest folly is to speak empty words, whether they be the vaunting boasts of Kay, the unconsidered advice of Gawain, or the unkept promises of Yvain himself. In sum, Chrétien plays his romance off against the simplistic concept of authentication that motivates Wace's foolish journey. Far from evading the norms of historiographical verification—what Bede had called the *vera lex historiae*—Chrétien confronts and transcends them by asserting the priority of his own conception of narrative truth.[27] For just as Calogrenant's tale provides the model for subsequent actions in the world of romance, so the romance as a whole is directed to a historical world that has fallen away from old ideals and must be inspired by fictively generated norms of rectitude. "Or est Amors tornee a fable" (line 24), says Chrétien in the prologue, and the task of his narrative is to provide a model of virtuous behavior that will make true that which is now only "fable et mançonge" (line 27). This is the folly of the wise, the *stultitia praedicationis* (1 Cor. 1:21) that is exemplified in the fabling of the biblical parables that Calogrenant had himself allusively invoked in his introductory injunction to his audience to open their ears and hearts (see lines 169–74, cited above, and Matt. 13:14–15, Mark 8:18).

Another text that exploits the distinction between history and romance—the factual and the fictive—for strategic purposes is *Sir Gawain and the Green Knight,* which frames its Arthurian narrative with references to the fall of Troy and Brutus' conquest of England. The poet's purpose is not to persuade us that he is writing history—no poem about a green giant who replaces his severed head at will could ever have such pretensions—but rather to tell us that his story's range of relevance includes the pattern of British history as Geoffrey described it. If we do then locate the poem in this context, certain otherwise-muted themes become visible. When Brutus first conquered the island he suppressed the giants who were its native inhabitants, but the poem suggests that these original creatures are in some sense still at large, and with them the spirit of divisiveness that tragically undermined the Arthurian project and that reappears in this poem as Morgan le Fay's malevolent jealousy. Gawain's culpable if unknowing compact with these forces, then, has more than an individual significance, and his *untrawþe* to his own ideal

---

27. In the Preface to his *Historia ecclesiastica,* Bede defines the *vera lex historiae* as a reliance upon "common report" (*fama vulgata*), by which he means the "countless faithful witnesses who either know or remember the facts;" see *A History of the English Church and People,* trans. Leo Sherley-Price (Harmondsworth: Penguin Books, 1955), p. 35.

self is as well a betrayal of the ideal court of which he is the representative. Obviously the poem is no political allegory, but in locating its subtle meditations on personal and cultural failure within a historical context it both speaks to a fourteenth-century England torn by dissension and comments on the meaning of the historical process per se.[28] Like Benoît's *Roman* and Geoffrey's *Historia, Sir Gawain and the Green Knight* is a fabrication—a romance—that tries to tell a truth about history. Moreover, in defining as its central value *trawþe,* and then committing itself to a magical narrative, the poem forces us to recognize that the crucial events by which history is shaped often present themselves in unprepossessing and even deceptive forms.

Finally, if the formal status of these texts can be seen as itself relevant to the problematic of historical action that they confront, we should also be aware that their thematic interests are similarly paradoxical. For they bespeak a historical imagination located between a past that is thought to be all-powerful (*verum quia vetus*) but is in fact pliable, and a present that feels itself to be always in need of support but is in fact intransigent in its demands. The result, in general terms, is an overwhelming concern in these texts with just these subterranean shuntings of influence and authority that bind together "then" and "now," "it was" with "it might have been." These texts not only create the past but meditate upon that process, committing themselves to the endless negotiation that constitutes historicism. Specifically, the issues raised by this discussion can provide us with an interpretive purchase upon Arthurian literature, and in particular upon one of its finest Middle English representatives, the Alliterative *Morte Arthure*. The history of the genre and the history of the times are mutually inscribed in this poem, providing occasions of form and theme that allow for a meditation on the meaning of history per se— for, that is, a historical consciousness.

2

The Alliterative *Morte Arthure* is a work that despite its major importance has not yet achieved a secure place in the canon of English literature. Perhaps, then, a summary will not be out of place. The poem retells the story of Arthur's nearly successful campaign against the Roman emperor Lucius, a campaign that functions as the major episode in Geoffrey

---

28. On the historical situating, see Theodore Silverstein, "*Sir Gawain,* Dear Brutus, and Britain's Fortunate Foundling: A Study in Comedy and Convention," *Modern Philology* 62 (1965), 189–206. In *Old English and Middle English Poetry* (London: Routledge and Kegan Paul, 1977), Derek Pearsall notes that this kind of historical preface occurs in six alliterative poems and calls it "something of a signature of alliterative poetry" (p. 158).

of Monmouth's account of the Arthurian tragedy. Challenged by Lucius to pay tribute to Rome, an act of homage dating back to Julius Caesar and recently reconfirmed on the British side by Uther Pendragon, Arthur not only rejects submission but asserts instead his own claim to the imperial throne. The outraged Lucius assembles his allies and marches into France, where Arthur—having paused to exterminate the monstrous giant of Mont St. Michel—joins him in battle. Arthur destroys Lucius and his host, reduces the city of Metz, then enters Italy and marches on Rome. The few senators left alive are eager to crown him emperor, but the night before his coronation Arthur is visited by a terrible dream, in which he is at once enrolled as one of the Nine Worthies and then subjected, like them, to the tyranny of Fortune's wheel, on which he rises only to be thrown down. The next morning he learns from an English pilgrim named Sir Cradoke that his regent in Britain, Mordred, has formed a liaison with Guenevere and seized the throne. Returning home, Arthur immediately suffers the loss of his chief retainer Gawain, who heroically if foolishly attacks Mordred's massive force with a handful of men, and then tracks Mordred down in the West where the final battle is fought. In this version of the story, both men are definitively killed: there is a *rex quondam* but no *rex futurus*.[29]

The poem survives in a single manuscript of about 1440, but was probably composed in the form in which we now have it about forty years earlier.[30] Recent scholarship has shown that some of the details almost certainly refer to the deposition of Richard II in 1399,[31] although these are by no means the only historical allusions, nor does the poem speak only to a single event in the life of the times. It has usually been thought that Arthur's invasion of Europe bears an unmistakable rele-

29. When this chapter was first written, the best edition was by Valerie Krishna (New York: Burt Franklin, 1976). It has now been superseded by Mary Hamel's excellent *Morte Arthure: A Critical Edition* (New York: Garland, 1984), which contains a hundred-page introduction, elaborate notes, bibliography, and glossary. Although I have been unable to take advantage of Hamel's supporting materials, I have checked my citations against her text. A recent survey of criticism is provided by Karl Heinz Göller in a collection of essays he has edited, *The Alliterative Morte Arthure: A Reassessment of the Poem* (Cambridge: D. S. Brewer, 1981), pp. 7–14.

30. The manuscript is Lincoln Cathedral MS 91, written by Robert Thornton; there is a facsimile with an introduction by D. S. Brewer and A. E. B. Owen, 2d ed. (London: Scolar Press, 1977). On Thornton, see the important articles by George R. Keiser, "Lincoln Cathedral Library MS. 91: Life and Milieu of the Scribe," *Studies in Bibliography* 32 (1979), 158–79, and "More Light on the Life and Milieu of Robert Thornton," *Studies in Bibliography* 36 (1983), 111–19.

31. Larry D. Benson, "The Date of the Alliterative *Morte Arthure*," in Jess B. Bessinger, Jr., and Robert K. Raymo, eds., *Medieval Studies in Honor of Lillian Herlands Hornstein* (New York: New York University Press, 1976), pp. 19–40.

vance to the adventures of Edward III in France, and indeed the fact that both campaigns have the same *casus belli*—the English king's refusal to pay homage to a foreign monarch and his subsequent claims to the foreign throne—makes a comparison inevitable.[32] This range of historical relevance suggests that the poem may well have been composed over a considerable period of time, through a process of accretion and revision familiar to medieval literature, and that it embodies a kind of historical layering, with level laid on level. In fact, as we shall see, this geological structure is a part of the poem's subject as well as of its form.[33]

Moreover, while the poem resists any restricted or exclusive application to the issues of any one time, it insists upon rendering its world with the kind of circumstantial detail we associate with fact, not fiction. Whether he has relied upon his own experience of the Hundred Years' War or upon literary accounts such as the *Life of the Black Prince* by the Chandos Herald, the poet has immersed his narrative in the gritty particulars of late-medieval military life.[34] Not only are the grim details of the battlefield undisguised by the cultic language of chivalry, but the effects of war on society as a whole are rendered with a dispassionate attention that is all the more moving for its self-restraint.[35] More generally, the poem aspires throughout to representational fidelity, carefully including specifics of dress, diplomacy, language, geography, and chronology— Arthur's campaign can be followed on both map and calendar[36]—that

---

32. See Göller's summary of the critical debate, Alliterative *Morte Arthure,* pp. 11–14.

33. As evidence, let me cite just two instances—one large, one tiny—of awkwardness that bespeak a poem in process. In the dream of Fortune, the evidence of Arthur's good fortune is not the triumph he has just achieved but his earlier victory over King Frollo of France, which has not in fact been previously mentioned in the poem (lines 3345–46, 3404–5); second, the line that describes Mordred's allies as including the Montagues (a crucial piece of evidence for Benson's argument on dating) is metrically defective: "With the Mownttagus and oþer gret lordys" (line 3773). It may be that we see here the hand of a scribe, whether Thornton or an earlier copyist.

34. In "Edward III and the Alliterative *Morte Arthure,*" *Speculum* 48 (1973), 37–51, George R. Keiser argues for literary sources; and see John Finlayson, "*Morte Arthure:* The Date and a Source for the Contemporary References," *Speculum* 42 (1967), 624–38. Personal experience is invoked, most recently, by Juliet Vale, "Law and Diplomacy in the Alliterative *Morte Arthure,*" *Nottingham Medieval Studies* 23 (1979), 31–46.

35. See, for example, the gruesome description of the death of Gawain (lines 3840–59) and the accounts of the taking of Metz (lines 3068–71) and Como (lines 3110–27). It has often been argued, especially by William Matthews, *Tragedy of Arthur,* that this is an antiwar poem, but such a reading overvalues certain details at the expense of larger interests (as I hope to show) as well as ascribing to the poet a narrow moral purpose that ill befits his commitment to the tradition of heroic (i.e., martial) poetry. For a useful discussion, see John Barnie, *War in Medieval English Society: Social Values in the Hundred Years War, 1337–99* (Ithaca: Cornell University Press, 1974), pp. 147–50.

36. Valerie Krishna prints a useful map in her edition (there have of course been scholarly disputes over the details of the journey); for temporal references, see lines 64, 78, 415,

are so precisely rendered that critics have considered the poem an anti-romance, an epic, and a pseudochronicle.[37] Interestingly enough, the poem itself shows an unusual awareness of its place in the tradition of Arthurian literature. It recognizes that there are two streams of Arthurian writing, "romaunce" (lines 3200, 3440) and "croncycle" (lines 3218, 3445), but locates itself at the source of both by designating them as later developments and calling itself a history: "herkenes now hedyrwarde and herys this *storye*" (line 25).[38] The point is not to make a claim for veracity—although based largely on Wace's translation of Geoffrey, the poem includes, as we shall see, large chunks of ostentatiously fictive material—but to insist that its focus is upon the historical world and its meaning.[39]

For it is not realism for its own sake that informs the attention to specificity. In its quest for historical meaning, the poem insists that what must be raised to significance is not a schematic outline of events but the historical world in all its random particularity. The itinerary of Arthur's triumphant sweep through France and Lorraine, across the Alps and into Lombardy and Tuscany, is studded with place names that serve to locate this campaign in a world that is reassuring in its historicity and yet troubling in its diversity, at once recognizable and alien. We are throughout reminded that Arthur's enemies, for all their conformity to the codes of medieval warfare, are foreigners who literally speak a different language. This fact is significantly insisted upon just as Arthur reaches the frustrated conclusion of his campaign. While walking in the Italian countryside the king engages a pilgrim in conversation in the "Latin corroumppede all" (line 3478) that, we are told, is the local language, and it

---

436, 462, 554, 625, 634, 1006, 2371, 2482, 3078, 3145, 3176, 3183, 3900, 4057 (an incomplete list). The campaign begins on New Year's Day with the arrival of Lucius' ambassadors and concludes the same autumn with Arthur's death, in October or November.

37. For these labels, see, respectively, Karl Heinz Göller, *Alliterative Morte Arthure,* p. 16; John Finlayson, in the introduction to his edition (Evanston: Northwestern University Press, 1967), pp. 6ff., where he compares the poem to the chansons de geste; and C. S. Lewis, "The English Prose *Morte,*" in J. A. W. Bennett, ed., *Essays on Malory* (Oxford: Clarendon Press, 1963), p. 26, where he berates the poem for its "vast contradictions of known history scrawled across a whole continent." One of the best accounts of medieval attitudes toward historical legend may be found in Lewis' *The Discarded Image* (Cambridge: Cambridge University Press, 1964): "I am inclined to think that most of those who read 'historial' works about Troy, Alexander, Arthur, or Charlemagne, believed their matter to be in the main true. But I feel much more certain that they did not believe it to be false. I feel surest of all that the question of belief or disbelief was seldom uppermost in their minds. That, if it was anyone's business, was not theirs. Their business was to learn the story" (p. 181).

38. On *storye* as "history," see Paul Strohm, "*Storie, Spelle, Geste, Romaunce, Tragedie:* Generic Distinctions in the Middle English Troy Narratives," *Speculum* 46 (1971), 348–59.

39. On Wace as the source, rather than Geoffrey or Layamon, see Finlayson's Introduction, pp. 31–32; his opinion is supported in his 1962 Cambridge dissertation.

is only after the pilgrim has similarly replied that Arthur realizes by his accent that he is conversing not with an Italian but with a fellow Englishman—with, indeed, a knight of his own chamber, Sir Cradoke.[40]

Arthur inhabits a world that is not merely various but fragmented, and whose disunities witness to the attritions of time. The war between Arthur and the Christian emperor Lucius reveals Christendom to be shattered within itself, just as the language of Christendom, Dante's "latino . . . perpetuo e non corruttibile," has become "Latin corroumppede all."[41] This is apparently a world grown old, a *mundus senescens* declining into its last age.[42] But decadence inevitably implies restoration, and there is much in the poem that would encourage us to see in Arthur the agent of historical renewal.[43] For one thing, his campaign against Lucius is presented as part of the inevitable process of *translatio imperii,* the westering of empire from Troy to Rome, where it will eventually serve as, in Father Chenu's words, "a providential preparation for the age of Christ."[44] As the *pax Augusta* was the cradle in which Christ was first born, so a renovated Empire will provide the context for his rebirth.[45] The idea of *translatio* was already, as we have seen, an important theme

---

40. This passage, and Chaucer's "a maner Latyn corrupt" from line 519 of the Man of Law's Tale, are discussed by John Burrow in *Medium Aevum* 30 (1961), 33–37.

41. Dante, *Convivio* 1.5; in the *De vulgari* 1.1 this immutable language is called *grammatica* and identified with both Latin and Greek, but is regarded not as prior to the vernaculars but as *secundaria,* an artificial abstract drawn from the living if corrupted *diversa vulgaria.*

42. This theme is well discussed in relation to other late-medieval English writing by James Dean, "Time Past and Time Present in Chaucer's Clerk's Tale and Gower's *Confessio Amantis,*" *ELH* 44 (1977), 401–18, and in "The World Grown Old and Genesis in Middle English Historical Writing," *Speculum* 57 (1982), 548–68.

43. See, e.g., Augustine, *Enarrationes in Ps. 38.9:* "Looking, therefore, upon sin, upon mortality, upon time flying by, upon moaning and labor and sweat, upon ages succeeding one another without rest, senselessly from infancy into old age—looking at these things, let us see in them the old man, the old day, the old canticle, the Old Testament. But if we turn to the inward man, to the things that are to be renewed, let us find . . . a new man, a new day, a new canticle, the New Testament—and we shall love this newness so that we shall not fear there any oldness." Quoted by Gerhart B. Ladner, *The Idea of Reform* (Cambridge: Harvard University Press, 1959), pp. 236–37. While Augustine's renewal is personal rather than historical, by the twelfth century, as Amos Funkenstein ("Periodization and Self-Understanding in the Middle Ages and Early Modern Times," *Medievalia et Humanistica* n.s. 5 [1974], 3–23) points out, Augustine's radical separation of "the course of the *civitas dei peregrinus in terris* from that of the *civitas terrena*" had been overcome, most explicitly by Otto of Freising. For Otto, the great promoter of the idea of *translatio imperii,* the Augustinian scheme is used in the service of a historiographical attitude that is at heart anti-Augustinian.

44. Chenu, *Nature, Man, and Society in the Twelfth Century,* p. 185.

45. Werner Goez, *Translatio Imperii* (Tübingen: Mohr, 1958); Robert Folz, *The Concept of Empire in Western Europe,* trans. S. A. Ogilvie (London: Edward Arnold, 1969); Charles T. Davis, *Dante and the Idea of Rome* (Oxford: Clarendon Press, 1957).

in Geoffrey's *Historia*. Brutus is not merely a Trojan refugee but a Roman exile, expelled for having inadvertently slain his father. He at once embodies the Roman line—he is Aeneas' great-grandson—and stands as a deadly challenge, and he founds in Britain the nation that will become Rome's greatest rival.[46] Geoffrey structures his narrative on just this Rome-Britain opposition, but while Rome is thrice subdued it is never finally conquered: the British are on each occasion undone by treachery at home. Arthur's campaign against Lucius, then, is in the *Morte Arthure* as in Geoffrey's *Historia* both the summation of these efforts and an analysis of their failure.

The *Morte Arthure,* however, goes well beyond Geoffrey and the other versions dependent on him in stressing both the legitimacy of Arthur's claim on Rome and the eschatological meanings that his imperial ambitions imply. When Lucius' ambassadors demand tribute of Arthur, Geoffrey has him first reply by asserting that the right of conquest supersedes any historical precedents: "Let him who comes out on top carry off what he has made up his mind to take!"[47] Only after thus dismissing the claims of history does Geoffrey's Arthur then invoke them, with breathtaking inconsistency, on his own behalf. But the poet of the *Morte Arthure* suppresses the argument from might entirely, and has his Arthur speak only to historical rights: "Myne ancestres ware emperours" (line 276), he says, and later adds, "Myn enmy . . . ocupyes myn heritage, þe Empyre of Rome" (lines 642–43). The past provides not only a precedent, as with Geoffrey, but a coherent lineage that has been broken and must now be restored. The Emperor Lucius is defined throughout as a usurper, and nowhere more explicitly than in the speech flung in his face by Arthur's tactless ambassador Gawain:

And þe fals heretyke þat emperoure hym calleȝ,
That occupyes in errour the empyre of Rome,
Sir Arthure herytage, þat honourable kynge,
That all his auncestres aught bot Vtere hym one,
That ilke cursynge þat Cayme kaghte for his brothyre

---

46. In *The Vision of History in Early Britain* (New York: Columbia University Press, 1966), Robert Hanning argues that Brutus' early history was originally, in the *Historia Britonnum,* a device to cut him free from the Roman past: "The Britons are a new order, free from the traditions of war and vengeance which in effect condemn the individual of the old society before he can help himself" (p. 105). But in its new context in Geoffrey's *Historia,* in which Britain is bedeviled precisely with war and vengeance, Brutus is now seen to have brought his past with him in the very effort to separate himself from it.

47. Geoffrey of Monmouth, *History of the Kings of Britain,* trans. Lewis Thorpe (Harmondsworth: Penguin, 1966), p. 233. For the Latin, see Edmond Faral, ed., *La légende Arthurienne,* Vol. 3 (Paris: H. Champion, 1929), p. 249: "et qui fortior supervenerit ferat quod habere exoptavit."

Cleffe on þe, cukewalde, with crounne ther thow lengeȝ,
For the vnlordlyeste lede þat I on lukede euer!

(Lines 1307–13)

The reference to Cain is only a small part of the defamation to which the poem subjects the Emperor. His allies are designated not just as from the East, as in Geoffrey, but specifically as heathens, "Sowdanes and Sarazenes owt of sere landes" (line 607).[48] Before undertaking the campaign Arthur's knights swear solemn vows on the "vernicle," the veil with which Veronica wiped the face of Christ and that was preserved at Rome.[49] Arthur's knights are embarking upon a quest that is in part to recover the holy relics of Christendom, and as the campaign proceeds Arthur is embraced with an aura of election. As he walks the fortifications before Metz, he is warned to take cover but replies with equanimity that "a corownde kynge with krysom enoynttede" (line 2447) need fear no casual attack. In short, we are made aware that Arthur is engaged not merely in a war of territorial ambition but in a crusade; and as he approaches his coronation at Rome, he is already planning to extend his conquests toward the hoped-for destination of all medieval monarchs, the Holy Land, where he will, he says, "reuenge the Renke that on the Rode dyede" (line 3217). Given this coalescence of political and religious motifs, both the reader and Arthur might be forgiven the thought that he is to become not merely a Roman emperor but that last emperor for whom the Middle Ages had waited so long, the "prince of the west," as "Mandeville" put it, who "shal conquer the Holy Land with helpe of othere Cristene" and for whom the withered tree of Paradise shall again bear fruit.[50]

That Arthur is not the agent of a providential history is the meaning of both the dream of Fortune and Cradoke's message about Mordred's rebellion. Having tried to restore a divided political world to its original (and final) unity, Arthur is recalled home by a division that continues to

---

48. Lucius is also accompanied by heathens from the Baltic lands—"Pruyslande" and "Lettow" (lines 604–5).

49. The structure of this episode derives from the *Voeux de paon* by Jacques de Longuyon (1312), a narrative poem loosely attached to the Alexander romances; in the original the Alexandrian heroes vow to do great deeds upon a baked peacock, a device our author significantly revises in a religious direction. The *Voeux de paon* provides as well the first literary account of the Nine Worthies. Perhaps also relevant is the satiric *Voeux du héron*, which uses the premise of Jacques de Longuyon's poem to provide a bitterly anti-English account of the beginnings of the Hundred Years' War; see B. J. Whiting, "The Vow of the Heron," *Speculum* 20 (1945), 261–78.

50. *The Bodley Version of Mandeville's Travels,* ed. M. C. Seymour, EETS 253 (London: Oxford University Press, 1963), p. 49; cf. EETS 153 (London: Oxford University Press, 1919), p. 45. The opening lines of the poem cater to the hopes for Arthurian success by summarizing the narrative as if it recorded only the victory over Lucius (lines 22–25).

fester within his own nation and his own family.[51] That he bears some
responsibility for his failure is clear, as he himself almost too eagerly
acknowledges; but while the kind and degree of this responsibility are at
the center of most critical discussion, they are not, I think, finally at the
heart of the poem.[52] Rather, it is the very pattern of expansion and collapse that is the poem's deepest concern, the rhythm of striving and disappointment, of aspiration toward transcendence followed by a tragic
submission to the iron law of historical recurrence. This is the pattern
that is enacted in the poem's geography and chronology, and that in the
image of the Wheel of Fortune is given a philosophical embodiment. But
it is not, we should be careful to note, a philosophy that the poem single-
mindedly espouses. Rather, the theme of recurrence functions as one element in a complex and difficult meditation on the meaning of historical
action in a world in which history is given and not made.

3

We can make the terms of this meditation clearer by examining in
detail the two major additions that the poet makes to his source: Gawain's
foraging expedition—undertaken while Arthur is beseiging Metz—and
the dream of Fortune itself. Apparently a romance intrusion in a poem
that aspires to representational fidelity, the foraging expedition has suf-
fered almost total critical neglect, although I believe it provides a paradigm of the poem's method and meaning.[53] The episode begins when

---

51. C. L. Regan, "The Paternity of Mordred in the Alliterative *Morte Arthure*," *Bulletin
bibliographique de la Société Internationale Arthurienne* 25 (1973), 153–54, argues that the poem
knows nothing of Arthur's incestuous begetting of Mordred, but there are in fact several
clear references to Mordred's irregular genealogy (lines 3741–44, 3776) as well as some less
explicit allusions (lines 689–92, 4062, 4174).

52. Matthews, *Tragedy of Arthur,* sees Arthur as culpable from the beginning by engaging in an imperialistic war; John Finlayson, "The Concept of the Hero in *Morte Arthure*,"
in *Chaucer und seine Zeit: Symposion für Walter Schirmer* (Tübingen: M. Niemeyer, 1968), pp.
249–74, argues instead that it is only after the defeat of Lucius that Arthur's behavior becomes culpable; while Larry Benson, "The Alliterative *Morte Darthur* and Medieval Tragedy," *Tennessee Studies in Literature* 11 (1966), 75–87, suggests more thoughtfully that the
poem records the conflict of two goods, "the Christian detachment that is necessary for
ultimate happiness even on this earth and the complete engagement with an earthly ideal
that is necessary for heroism" (pp. 80–81). All of these readings—and others—share the
common assumption that the poem's raison d'être is ethical judgment. To be sure, here as
elsewhere in medieval literature the reader is invited to pass judgment and to extract a moral
from his reading; but it would be a mistake to regard this self-justifying process as the
single purpose toward which all of the elements of the work are directed.

53. Only Finlayson, Introduction, pp. 18–19, has provided any critical commentary;
he suggests that in its explicit romanticism and individualism the episode marks the point
at which Arthur's campaign loses its moral justification. The reading that follows, although
different, is consistent with this interpretation.

Arthur sends Gawain and some French allies in search of forage, but instead of finding supplies they become engaged in two separate actions against the enemy. The first is a single combat between Gawain and a pagan warrior called Priamus, in which the Arthurian knight is victorious. The second is against a huge enemy force en route to raise the siege. The French, intimidated by the disparity in numbers, try to retire, but in a series of heroic speeches Gawain goads them on and together French and English achieve a magnificent victory, returning to Arthur in triumph.

Now in constructing this episode our poet relied upon two sources. One is the *Fuerres de Gadres* (or *Foray of Gaza*), a self-contained narrative attached to the twelfth-century *Roman d'Alexandre*.[54] In the *Fuerres* the foraging expedition is sent out by Alexander while he is besieging Tyre. The Greeks discover some cattle but are immediately attacked, first by a small group of knights, then by a huge army of Gadarenes en route to relieve Tyre. Here the disparity in numbers also elicits heroic speeches and deeds, although now the argument is over who will forgo the opportunity for heroic achievement in order to return for help, and only after a gallant (and interminable) dispute is Alexander finally summoned to rescue the few Greeks who now remain. Despite this minor difference, however, it is clear that the *Fuerres* provided the basic structure for Gawain's expedition, and the reliance is in fact also enforced by several similarities in detail.[55]

But in the *Morte Arthure* our poet chose to substitute for the first battle against the Gadarene knights the single combat between Priamus and Gawain. Here too there is a source, creating the total effect of an interpolation inset within an interpolation. The source in this case is a late-twelfth- or early-thirteenth-century chanson de geste called *Fierabras,* a crusade poem that deals with the Charlemagne, Roland, and Oliver legend.[56] In the *Fierabras,* the severely wounded Oliver engages the pagan giant Fierabras in single combat, a responsibility that has fallen to him because Roland, offended by a slight from Charlemagne, has refused; and Oliver not only defeats Fierabras but converts him to Christianity. But from this high-minded beginning, the chanson de geste de-

---

54. The *Fuerres* is printed in *The Medieval French Roman d'Alexandre, 2: Version of Alexandre de Paris,* ed. E. C. Armstrong et al., Elliott Monographs 37 (Princeton: Princeton University Press, 1937), pp. 60–127.

55. See Matthews, *Tragedy of Arthur,* pp. 44–46.

56. *Fierabras,* eds. A. Kroeber and G. Servois (Paris: F. Viewig, 1860). This source was first proposed by R. H. Griffith, "Malory, *Morte Arthure,* and *Fierabras,*" *Anglia* 32 (1909), 389–98. John Finlayson, "The Alliterative *Morte Arthure* and Sir Firumbras," *Anglia* 92 (1974), 380–86, suggested that the direct source was one of the two Middle English translations. The points I wish to make about this source are the same in either case.

clines into frivolity. The peers get themselves trapped in a luxuriously provisioned Saracen castle, and it is not long before the crusade has subsided into an Eastern wish fulfillment of maidens to be seduced, magic trinkets to be fiddled with, and (best of all) Saracens to be killed.

What could have been the motives of the poet of the *Morte Arthure* in alluding to this improbable material? To begin to answer that question, we need to understand what each of the two sources could themselves have been thought to mean. In the *Fierabras* Oliver's initial championing of the Carolingian court against its pagan enemy stands as an ideal of Christian heroism that passes judgment on the rest of the poem. The purpose of the crusade is to recover the relics of the Passion, and it is Fierabras, conqueror of Jerusalem and Rome, who possess them. In defeating and converting Fierabras, then, Oliver has in effect accomplished the crusade single-handedly. But the starkly simple crusading ideology— "Paien unt tort e crestiens unt dreit"[57]—is here somewhat troubled. For if the poet carefully contrasts Oliver's humility and loyal self-sacrifice to Fierabras' arrogant contempt, he also contrasts it to Roland's pride, to Charlemagne's indolence, and to Ganelon's treachery; and the narrative as a whole shows how thoroughly compromised the crusading ideology has become. By the end of the poem, in fact, it is to be found embodied not in Charlemagne's peers at all, but rather—ironicallly—in the converted pagan Fierabras.

The *Fierabras* is, then, a poem about the corruption of the crusading spirit: in their foray into Saracen territory the Christians have become mired in the faithlessness they have come to punish. The Alexandrian *Fuerres de Gadres,* the episode's other source, provides a similar interpretive context. Set in the Holy Land—the battle takes place in the highly significant Vale of Josephas or Jehosephat, as the *Morte Arthure* itself notes[58]—and deploying the traditional motif of a conflict between heroic self-fulfillment and submission to a larger cause, the *Fuerres* also gestures toward the crusading ideal. But the legions of Alexander are on no pilgrimage to a holy place but rather a futile journey to the ends of the earth; and when they arrive there, at the gates of the Earthly Paradise,

---

57. *La chanson de Roland,* ed. Joseph Bédier (Paris: H. Piazza, 1964), line 1015, p. 86.

58. "Was neuer siche a justynge at journé in erthe / In the vale of Josephate, as gestes vs telles, / When Julyus and Joatall ware juggede to dy" (lines 2875–77). Jehosephat is the locale not only for this confrontation but for Titus' battle against the Jews when he revenged Christ's death—recounted in the ME *Siege of Jerusalem,* from which the poet probably got the detail—and, of course, for the Last Judgment. The *Fuerres de Gadres* gestures toward these two progressively more exalted contests but is unable to elevate its own battle to either level. Julius and Joatall do not appear, to my knowledge, in the *Fuerres,* and the allusion has not been explained; Hamel calls these names "meaningless and certainly scribal" (p. 348, note to lines 2876–77).

they will be denied entrance and told to retrace their steps. For them the capture of Jerusalem is not the climax of their efforts but just one step on a meaningless circuit.[59] The poet of the *Morte Arthure* has therefore interpolated, as seemingly victorious episodes in Arthur's campaign, fragments of two failed heroic expeditions, making the point clearer by repetition while at the same time allowing each fragment to reveal the meaning of the other.

But while our poet's interpretation includes the meanings proffered by his two sources, separately and together, it goes beyond them, even to the extent of providing both a historiographical statement and a comment upon his own strategies of allusion and revision. He not only passes judgment upon the Arthurian project but in the details of the episode analyzes its failure by focusing on the ideology of allusion itself, whether its context be political or literary. The single combat between Gawain and Priamus might be supposed to be a sign of Arthur's eschatological destiny, especially since the Oliver-Fierabras contest stands itself as a norm of crusading rectitude. But in fact the more dubious context established by the whole of the *Fierabras* controls its presentation here and redirects its force, as several crucial revisions show. For what is unsettling here is that the *Morte Arthure* omits the very topos of conversion that gives the episode its raison d'être in the *Fierabras*. Priamus is a pagan, but at no point does he ask for baptism or lament its absence, as does Fierabras.[60] The point is underlined by the presence in both texts of magic fluids. Fierabras, among other relics of the Passion, improperly possesses flasks filled with the fluid with which Christ was embalmed, and whenever wounded by Oliver he simply douses and heals himself. This detail is more than a mere romance exoticism, for it functions to underline the contrast between Fierabras' constantly restored body and his unregenerate soul, which requires and receives another, symbolic laving. Priamus' magic fluid is of a different order, however, as is his paganism. He is in fact not a Saracen but a classical warrior, heir to the heroic virtues of the antique world and descended, he tells us, not only from Hector of Troy and Alexander but also from Judas Maccabeus and Joshua (lines 2602–5). He embodies, in short, the virtue of the non-Christian world as it is later to be manifested in the figure of the Nine Worthies. Appropriately, then, his flask "es full of þe flour of þe four well / þat

---

59. Interestingly, the full version of the *Fuerres de Gadres* was heavily influenced by the crusading narrative of William of Tyre; see *The Medieval French Roman d'Alexandre, 4: Le Roman de Fuerre de Gadres D'Eustache,* ed. E. C. Armstrong and Alfred Foulet, Elliott Monographs 39 (Princeton: Princeton University Press, 1942), p. 23.

60. *Fierabras,* lines 1510–12 (p. 46); *Sir Ferumbras,* ed. Sidney J. Herrtage, EETS, ES 34 (London: Trübner, 1879), line 760.

flowes owte of Paradice" (lines 2705–6), clearly a reference to the aqua vitae discovered by Alexander in his journey to the Earthly Paradise.[61] With this balm Priamus heals a wound that would otherwise prove fatal to Gawain, but he neither asks for nor does he receive in return a baptismal anointing.[62] It appears that in this poem there is no superior fluid by which the essence of pagan heroism can be redeemed.

As a brief allegory of the transactions of past and present this episode represents the appropriation of the old, Alexandrian values by the new order. Priamus initially identified himself as "apparaunt . . . ayere" (line 2606) to the classical world, but after his defeat he realizes that his virtue will pass in the Christian era to Arthur: "*He* will be Alexander ayre, that all þe erthe lowttede, / Abillere þan euer was sir Ector of Troye" (lines 2634–35). Gawain's defeat of Priamus is a metaphor for historical transition, a *translatio virtutis* from past to present. But if the dominion of the present over the past is asserted, so too is the continuity between them. For the axial fact of discontinuity, the entrance into history of Jesus Christ, is here barely acknowledged.[63] Inevitably, then, value is conveyed in only one direction, from past to present: Priamus can heal Gawain's wounds but cannot himself be spiritually healed. Nor is the inheritance that he hands over subject to any redemptive transformation: the past is superseded but the act of supersession is itself without spiritual or even

---

61. Matthews, *Tragedy of Arthur,* p. 62. For this theme, and others relevant to the poem, see Mary Lascelles, "Alexander and the Earthly Paradise in Medieval English Writings," *Medium Aevum* 5 (1936), 31–47, 79–104, 173–88. Matthews stresses throughout the analogy between Arthur and Alexander, a comparison that was present at the legend's learned origin when Geoffrey of Monmouth drew upon the Alexander stories for his account of Arthur; see J. S. P. Tatlock, *The Legendary History of Britain* (Berkeley: University of California Press, 1950), pp. 312–20. It is relevant to note that according to the most recent paleographical report, the Thornton MS originally began with the *Morte Arthure* and that a prose *Alexander* was added later, apparently as an appropriate introduction: see Keiser, "Lincoln Cathedral Library MS. 91," pp. 177–78.

62. Unfortunately, the useful edition by Larry D. Benson, *The Death of Arthur* (Indianapolis: Bobbs-Merrill, 1974), includes an emendation at this point—derived from Malory—that makes Priamus ask for baptism (p. 189). Hamel, on the other hand, argues that since Priamus asks to be allowed "to schewe schortly my schrifte and schape for myn ende" (line 2588) he must already be a Christian; see p. 340, note to lines 2587–88, and Hamel's "The 'Christening' of Sir Priamus in the Alliterative *Morte Arthure,*" *Viator* 13 (1982), 295–307. But Priamus asks Gawain for this opportunity "for sake of *thy* Cryste" (line 2587), and there is no reason to think that the poet did not assume that virtuous pagans conducted their final moments on earth in much the same way as did Christians.

63. Priamus first asks Gawain, "Will thow, for knyghthede, kene me thy name?" (line 2619), and Gawain replies by falsely identifying himself as a chamber knave; Priamus then asks Gawain his identity "fore the krisome þat þou kaght þat day þou was crystenede" (line 2636) and Gawain replies with the truth. While the purpose of this conversation is uncertain, Priamus' invocation of the baptismal anointing at once acknowledges its historical existence and reminds us of its absence in this narrative.

historical value. Classical heroism is transferred but not transformed, and no answer is given to the question of how Arthur, invested with Alexander's force, can avoid Alexander's fate. Moreover, if the past authenticates the present it cannot be itself redeemed, cannot, that is, be seen as valid because it humbly prepares for a present that is inarguably different and better. There is here no typology, no old dispensation prefiguring a new. We are offered instead a wholly secular patrimony, a natural process of succession; hence Priamus' name, in allusion to the Trojan patriarch. It is only a brief step from here to the Nine Worthies on the Wheel of Fortune, a vision of history that undermines the very possibility of meaningful historical action.

But let me not move ahead to Arthur's dream without first stressing the fatal economy of this kind of historical consciousness. The poem sees the past as harboring a legitimizing authority of such value that it must be retained even if it costs the present its own historical identity. Arthur must be another Alexander even if it means that his career will enact the same curve of aspiration and disappointment. Not that this risk is lightly undertaken. The fear of recursion haunts the poem, and if it sees the past as uniquely valuable it ascribes to the present a desire for ascendancy, an ardor for selection and control that would grant to the past only so much survival as the present would wish. The stance toward the past remains as aggressive as Gawain's attack upon Priamus. When, in the subsequent battle against the men of Lorraine, Gawain urges on his troops, he compares them favorably in point of honor to their "elders" (line 2867), Absolon and Unwine, types, in scriptural and Germanic legend respectively, of rebellion against the father;[64] and when Arthur's knights first promote the campaign against Lucius they urge it in terms of redeeming and so surpassing the ancestral past. "Now schall we wreke full wele the wrethe of oure elders" (line 321), says the Welsh king, and King Lot adds, more ominously, "It es owre weredes to wreke the wrethe of oure elders" (line 385).[65] Moreover, since Uther Pendragon paid tribute to Rome the war is for Arthur personally a way to cancel a filial shame. And yet, with bitter irony, his efforts are undone by his own rebellious son Mordred: there is, it seems, no end to filial antagonism.

It is to be expected, then, that generational hostility should run in

---

64. On Absalom's revolt against his father, David, see 2 Kings 13–18. Of Unwine we know only that his name means "son born beyond hope" or "the unexpected one" and that he did not succeed his father Eastgota: see R. W. Chambers, *Widsith* (Cambridge: Cambridge University Press, 1912), pp. 219, 254; R. M. Wilson, *The Lost Literature of Medieval England* (London: Methuen, 1970), pp. 7–8.

65. These details, and the insistent foregrounding of the theme of generational conflict, are unique to the *Morte Arthure* among the chronicle versions.

both directions: sons not only challenge their fathers but are themselves at risk from paternal violence. When the foraging party is sent out by Arthur he makes it clear that the Frenchman Florent is in immediate charge but that Gawain, denominated here and nowhere else in the poem as "Wardayne" (lines 2494, 2678, 2740), is to maintain an ultimate authority. Moreover, the relationship between Gawain and the Frenchman has a familial value: Florent addresses him as "Fadyr" (line 2735) and describes himself as "bot a fawntkyn vnfraystede in armes" (line 2736), and Gawain urges them to attack the enemy because they have "faughte noghte þeire fill this fyftene wynter" (line 2822) but refuses to help them until they are challenged by more than the "gadlyngez" (line 2854) and "boyes" (line 2856) of the enemy's first wave. But Gawain's paternal condescension has telling consequences. Among the English contingent is "Chastelayne, a childe of þe kynges chambyre / [And] warde to sir Wawayn" (lines 2952–53), and the only significant casualty in the encounter is precisely this youth, overmatched by a Swedish knight. The point is not just Gawain's failure as warden, which matches the later and more deliberate failure of Mordred, appointed by his father as "Wardayne" (lines 650, 3523) of England. Rather, we see expressed in Gawain's failure to protect Chastelayne a dark and terrible motif that weaves itself throughout the narrative: the sacrifice of children.

This theme comes to us first in a lurid, almost comically grotesque form. The giant of Mont St. Michel, in a detail unique to this version, feeds on "crysmede childyre" (line 1051) roasted on spits, a scene whose horror is perhaps disarmed by its fairy-tale context. But we are forced to recall it in less protected circumstances when at the end of the poem the dying Arthur, in another unique detail, commands that Mordred's children "bee sleyghely slayne and slongen in watyrs" (line 4321).[66] The thematic import seems clear: just as the present feels itself tyrannized by the past so does it dominate the future, conveying a burdensome legacy of not only heroic achievement but also intolerable violence. It is this motif, moreover, that gives special point in the description of the Nine Worthies to the designation of Charlemagne and Godfrey of Bouillon as "childire" (line 3328) and the insistence—present only in their cases—that they achieved their positions only by inheritance: Charlemagne is "the kyng son of Fraunce" (line 3423), Godfrey "sall of Lorrayne be lorde be leefe of his fadire" (line 3432). Historically belated, they are above all children who will bear the burden of the example and fate of their ideological

---

66. Arthur's motives are of course dynastic, but the *Morte Arthure* adds a detail to the traditional narrative that suggests that this effort by the past to control the future will in the event be undone: Mordred has, we are told, gotten Guenevere with child (lines 3552, 3576), and of her fate and the child's the poem tells us nothing.

father, the first Christian worthy, Arthur, just as Arthur is himself subject to the fatal prototype defined by Alexander. But let us not forget that if the *moderni* of whatever period are tyrannized by the past, it is a past that they have themselves empowered. The reality, the poem suggests, is far different. When Alexander is finally granted a literal rather than a merely textual existence in the poem, in the portrait that appropriately stands at the head of the Nine Worthies, he is revealed to be "a lityll man that laide was benethe: / His leskes laye all lene and latheliche to schewe" (lines 3278–79). Far from being a figure of incomparable achievement, he is in fact an almost shocking representation of the impotent father.

I have been investigating here the genealogical and psychological meaning of historical repetition. We should always remember that the great defense against repetition is the destinal linearity entailed by the linked ideas of *translatio imperii* and the crusade. I have suggested that the foraging episode, despite or perhaps because of its conspicuous irrelevance, is the point at which the effort to sustain a linear conception of historical process breaks down. It is here that the present is revealed to be not a fulfillment of the past but a reenactment, and where the value that is conveyed from past to present is finally seen to have been illusory, an authority projected onto the past by the present and then read back in impossibly exaggerated terms. The literary analogue to this process is the tyranny of the source, and it is a striking fact that for all his revisions the poet does not deviate from the essential meaning of either the *Fierabras* or the *Fuerres de Gadres*. Written as poems about the secularization of the crusading ideology, they remain in their new habitat precisely that, never able to invest chivalric action with a meaning beyond itself. The layers of literary history reveal themselves to be identical, successive pages that are all inscribed with the same disabling message. Just as Arthur is recalled to Britain to confront the sins of his past, so the corpus of medieval literature can only recall the reader to the knowledge of his irreparably flawed origin.

The dream of Fortune both represents historical recurrence and functions in the narrative as the agency of recall. But in its detail it bespeaks a concern to place this historiography within the economy of the heroic life. The dream falls into two distinct parts. In the first Arthur is lost in a wood filled with savage beasts, including lions that "full lothely lykkyde þeire tuskes, / All fore lapynge of blude of [his] lele knyghtez" (lines 3234–35). Terrified by these "foule thyngez" (line 3237), Arthur escapes "to a medowe with montayngnes enclosyde, / The meryeste of medill-erthe that men myghte beholde" (lines 3238–39). Here are vines of silver adorned with grapes of gold, every fruit that flourishes on earth, and birds on every bough—details that recall unmistakably the Earthly

Paradise.[67] It is here that the second, longer movement of the dream takes place. Lady Fortune and her bejeweled wheel descend from the clouds with eight of the Nine Worthies.[68] Six of the eight (Alexander, Hector, Julius Caesar, Judas Maccabeus, Joshua, and David) have already fallen from the wheel; they first issue a collective lament—"That euer I rengnede on þi rog, me rewes it euer!" (line 3272)—and are then individually described and given a few lines of regret to speak. The two remaining Worthies (Charlemagne and Godfrey) are preparing to mount the wheel: "'This chaire of charbokle,' they said, 'we chalange hereaftyre'" (line 3326). Lady Fortune then places Arthur on the wheel, gives him a scepter, diadem, and a "pome" (line 3354) or orb engraved with a map of the world "In sygne þat [he] sothely was souerayne in erthe" (line 3357), and proffers him the fruit and wine of the garden. But at midday her mood changes: she berates Arthur, whirls the wheel about, and crushes him beneath.

The "philosophre" (line 3394) to whom Arthur turns for an interpretation tells him, with the smug obviousness of the medieval moralist, that his "fortune es passede" (line 3394) and that he should prepare for death: "Schryfe the of thy schame and schape for thyn ende" (line 3400). But both in its structure and in its inclusion of the Nine Worthies the dream has a broader relevance. The concept of Fortune inevitably expresses a historiography of recurrence: Alexander is the prototype whose achievements are endlessly, and meaninglessly, reenacted. Arthur's dream is itself, ironically, part of this reenactment. When Alexander reached the Earthly Paradise he demanded tribute and was given a stone with the remarkable property that when placed in a scale it outweighed everything set against it but when covered with a light sprinkling of dust it was itself similarly outweighed. Alexander's own philosopher, Aristotle, interpreted this Wonderstone (as it came to be known) as representing Alexander himself: he is now the weightiest thing in the world but when in the grave and covered with dirt will become insignificant.

---

67. See John Finlayson, "Rhetorical 'Descriptio' of Place in the Alliterative *Morte Arthure*," *Modern Philology* 61 (1963), 1–11. There are three descriptions of pleasant landscapes, the first two (in the episodes of the giant and of Priamus and Gawain) prefiguring in their naturalism the supernaturalism of the third description in the dream of Fortune. The placing of these episodes links these three crucial thematic moments together, three episodes that are in narrative terms expendable. They also foreground the motif of wilderness and paradise, which is part of the poem's larger eschatological theme; on this motif, see George H. Williams, *Wilderness and Paradise in Christian Thought* (New York: Harper, 1962).

68. The most complete discussion of the Worthies in the *Morte Arthure*, and in general, is by Horst Schroeder, *Der Topos der Nine Worthies in Literatur und bildender Kunst* (Göttingen: Vandenhoeck & Ruprecht, 1971), pp. 309–18.

Demanding tribute, Alexander received an object that marked the limits of the very sovereignty it was supposed to acknowledge,[69] just as the Earthly Paradise itself stood as an impassable limit to his geographical conquests.[70] So too for Arthur, whose venture into the Earthly Paradise of the dream that stands at the end of his journey reveals a similarly dark message, and one also to be expounded by a philosopher. The gestures toward chronology in the presentation of the Nine Worthies, then, are revealed to be empty signs that can only recall an alternative view of time by which to measure the insufficiency of this one. Arthur follows upon classical and Jewish heroes but remains simply a Christian version of the same thing—Christianity is a distinction without a difference, just as Charlemagne and Godfrey follow upon Arthur but derive from his example no guidance that might allow them to shape their ends differently. When in the *City of God* Augustine attacked the pagan's cyclic conception of history he cited a phrase from the Psalms: "In circuitu impii ambulabunt"—"The wicked will walk in a circle" (Ps. 11:9).[71] It is precisely this tragic view of history that stands, almost a millennium later, as the brooding truth at which the hero arrives.

Moreover, the structure of the dream is itself repetitive: Arthur turns first from the *oscura selva* to the garden, then from the laments of the fallen worthies to his own elevation.[72] Twice he is presented with a monitory teaching and twice he turns aside. This is a pattern of recognition and evasion that continues into the philosopher's exposition of the dream. For while the philosopher insists that the dream shows Arthur that all is *vanitas vanitatum* he nonetheless celebrates Arthur's fame as one of "nynne of þe nobileste namede in erthe" (line 3439; and see lines 3444–45). Similarly, while Arthur is told to prepare for his end by penitential lament and ecclesiastical endowment, he is also informed that the opening scene in the wild wood foretells trouble at home. If Arthur does

---

69. In the *Morte Arthure* this pattern is ironically enacted by Lucius, who demands a tribute from Arthur that is then paid with silver caskets enclosing the bodies of Lucius himself and his senators.

70. In at least one Alexander romance, the orb is referred to as a "pome"; Lascelles, "Alexander and the Earthly Paradise in Medieval English Writings," p. 42. On the conjunction of sovereignty, the garden, and the *Reichsapfel,* see Terry Comito, *The Idea of the Garden in the Renaissance* (New Brunswick: Rutgers University Press, 1978), pp. 8–9.

71. Augustine, *De Civ. Dei* 12.14. Augustine did not of course mean that in pre-Christian times history actually was cyclic but was attacking rather what he took to be the ruling idea of classical historiography. For a criticism of this now common (mis)conception, see Momigliano, *Essays in Ancient and Modern Historiography,* pp. 179–204, esp. pp. 184–85.

72. A possibly Dantean background to the dream is discussed by Mary Hamel, "The Dream of a King: The Alliterative *Morte Arthure* and Dante," *Chaucer Review* 14 (1979–80), 298–312.

"amende [his] mode," as the philosopher enjoins, "And mekely aske mercy for mede of [his] saule" (lines 3454–55), then who will free Britain from Mordred's barbarism, whose atrocities Cradoke is soon vividly to detail (lines 3523–56)? Cradoke is himself, in fact, a pilgrim who now lives the life of penance to which Arthur has been directed, but it is a life which is, for the moment at least, closed to the king. Participation in the historical world is simultaneously proscribed and required, both revealed as without value and imposed as a duty. But for this duty to be taken up, the poem suggests, the emptiness of the historical process must be simultaneously acknowledged and repudiated. It is just this double act of recognition and evasion that the dream of Fortune both records and, in its reception, occasions. Doubled in its own structure, then, the dream gives rise to two equally conflicted imperatives, the philosopher's disjunctive interpretation and the mixed message of Cradoke, whose example urges pilgrimage to Rome but whose words send Arthur back to his final battle in England.

The final movement of the poem—the return to England, the death of Gawain, the mutual annihilation of Mordred and Arthur—records the nature of action in a world that no longer believes in history. That participation in the world is itself a mode of penance is of course a common medieval attitude. Man is tested by the world, and the whirligig of time, meaningless in itself, finds its significance in the trials it imposes on the individual soul. Throughout its course the poem has entertained the possibility that its events are to be understood not eschatologically, as part of a providential *consummatio saeculi,* but rather penitentially, in their effect on the soul. The vow on the vernicle—a pilgrim's badge—can be read this way, and so can Arthur's battle with the giant of Mont St. Michel. As he leaves to climb the mountain, he laconically tells his companions to wait behind, "Fore I will seke this seynte by my selfe one" (line 937); and Bedivere later sarcastically refers to the giant's huge corpse as a "corsaint" (line 1164) and suggests that it should be enclosed in silver like a relic. In reminding us that Mont St. Michel was a popular pilgrimage shrine, this byplay raises disquieting questions. Ought the battle between Arthur and the giant to be placed in the same apocalyptic category as the Archangel Michael's battle with the dragon?[73] Or ought it not rather to be read with reference to Arthur's own human limitations, as a

---

73. For a wholly positive, although not explicitly apocalyptic, reading of the battle with the giant, see John Finalyson, "Arthur and the Giant of St. Michael's Mount," *Medium Aevum* 33 (1964), 112–20. Also relevant to this kind of reading is the notion of giants as representatives of an evil at once primitive and terminal, as in the monstrous figures Gog and Magog, who came to embody the barbaric tribes whose depredations would mark the coming of the last days.

confrontation with an unbridled appetitive self that embodies some of Arthur's own preoccupations? Is it, in other words, an eschatological event and so relevant to the largest of historical movements, or is it rather penitential, relevant only to the spiritual progress of a single hero? Finally, when Priamus is defeated by Gawain he confesses that he was "hawtayne of herte" (line 2612) and has been "for cyrqwitrye schamely supprisede" (line 2616), a literal act of penance that might cause us, at least in retrospect, to revalue this episode by placing it in a pattern of significance that is less apocalyptic than confessional.

It is in the final movement of the narrative that this penitential theme, implicit throughout, threatens to dominate the meaning of the poem as a whole. *Disce mori*—learn to die—is one of the great watchwords of late-medieval spiritual life, and everywhere present in these final confrontations is the ideal of the good end. Religious values coalesce about the figures of Gawain and Arthur in their final acts of self-fulfillment. The dead Gawain is represented by his stricken king as a martyred innocent whose blood must be "schrynede in golde, / For it es sakles of syn, sa helpe me oure Lorde" (lines 3991–92); and Arthur himself dies in the odor of sanctity: "He saide 'In manus' with mayne one molde whare he ligges, / And thus passes his speryt, and spekes he no more" (lines 4326–27).

But lest we too easily assume that the poem has finally been chastened into abandoning its eschatological ambitions, we must note in closing two contra-indications. One is the refusal to abandon the language of crusade that has for so long sustained Arthur's imperial ambitions. Even now that he is fighting an internecine civil war at home in England the poem insists, against all logic, that the religious imperatives that validated his earlier efforts are still in effect. Mordred's allies are as much pagans as those who supported Lucius, and both Gawain and Arthur exhort their men in terms that derive from crusading literature. "We sall ende this daye alls excellent knyghttes," says Gawain, "Ayere to endelesse joye with angells vnwemmyde" (lines 3800–3801), and Arthur later promises the same reward: "Зif vs be destaynede to dy to-daye one this erthe, / We sall be hewede vnto heuen or we be halfe colde" (lines 4090–91). The poem's unwillingness to forgo this crusading rhetoric, and the ideology that supports it, witnesses to a deeper unwillingness to hand the narrative over to Fortune and so to narrow the range of its relevance to a merely individual fate.

The other unsettling element of the poem's final movement is the presence of an insistent desire for closure that refuses to be accommodated to the usual patterns of religious fulfillment. Gawain's hopeless attack on Mordred is the act of a man, says Mordred, "þat wold wilfully wasten hym selfen" (line 3835), and after he is gone Arthur proclaims that "my were [is] endide" (line 3957) and hastens after Mordred despite warnings that his forces are fatally insufficient. In these acts of almost nihilistic finality we witness a pattern of behavior that harks back to traditions more ancient even than Christianity. We inevitably call to mind the futile concluding gestures of other heroes—men such as Bryhtnoth and Beowulf, Siegfried and Njal, Turnus and Achilles. These are men whom history failed, whose time never came, and for whom only a fierce nobility made their situation endurable. The *Morte Arthure* is a poem that supplicates the past in order to speak to the present, and in its conclusion it achieves an almost incantatory power by which to measure tragic failure. As Arthur returns home to the west to be slain by his own sword at the hands of his own son, so the poem returns to the deepest sources of heroic poetry in an act of solicitation that courts possession. Perhaps now we can understand some of the reasons why the poet concludes his poem with his hero's irremediably ambiguous genealogy:

> Thus endis Kyng Arthure, as auctors alegges,
> That was of Ectores blude, the kynge son of Troye,
> And of sir Pryamous the prynce, praysede in erthe;
> Fro thythen broghte the Bretons all his bolde eldyrs
> Into Bretayne the brode, as þe Bruytte tellys.

(Lines 4342–46)

4

"For God's sake let us sit upon the ground / And tell sad stories of the death of kings" (3.2.155–56). Richard II's invitation to rehearse the repertory of royal tragedies, his own included, correctly assumes that the relationship between monarchy and tragedy is reciprocal. One side of that mutuality—the tragic prescription of a noble protagonist—is familiar enough, but we less often remember that most kingly stories, and especially medieval ones, are profoundly, distressingly unhappy. Nor was this a fact that medieval monarchs avoided. Like his Shakespearean counterpart, the historical Richard II also seems to have had an affinity for sad stories, choosing as his political patron saints neither his immensely popular father (the Black Prince) nor his equally popular grandfather (Edward III) but two of the least successful of English kings, the sanctified Edward the Confessor and the "martyred" Edward II, whom Richard assiduously promoted for canonization.[74] And as we have seen, when even the astute Henry II and the manly Edward III chose to assume

---

74. See McKisack, *Fourteenth Century*, p. 498.

the Arthurian aura they were simultaneously darkened with the shadow of the Arthurian fate. If kings wanted national heroes to exemplify and authorize their own heroism, they seem also to have wanted them, paradoxically, to have come to tragic ends. In part this insistence on final adversity can be understood as an inevitable aspect of the ethic of the *Fürstenspiegel:* prideful in their emulation of the great heroes of the past, monarchs are subjected to the compensatory message that all heroism comes to dust. But moral explanations are as partial here as elsewhere, as is the almost atavistic superstition that by gazing upon the downfall of our ancestors we can avoid downfall ourselves. On the contrary, these narratives deliberately complicate moral response, soliciting our engagement by both episodic complexity and empathic identification. The hero's fall is cause not for righteous celebration but for tears.

Perhaps it is in these tears that we find this literature's deepest apologetics. The hero is a man condemned to historical action even when everything proclaims its futility, and royal worldliness imposes a burden on both soul and body. Arthur, as we have seen, must forego the certain consolations of the penitential way to return to the vain heroics of another battle, and he is not alone in this sacrifice, as other poets show about other kings. In canto 7 of the *Purgatorio* Dante describes in the Valley of the Princes one of his gentlest locales, the habitation of those melancholy rulers who were seduced from their true end by the magnificence of their royal means and are now imprisoned in a gilded imitation of their own gardens. Correlatively, when at the end of the *Chanson de Roland* Charlemagne is told to reassume the crusade his eyes fill with tears and he pulls helplessly at his beard. "'Deus,' dist li reis, 'si penuse est ma vie!'"[75] Denied Roland's opportunity for heroic *desmesure,* Charlemagne must submit to a life in history that requires him to bear up the weight of temporality itself, a life that has already lasted (the poem tells us) more than two hundred years. As a royal apologetics, these moments aim not at elevation but at sympathy: it is less the king whom we are to admire than the man who must be king whom we are to pity. This is an empathy that encourages us to forego criticism in the recognition that royal prerogatives are at best only consolations for the heavy imposts of the public life. The pathos of monarchy solicits our political consent, and tragic spectacle becomes a final, ironic justification for the recursive futility of the historical life.

---

75. This is the last line of the *Chanson de Roland.*

INDEX

Index

DESIGNED BY JIM MENNICK
COMPOSED BY GRAPHIC COMPOSITION, INC., ATHENS, GEORGIA
MANUFACTURED BY BOOKCRAFTERS, CHELSEA, MICHIGAN
TEXT AND DISPLAY LINES ARE SET IN BEMBO

Library of Congress Cataloging-in-Publication Data
Patterson, Lee.
Negotiating the past.
Includes bibliographical references and index.
1. English literature—Middle English, 1100–1500—
History and criticism.   2. French poetry—To 1500—
History and criticism.   3. Romances—History and
criticism.   4. Historical criticism (Literature)
5. History in literature.   6. Literature, Medieval—
History and criticism.   7. Chaucer, Geoffrey, d. 1400—
History and criticism.   I. Title.
PR255.P34   1987   821'.1'09   87-40144
ISBN 0-299-11040-0
ISBN 0-299-11044-3 (pbk.)